Austin Maxi 1500/1750 Owners Workshop Manual

by J H Haynes

Member of the Guild of Motoring Writers

and B L Chalmers - Hunt

TEng (CEI), AMIMI, AMIRTE, AMVBRA

Models covered:

Austin Maxi 1500. 1485 cc
Austin Maxi 1750. 1748 cc
Austin Maxi HL. 1748 cc
Includes coverage of automatic models

ISBN 0 900550 52 X

© J H Haynes and Company Limited 1976   2876/062

All rights reserved. No part of this book may be reproduced or
transmitted in any form or by any means, electronic or mechanical,
including photocopying, recording or by any information storage or
retrieval system, without permission in writing from the copyright
holder.

Printed in England *(052 - 1B2)*

Haynes

HAYNES PUBLISHING GROUP
SPARKFORD YEOVIL SOMERSET ENGLAND
distributed in the USA by
HAYNES PUBLICATIONS INC
861 LAWRENCE DRIVE
NEWBURY PARK
CALIFORNIA, 91320
USA

Acknowledgements

Thanks are due to BLMC Limited for their assistance with technical material and certain illustrations and to Castrol Limited for lubrication details.

Invaluable assistance was given by Brian Horsfall for help with the photographs and by Stanley Randolph on sorting out the text.

Champion Sparking Plug Company Limited for the provision of spark plug photographs. The bodywork repair photographs used in this manual were provided by Lloyds Industries Limited who supply 'Turtle Wax', Holts 'Dupli-Color' and a range of other Holts products.

Whilst every care is taken to ensure that the information in this manual is correct, no liability can be accepted by the authors and publishers for loss, damage or injury caused by any errors in, or omissions from, the information given.

Photographic captions and cross references

The book is divided into thirteen chapters. Each chapter is divided into numbered sections which are headed in bold type between horizontal lines. Each section consists of serially numbered paragraphs.

There are two types of illustration: (1) Figures which are numbered according to Chapter and sequence of occurrence in that chapter and having an individual caption to each figure. (2) Photographs which have a reference number in the bottom left hand corner. All photographs apply to the chapter in which they occur so that the reference figures pinpoint the pertinent section and paragraph numbers.

Procedures, once described in the text, are not normally repeated. If it is necessary to refer to another chapter the reference will be given in chapter number and section number thus: Chapter 1/16.

If it is considered necessary to refer to a particular paragraph in another chapter the reference is eg 'Chapter 1/65'. Cross references given without use of the word 'Chapter' apply to sections and/or paragraphs in the same chapter, eg, 'see Section 8' means also 'in this Chapter'.

When the left or right hand side of a car is mentioned it is as if one were looking in the forward direction of travel.

Austin Maxi Mk II Saloon

Introduction

This is a manual for the do-it-yourself minded MAXI motoring enthusiasts. It shows how to maintain these cars in first class condition, and how to carry out repairs when components become worn or break. By doing all maintenance and repair work themselves owners will gain three ways: they will know the job has been done properly; they will have had the satisfaction of doing the job themselves; and they will have saved garage labour charges which, although quite fair bearing in mind the high cost of capital equipment and skilled men. Regular and careful maintenance is essential if maximum reliability and minimum wear are to be achieved.

The author has stripped, overhauled, and rebuilt all the major mechanical and electrical assemblies and most of the minor ones as well. Only through working in this way can solutions be found to the sort of problems facing private owners. Other hints and tips are also given which can only be obtained through practical experience.

The step-by-step photographic strip and rebuild sequences show how each of the major components was removed, taken apart, and rebuilt. In conjunction with the text and exploded illustrations this should make all the work quite clear - even to the novice who has never previously attempted the more complex job.

Although the MAXI range of cars are hardwearing and robust it is inevitable that their reliability and performance will decrease as they become older. Repairs and general reconditioning will become necessary if the car is to remain roadworthy. Early models requiring attention are frequently bought by the more impecunious motorist who just cannot afford the repair prices charged in garages. It is in these circumstances that the manual will prove to be of maximum help, as it is the ONLY workshop manual written from practical experience especially for owners of cars covered in this manual (as opposed to service operators and garage proprietors).

Manufacturers official manuals are usually splendid publications which contain a wealth of technical information. Because they are issued primarily to help the manufacturers' authorised dealers and distributors they tend to be written in very technical language, and tend to skip details of certain jobs which are common knowledge to garage mechanics. Owner's workshop manuals are different as they are intended primarily to help the owner, and therefore contain details of all sorts of jobs not normally found in official manuals.

Owners who intend to do their own maintenance and repairs should have a reasonably comprehensive tool kit. Some jobs require special service tools, but in many instances it is possible to get round their use with a little care and ingenuity. For example a $3\frac{1}{2}$ inch diameter jubilee clip makes a most efficient and cheap piston ring compressor.

Throughout this manual ingenious ways of avoiding the use of special equipment and tools are shown. In some cases the proper tool must be used. Where this is the case a description of the tool and its correct use is included, and details are given of where it can usually be borrowed or hired.

When a component malfunctions garage repairs are becoming more and more a case of replacing the defective item with an exchange rebuilt unit. This is excellent practice when a component is thoroughly worn out, but it is a waste of good money when overall the component is only half worn, and requires the replacement of but a single small item to effect a complete repair. As an example, a non-functioning dynamo can frequently be repaired quite satisfactorily just by fitting new brushes.

A further function of this manual is to show the owner how to examine malfunctioning parts; determine what is wrong; then how to make the repair.

Although every care has been taken to ensure all the information in this manual is correct, bearing in mind current manufacturer's practice to make small alterations and design changes without re-classifying the model, no liability can be accepted for damage, loss or injury caused by any errors in or omissions from the information given.

Given the time, mechanical do-it-yourself aptitude, and a reasonable collection of tools this manual will show the enthusiastic owner how to maintain and repair his car really economically with minimum recourse to professional assistance and expensive tools and equipment.

Contents

Routine maintenance

The maintenance instructions listed are basically those recommended by the manufacturer. They are supplemented by additional maintenance tasks proven to be necessary.

The additional tasks are indicated by an asterisk and are primarily of a preventative nature in that they will assist in eliminating the unexpected failure of a component due to fair wear and tear.

When a new car is delivered the complete engine/transmission unit contains sufficient running-in oil for the running-in period. Providing the level is maintained between the low and high marks on the dipstick during this period, topping up is unnecessary. At the first "Free Service", the running-in oil is drained and the sump replenished to the level of the high mark on the dipstick.

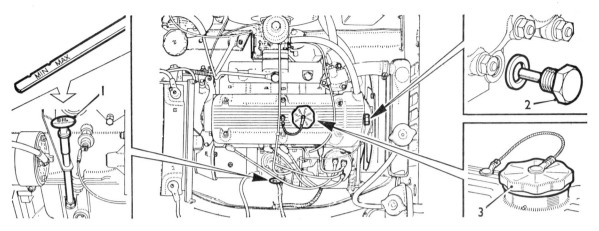

FIG. 1 LOCATION OF OIL LEVEL DIPSTICK AND DRAIN PLUG

No.	Description	No.	Description	No.	Description
1	Dipstick	2	Magnetic drain plug	3	Oil filler cap

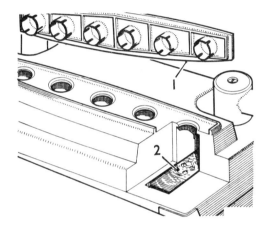

FIG. 2. LUCAS BATTERY FILLER

No.	Description	No.	Description
1	Manifold	2	Separator guards

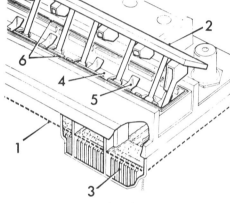

FIG. 3 LUCAS 'PACEMAKER' FILLER

No.	Description	No.	Description
1	Electrolyte level	4	Trough
2	Vent cover	5	Rectangular filler slots
3	Separator plates	6	Cover seating grooves

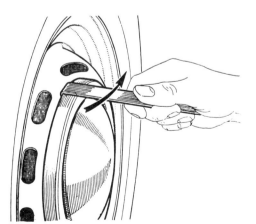

Fig. 4 Wheel trim removal

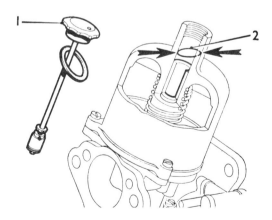

FIG. 5 CARBURETTOR DASHPOT OIL LEVEL

No.	Description	No.	Description
1	Damper assembly	2	Correct oil level

Weekly, before a long journey or every 250 miles (400 Km)

1   Remove the dipstick and check the engine/transmission unit oil level which should be up to the 'MAX' mark. Top up the oil with Castrol GTX. On no account allow the oil to fall below the 'MIN' mark on the dipstick. The distance between the 'MAX' and 'MIN' marks corresponds to approximately 2 pints. (Fig. 1).
2   Check the tyre pressures with an accurate gauge and adjust as necessary. As a safety precaution make sure that the tyre walls and treads are free of damage. Remember that the tyre tread should have a minimum of 1 millimetre depth across three quarters of the total width.
3   Check the battery electrolyte level and top up as necessary with distilled water. Make sure that the top of the battery is always kept clean and free of moisture. (Figs 2 and 3).
4   Refill the windscreen washer bottle with soft water. Add an antifreeze satchet in cold weather to prevent freezing (do not use ordinary antifreeze). Check that the jets operate correctly.
5   Remove the wheel trims and check all wheel nuts for tightness but take care not to overtighten. (Fig. 4).

Every 3000 miles (5000 Km) or 3 months

Complete the service items in the weekly service check plus:
1   Wipe the top of the carburettor dashpot and unscrew the damper. Check the level of oil using the damper as a dipstick. The level should be up to $\frac{1}{2}$ inch above the top of the hollow piston rod. Top up as necessary using Castrol GTX. (Fig. 5).
2   Check the level of coolant in the engine cooling system when the unit is cold. Remove the expansion tank pressure cap and check the level of coolant which should be at least up to the centre of the mounting strap. Top up as necessary with soft rain water. In winter an antifreeze solution must be used. It is very important that the radiator filler cap is not removed whilst the cooling system is hot. (Fig. 6).
3   Wipe the top of the clutch and brake master cylinder reservoirs, unscrew the caps and top up with Castrol Girling Brake Fluid. Take care not to spill any hydraulic fluid on the paintwork as it acts as a solvent. The correct level is when the fluid coincides with the fluid level line on the outside of the reservoirs. (Fig. 7).
4   Check the amount of brake pedal travel and if excessive adjust the rear brakes as described in Chapter 9, Section 2.
5   Carefully examine all hydraulic pipes and unions for signs of leakage and flexible hoses for signs of perishing. Make sure that the front brake flexible hoses are not in contact with any body or mechanical component when the steering is turned on both full locks.
6   Check the headlight alignment as described in Chapter 10, Section 38.
*7   Check the rubber gaiters on the constant velocity joints and steering assembly for leakage or damage and rectify accordingly.
*8   Check the operation of the lights, heater, screen washer and wipers, and warning lights fitting new bulbs or correcting faults as applicable.
*9   Lubricate all locks, hinges and striker plates. Wipe away any excess oil.

Every 6000 miles (10000 Km) or 6 months

Complete the service items in the 3000 miles service check as applicable plus:
1   Remove the engine top cover and check the valve clearances. Full information will be found in Chapter 1, Section 54.
2   The fan belt adjustment must be tight enough to drive the dynamo without overloading the bearings, including the water pump bearings. The method of adjusting the fan belt is described in Chapter 2, Section 12. It is considered to be correct when it can be pressed in $\frac{1}{2}$ inch at the mid point of its longest run - from the dynamo to the crankshaft pulley.
3   Check the operation of the automatic advance/retard system by first releasing the two distributor cap retaining clips and lifting off the distributor cap. Hold the rotor arm (1) Fig. 8 between the finger and thumb and turn in the normal direction of rotation (shown by arrow on rotor arm). Release the rotor arm and if all is well it should return to its original position without any signs of binding or sticking. Using a screwdriver check that the moving plate (2) is free to move.
4   Spring back the two clips and remove the distributor cap. Lift off the rotor arm. Apply a few drops of thin oil over the screw in the centre of the cam spindle and on the moving contact breaker pivot. Apply a smear of grease to the cam surface. Remove any excess oil or grease with a clean rag. Apply a few drops of oil through the hole in the contact breaker base plate to lubricate the automatic timing control. (Fig. 9).
5   Clean and adjust the distributor contact breaker points as described in Chapter 4, Sections 3 and 2.
6   Remove the spark plugs and inspect and clean them as described in Chapter 4, Section 11.
7   To ensure correct clutch operation there should be a clearance of 0.052 in, between the clutch release lever (4) Fig. 10 and its return stop (2). Pull on the clutch release lever to overcome the action of the spring and check the clearance using feeler gauges. If adjustment is necessary, slacken the locknut (1) and with an open ended spanner turn the squared shank of the stop (2) in an anticlockwise direction to decrease the clearance, or clockwise direction to increase the clearance. Retighten the locknut.
8   The front wheel alignment should be checked at the local BLMC garage.
9   Refer to Chapter 9, Section 10 and check the wear of the disc brake pads.
10   Working underneath the car, check the tightness of all nuts, bolts and fixing with particular reference to steering and suspension mountings.
11   Refer to Chapter 10, Section 3, and check the specific gravity of the battery electrolyte.
12   Run the engine until it is hot and then place a container of at least 10 pints capacity under the engine/transmission unit drain plug located as shown in Fig. 1. Unscrew and remove the drain plug and allow the oil to drain out for at least 10 minutes. Whilst this is being done change the oil filter as described in the next service operation. Clean the oil filler cap in petrol and shake dry. Refill the engine/transmission unit with 8¾ Imp pints (manual gearbox) 12 Imp pints (automatic transmission) of the recommended lubricants. Run the engine and check the oil level. The interval between oil changes should be reduced in very hot or dusty conditions or during cool weather with much slow or stop/start driving.

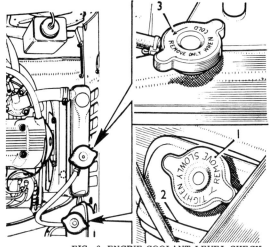

FIG. 6 ENGINE COOLANT LEVEL CHECK

No.	Description	No.	Description
1	Expansion tank pressure cap	2	Expansion tank
		3	Radiator filler cap

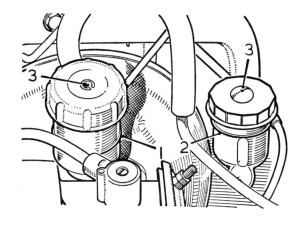

FIG. 7 CLUTCH AND BRAKE MASTER CYLINDER LOCATION

No.	Description	No.	Description
1	Brake master cylinder	3	Vent hole
2	Clutch master cylinder		

FIG. 8 CHECKING OPERATION OF AUTOMATIC ADVANCE AND RETARD MECHANISM

No.	Description	No.	Description
1	Rotor arm	2	Moving base plate

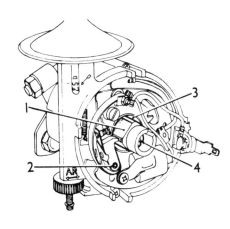

FIG. 9 DISTRIBUTOR LUBRICATION POINTS

No.	Description	No.	Description
1	Cam lobes		cation aperture
2	Pivot post	4	Cam spindle and centre screw
3	Centrifugal device lubri-		

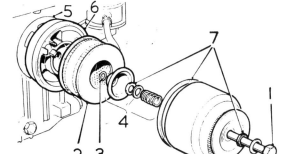

FIG. 11 COMPONENTS OF OIL FILTER ASSEMBLY

No.	Description	No.	Description
1	Centre bolt	5	Filter head gasket
2	Element	6	Filter head
3	Circlip - centre bolt	7	Rubber sealing washers and sealing ring
4	Pressure plate, rubber and steel washers and spring		

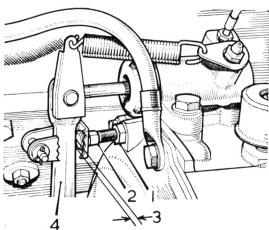

FIG. 10 CLUTCH OPERATING LEVER AND STOP CLEARANCE

No.	Description	No.	Description
1	Stop locknut	3	0.052 inch clearance
2	Stop	4	Operating lever

13 The engine oil filter is located on the front righthand side of the transmission casing and its components are shown in Fig. 11. Place a container having a capacity of at least 1 pint under the filter casing and unscrew the centre bolt. Lift away the complete filter assembly. Lift out the element and remove the circlip. Slide out the centre bolt and lift off the pressure plate, rubber washers, steel washer and the spring, from the casing. Thoroughly wash all components in petrol and wipe dry with a clean non-fluffy rag. Inspect the sealing rings and the rubber washer for signs of deterioration and fit new, if evident. Reassemble the components in the order shown. Fit a new filter element and fit the assembly to the side of the transmission casing. Secure with the retaining screw which must be tightened fully.

14 Inject a few drops of engine oil through the hole in the dynamo rear end cover to lubricate the bush. (Fig. 12).

*15 Wash the bodywork and chromium fittings and clean out the interior of the car. Wax polish the bodywork including all chromium and bright metal trim. Force wax polish into any joints in the bodywork to prevent rust formation.

*16 Check all fuel lines and union joints for leaks. Rectify any leaks found.

*17 Examine the exhaust system for leaks or holes and replace defective components as necessary.

*18 Balance the wheels to eliminate any vibration, especially from the steering. This may be done by the local BLMC garage.

*19 If it is wished, change over the tyres to equalise wear. (Fig. 13).

*20 Lubricate the washer around the wiper spindles with several drops of glycerine.

Every 12000 miles (20000 Km) or 12 months

Complete the service items in the 6000 mile service check as applicable plus:

1 Refer to Fig. 14 and unscrew the ventilation air cover retaining screw (1). Lift away the screw, washer and cover (2) followed by the element (3). Throw away the old element and fit a new one. Replace the cover and secure with the retaining screw and washer.

2 Refer to Fig. 15 and release the rubber clip holding the speedometer drive cable to the air intake tube. Unscrew the centre bolt (1) and lift away the air cleaner assembly. Remove the base (2) from the cover (3) and, using a screwdriver disengage the clip and remove the element (4). Wash out the air cleaner casing in petrol and wipe dry using a clean non-fluffy rag. Fit a new element and refit the cover to the base. Refitting to the carburettor is the reverse sequence to removal.

It will be seen that there are two positions of the air cleaner air intake depending on the ambient temperature. To adjust the position, slacken the centre bolt (1) and turn the whole air cleaner assembly either clockwise or anti-clockwise to the required position as shown in the inset to Fig. 15.

3 To remove the fuel pump gauge filter for cleaning, undo and remove the three cover retaining screws (1) Fig. 16. Lift away the domed cover (2) and joint washer (3) followed by the gauze filter (4) from its recess in the pump body. Use an absorbant cloth to soak up petrol in the filter chamber and then remove any sediment, if possible, carefully using an air jet. Clean the filter in petrol and remove any solid matter with an old toothbrush. Inspect the cover joint washer (3) for hardening or breaking and obtain a new one if necessary. Refit the filter and cover with joint washer and secure with the three retaining screws. These must be tightened progressively to ensure a petrol tight joint. With the engine running, check for signs of petrol leaks.

4 Fit new spark plugs of the correct type as given in the 'Specifications' in Chapter 4.

5 The steering system and suspension moving parts should be checked for wear and the necessary course of action taken as will be found in Chapter 11.

6 Refer to Chapter 9 and inspect the rear brake linings and drums for wear. Remove all traces of dust and fit new linings if necessary.

*7 Lubricate all moving parts of the handbrake system.

*8 Inspect the ignition HT leads for cracks and perishing and replace as necessary.

*9 Examine the dynamo brushes, replace them if worn and clean the commutator. Full details will be found in Chapter 10.

*10 Fit new windscreen wiper blades.

*11 Steam clean the underside of the body and clean the engine/transmission exterior as well as the whole of the front compartment.

Every 24000 miles (40000 Km) or 18 months

Complete the service items in the 6000 and 12000 miles service check as applicable plus:

*1 Examine the hub bearings for wear and replace as necessary. Full information will be found in Chapter 11.

*2 Check the tightness of the battery earth lead on the bodywork.

*3 Renew the condenser in the distributor. See Chapter 4, Section 4 for full information.

*4 Remove the starter motor, examine the brushes and replace as necessary. Clean the commutator and starter drive as described in Chapter 10.

*5 Test the cylinder compressions, and if necessary remove the cylinder head, decarbonise, grind in the valves and fit new valve springs. Full information will be found in Chapter 1.

6 Completely drain the brake hydraulic fluid from the system. All seals and flexible hoses throughout the braking system should be examined and preferably renewed. The working surfaces of the master cylinder, wheel and caliper cylinders should be inspected for signs of wear or scoring and new parts fitted as considered necessary. Refill the hydraulic system with Castrol Girling Brake Fluid.

Every 36000 miles (60000 Km) or 3 years

Complete the service items in the 6000 and 12000 miles service check as applicable plus:

1 Pull back the servo unit dust cover (1) Fig. 17 and ease off the end cap (2). Remove the old filter (3). To fit a new filter, cut it diagonally to the centre hole (4 inset) and then fit it over the push rod and into the housing. Replace the end cap and dust cover.

Every 60000 miles (100000 Km) or 5 years

1 Examine the alternator brushes for wear See Chapter 13, Section 24 for details.

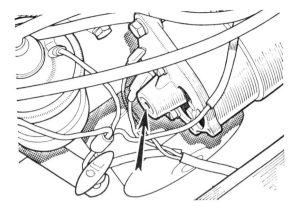

Fig. 12 Dynamo rear bearing lubrication point

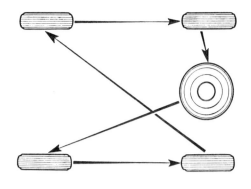

Fig. 13 Tyre change round pattern

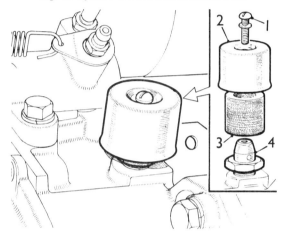

FIG. 14 VENTILATION AIR FILTER ASSEMBLY

No.	Description	No.	Description
1	Cover retaining screw	3	Filter element
2	Cover	4	Filter body

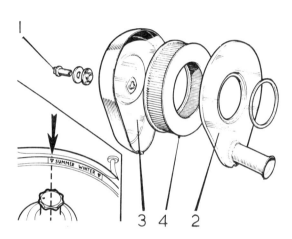

FIG. 15 AIR CLEANER ASSEMBLY

No.	Description	No.	Description
1	Centre bolt	3	Cover
2	Base	4	Element

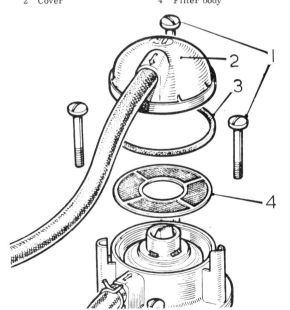

FIG. 16 FUEL PUMP FILTER LOCATION

No.	Description	No.	Description
1	Cover retaining screws	3	Joint washer
2	Fuel pump cover	4	Gauge filter

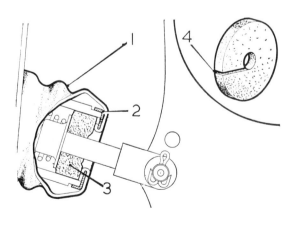

FIG. 17 SERVO UNIT AIR FILTER

No.	Description	No.	Description
1	Dust cover	3	Air filter
2	End cap	4	Cut in new element

LUBRICATION CHART

EXPLANATION OF SYMBOLS

CASTROL GTX.
An ultra high performance motor oil. Recommended for the engine in summer and winter.

CASTROL LM GREASE.
A multi-purpose high melting point lithium based grease, recommended for all greasing points.

DAILY

ENGINE
Check oil level in sump and replenish if necessary to the "full" mark on the dipstick with **Castrol GTX**.

EVERY 6,000 MILES
At the first 500 miles, thereafter every 6,000 miles, drain off old oil while warm and refill to correct level with **Castrol GTX**.

NOTE:—Owners are advised that more frequent sump draining periods are desirable if the operation of the car involves:—

(1) Frequent stop/start driving.
(2) Operation during cold weather, especially when appreciable engine idling is involved.
(3) Where much driving is done under dusty conditions.

Capacity 8¼ pts. including filter.

EVERY 6,000 MILES
Including 3,000 mile service

DYNAMO
To lubricate the dynamo bearing add a few drops of **Castrol GTX** through the central hole in the rear bearing housing. Avoid over-lubrication.

EVERY 6,000 MILES
Including 3,000 mile service

DISTRIBUTOR
Remove the distributor cover and rotor arm and lightly smear the cam and contact breaker pivot with **Castrol LM Grease**. Avoid over-greasing. Also add a few drops of **Castrol GTX** to the centre of the cam spindle after withdrawing the rotor arm.

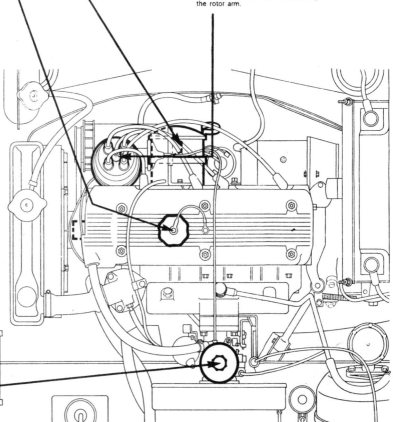

EVERY 3,000 MILES
Including DAILY service

CARBURETTOR
Unscrew and remove the damper unit, and pour **Castrolite** into the hollow piston rod until the level is ¼" above the piston, then screw the damper back into position.
Also apply **Castrolite** to the carburettor controls and cables.

Recommended lubricants

COMPONENT	CLIMATIC CONDITIONS PREDOMINATING	CORRECT CASTROL PRODUCTS
Engine and transmission distributor, carburettor dashpot, oil can	All temperatures above – 10° C (10° F)	Castrol GTX or Castrol XL 20 W/50
	Temperatures – 15° to – 5° C (0° to 20° F)	Castrolite or Castrol Super
	All temperatures below – 15° C (0° F)	Castrol CR 1 5W/20
All grease points	All conditions	Castrol LM Grease
Steering gear	All conditions	Castrol Hypoy
Upper cylinder lubricant	All conditions	Castrollo

Additionally Castrol 'Everyman' oil can be used to lubricate door, boot and bonnet hinges, locks, pivots etc.

Ordering spare parts

Always order Genuine British Leyland Unipart spare parts from your nearest BLMC dealer or local garage. BLMC authorised dealers carry a comprehensive stock of GENUINE PARTS and can supply most items 'over the counter'.

When ordering spare parts it is essential to give full details of your car to the storeman. He will want to know the commission, car, and engine numbers. When ordering parts for the transmission unit or body it is also necessary to quote the transmission casing and body numbers.

Commission number: Located on a plate mounted on the right hand side of the bonnet lock platform.

Car number: Located on a plate mounted on the right hand wing valance.

Engine number: Stamped on the cylinder block or on a metal plate secured to the cylinder block between the ignition coil and distributor.

Body number: Stamped on a plate fixed to the left hand side of the bonnet lock platform.

If you want to retouch the paintwork you can obtain an exact match (providing the original paint has not faded).

When obtaining new parts remember that many assemblies can be exchanged. This is very much cheaper than buying them outright and throwing away the old part. Normally parts used in the Factory Exchange Unit Scheme covers practically every major assembly on any BLMC car marketed in the last ten years. The following units are available under this scheme.

Engine and ancillaires
Clutches
Transmission units
Braking system units
Steering gears
Instruments
Electrical units
Bumper bars
Fuel pumps
Heaters

Chapter 1 Engine

Contents

Specifications

Designation	14 H, 1500 17 H, 1750
Number of cylinders...	4
Bore	76. 2 mm (3.00 inch)
Stroke...	81.28 mm (3.2 inch), 1500 95.75 mm (3.77 inch), 1750
Capacity	1485 cc (90.61 inch^3), 1500 1748 cc (106.69 inch^3), 1750
Valve operation...	Overhead camshaft (ohc)
Compression ratio	9.0:1 1500 8.75:1 1750
Firing order	1 3 4 2 (No 1 at left hand end)
Idle speed: 1500	700 rpm
1750	750 rpm

Specifications

Fast idle speed	1000 to 1100 rpm
Bhp	74 at 5500 rpm 1500
	84 at 5000 rpm 1750

Valve clearance:

Standard – Inlet	0.016 to 0.018 inch (0.41 to 0.46 mm)
– Exhaust	0.020 to 0.022 inch (0.51 to 0.56 mm)
Minimum – Inlet...	0.012 inch (0.31 mm)
– Exhaust	0.012 inch (0.31 mm)

Camshaft

Valve timing marks	Camshaft sprocket and carrier marks in conjunction with flywheel marks
Inlet valve: opens	9° 4' BTDC*
closes	50° 56' ABDC*
Exhaust valve:opens	48° 56' ABDC*
closes...	11° 4' ATDC*
	* At 0.021 inch (0.53 mm) valve clearances
End thrust	Taken on front and locating plate
End float	0.002 to 0.007 inch (0.05 to 0.17 mm)
Adjustment...	renew locating plate
Bearings	3. Run direct in aluminium carrier
Journal diameter: Front	1.9355 to 1.9365 inch (49.185 to 49.197 mm)
Centre	1.9668 to 1.9678 inch (49.975 to 49.987 mm)
Rear	1.998 to 1.999 inch (50.762 to 50.775 mm)
Drive	chain. 3/8 inch (9.52 mm) pitch x 108 pitches

Connecting rods

Type	Big end: split horizontally, small end: solid.
Length between centre	5.828 to 5.832 inch (148.02 to 148.12 mm)
End float or crankpin (nominal)	0.006 to 0.01 inch (0.15 to 0.25 mm)
Small end diameter	0.811 to 0.8115 inch (20.59 to 20.61 mm)
Big end bearing material	Steel backed, reticular tin.

Gudgeon pin

Type	press fit in small end
Outside diameter	0.8123 to 0.8125 (20.6 to 20.65 mm)

Pistons

Type	Aluminium, (slotted) solid skirt
Oversize	0.020 inch (0.51 mm)
Clearance in cylinder:	
Top (below oil control groove)	0.0018 to 0.0024 inch (0.045 to 0.061 mm)
Bottom	0.001 to 0.0016 inch (0.025 to 0.039 mm)
Width of ring grooves:	
Top	0.064 to 0.065 inch (1.64 to 1.66 mm)
Second	0.064 to 0.065 inch (1.64 to 1.66 mm)
Third (1500 models)	0.064 to 0.065 inch (1.64 to 1.66 mm)
Oil control	0.1565 to 0.1575 inch (4.962 to 4.987 mm)

Piston rings

Compression

Type: Top	Plain chrome
Second	Tapered
Third (1500 only)	Tapered
Width: Top	0.0615 to 0.625 inch (1.55 to 1.60 mm)
Second	0.0615 to 0.625 inch (1.55 to 1.60 mm)
Third (1500 only)	0.0615 to 0.625 inch (1.55 to 1.60 mm)
Fitted gap: Top	0.011 to 0.022 inch (0.305 to 0.55 mm)
Second	0.011 to 0.022 inch (0.305 to 0.55 mm)
Third (1500 only)	0.011 to 0.022 inch (0.305 to 0.55 mm)
Ring to groove clearance:	
Top	0.0015 to 0.0035 inch (0.03 to 0.08 mm)
Second	0.0015 to 0.0035 inch (0.03 to 0.08 mm)
Third (1500 only)	0.0015 to 0.0035 inch (0.03 to 0.08 mm)

Specifications

Piston rings:

Material 1500	sintered alloy	
1750	spun cast	

Oil control

Type	Two chrome faced rings with expander
Width	0.100 to 0.105 inch (2.54 to 2.66 mm)
Fitted gap	0.015 to 0.045 inch (0.38 to 1.14 mm)

Valves

Seat angle	$45\frac{1}{4}°$
Head diameter: Inlet	1.5 inch (38.1 mm)
Exhaust	1.216 to 1.220 inch (30.88 to 31.04 mm)
Stem diamter*: Inlet	0.3110 to 0.3115 inch (7.89 to 7.91 mm)
Exhaust	0.3100 to 0.3105 inch (7.87 to 7.89 mm)
Stem to guide clearance: Inlet	0.002 inch (0.051 mm)
Exhaust	0.003 inch (0.076 mm)
Stem diameter**: Inlet	0.3115 to 0.3120 inch (7.91 to 7.93 mm)
Exhaust...	3.115 to 0.3120 inch (7.91 to 7.93 mm)
Stem to guide clearance**: Inlet	0.0015 inch (0.038 mm)
Exhaust...	0.0015 inch (0.038 mm)
Valve lift	0.36 (0.914 mm)
Running clearance: Inlet	0.018 inch (0.46 mm)
Exhaust	0.022 inch (0.56 mm)
Valve timing clearance: Inlet	0.021 inch (0.53 mm)
Exhaust	0.021 inch (0.53 mm)

* Early engines up to engine number 14H/283EH/39163, 14H/288EH/1102
** Later engines from engine numbers 14H/283EH/39164, 14H/288EH/1103

Valve springs

Free length...	1.797 inch (45.70 mm)
Fitted length	1.38 inch (35.05 mm)
Load at top of lift	96 lbs (43.5 Kg)
Load at fitted length	$5\frac{1}{2}$

Valve timing marks	On boss of camshaft sprocket and camshaft housing. Also on flywheel.

Oil pump

Type	concentric (serviced as a unit)
Outer ring end float	0.004 to 0.005 inch (0.10 to 0.12 mm)
Inner rotor end float	0.0045 to 0.0055 inch (0.11 to 0.14 mm)
Outer ring to body clearance	0.011 inch (0.25 mm)
Rotor lobe clearance	0.0035 inch (0.089 mm)

Oil pressure

Idling	15 lb/sq in
Running	60 lb/sq in

Oil filter	Purolator full flow, paper element

Oil Capacity (total)

Engine sump with filter	$9\frac{3}{4}$ pints, 5.6 litres
Oil filter	1 pint, 0.6 litre

Torque wrench settings

	lb ft	Kg m
Oil filter bolt	20	2.8
Cylinder head bolts	60	8.3
Lifting bracket set screws	30	4.1
Cam carrier to cylinder head	20	2.8
Camshaft sprocket	35	4.8
Camshaft cover	6	0.8
Thermostat housing to cylinder head	8 to 10	1.1 to 1.4
Water outlet elbow	8 to 10	1.1 to 1.4

Specifications

Torque wrench settings	lb ft	Kg m
Manifold to cylinder head	18 to 20	2.5 to 2.8
Adaptor plugs	30	4.1
Carburettor studs	6 to 8	0.8 to 1.1
Water pump set screws	18 to 20	2.5 to 2.8
Plug – water pump body	35	4.8
Pulley	18	2.5
Front cover – studs	6	0.8
Front cover – nuts	17 to 19	2.4 to 2.6
Petrol pump – studs	6	0.8
Petrol pump – nuts	15 to 18	2.1 to 2.5
Flywheel housing – studs	6	0.8
Flywheel housing – nuts	17 to 19	2.4 to 2.6
Flywheel housing – set screws...	17 to 19	2.4 to 2.6
Crankshaft pulley bolt	60 to 70	8.3 to 9.7
Timing cover	18 to 20	2.5 to 2.8
Timing chain guide strips	18 to 20	2.5 to 2.8
Pivot pin	18 to 20	2.5 to 2.8
Big end nuts	30	4.1
Main bearing bolts	70	9.7
Flywheel bolts	60	8.3
Oil pump	18 to 20	2.5 to 2.8

1 General description

The Maxi is fitted with a four cylinder overhead cam-shaft engine, with a single SU HS6 horizontal mounted car-burettor. It is transversely mounted in the car and supported by rubber mountings.

Two valves per cylinder are mounted at an angle in the cast iron cylinder head. They are operated by tappets in direct contact with the camshaft lobes.

The cylinder head has all eight inlet and exhaust ports on one side of the cylinder head.

The cast iron cylinder block and upper half of the crank-case are cast together, whilst the bottom half of the crankcase is incorporated within the combined transmission casing and oil sump.

The flat top pistons are made from anodised aluminium with slotted solid skirts. Three compression rings are fitted to 1500 cc engines, only two compression rings are fitted to 1750 cc engines. One oil control ring located above the gudgeon pin is fitted to both engines. The gudgeon pin is a tight press fit into the connecting rod small end and fully floating in the piston bosses.

The crankshaft is machined from cast iron and runs in five main bearings. Fitted to the front of the crankshaft is a combined torsional vibration damper and crankshaft pulley. Situated behind this is the front oil seal followed by the cam-shaft chain driving sprocket and a skew gear, in mesh with a shaft, which drives the oil pump and distributor.

Located at the lower end of the shaft is a cam which operates the fuel pump via a short push rod.

At the rear end of the crankshaft is bolted the flywheel and clutch which transmits engine torque via a single helical gear to the transmission mounted beneath the engine. The crankshaft main bearings run in reticular tin steel backed shell bearings.

Connecting the pistons to the crankshaft are four short connecting rods. The big ends may be split horizontally like the crankshaft main bearings. The big end bearings are of re-ticular tin steel back shell design.

Mounted onto the top face of the cylinder head is the alu-minium casting in which the camshaft is fitted. The camshaft rotates in three bearings which are machined directly in the casting. Placed below each camshaft cam lobe is a large bore machined in the aluminium casting, and in each bore is a bucket type tappet. The hollow part of the tappet sits on the top of the valve stem and spring. There should be a clear-ance between the top of the tappet and cam lobe which may be adjusted by placing shims between the underside of the top of the tappet and the valve stem.

The camshaft is driven by a sprocket which is twice the size of the one fitted to the crankshaft.

Because of the length of drive chain, one automatic adjusting chain tensioner is used and two chain guides.

The centrifugal water pump and radiator cooling fan are driven, together with the generator, from the crankshaft pulley wheel by a rubber/fabric belt. The cooling fan is mounted on the front end of the water pump spindle.

Engine lubrication is accommodated by an oil pump which draws oil from the bottom of the transmission casing and passes it through a full flow replaceable element oil filter and then to the oil galley and distribution drillings within the engine. Oil pressure is controlled by a non-adjustable oil relief valve which is located in the transmission casing just below the filter head.

From the 'Specifications' given at the beginning of this Chapter it will be seen that two engine sizes are available, the increase in capacity being obtained by increasing the stroke.

Any references in the text to the left hand side or right hand side of the engine are applicable when sitting in the drivers seat. The front of the engine is the side nearest to the front grille and the rear is that nearest the bulkhead.

2 Operations with engine in place

No major operations can be carried out on the Maxi en-gine with it in place becuase it is impossible to drop the sump.

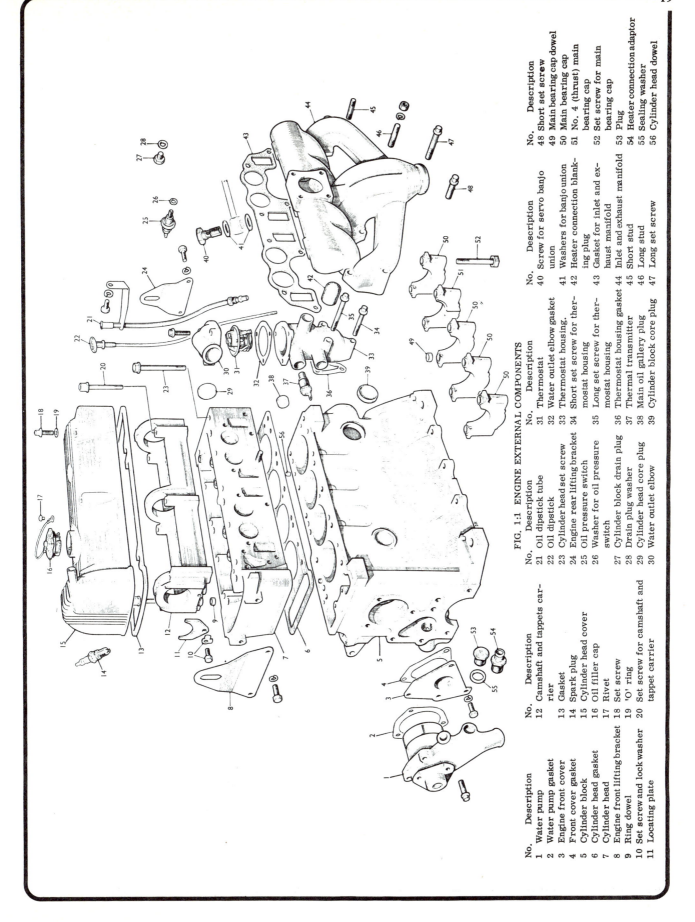

FIG. 1:1 ENGINE EXTERNAL COMPONENTS

No.	Description
1	Water pump
2	Water pump gasket
3	Engine front cover
4	Front cover gasket
5	Cylinder block
6	Cylinder head gasket
7	Cylinder head
8	Engine front lifting bracket
9	Ring dowel
10	Set screw and lock washer
11	Locating plate
12	Camshaft and tappets carrier
13	Gasket
14	Spark plug
15	Cylinder head cover
16	Oil filler cap
17	Rivet
18	Set screw
19	'O' ring
20	Set screw for camshaft and tappet carrier
21	Oil dipstick tube
22	Oil dipstick
23	Cylinder head set screw
24	Engine rear lifting bracket
25	Oil pressure switch
26	Washer for oil pressure switch
27	Cylinder block drain plug
28	Drain plug washer
29	Cylinder head core plug
30	Water outlet elbow
31	Thermostat
32	Water outlet elbow gasket
33	Thermostat housing.
34	Short set screw for thermostat housing
35	Long set screw for thermostat housing
36	Thermostat housing gasket
37	Thermal transmitter
38	Main oil gallery plug
39	Cylinder block core plug
40	Screw for servo banjo union
41	Washers for banjo union
42	Heater connection blanking plug
43	Gasket for inlet and exhaust manifold
44	Inlet and exhaust manifold
45	Short stud
46	Long stud
47	Long set screw
48	Short set screw
49	Main bearing cap dowel
50	Main bearing cap
51	No. 4 (thrust) main bearing cap
52	Set screw for main bearing cap
53	Plug
54	Heater connection adaptor
55	Sealing washer
56	Cylinder head dowel

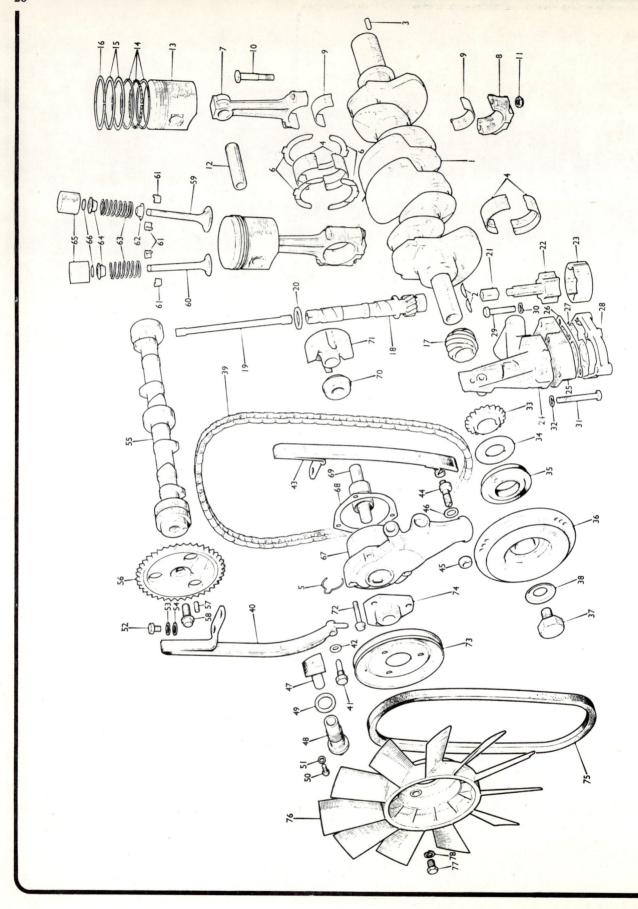

FIG. 1:2 ENGINE INTERNAL COMPONENTS

No.	Description
1	Crankshaft
2	Keys for timing gear and sprocket
3	Dowel for flywheel
4	Main bearing shells
5	Retainer for water pump bearing
6	Crankshaft thrust washers
7	Connecting rod
8	Big-end bearing cap
9	Big-end bearing shell
10	Big-end bolt
11	Nut for bolt
12	Gudgeon pin
13	Piston
14	Oil control ring
15	Tapered compression rings
16	Top compression ring
17	Distributor, oil pump and fuel pump drive gear
18	Distributor and fuel pump drive shaft
19	Oil pump drive coupling
20	Thrust washer for shaft
21	Oil pump drive coupling
22	Oil pump rotor
23	Oil pump outer ring
24	Oil pump body
25	Oil strainer body
26	Gasket

No.	Description
27	Oil strainer
28	Oil strainer cover
29	Bolt for oil pump—short
30	Spring washer
31	Bolt for oil pump—long
32	Spring washer
33	Crankshaft sprocket
34	Oil thrower
35	Crankshaft front oil seal
36	Crankshaft pulley and vibration damper
37	Pulley bolt
38	Lock washer for bolt
39	Chain for camshaft
40	Chain guide—tensioner side
41	Dowel bolt for guide
42	Washer for bolt
43	Chain guide—tight side
44	Adjuster for chain guide
45	Locknut for adjuster
46	Washer for nut
47	Chain tensioner assembly
48	Chain tensioner adaptor
49	Washer for adaptor
50	Bolt for adaptor
51	Washer for bolt
52	Set screw for chain guides

No.	Description
53	Spring washer
54	Plain washer
55	Camshaft
56	Camshaft sprocket
57	Dowel for sprocket
58	Bolt for sprocket
59	Inlet valve
60	Exhaust valve
61	Valve cotters
62	Oil seal (Inlet valve only)
63	Valve springs
64	Valve spring cup
65	Tappets
66	Shim for tappets
67	Water pump body
68	Water pump gasket
69	Bearing and shaft assembly
70	Seal for water pump
71	Vane for water pump
72	Set screw for water pump
73	Pulley for water pump and fan
74	Hub for fan and pulley
75	Fan belt
76	Fan
77	Bolt for fan
78	Spring washer for bolt

The following operations are possible however:
a)   Removal and replacement of the cylinder head assembly.
b)   Removal and replacement of camshaft and carrier.
c)   Removal and replacement of clutch and flywheel.
d)   Removal and replacement of engine mountings.

3   Major operations with engine removed

The following major operations can be carried out with the engine out of the body:
a)   Removal and replacement of the main bearings.
b)   Removal and replacement of the crankshaft.
c)   Removal and replacement of the oil pump.
d)   Removal and replacement of the big end bearings.
e)   Removal and replacement of the pistons and connecting rods.
f)   Removal and replacement of the camshaft drive sprocket and chain.

4   Engine and transmission (cable gear change models) - removal

The sequence of operations listed in this section is not critical as the position of the person undertaking the work, or the tool in his hand, will determine to a certain extent the order in which the work is tackled. Obviously the power unit cannot be removed until everything is disconnected from it and the following sequence will ensure nothing is forgotten.
1   Refer to Chapter 2/2 and drain the cooling system.
2   Preferably whilst the engine is warm, place a container having a capacity of at least 10 pints under the transmission unit drain plug and unscrew the drain plug. This is located on the radiator side of the transmission unit casing.
3   Using a soft pencil, mark the outline position of both the hinges at the bonnet to act as a datum for refitting.
4   With the help of a second person to take the weight of the bonnet, undo and remove the two lower stay retaining screws. (photo).
5   Undo and remove the hinge to bonnet securing bolts with plain and spring washers (photo). There are two bolts to each hinge.
6   Lift away the bonnet and put in a safe place so that it will not be scratched (photo).
7   Disconnect the positive and then the negative terminals from the battery.
8   Undo and remove the nuts and plain washers holding the battery clamp bar to the support rods and lift away the clamp bar and two rods (photo).
9   Life away the battery from its tray (photo). The tray may next be lifted out.
10   Undo and remove the two nuts and shakeproof washers securing the air cleaner to the carburettor air intake flange. (photo). Lift away the air cleaner.
11   Pull the H.T. lead from the centre of the ignition coil (photo).
12   Mark the high tension cables relative to the spark plugs for correct refitting, and disconnect the four leads. (photo)
13   Release the two distributor cap retaining clips and lift away the distributor cap and H.T. leads (photo).
14   Undo and remove the two exhaust manifold to downpipe clamp securing nuts, bolts and washers (photo). Lift away the clamp.
15   Make a note of the manner in which the throttle return

spring is fitted and unhook the spring (photo). Put the spring in a safe place.
16   Release the throttle cable connector from the cable by slackening the centre screw and drawing the connector from the end of the cable (photo).
17   Pull the throttle outer cable from its support bracket (photo).
18   Slacken the choke cable connector centre screw and pull the inner cable from the connector. Lift away the connector (photo).
19   Draw the water temperature gauge thermal transmitter cable from the transmitter (photo).
20   Pull the distributor automatic advance/retard pipe connector from its union on the induction manifold side of the carburettor body (photo).
21   Pull the advance/retard pipe from the end of the distributor vacuum unit (photo). Lift away the complete pipe.
22   Slacken the clip securing the heater hose to the union on the water pump and carefully draw off the hose (photo).
23   Slacken the clip securing the second heater hose to thermostat (photo). Carefully draw off the hose (photo).
24   Undo and remove the union bolt and copper washers securing the brake servo unit hose to the induction manifold (photo).
25   Apply the handbrake, chock the rear wheels, remove the front wheel trims, slacken the front wheel nuts, jack up the front of the car until the wheels are just off the ground and place on firmly based axle stands. Remove the front wheels
26   Working under the right hand wheel arch, soak with penetrating oil the four nuts securing the battery tray support to the inner wing panel. Undo and remove the four nuts and spring washers and lift away the support (photo).
27   Note which way round the clutch release arm return spring is fitted and detach the spring (photo).
28   Undo and remove the two bolts with spring washers securing the clutch slave cylinder to the clutch/flywheel housing (photo).
29   Carefully draw the clutch slave cylinder rearwards out of engagement of the pushrod and tie back out of the way. ON NO ACCOUNT DEPRESS THE CLUTCH PEDAL AFTER THIS HAS BEEN DONE.
30   Undo and remove the bolt and spring washer securing the battery earth strap to the clutch housing cover (photo).
31   Using a pair of pliers, release the clip securing the pipe to the expansion tank at the take off pipe on the radiator filter neck. (photo).
32   Undo and remove the two expansion tank clamp securing self tapping screws (photo).
33   Lift away the expansion tank and connecting hose (photo).
34   Pull the cable Lucar connector from the oil warning light switch located just beneath the ignition coil (photo).
35   Make a note of the cable connections to the rear of the dynamo and pull off the two Lucar connectors (photo).
36   Ease back the cap on the ignition coil and note the low tension electrical cable connections. Carefully pull off the Lucar connectors (photo).
37   Pull off the Lucar connector from the side of the distributor body (photo).
38   Undo and remove the nut securing the heavy duty cable to the terminal at the rear of the starter motor (photo). Lift off the cable from the terminal.
39   If a pre-engaged starter motor is fitted, note the electrical cable connections and release the cables from the solenoid.
40   Undo and remove the one bolt securing the dip stick bracket to the ignition coil mounting bracket (photo).
41   With a pair of pliers, compress the ears of the fuel pump

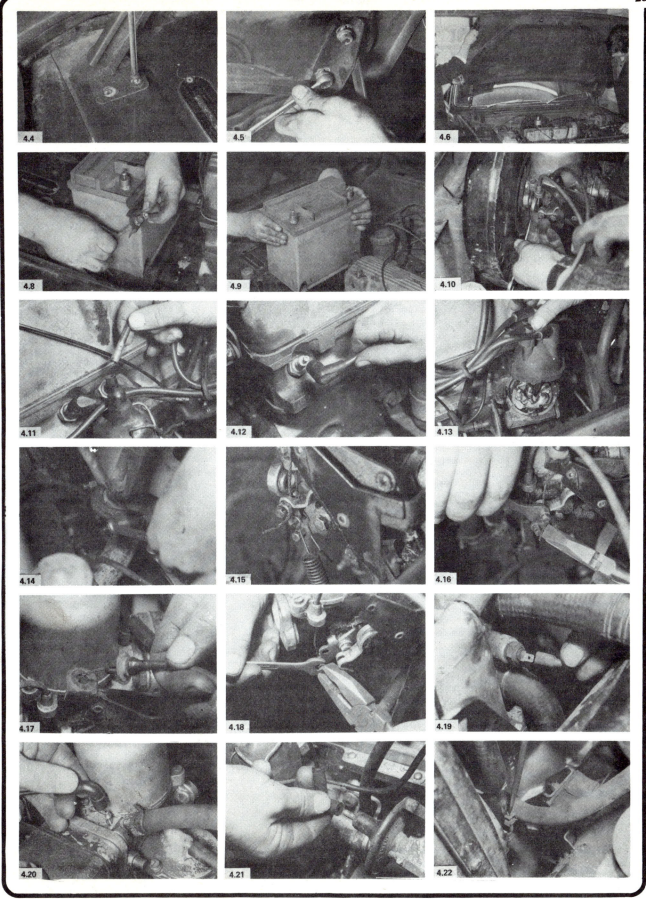

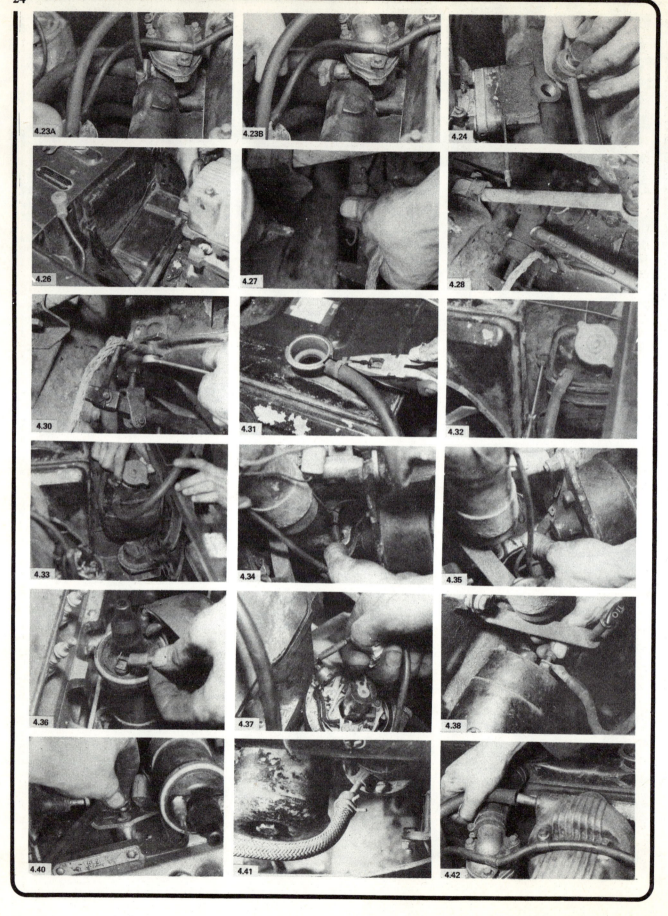

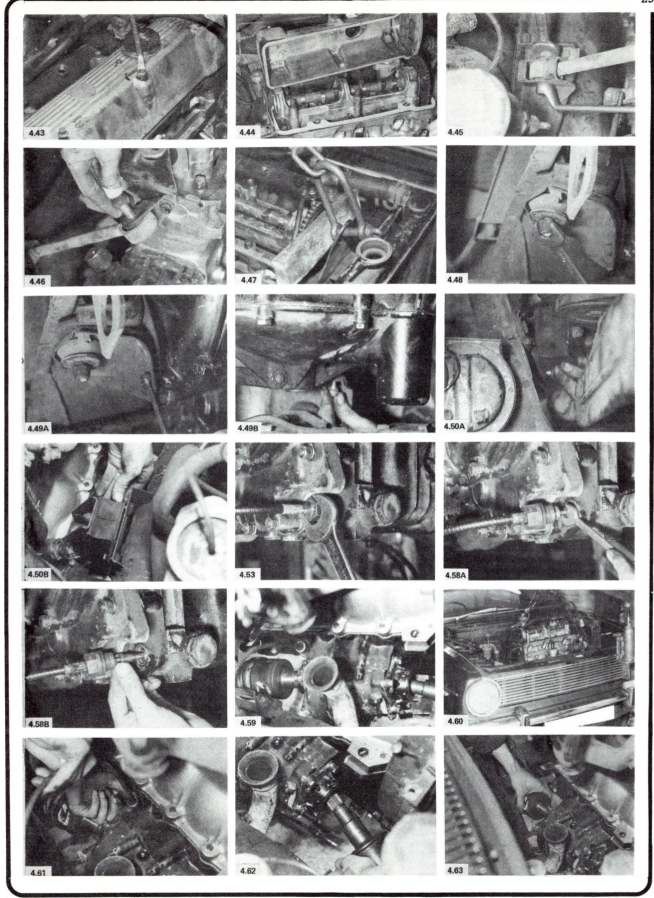

4.43

4.44

4.45

4.46

4.47

4.48

4.49A

4.49B

4.50A

4.50B

4.53

4.58A

4.58B

4.59

4.60

4.61

4.62

4.63

4.64A

4.64B

4.64C

4.65

4.66

feed pipe flexible hose clip and carefully draw off the hose (photo).

42   Carefully pull off the breather pipe from the radiator end of the camshaft cover (photo).

43   Undo the camshaft cover securing bolts in a progressive manner and withdraw the bolts (photo).

44   Carefully lift the camshaft cover and gasket from the top of the cylinder head (photo).

45   Undo and remove the nut and bolt securing the engine steady bracket to the body (photo).

46   Undo and remove the nut and bolt securing the engine steady bracket to the mounting bracket on the side of the cylinder head (photo).

47   Fit lifting chains or strong rope to the two engine lifting brackets and, with an overhead hoist or crane, take the weight of the complete unit from the mountings (photo).   Reference to photo 4:66 will show chains correctly fitted preventing damage to camshaft sprocket.

48   Working under the car undo, but do not remove, the centre nut plain washer from the right hand mounting (photo).

49   Undo and remove the bolts with spring washers securing the right hand mounting to the transmission unit (photos).

50   Undo and remove the bolts with spring washers securing the left hand mounting to the sub frame (photos).

51   Move the gear change lever to the neutral position and mark the cables so that they may be refitted correctly.

52   Working under the car, unscrew the cable locking nut from each cable (if fitted).

53   Unscrew the outer cable gland nut from each cable (photo).

54   Pull the fifth/reverse cable outwards from the transmission unit.

55   Unscrew the inner cable gland nut and detach the cable.

56   Repeat the instructions given in paragraphs 54 and 55 for the first/second speed cable.

57   Push the first/second speed selector rod back into the neutral position using a suitable diameter metal rod.

58   Repeat the instructions given in paragraphs 54 and 55 for the third/fourth speed cable (photos).

59   Check that no electric cables or controls have been left connected, with the exception of the speedometer cable, and then raise the engine about three inches.   This can be judged by the gap between exhaust manifold and downpipe flange. (photo).   It will be necessary to lower the rear of the unit so as to disengage the rear mounting.

60   Push the engine forwards as far as possible and then raise it sufficiently for the rear mounting to be completely disengaged (photo).

61   Release the speedometer drive from the rear of the transmission unit (photo).

62   Move the engine as far as possible to the left hand side of the car and disengage the right hand drive shaft (photo).

63   Move the engine to the right and disengage the left hand drive shaft (photo).

64   Continue to raise the engine and transmission until the underside is just clear of the front panel (photos).

65   Either tie the drive shafts to support their weight (photo) and push the car rearwards, or pull the crane forwards from the car until the complete power unit is clear of the car.

66   Carefully lower the power unit to the ground (photo).

67   Thoroughly wash the exterior with paraffin or 'Gunk'. Wash off with a strong water jet and dry thoroughly.   The engine unit is now ready to have the radiator removed and then separated from the transmission as described in Section 8.

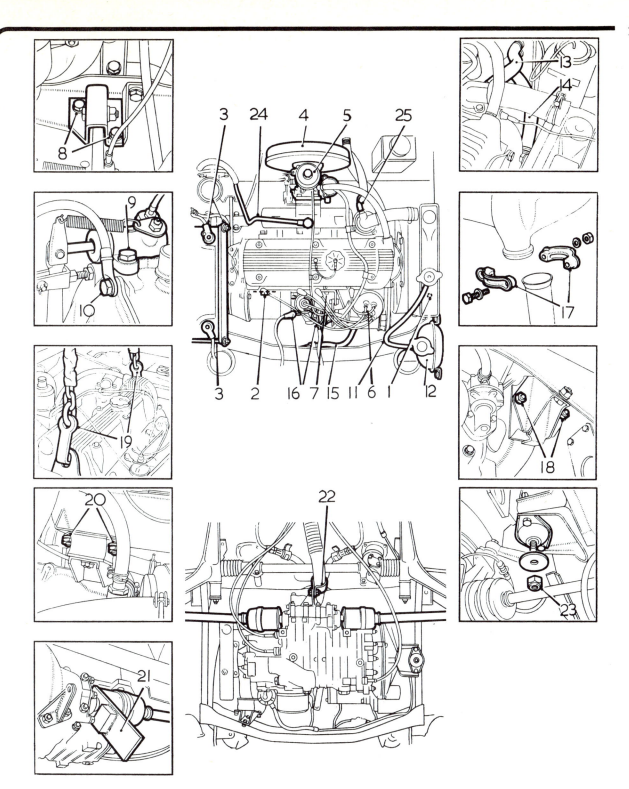

FIG. 1:3 POWER UNIT REMOVAL - CABLE GEAR CHANGE. SUMMARY OF ITEMS TO BE DISCONNECTED

No.	Description	No.	Description	No.	Description	No.	Description
1	Radiator drain plug	9	Clutch slave cylinder	15	Fuel pipe to fuel pump	21	Drive shaft removal from final drive unit
2	Cylinder block drain plug	10	Earth cable	16	Electric cables	22	Exhaust down pipe clip
3	Battery terminals and carrier	11	Radiator spill pipe	17	Exhaust pipe to manifold clamp	23	Rear engine mounting
4	Air cleaner	12	Expansion tank	18	LH engine mounting	24	Vacuum servo unit manifold pipe connection
5	Carburettor (optional)	13	Heater hose to thermostat housing	19	Engine lifting brackets and chains	25	Thermal transmitter
6	Distributor and cap (optional)	14	Heater hose to water pump	20	LH rear engine mounting		
7	Oil pressure warning light switch						
8	Steady bracket						

5   Engine and transmission (rod gear change models) - removal.

1   Follow the sequence given in Section 4:1 to 50 inclusive.
2   Undo and remove the large bolt and nut securing the steady rod to the differential housing. Separate the rod yoke from the casting and recover the two washers.
3   Undo and remove the two nuts and spring washers securing the exhaust bracket to the differential housing.
4   Slacken the exhaust bracket U bolt nuts and slide the bracket down the exhaust pipe.
5   Undo and remove the two nuts, bolts and spring washers that secure the front left hand mounting to the subframe bracket.
6   Undo and remove the two bolts that secure the rear left hand mounting to the displacer housing.
7   Using a piece of metal bar shaped as shown in Fig. 1:4(27). carefully release the two drive shafts from their locator rings. For this it may be necessary to jack up the lower suspension arms.
8   Slacken the two nuts and bolts that secure the rear engine mounting to the subframe bracket.
9   Undo and remove the two nuts retaining the rear engine mounting to the bracket on the clutch cover.
10   Using a parallel pin punch, carefully drift out the pin that retains the extension rod to the selector shaft.
11   Undo and remove the two nuts and spring washers that secure the damper mounting bracket to the transmission.
12   The removal procedure is now identical to that for cable operated gear change models. Refer to Section 4 and follow the sequence described in paragraphs 59 to 67 inclusive.

6   Engine and transmission with subframe (cable gear change models) - removal

1   For this method of engine and transmission removal it is necessary to depressurise the hydrolastic suspension system. Refer to Chapter 11/13 for information on this subject.
2   Refer to Section 4 and follow the sequence given in paragraphs 1 to 47 inclusive.
3   Undo the two nuts and bolts securing the heat control valve to the subframe. Lift away the heat control valve.
4   Disconnect the speedometer cable from the rear of the transmission unit casing.
5   Undo and remove the bolt, nut and spring washer that secures the brake servo unit to the subframe.
6   Release the gear change lever knob locknut. Unscrew and remove the knob and the locknut.
7   Disconnect the cables to the reverse light switch located on the transmission unit casing.
8   Undo and remove the nut and bolt securing the exhaust pipe clip to the exhaust down pipe.
9   Undo and remove the four bolts securing the exhaust pipe to the silencer mountings.
10   Slacken the two nuts on the exhaust pipe to rear silencer joint clip and carefully remove the exhaust pipe.
11   Undo and remove the nuts and spring washers from the exhaust pipe and silencer heat shield.
12   Carefully lower the gear change control from the underside of the body.
13   With a scriber, or small file, mark the steering column flange and pinion so that the two parts may be correctly fitted on reassembly.

14   Disconnect the steering column from the coupling by undoing and removing the two nuts, bolts and spring washers.
15   Wipe the top of the brake master cylinder and unscrew the cap. Place a piece of thick polythene sheet over the top and refit the cap. This is to prevent hydraulic fluid syphoning out in subsequent operations.
16   Wipe the brake pipe connections at the joint between the front hub flexible hoses and main metal pipe lines and detach the brake pipes at these connections. Further information will be found in Chapter 9/22.
17   Open the boot lid and remove the boot compartment floor covering. Undo and remove the two self tapping screws securing each of the two suspension access plates to the floor. Remove the access plates.
18   The suspension may now be depressurised. For this it is usually necessary to use special equipment, but it may be done by unscrewing the valve cap, using a large jam jar to catch the fluid, and very carefully depressing the centre of the valve. Do not depress it fully as the Hydrolastic suspension is pressurised to approximately 245 lb/sq in. Use a small screwdriver.
19   Using the same technique for the disconnection of brake flexible hoses, disconnect the suspension pipes at their front connectors.
20   Next release the flexible suspension pipes from the body clips.
21   Undo and remove the four bolts that secure the lower suspension arm bearings to the body.
22   Undo and remove the two bolts that secure the subframe to the tow board.
23   Undo and remove the three bolts, nuts and spring washers that secure each side of the subframe to the wing valance.
24   Very carefully lower the complete subframe assembly.
25   Place a rope sling, suitably padded, around the front of the body and raise the body to a sufficient height to clear the top of the engine. Either move the body rearwards and swing the front away from the complete power unit and subframe assembly, or draw the assembly forwards from under the car.

7   Engine and transmission with subframe (rod gear change models) - removal

The sequence for removal is basically identical to that for removal of the cable operated gear change models as described in Section 6. The main difference is confined to the removal of the gear change remote control system. Full information will be found in Chapter 6. The following additional points should be carried out:
1   Remove the complete exhaust system from the underside of the car.
2   Slacken the screws that secure the front door kicking plates and completely remove the front carpeting.
3   When the subframe has been removed, recover the rubber mountings and sleeves from the subframe mounting points. These are shown in Fig. 1:6(27).

8   Engine - separation from transmission unit.

Full information of this operation is given in Chapter 6/4.

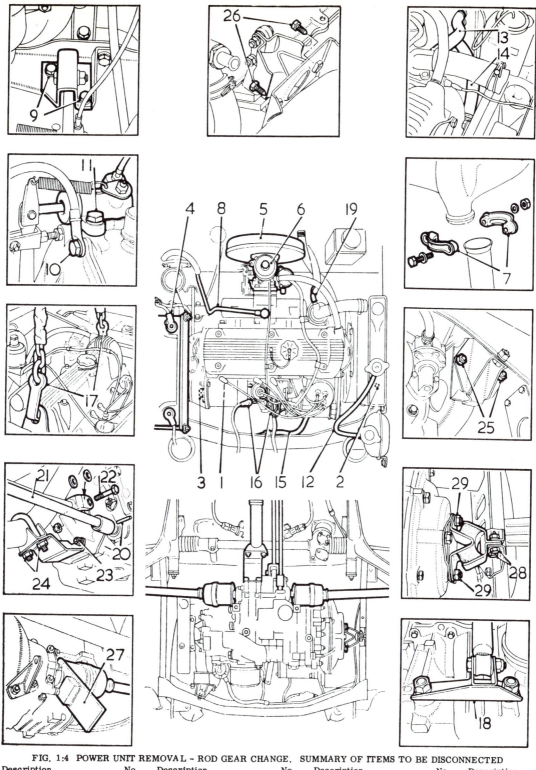

FIG. 1:4 POWER UNIT REMOVAL - ROD GEAR CHANGE. SUMMARY OF ITEMS TO BE DISCONNECTED

No.	Description	No.	Description	No.	Description	No.	Description
1	Cylinder block drain plug	10	Earth cable		chain	24	'U' bolt nuts
2	Radiator drain plug	11	Clutch slave cylinder	18	Damper bracket	25	LH engine mounting
3	Oil drain plug *	12	Spill pipe	19	Thermal transmitter	26	Rear LH engine mounting
4	Battery terminals and carrier	13	Heater hose to thermostat housing	20	Extension rod to selector shaft retaining pin	27	Drive shaft removal from final drive unit
5	Air cleaner	14	Heater hose to water pump	21	Extension rod	28	Rear engine mounting fixings to sub frame fixings
6	Carburettor	15	Fuel pipe to fuel pump	22	Steady rod securing bolt	29	Rear engine mounting fixings to clutch housing
7	Exhaust pipe to manifold clamp	16	Electric cables	23	Exhaust bracket to transmission securing nuts		
8	Vacuum servo to inlet manifold pipe connection	17	Engine lifting brackets and				
9	Steady bracket						

Later models have the oil drain plug on the left-hand side of the block

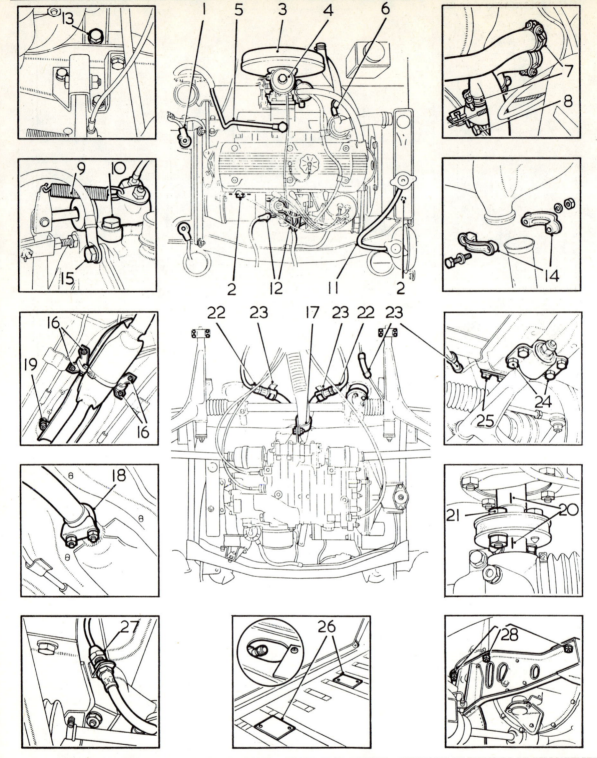

FIG. 1:5 POWER UNIT REMOVAL WITH SUB FRAME – CABLE GEAR CHANGE. SUMMARY OF ITEMS TO BE DISCONNECTED

No.	Description
1	Battery terminals and carrier
2	Radiator and cylinder block drain plug
3	Air cleaner
4	Carburettor
5	Vacuum servo to inlet manifold pipe connection
6	Thermal transmitter
7	Heater hoses at heater and control valve

No.	Description
8	Control valve mounted on sub frame
9	Clutch arm return spring
10	Clutch slave cylinder
11	Spill pipe
12	Electric cables
13	Brake servo to subframe mounting
14	Exhaust pipe to manifold clamp
15	Earth cable

No.	Description
16	Exhaust silencer mountings
17	Exhaust pipe clip
18	Exhaust pipe to rear silencer joint
19	Heat shield mountings
20	Alignment marks
21	Steering column coupling nuts and bolts
22	Hydrolastic suspension pipe union
23	Fuel pipe flexible connector

No.	Description
24	Lower suspension arm bearing mounting to body
25	Sub frame to toe board securing bolts
26	Suspension pipes access plate
27	Brake pipe union
28	Sub frame to wing valance securing bolts

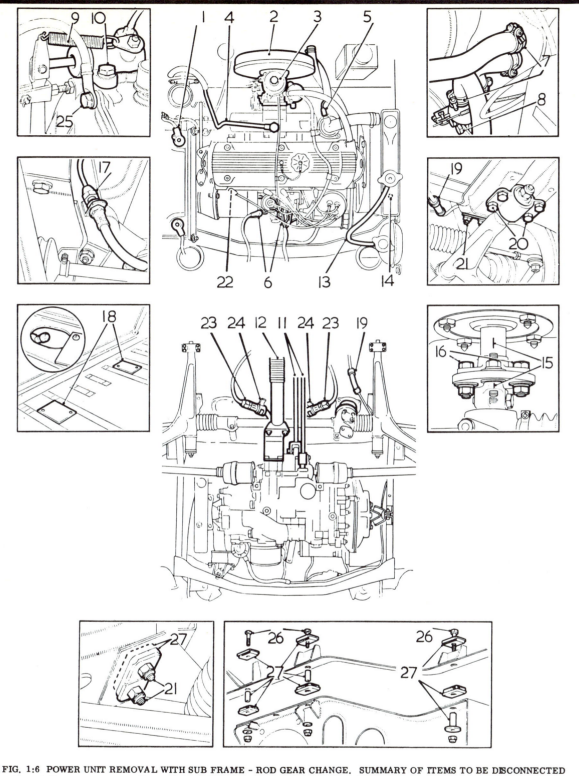

FIG. 1:6 POWER UNIT REMOVAL WITH SUB FRAME - ROD GEAR CHANGE. SUMMARY OF ITEMS TO BE DISCONNECTED

No.	Description	No.	Description	No.	Description	No.	Description
1	Battery terminals and carrier		frame		and bolts		ion
2	Air cleaner	9	Clutch aim return spring	17	Brake pipe union	24	Hydrolastic suspension pipe clips
3	Carburettor	10	Clutch slave cylinder	18	Suspension pipes access plate		
4	Vacuum servo to inlet manifold pipe connection	11	Remote control assembly	19	Fuel pipe flexible connector	25	Earth cable
5	Thermal transmitter	12	Exhaust system	20	Lower suspension arm bearing mounting to body	26	Sub frame to wing valance securing bolts
6	Electric cables	13	Spill pipe	21	Sub frame to body mounting	27	Rubber mountings and sleeves
7	Heater hoses at heater and control valve	14	Radiator drain plug	22	Cylinder block drain plug		
		15	Alignment marks	23	Hydrolastic suspension pipe un-		
8	Control valve mounted on sub	16	Steering column coupling nuts				

9 Engine - dismantling (general)

1   It is best to mount the engine on a dismantling stand, but if this is not available, stand the engine on a strong bench at a comfortable working height. Failing this, it can be stripped down on the floor.

2   During the dismantling process, the greatest care should be taken to keep the exposed parts free from dirt. As an aid to achieving this thoroughly clean down the outside of the engine, first removing all traces of oil and congealed dirt.

3   A good grease solvent such as 'Gunk' will make the job much easier, for, after the solvent has been applied and allowed to stand for a time, a vigorous jet of water will wash off the solvent and the grease with it. If the dirt is thick and deeply embedded, work the solvent into it with a strong stiff brush.

4   Finally wipe down the exterior of the engine with a rag and only then, when it is quite clean, should the dismantling process begin. As the engine is stripped, clean each part in a bath of paraffin or petrol.

5   Never immerse parts with oilways in paraffin, e.g. crankshaft. To clean these parts, wipe down carefully with a petrol dampened rag. Oilways can be cleaned out with nylon pipe cleaners. If an air line is available, all parts can be blown dry and the oilways blown through as an added precaution.

6   Re-use of old gaskets is false economy. To avoid the possibility of trouble after the engine has been reassembled ALWAYS use new gaskets throughout.

7   Do not throw the old gaskets away, for sometimes it happens that an immediate replacement cannot be found and the old gasket is then very useful as a template. Hang up the gaskets as they are removed.

8   To strip the engine, it is best to work from the top down. The crankcase provides a firm base on which the engine can be supported in an upright position. When the stage is reached where the crankshaft must be removed, the engine can be turned on its side and all other work carried out with it in this position.

9   Wherever possible, replace nuts, bolts and washers finger tight from wherever they were removed. This helps to avoid loss and muddle. If they cannot be replaced, then lay them out in such a fashion that it is clear from whence they came.

10 Engine - removing ancilliary components

Before basic engine dismantling begins, it is necessary to strip it of ancilliary components. These are as follows:-

a)   Fuel system components
        Carburettor and manifold assembly
        Fuel pump
        Fuel lines
b)   Ignition system components
        Spark plugs
        Distributor
        Coil and mounting bracket
c)   Electrical system components
        Generator
        Starter motor
d)   Cooling system components
        Radiator and mountings
        Fan and hub
        Water pump

Thermostat housing and thermostat
        Water temperature sender unit
e)   Engine
        Crankcase ventilation tube
        Oil pressure sender unit
        Oil level dipstick and guide tube
        Oil filler cap and camshaft cover
        Engine mountings
f)   Clutch
        Clutch pressure plate assembly
        Clutch friction plate assembly
     All nuts and bolts associated with the foregoing.

Some of these items have to be removed for individual servicing or renewal periodically and details can be found under the appropriate chapter.

11 Cylinder head removal - engine in car

1   Undo and remove the two nuts and spring washers securing the air cleaner to the air intake flange of the carburettor (photo). Lift away the air cleaner.

2   Detach the distributor automatic advance/retard pipe from the distributor vacuum unit and the induction side of the carburettor body. Lift away the pipe.

3   Detach the engine breather hose from the camshaft cover.

4   With a pair of pliers, compress the ears of the clip holding the fuel supply hose to the float chamber union. Pull off the fuel supply hose.

5   Make a note of the manner in which the throttle return spring is fitted and unhook the spring. Put the spring in a safe place.

6   Release the throttle cable connector from the cable by slackening the centre screw and drawing the connector from the end of the cable.

7   Pull the throttle outer cable from its support bracket.

8   Slacken the choke cable connector centre screw and pull the inner cable from the connector. Lift away the connector (photo).

9   Undo the brake servo unit pipe union bolt from the induction manifold. Lift away the union bolt and recover the two copper washers.

10   Undo and remove the two nuts, bolts and washers from the clamp securing the exhaust down pipe to the exhaust manifold. Lift away the two halves of the clamp (photo).

11   Refer to Chapter 2/2 and drain the cooling system.

12   Slacken the clips securing the radiator, water pump and heater hoses to the thermostat housing. Ease the hoses from the thermostat housing.

13   Disconnect the Lucar terminal from the temperature gauge thermal transmitter.

14   Mark the high tension cables relative to the spark plugs for correct refitting and disconnect the four leads.

15   Undo and remove the bolts and spring washers securing the engine steady arm bracket and right hand lifting bracket to the cylinder head.

16   Undo and remove the bolts and spring washers securing the radiator bracket and left hand lifting bracket to the cylinder head.

17   The six shaped bolts which hold the camshaft cover to the top of the cylinder head should now be unscrewed in a progressive diagonal manner. Lift away the cover and the gasket.

18   The crankshaft should now be turned until the timing marks 1/4 TDC on the flywheel are in alignment with number

FIG.1:7 CYLINDER HEAD
                  REMOVAL

No.	Description
1	Air cleaner
2	Fuel, heater and distributor vacuum pipe
3	Throttle and choke cables
4	Brake servo unit pipe
5	Exhaust down pipe
6	Exhaust down pipe to manifold clip
7	Thermal transmitter
8	Spark plug leads
9	Rear lifting bracket
10	Front lifting bracket
11	Cylinder head cover
12	Flywheel and camshaft alignment marks
13	Chain tensioner adaptor
14	1/8 inch Allen key
15	Camshaft sprocket
16	Cylinder head bolts
17	Cylinder head and gasket

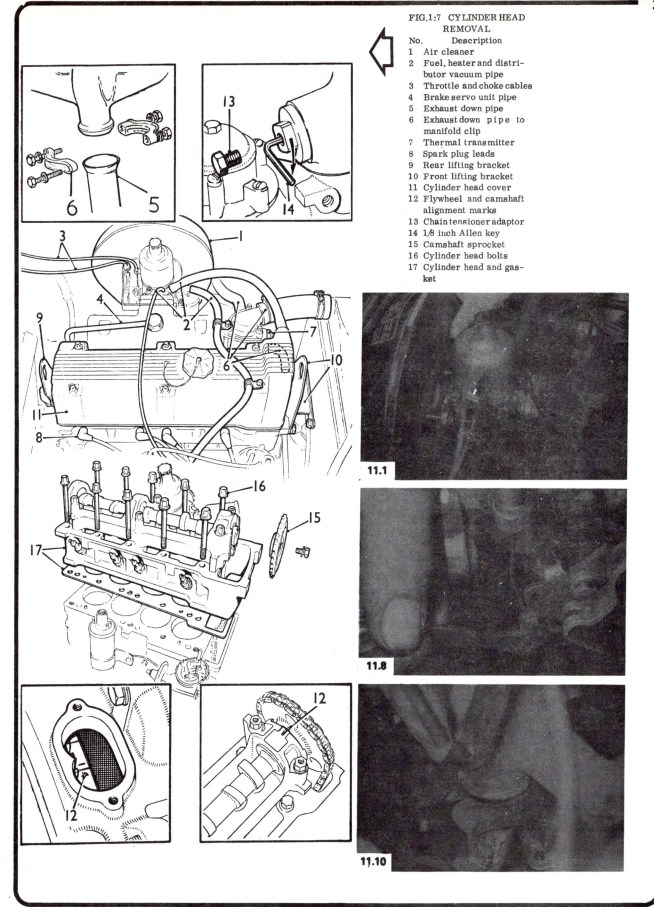

11.1

11.8

11.10

1 cylinder on commencement of the firing stroke. The marks can be seen once the timing cover has been removed.

19 Carefully adjust the camshaft sprocket until the camshaft timing marks are in alignment. These are to be found on the sprocket hub and adjoining bearing boss.

20 Undo and remove the chain tensioner adaptor bolt and then, using an 1/8 inch Allen key placed through the bolt aperture, turn the tensioner plunger in a clockwise direction to retract the tensioner slipper from the chain.

21 Undo and remove the bolt and spring washer securing the camshaft sprocket to the camshaft and detach the sprocket from the camshaft.

22 Slacken the cylinder head securing bolts in a diagonal and progressive manner until all are free from tension. Remove the ten bolts noting that because of the shape of the bolt head no washers are used.

23 The cylinder head may now be removed by lifting upwards. If the head is jammed, try to rock it to break the seal. Under no circumstances try to prise it apart from the cylinder block with a screwdriver or cold chisel, as damage may be done to the faces of the cylinder head and block. If the head will not readily free, turn the engine over by the flywheel using the starter motor, as the compression in the cylinders will often break the cylinder head joint. If this fails to work, strike the head sharply with a plastic headed or wooden hammer, or with a metal hammer with an interposed piece of wood to cushion the blow. Under no circumstances hit the head directly with a metal hammer as this may cause the iron casting to fracture. Several sharp taps with the hammer, at the same time pulling upwards, should free the head. Lift the head off and place on one side.

12 Cylinder head removal - engine on bench

The procedure for removing the cylinder head with the engine on the bench is similar to that for removal when the engine is in the car, with the exception of disconnecting the controls and services. Refer to Section 11 and follow the sequence given in paragraphs 12, and 15 to 22 inclusive.

Instead of turning the crankshaft using the starter motor as mentioned in Section 11/23, use a large socket spanner on the pulley retaining bolt to turn the crankshaft.

13 Camshaft and tappets - removal

1 Undo and remove the two bolts and spring washers securing the timing cover to the flywheel housing.

2 Undo and remove the six shaped bolts which hold the camshaft cover to the top of the cylinder head in a diagonal and progressive manner. Lift away the cover and the gasket.

3 The crankshaft should now be turned until the timing marks 1/4 TDC on the flywheel are in alignment with number 1 cylinder on the commencement of the firing stroke.

4 Carefully check that the camshaft sprocket and adjoining bearing boss marks align correctly and if necessary turn the crankshaft in the normal direction of rotation until the marks do align correctly.

4 Remove the positive and then negative terminals from the battery.

5 Undo and remove the nuts and plain washers holding the battery clamp bar to the support rods and lift away the clamp bar and two rods.

6 Lift away the battery from its tray. The tray may be lifted out next.

7 Undo and remove the bolts and spring washers securing the radiator stay and left hand lifting bracket to the end of the cylinder head.

8 Undo and remove the bolts and spring washers securing the engine steady and right hand lifting bracket to the end of the cylinder head.

9 Undo and remove the chain tensioner adaptor bolt and then, using an 1/8 inch Allen key placed through the bolt adaptor, turn the tensioner plunger in a clockwise direction to retract the tensioner slipper from the chain.

10 Undo and remove the bolt and spring washer securing the camshaft sprocket to the camshaft and detach the sprocket from the camshaft.

11 Slacken the camshaft housing bolts in a diagonal and progressive manner until the valve spring pressure is released.

12 Lift up the camshaft housing by a sufficient amount for the tappets to fall clear of the camshaft. Give the housing a little shake if necessary.

13 Recover the tappets and place in order so that they can be refitted in their original positions.

14 The camshaft can be removed from the housing by the end opposite to the sprocket.

14 Valve - removal

1 The valves can be removed from the cylinder head by the following method. Compress each spring in turn with a valve spring compressor until the two halves of the collets can be removed (photo).

2 Release the compressor and remove the valve spring cup and spring (photo).

3 Lift away the oil seal fitted to inlet valves only (photo).

4 If, when the valve spring compressor is screwed down, the valve spring cup refuses to free and expose the split collet, do not continue to screw it down as there is a likelihood of damaging it.

5 Gently tap the top of the tool directly over the cup with a hammer. This will free the cup. To avoid the compressor jumping off the valve retaining cup when it is tapped, hold the compressor firmly in position with one hand.

6 It is essential that the valves are kept in their correct sequence unless they are so badly worn that they are to be renewed. If they are going to be used again, place them in a sheet of card having eight numbered holes corresponding with the relative positions of the valves when fitted. Also keep the valve springs, cups etc., in the correct order.

7 Should a case of noisy valve gear be under investigation on early engines up to engine number 14H/283 EH/13472 the cause could be due to the valve stem either scuffing or picking up in the guide. If this is evident new valves must be fitted. On engines produced after this number, the finish of the guides and method of assembly into the cylinder head were changed to eliminate this problem.

15 Timing chain and sprockets - removal

1 Before commencing work it should be noted that a special tool is required to split the chain. If this tool, having a part number 18G1151, cannot be borrowed the job should be left to the local BLMC garage.

2 For this work to be carried out the power unit must first be removed from the car.

3 Refer to Chapter 6/4 and separate the engine from the transmission unit.

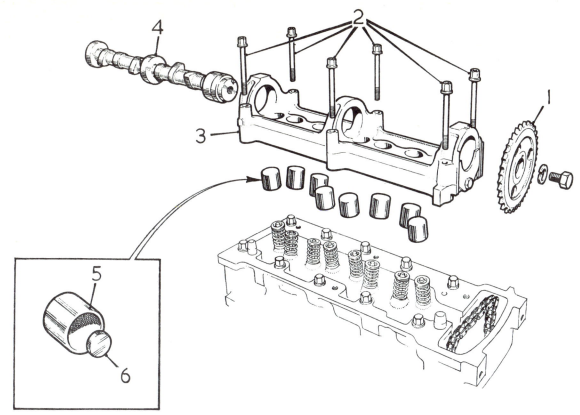

FIG. 1:8 CAMSHAFT AND TAPPETS REMOVAL

No.	Description	No.	Description	No.	Description	No.	Description
1	Camshaft sprocket	3	Camshaft housing	5	Tappet	6	Tappet adjustment shim
2	Camshaft housing bolts	4	Camshaft				

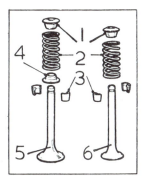

FIG. 1:9 INLET AND EX-
HAUST VALVE ASSEM-
BLIES

No.   Description
1   Valve spring cups
2   Valve springs
3   Collets
4   Oil seal (inlet valve only)
5   Inlet valve
6   Exhaust valve

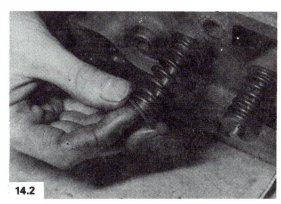

14.2

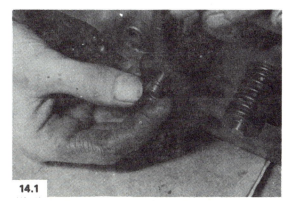

14.1

14.3

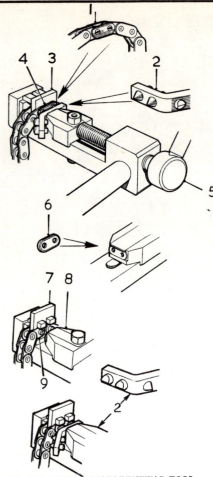

FIG. 1:10 TIMING CHAIN RENEWAL TOOL

No.	Description	No.	Description
1	Timing chain	6	Side plate fitted to moving jaw
2	Pointed extractor pins	7	Loose bridge piece reversed
3	Loose bridge piece	8	Moving jaw
4	Side plate removal	9	Press tightened onto pins
5	Service tool 18G 1151		

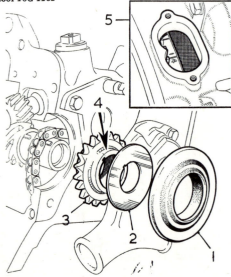

FIG. 1:11 CRANKSHAFT SPROCKET REMOVAL

No.	Description	No.	Description
1	Oil seal	4	Tapered face of sprocket to face forwards
2	Oil thrower		
3	Crankshaft sprocket	5	Flywheel timing marks

4   Using a suitable sized socket and, to lock the flywheel, a screwdriver inserted through the timing cover, undo and remove the crankshaft pulley securing bolt and lockwasher.

5   With either a universal puller or tyre levers draw the crankshaft pulley from the end of the crankshaft.

6   Turn the crankshaft until the timing marks 1/4 TDC on the flywheel are in alignment with number 1 cylinder on the commencement of the firing stroke.

7   Carefully check that the camshaft sprocket and adjoining bearing boss marks align correctly and, if necessary, turn the crankshaft in the normal direction of rotation until the marks do align correctly.

8   Undo and remove the chain tensioner adaptor bolt and then, using a 1/8 inch Allen key placed through the bolt adaptor, turn the tensioner plunger in a clockwise direction to retract the tensioner slipper from the chain.

9   Undo and remove the bolt and spring washer securing the camshaft sprocket to the camshaft and detach the sprocket from the camshaft.

10   Using a screwdriver, carefully ease the front oil seal from its location in the cylinder block. (Fig. 1:11).

11   Lift out the oil thrower and ease the crankshaft sprocket off the end of the crankshaft.

12   To remove the chain it is now necessary to use the special tool as mentioned in paragraph 1.

13   Locate the bright link of the chain.

14   Fit the pointed extractor adaptor into the head of the tool sliding press.

15   Fit the bridge piece of the tool into the bright link.

16   Position the bright link in the front of the tool anvil with the riveted side of the link (link pin heads with horizontal depression) towards the sliding press of the tool.

17   Tighten the press until the link pins shear through the link plate.

18   Retract the press and remove the chain.

___

16   Chain tensioner - removal

___

1   This operation may be carried out with the engine still in the car.

2   Refer to Chapter 2/5:1 to 7 inclusive and remove the radiator and cowling.

3   Slacken the dynamo mountings and push the dynamo towards the cylinder block. Lift off the fan belt.

4   Undo the two bolts that secure the fan blade hub to the water pump spindle and lift away the two bolts, metal bushes and the fan blades.

5   Undo and remove the two bolts and spring washers that secure the radiator lower support bracket. Lift away the support bracket.

6   Using a suitable sized socket, and to lock the flywheel a screwdriver inserted through the timing cover, undo and remove the crankshaft pulley securing bolt and lockwasher.

7   With either a universal puller or tyre levers, draw the crankshaft pulley from the end of the crankshaft.

8   Refer to Section 15 and follow the sequence described in paragraphs 6 to 9 inclusive.

9   Using a small open ended spanner, unscrew and remove the dynamo adjusting link pivot and spring washer.

10   Undo and remove the three bolts and spring washers securing the engine cover to the cylinder block just below the water pump. Lift away the cover and joint washer.

11   Unscrew and remove the chain tensioner adaptor and withdraw the tensioner through the front cover aperture.

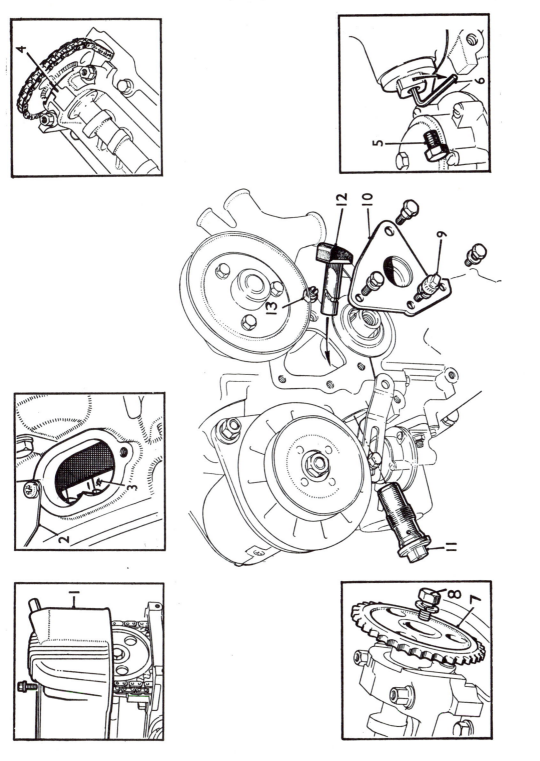

FIG. 1:12 TIMING CHAIN TENSIONER REMOVAL

No.	Description	No.	Description	No.	Description
1	Cylinder head cover	7	Camshaft sprocket	13	Adjuster for right hand chain guide
2	Flywheel housing cover	8	Camshaft sprocket securing bolt	11	Tensioner adaptor
3	Flywheel marking	9	Generator link pivot bolt	12	Tensioner
4	Camshaft alignment marks	10	Engine front cover		
5	Tensioner adaptor bolt				
6	1/8 inch Allen key				

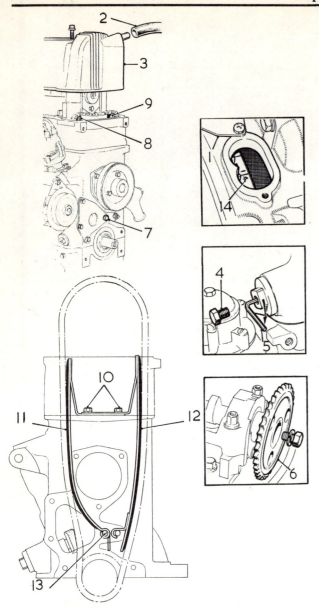

FIG. 1:13 TIMING CHAIN GUIDE REMOVAL

No.	Description	No.	Description
1	Flywheel housing timing cover	8	LH guide
2	Breather hose	9	RH guide
3	Cylinder head cover	10	Guide retaining bolts
4	Tensioner adaptor bolt	11	LH guide
5	1/8 inch Allen key	12	RH guide
6	Camshaft sprocket	13	Dowel bolt for LH guide
7	Dowel bolt for LH guide	14	Flywheel mark

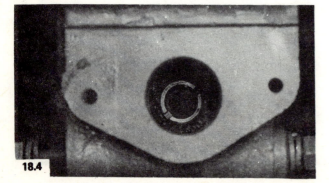

17   Chain guides - removal

1   Refer to Chapter 2/5:1 to 7 inclusive, and remove the radiator and cowling.
2   Refer to Section 16:3 to 7 inclusive, and remove the fan belt, fan blades, radiator lower support bracket and crankshaft pulley.
3   Unscrew and remove the two bolts and spring washers securing the timing cover to the flywheel housing.
4   Pull the breather hose from the radiator end of the camshaft cover.
5   Unscrew the six camshaft cover securing bolts in a diagonal and progressive manner.   Lift away the camshaft cover and its gasket.
6   Turn the crankshaft until the timing marks 1/4 TDC on the flywheel are in alignment with number 1 cylinder on the commencement of the firing stroke.
7   Carefully check that the camshaft sprocket and adjoining bearing boss marks align correctly and, if necessary, turn the crankshaft in the normal direction of rotation until the marks do align.
8   Undo and remove the chain tensioner adaptor bolt and then, using a 1/8 inch Allen key placed through the bolt adaptor, turn the tensioner plunger in a clockwise direction to retract the tensioner slipper from the chain.
9   Undo and remove the bolt and spring washer securing the camshaft sprocket to the camshaft and detach the sprocket from the camshaft.
10   Undo and remove the dowel bolt and spring washer from the lower end of the fixed guide.
11   Undo and remove the two guide upper retaining bolts and spring washers.
12   The fixed guide (tensioner side) may now be lifted away from the engine.
13   Carefully detach the lower end of the adjustable guide from the eccentric adjuster, turn the guide through 90º and lift it from the engine.

18   Distributor and fuel pump drive shaft - removal

1   For this operation it is necessary to remove the power unit from the car.
2   Refer to Chapter 6/4 and separate the engine from the transmission unit.
3   Refer to Section 15:4 to 11 inclusive and remove the camshaft and crankshaft sprocket.
4   Note the position of the distributor drive and the slot at the 2 o'clock position with the large lobe uppermost (photo).
5   The distributor drive gear may now be withdrawn from the crankshaft.   Note that the drive gear shaft will turn through approximately 90º as the gear is withdrawn.   Lift out the drive shaft and thrust washer.

19   Piston, connecting rod and big end bearing - removal

Unlike the conventional engine it is not possible to remove the pistons or connecting rods whilst the engine is still in the car as it is necessary first to remove the flywheel housing and primary drive gear cover and then separate the transmission unit as described in Chapter 6/4.   Then proceed as follows:
1   Undo the big end nuts and place to one side in the order in which they were removed.

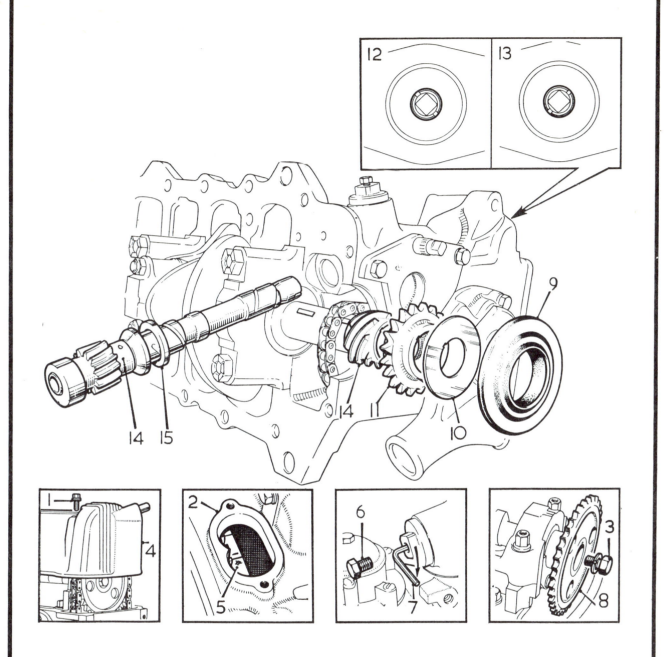

FIG. 1:14 DISTRIBUTOR AND FUEL PUMP DRIVE SHAFT REMOVAL AND REFITTING

No.	Description	No.	Description	No.	Description	No.	Description
1	Cylinder head cover securing bolts	4	Cylinder head cover	9	Front oil seal	13	Position of offset after meshing gears
2	Flywheel housing	5	Flywheel marks	10	Oil thrower	14	Distributor and fuel pump drive shaft
3	Camshaft sprocket securing bolt	6	Tensioner adaptor bolt	11	Crankshaft sprocket	15	Thrust washer
		7	1/8 inch Allen key	12	Position of offset before meshing gears		
		8	Camshaft sprocket				

2   Remove the big end caps, taking care to keep them in the right order and the correct way round. Also ensure that the shell bearings are kept with their correct connecting rods and caps unless they are to be renewed. Normally, the numbers 1 - 4 are stamped on adjacent sides of the big end caps and connecting rods, indicating which cap fits on which rod and which way round the cap fits. (See Fig. 1.15). If no numbers or lines can be found, then with a scriber or file scratch mating marks across the joint from the rod to the cap. One line for connecting rod No. 1, two for connecting rod No. 2 and so on. This will ensure that there is no confusion later. It is most important that the caps go back in the correct positions on the connecting rods from which they were removed.

3   If the big end caps are difficult to remove, they may be gently tapped with a soft hammer.

4   To remove the shell bearings, press the bearing opposite the groove in both the connecting rod and its caps, and the bearings will slide out easily.

5   Withdraw the pistons and connecting rods upwards and ensure they are kept in the correct order for replacement in the same bore.

20   Gudgeon pin - removal

1   A press fit gudgeon pin is used and a special BLMC tool No. 18G1150 with adaptors 18G1150C is required to remove and replace it. The tool is shown in Fig. 1:16 and must be used in the manner described in the following paragraphs:

2   Securely hold the hexagonal body in a firm vice and screw back the large nut until it is flush with the end of the main centre screw. Well lubricate the screw and large nut as they have to withstand high loading. Now push the centre screw in until the nut touches the thrust race.

3   Fit the adaptor number 18G1150C onto the main centre screw with the piston ring cut away positioned uppermost. Then slide the parallel sleeve with the groove end first onto the centre screw.

4   Fit the piston with the 'Front' or '△' mark towards the adaptor, on the centre screw. This is important because the gudgeon pin bore is offset and irreparable damage will result if fitted the wrong way round. Next fit the remover/replacer bush on the centre screw with the flange end towards the gudgeon pin.

5   Screw the stop nut onto the main centre screw and adjust it until approximately 1/32 inch end play ('A' in Fig. 1:16) exists, and lock the stop nut securely with the lock screws. Now check that the remover/replacer bush and parallel sleeve are positioned correctly in the bore on both sides on the piston. Also check that the curved face of the adaptor is clean and slide the piston onto the tool so it fits into the curved face of the adaptor with the piston rings over the cut away.

6   Screw the large nut up to the thrust race and, holding the lock screw, turn the large nut with a ring spanner or long socket until the gudgeon pin is withdrawn from the piston.

21   Piston ring - removal

1   To remove the piston rings, slide them carefully over the top of the piston, taking care not to scratch the aluminium alloy; never slide them off the bottom of the piston skirt. It is very easy to break the cast iron piston rings if they are pulled off roughly, so this operation should be done with extreme care. It is helpful to make use of an old 0.020 inch feeler gauge.

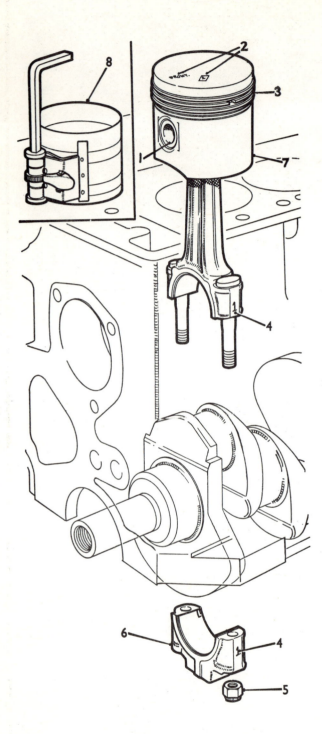

FIG. 1:15 PISTON AND CONNECTING ROD ASSEMBLY

No.	Description	No.	Description
1	Gudgeon pin	5	Big end nut
2	Piston identification marks	6	Big end cap
3	Piston rings	7	Piston
4	Connecting rod and cap/bore identification number.	8	Piston ring compression.

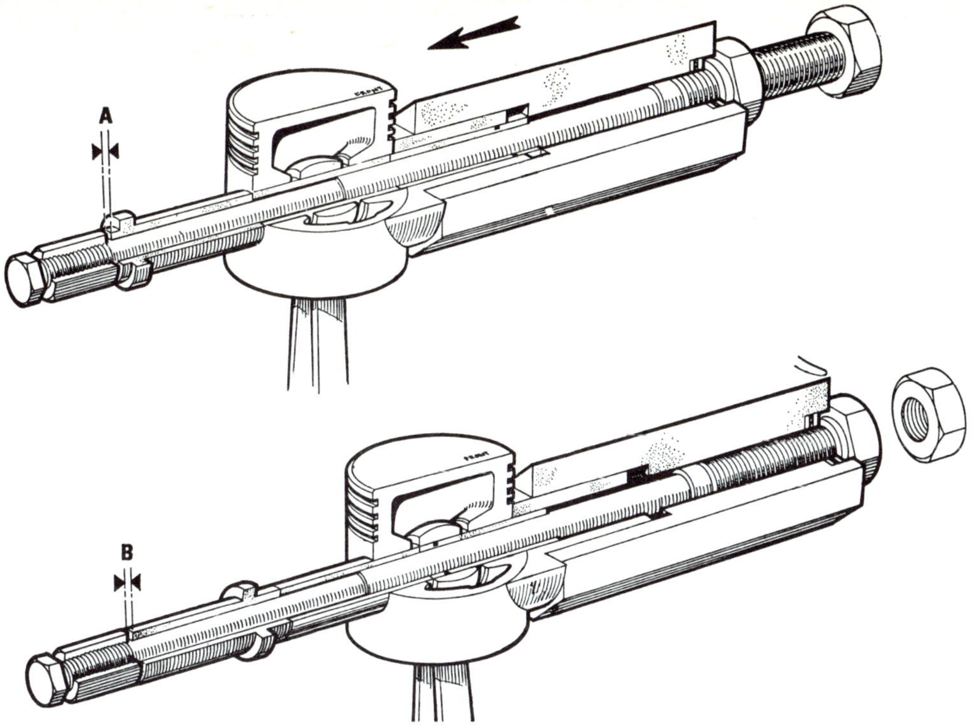

Fig. 1:16 Gudgeon pin removal and refitting

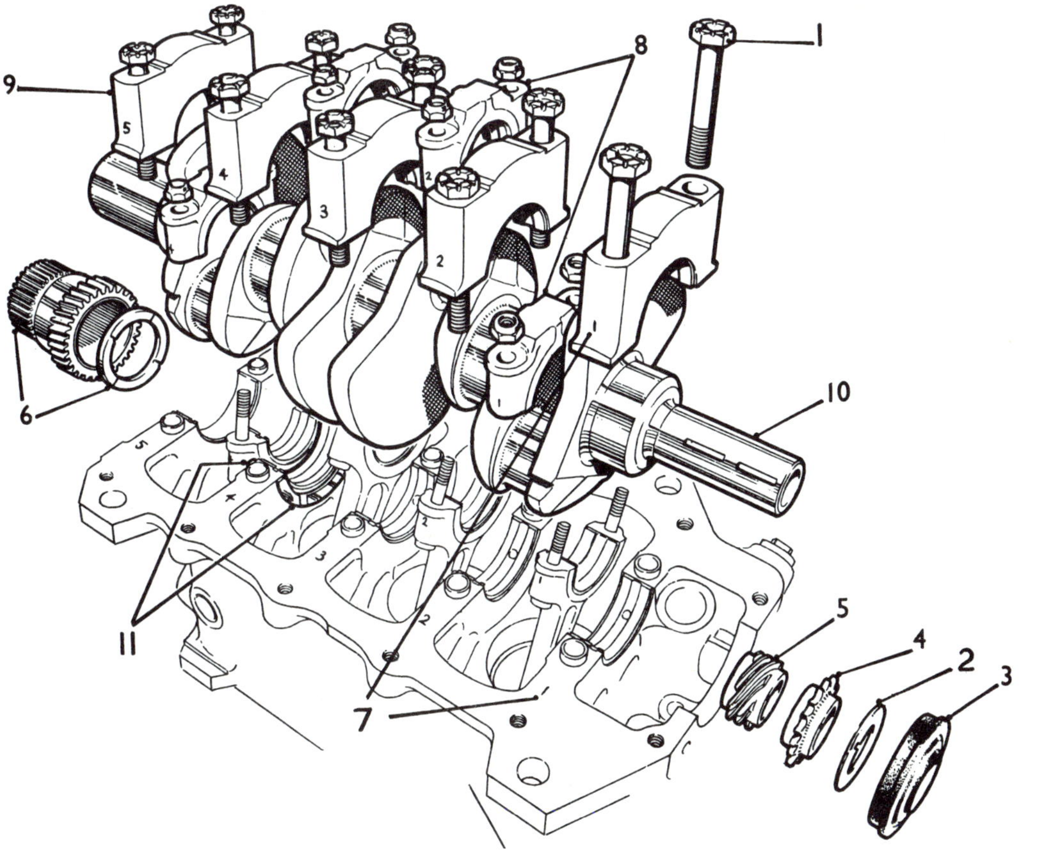

FIG. 1:17 CRANKSHAFT AND MAIN BEARING ASSEMBLIES

No.	Description	No.	Description	No.	Description	No.	Description
1	Main bearing cap bolt	4	Crankshaft sprocket	7	Main bearing cap and crankcase web mating marks	9	Main bearing cap
2	Oil thrower	5	Distributor drive gear			10	Crankshaft
3	Front oil seal	6	Primary gear and thrust washer	8	Big end bearing caps	11	Crankshaft thrust washers

2   Lift one end of the piston ring to be removed out of its groove and insert under it the end of the feeler gauge.
3   Turn the feeler gauge slowly round the piston and, as the ring comes out of its groove, apply slightly upward pressure so that it rests on the land above. It can then be eased off the piston with the feeler gauge stopping it from slipping into an empty groove if it is any but the top piston ring that is being removed.

22   Flywheel and flywheel housing - removal

Full details of this operation are given in Chapter 6/4.

23   Crankshaft and main bearing - removal

With the engine r e m o v e d from the car and separated from the transmission, remove the camshaft drive chain and sprocket. Also remove the crankshaft sprocket, flywheel and flywheel housing, big end bearings and pistons.
It will also be necessary to remove the distributor drive gear, the crankshaft primary gear and thrust washer.
Removal of the crankshaft can be attempted only with the engine on the bench or a clean floor.
1   Undo by one turn at a time the bolts which hold the five bearing caps.
2   Unscrew the bolts and remove them. Check that each bearing cap is marked as shown in Fig. 1.17. If no marks are evident these should be made with a file or scriber.
3   Remove the main bearing caps and the bottom half of each bearing shell, taking care to keep the bearing shells in the right caps.
4   When removing the number 4 main bearing cap, note the bottom semi-circular halves of the thrust washers, one half lying on either side of the main bearing. Lay them with the number 4 main bearing along the correct side.
5   Slightly rotate the crankshaft to free the upper halves of the bearing shells and thrust washers which can be extracted and placed over the correct bearing cap.
6   Remove the crankshaft by lifting it away from the crankcase.

24   Lubricating system - description

1   A forced feed system of lubrication is used so that oil circulates round the engine from the transmission unit below the cylinder block. The level of oil is indicated on the dipstick which is fitted to the front of the cylinder block. It is marked to i n d i c a t e the maximum and minimum oil level (photo).
2   The level of oil ideally should not be above or below the MAX mark. Oil is replenished via the filler cap on the top of the camshaft cover.
3   The oil pump, located in the transmission unit, draws oil from the supply in the transmission casing and passes it to a full flow oil filter which is fitted with a renewable element. To control the oil pressure, an oil pressure relief valve is located in the transmission unit under the filter head.
4   Oil passes from the filter to the main gallery, which runs the length of the cylinder block, and from there it is distributed by means of drillings to the various bearings.
5   Oil passes from the main gallery to the big end and main crankshaft bearings. A small hole in each connecting rod lets a jet of oil lubricate the cylinder wall on each revolution.

6   Oil passes up through a drilling in the cylinder head to lubricate the overhead camshaft and valve assemblies. From the top of the cylinder head, oil is able to pass back into the crankcase via the camshaft drive chain chest and from there into the transmission casing for re-circulation.

25   Oil filter - removal and replacement

1   The full flow oil filter is located at the front of the transmission casing in the vicinity of the fuel pump.
2   It is removed by first unscrewing the centre bolt and withdrawing the complete filter assembly.
3   Remove the filter head from the transmission casing.
4   Remove and discard the element and then remove the circlip. Withdraw the centre bolt and lift out the pressure plate, rubber washer, steel washer and spring from the casing.
5   Remove the old sealing ring from the filter head and the old gasket located between the filter head and transmission casing.
6   Thoroughly wash all components in petrol and wipe dry with a clean non-fluffy rag. Make sure that the mating faces of the filter head and transmission casing are really clean.
7   Fit the centre bolt to the f i l t e r bowl and slide on the spring, steel washer and new rubber washer followed by the pressure plate. (photo).
8   Secure the pressure plate in position with the circlip (photo).
9   Using a screwdriver, carefully ease a new sealing ring into the filter head by first fitting the ring into the groove at four equidistant points. Press it home a segment at a time (photo).
10   Do not insert the ring at just one point and work round the groove by pressing it home as, using this method, it is easy to stretch the ring and be left with a small loop of rubber which will not fit into the locating groove.
11   Insert a new oil filter element into the filter bowl (photo).
12   If the filter head centre seal is damaged or perished, ease out the old and fit a new one (photo).
13   Fit the filter head over the centre bolt, making sure that filter bowl locates correctly on the rubber sealing ring in the filter head (photo).
14   Smear a little grease onto the transmission casing filter head mating face and fit the new gasket noting that the oil filter face is marked (photo).
15   Refit the complete filter assembly and secure with the centre bolt (photo).

26   Ventilation air filter - removal and replacement

1   To provide air for ventilating the engine, a filter is located on the flywheel housing.
2   The filter element may be renewed by unscrewing the cover retaining screw and lifting off the cover and finally the filter element (photo).
3   Throw away the old element and place a new element onto the filter body. Refit the cover and secure with the screw and plain washer.

27   Oil pressure relief valve

1   The oil pressure relief valve is non-adjustable so, if its

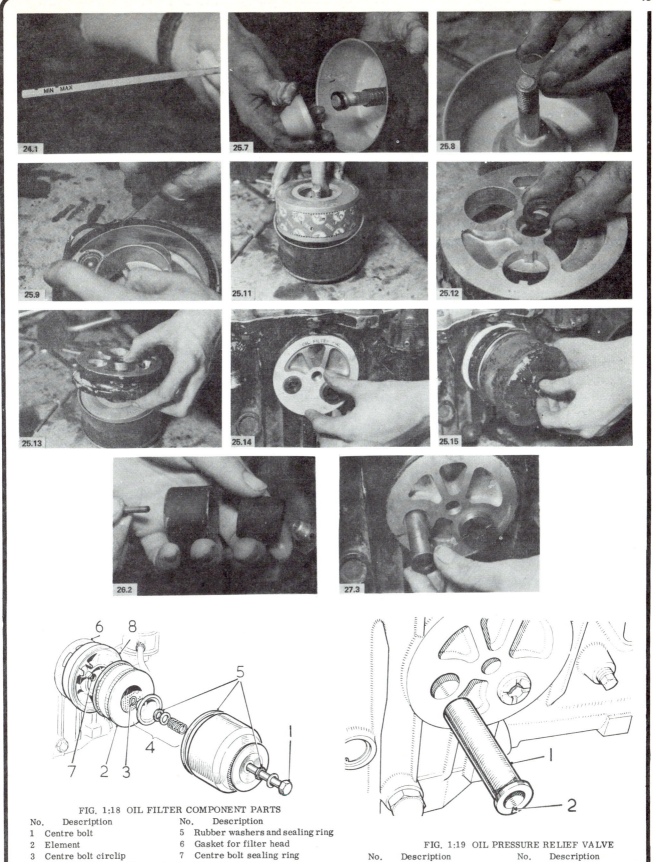

FIG. 1:18 OIL FILTER COMPONENT PARTS

No.	Description	No.	Description
1	Centre bolt	5	Rubber washers and sealing ring
2	Element	6	Gasket for filter head
3	Centre bolt circlip	7	Centre bolt sealing ring
4	Pressure plate, rubber and steel washers and spring.	8	Filter head

FIG. 1:19 OIL PRESSURE RELIEF VALVE

No.	Description	No.	Description
1	Relief valve		tion of release hole.
2	Identification mark for posi-		

operation is suspect, a new assembly must be obtained and fitted. It is located under the oil filter head.

2   Refer to Section 25 and remove the oil filter and head assembly.

3   Draw the oil pressure relief valve from its bore in the transmission case. Note the location of the release hole which must point downwards (photo).

4   There is a line scribed on the face of the pressure relief valve to act as a guide for refitting. This is shown in Fig. 1.19.

5   Refitting is the reverse procedure to removal.

---

28   Oil pump - removal and dismantling

To gain access to the oil pump remove the complete power unit and then separate the transmission unit from the engine. Full information on this operation will be found in Chapter 6/4. Then proceed as follows:

1   Bend back the tab washer locking the baffle plate securing bolt in the centre web of the transmission unit. Undo and remove the bolt, tab washer and baffle.

2   Unscrew the oil pump outlet connection which will be found under the oil filter head adjacent to the pressure relief valve. Although a special tool is recommended it is possible to remove it with a mole wrench provided it is clamped securely to the large boss of the outlet connection.

3   Undo and remove the two bolts with spring and plain washers that secure the oil pump to the side of the transmission unit.

4   The oil pump may now be lifted out of the transmission unit.

5   Should it be necessary to remove the oil pump pick up, it is necessary to remove the fifth speed gear.

6   To dismantle the oil pump, first undo and remove the three bolts and spring washers which secure the suction filter housing to the body.

7   Lift away the intake filter assembly.

8   The motor and shaft assembly and outer ring may now be withdrawn from the body.

9   Undo and remove the bolts and spring washers holding the two parts of the intake filter assembly together. Separate the two parts and lift away the strainer and joint washer.

---

29   Chain tensioner - dismantling

With the tensioner removed from the engine as described in Section 16, fit a 1/8 inch Allen key to its socket in the cylinder and, holding the slipper and plunger firmly, turn the key clockwise to free the cylinder and spring from the plunger.

---

30   Engine - examination and renovation - general

---

1   With the engine stripped down and all parts thoroughly clean it is time to examine everything for wear or damage. The items in Sections 31 to 41 following should be checked and where necessary renewed or renovated.

2   In any border line case it is always best to decide in favour of a new part. Even if a part may still be serviceable its life will have been reduced by wear and the degree of trouble needed to replace it in the future must be taken into consideration.

3   This is a relative situation; it depends on whether a quick

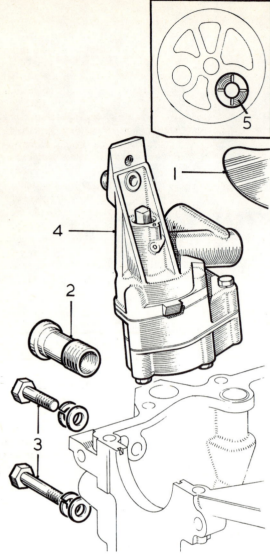

FIG. 1:20 OIL PUMP REMOVAL

No.	Description	No.	Description
1	Transmission unit baffle	4	Oil pump
2	Pump outlet	5	Oil pump outlet location
3	Pump securing bolts		

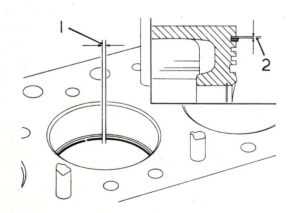

FIG. 1:21 PISTON RING WEAR MEASUREMENT

No.	Description	No.	Description
1	Ring gap measurement	2	Ring groove measurement

'survival' job is being done or the car as a whole is being regarded as having many thousands of miles of useful and economical life remaining.

---

31 Crankshaft - examination and renovation

---

1   Look at the main bearing journals and the crankpins. If there are any scratches or score marks then the shaft will need regrinding. Such conditions will nearly always be accompanied by similar deterioration on the matching bearing shells.
2   Each bearing journal should also be round and can be checked with a micrometer or caliper gauge around the periphery at several points. If there is more than 0.001 inch of ovality regrinding is necessary.
3   A BLMC garage or motor engineering specialist will be able to decide to what extent regrinding is necessary and supply the special undersize bearings to match.
4   Before taking the crankshaft for regrinding, check the cylinder bores and pistons, as it may be advantageous to have the whole unit done together.

---

32 Crankshaft (main) bearings and big end (connecting rod) bearings - examination and renovation

---

1   With careful servicing and regular oil and filter changes, bearings will last for a very long time but they can still fail for unforseen reasons. With big end bearings, the indication of failure is a regular rythmic loud knocking from the crankcase. The frequency depends on engine speed and is particularly noticeable when the engine is under load. This sympton is accompanied by a fall in oil pressure, although this is not noticeable unless an accurate oil pressure gauge is fitted. Main bearing failure is usually indicated by serious vibration, particularly at higher engine revolutions, accompanied by a more significant drop in oil pressure and a 'rumbling' noise.
2   Bearing shells in good condition have bearing surfaces with a smooth, even matt silver/grey colour all over. Worn bearings will show patches of a different colour when the bearing metal has worn and exposed the underlay. Damaged bearings will be pitted or scored. Always fit new shells. Their cost is relatively low. If the crankshaft is in good condition it is merely a question of obtaining another set of standard size shells. A reground crankshaft will need new bearing shells as a matter of course.

---

33 Cylinder bores - examination and renovation

---

1   A new cylinder bore is perfectly round and the walls parallel throughout its length. The action of the piston tends to wear the walls at right angles to the gudgeon pin due to side thrust. This wear takes place principally on that section of the cylinder swept by the piston rings.
2   It is possible to get an indication of bore wear by removing the cylinder head with the engine still in the car. With the piston down in the bore, first signs of wear can be seen and felt just below the top of the bore where the top piston ring reaches, and there will be a noticeable lip. If there is no lip evident, it is reasonable to expect that bore wear is not severe and any lack of compression or excessive oil consumption is due to either worn or broken piston rings, pistons, valves or guides.

3   If it is possible to obtain an internal micrometer, measure the bore in the thrust plane below the lip and again at the bottom of the cylinder bore in the same plane. If the difference is more than 0.003 inch then a rebore is necessary. Similarly a difference of 0.003 inch or more across the bore diameter is a sign of ovality calling for a rebore.
4   Any bore which is significantly scratched or scored will need reboring. This symptom usually indicates that the piston or rings are also damaged in that cylinder. In the event of any one cylinder being in need of reboring, it will still be necessary for all four to be bored and fitted with new oversize pistons and rings. Your BLMC garage or local motor engineering specialist will be able to rebore and obtain the necessary matched pistons. If the crankshaft is undergoing regrinding, it is a good idea to let the same firm renovate and reassemble the crankshaft and pistons to the cylinder block. A reputable firm normally gives a guarantee for such work. In cases where engines have been rebored already to their maximum, new cylinder liners are available which may be fitted. In such cases the same reboring processes have to be followed and the services of a specialist engineering firm are required.

---

34 Pistons and piston rings - examination and renovation

---

1   Worn pistons and rings can usually be diagnosed when the symptoms of excessive oil consumption and low compression occur and are sometimes, though not always, associated with worn cylinder bores. Compression testers that fit into the spark plug holes are available and these can indicate where low compression is occuring. Wear usually accelerates the more it is left, so when the symptoms occur early action can possibly save the expense of a rebore.

2   Another symptom of piston wear is piston slap - a knocking noise from the crankcase not to be confused with big end bearing failure. It can be heard clearly at low engine speed when there is no load (idling for example) and is much less audible when the engine speed increases. Piston wear usually occurs in the skirt or lower end of the piston and is indicated by vertical streaks in the worn area which is always on the thrust side. It can be seen where the skirt thickness is different.

3   Piston ring wear can be checked by first removing the rings from the pistons as described in Section 21. Then place the rings in the cylinder bores from the top, pushing them down about $1\frac{1}{2}$ inches with the head of a piston (from which the rings have been removed) so that they rest squarely in the cylinder bore. Then measure the gap at the ends of the ring with a feeler gauge. If it exceeds 0.022 inch for the compression rings or 0.045 inch for the lower oil control ring, then they need renewal.

4   The grooves in which the rings locate in the piston can also become enlarged in use. The clearance between ring and piston, in the groove, should not exceed 0.035 inch for each ring.

5   However, it is rare that a piston is only worn in the ring grooves, and the need to replace them for this fault alone is hardly ever encountered. When ever pistons are renewed, the weight of the four piston/connecting rod assemblies should be kept within the limit variation of 8 grms. to maintain correct engine balance.

38.2

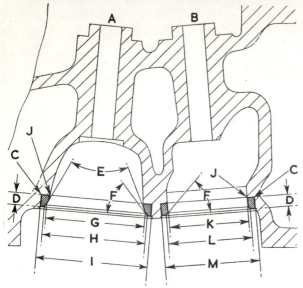

FIG. 1:22 VALVE SEAT DIMENSIONS
INLET (A)

C   Maximum radius .010 in. (.25 mm)
D   2.175 in. (55.25 mm) to 2.174 in. (55.23 mm)
E   Included angle 50°
F   45°
G   1.395 in. (35.44 mm) to 1.405 in. (35.69 mm)
H   1.498 in. (38.05 mm) to 1.501 in. (38.13 mm)
J   Blend insert to throat

EXHAUST (B)

C   Maximum radius .010 in. (.25 mm)
D   2.175 in. (55.25 mm) to 2.174 in. (55.23 mm)
F   45°
J   Blend insert to throat diameter
K   1.11 in. (28.19 mm) to 1.13 in. (28.7 mm)
L   1.215 in. (30.86 mm) to 1.218 in. (30.94 mm)
M   1.3456 in. (33.20 mm) to 1.3475 in. (34.23 mm)

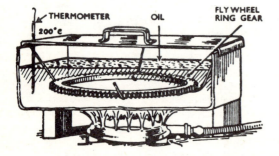

Fig. 1:23 Alternative method of heating starter ring gear.

35 Connecting rods and gudgeon pins - examination and renovation

1   Gudgeon pins are a tight fit in the little end of the connecting rods. Neither of these would normally need replacement unless the pistons are being changed, in which case the new pistons would automatically be supplied with new gudgeon pins.

2   Connecting rods are not subject to wear but, in extreme circumstances such as engine seizure, they could be distorted. Such conditions may be visually apparent, but where doubt exists they should be changed. The bearing caps should also be examined for indications of filing down which may have been attempted in the mistaken idea that bearing slackness could be remedied in this way. If there are such signs then the connecting rods should be replaced.

36 Camshaft and camshaft bearings - examination and renovation

1   The camshaft itself should show no sign of wear, but if very slight score marks on the cams are noticed, they can be removed by very gentle rubbing down with very fine emery cloth or an oil stone. The greatest care should be taken to keep the cam profiles smooth.

2   Carefully examine the camshaft bearing surfaces for wear and, if evident, the camshaft must be renewed.

3   Check the camshaft fit in the cast aluminium housing and, if side movement is evident, a new housing must be obtained. The camshaft runs directly in the aluminium housing and does not have white metal bushes.

37 Tappets - examination and renovation

1   The little shims found inside the tappet bucket must be kept with the relative tappet and not interchanged.

2   The faces of the tappets which bear on the camshaft lobes should show no signs of pitting, scoring, fracturing or other forms of wear. They should not be a loose fit in the aluminium housing. Wear is normally encountered at very high mileages or in cases of neglected engine lubrication. Renew the tappets or housing as necessary.

38 Valves and valve seats - examination and renovation

1   With the valves removed from the cylinder head, examine the heads for signs of cracking, burning away and pitting of the edges where they seat in the ports. The seats of the valves in the cylinder head should also be examined for the same signs. Usually it is the valve that deteriorates first, but if a bad valve is not rectified the seat will suffer and this is more difficult to repair.

2   Provided there are no obvious signs of serious pitting, the valve should be ground into its seat. This may be done by placing a smear of carborundum paste on the edge of the valve and using a suction type valve holder, grinding the valve in situ. Use a semi rotary action; rotating the handle of the valve holder between the hands and lifting it occasionally to re-distribute the traces of paste. Start with a coarse paste (photo).

3   As soon as a matt grey unbroken line appears on both the valve and seat, the valve is 'ground in'. All traces of carbon

should also be cleaned from the head and neck of the valve stem. A wire brush mounted in a power drill is a quick and effective way of doing this.

4 If the valve requires renewal, it should be ground into the seat in the same way as the old valve.

5 Another form of valve wear can occur on the stem where it runs in the guide in the cylinder head. This can be detected by trying to rock the valve from side to side. If there is any movement at all, it is an indication that the valve stem or guide is worn. Check the stem first with a micrometer at points along and around its length, and if they are not within the specified size new valves will probably solve the problem. If the guides are worn however, they will need reboring for oversize valves or for fitting guide inserts. The valve seats will also need recutting to ensure they are concentric with the stems. This work should be given to your local BLMC garage or engineering works.

6 When valve seats are badly burnt or pitted, requiring replacement, inserts may be fitted - or replaced if previously fitted - and once again this is a specialist task to be carried out by a suitable engineering firm.

7 When all valve grinding is completed, it is essential that every trace of grinding paste is removed from the valves and ports in the cylinder head. This should be done by thorough washing in petrol or paraffin and blowing out with a jet of air. If particles of carborundum paste should work their way into the engine this would cause havoc with bearings or cylinder walls.

39 Crankshaft and camshaft sprockets and chain - examination and renovation.

1 Carefully examine the teeth on both the crankshaft and camshaft sprockets for wear. Each tooth forms an inverted V with the gear wheel periphery and if worn, the side of each tooth under tension will be slightly concave in shape when compared with the other side of the tooth. If any sign of wear is present, the sprockets must be renewed.

2 Examine the links of the chain for side slackness and renew the chain if any slackness is noticeable when compared with a new chain. It is a sensible prevaution to renew the chain at about 30,000 miles and at a lesser mileage if the engine is stripped down for major overhaul. The actual rollers on a very badly worn chain may be slightly grooved.

40 Flywheel starter ring - examination and renovation

1 If the teeth on the flywheel starter ring gear are badly worn, or if some are missing, then it will be necessary to remove the ring. This is achieved by splitting the old ring with a cold chisel. The greatest care must be taken not to damage the flywheel during this process.

2 To fit a new ring gear, heat it gently and evenly with an oxy-acetylene flame until a temperature of approximately 350°C is reached. This is indicated by a light metallic surface colour. With the ring gear at this temperature, fit it to the flywheel with the front of the teeth furthermost from the clutch mounting face. The ring gear should be either pressed or lightly tapped onto its register and left to cool naturally when the contraction of the metal on cooling will ensure that it is a secure and permanent fit. Great care must be taken not to overheat the ring gear as if this happens the temper of the ring will be lost.

3 Alternatively the local BLMC garage or engineering works may have a suitable oven in which the ring gear can be heated. The normal domestic oven will only give a maximum temperature of about 250°C, except for the latest self cleaning type which will give a higher temperature. With the former it may just be possible to fit the ring gear with it at this temperature, but it is unlikely. No great force should have to be used. See alternative method of heating in Fig. 1.23.

41 Oil pump - examination and renovation

1 Thoroughly clean all the component parts in petrol and then check the rotor end float and lobe clearance in the following manner:

2 Position the rotor and outer ring in the pump body and place the straight edge of a steel rule across the joint face of the pump. Measure the gap between the bottom of the straight edge and the top of the rotor and outer ring as shown in Fig. 1.25 (A). If the measurement exceeds 0.005 inch (outer ring) and 0.0055 inch (inner rotor) a new pump must be obtained as no individual parts are obtainable.

3 Measure the gaps between the peaks of the lobes and peaks of the outer ring with feeler gauges. If the measurement exceeds 0.0035 inch a new pump must be obtained, (Fig. 1.25 (B)).

4 Measure the clearance between the outer ring and the pump body and if it exceeds 0.011 inch a new pump must be obtained (Fig. 1.25 (C)).

5 If all parts are satisfactory, assembly is the reverse sequence to dismantling as described in Section 28. Always make sure the strainer is clean and use a new joint washer between the two halves of the strainer body.

42 Cylinder head - decarbonisation

1 This operation can be carried out with the engine either in or out of the car. With the cylinder head off, carefully remove, with a wire brush and blunt scraper, all traces of carbon deposits from the combustion spaces and the ports. The valve stems and valve guides should also be free from any carbon deposits. Wash the combustion spaces and ports down with petrol and scrape the cylinder head surface free of any foreign matter with the side of a steel rule or a similar article. Take care not to scratch the surfaces.

2 Clean the pistons and top of the cylinder bores. If the pistons are still in the cylinder bores, it is essential that great care is taken to ensure that no carbon gets into the bores as this could scratch the cylinder walls or cause damage to the piston and rings. To ensure that this does not happen first turn the crankshaft so that two of the pistons are at the top of the bores. Place clean non-fluffy rag into the two bores, or seal them off with paper and masking tape. The water and oil ways should also be covered with a small piece of masking tape to prevent particles of carbon entering the cooling system and damaging the water pump, or entering the lubrication system and causing damage to a bearing surface.

3 There are two schools of thought as to how much carbon ought to be removed from the piston crown. One is that a ring of carbon should be left around the edge of the piston and on the cylinder bore wall as an aid to keeping oil consumption low. The other is to remove all traces of carbon during decarbonisation, and leave everything clean.

4 If all traces of carbon are to be removed, press a little grease into the gap between the cylinder walls and the two

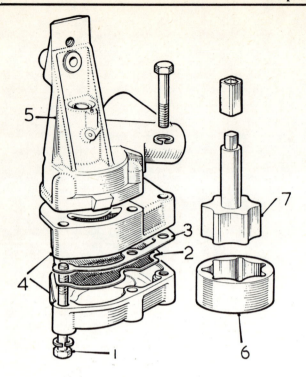

FIG. 1:24 COMPONENT PARTS OF OIL PUMP

No.	Description	No.	Description
1	Filter housing bolts		lower halves.
2	Filter	5	Oil pump body
3	Gasket	6	Outer ring
4	Filter housing - upper and	7	Rotor and shaft assembly

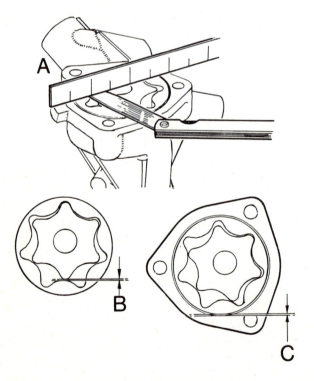

Fig. 1:25 Checking oil pump for wear

pistons which are to be worked on. With a blunt scraper carefully scrape away the carbon from the piston crown, taking care not to scratch the aluminium. Also scrape away the carbon from the surrounding lip of the cylinder wall. When all carbon has been removed, scrape away the grease which will now be contaminated with carbon particles, taking care not to press any into the bores. To assist prevention of carbon build up, the piston crown can be polished with a metal polish such as 'Brasso'. Remove the rags or masking tape from the other two cylinders and turn the crankshaft so that the two pistons which were at the bottom are now at the top. Place non-fluffy rag into the other two bores, or seal them with paper and masking tape. Do not forget the waterways and oilways as well. Proceed as previously described.

5   If a ring of carbon is going to be left round the piston, this can be helped by inserting an old piston ring into the top of the bore to rest on the piston and ensure that carbon is not accidently removed. Check that there are no particles of carbon in the cylinder bores. De-carbonisation is now complete.

---

43   Engine - reassembly - general

---

1   To ensure maximum life with minimum trouble from a rebuilt engine, not only must every part be correctly assembled, but everything must be spotlessly clean. All the oilways must be clear, locking washers and spring washers must always be fitted where indicated, and all bearings and other working surfaces must be thoroughly lubricated during assembly. Before assembly begins, renew any bolts or studs the threads of which are in any way damaged, and whenever possible use new spring washers.

2   Apart from your normal tools, a supply of non-fluffy rag, an oil can filled with Castrol GTX (an empty washing up fluid bottle thoroughly cleaned and washed out will do just as well), a supply of new spring washers, a set of new gaskets and a torque wrench should be collected together.

---

44   Crankshaft - replacement

Ensure that the crankcase is thoroughly clean and that all the oilways are clear. A thin drill is useful for clearing them out. If possible, blow them out with compressed air. Treat the crankshaft in the same fashion and then inject engine oil into the crankshaft oilways.

Commence work on rebuilding the engine by replacing the crankshaft and main bearings.

1   Replace the main bearing shells by fitting the five upper halves of the main bearing shells to their location in the crankcase, after wiping the location clean (photo).

2   Note that on the back of each bearing is a tab which engages in locating grooves in either the crankcase or the main bearing cap housings (photo).

3   New bearings are coated with protective grease; carefully clean away all traces of this with paraffin.

4   With the five upper bearing shells securely in place, wipe the lower bearing cap housings and fit the five lower shell bearings to their caps ensuring that the right shell goes into the right cap, if the old bearings are being refitted (photo)

5   Wipe the recesses either side of the number 4 main bearing which locate the upper halves of the thrust washers.

6   Smear a little Castrol LM Grease onto the recesses for the upper thrust washers within the crankcase. Fit the thrust washers with their grooves facing outwards (photo).

49

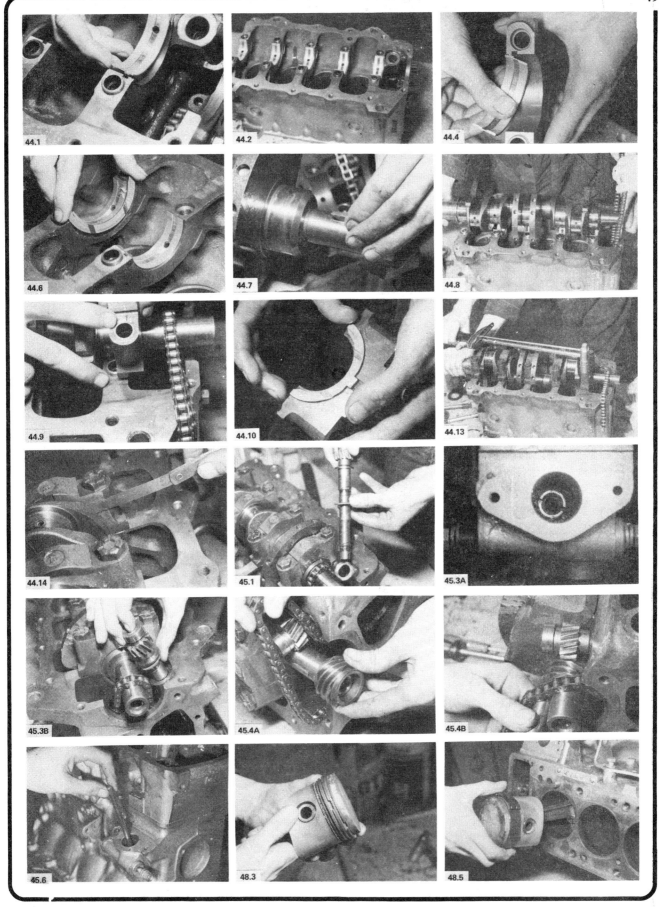

7   Fit the innermost Woodruff key to the nose of the crank-shaft (photo).

8   Generously lubricate the crankshaft journals and the up-per and lower main bearing shells and carefully lower the crankshaft into position. Make sure that it is the right way round. (photo).

9   Fit the main bearing caps into position ensuring that they locate properly on the dowels and that the mating num-bers correspond (photo).

10   Apply a little Castrol LM Grease to the location for the thrust washers on number 4 main bearing cap. Fit the thrust washers with the grooves facing outwards. Refit the cap to the main bearing web. (photo).

11   Replace the long bolts that secure the main bearing caps and screw them up finger tight.

12   Test the crankshaft for freedom of rotation. Should it be very stiff to turn, or possess high spots, a most careful in-spection must be made, preferably by a skilled mechanic with a micrometer to trace the cause of the trouble. It is very seldom that any trouble of this nature will be experienced when fitting the crankshaft.

13   Tighten the main bearing bolts, using a torque wrench setting of 70 lb ft, and recheck the crankshaft for freedom of rotation (photo).

14   The end float of the crankshaft may next be checked. Using a screwdriver as a lever at one of the crankshaft webs and main bearing caps, move the crankshaft longitudinally as far as possible in one direction. Measure the gap between the side of number 4 journal and the thrust washer. Maxi-mum end float should be between 0.002 and 0.003 inch and is adjustable by means of selective thrust washers (photo).

45   Distributor and fuel pump drive shaft - refitting

1   Fit the thrust washer to the drive shaft (photo).

2   Turn the crankshaft until the big end journals are paral-lel with the cylinder bores. This would be an equivalent TDC position for two of the four pistons.

3   Fit the drive shaft with the drive slot at the 10 o'clock position with the large lobe uppermost (photos).

4   Fit the distributor drive gear. It will be noticed that as the teeth mesh, the shaft will turn anti-clockwise through ap-proximately 90° to bring the drive slot to the 2 o'clock posi-tion with the large lobe uppermost. (photos).

5   Refer to page 38, photo 18:4 which shows the correct position of the drive slot.

6   Insert the oil pump drive shaft into the distributor and fuel pump drive shaft (photo).

7   As a further check, temporarily refit the distributor and make sure that the rotor arm is set to fire number 1 cylinder.

46   Piston and connecting rod - reassembly

If the same pistons are being used, then they must be mated to the same connecting rod with the same gudgeon pin. If new pistons are being fitted it does not matter with which connecting rod they are used, but the gudgeon pin must be kept matched to its piston.

Upon reference to Section 20 it will be seen that a special tool was required to remove the gudgeon pin from the piston and connecting rod assembly. This tool is now required to refit the gudgeon pin.

1   Unscrew the large nut and withdraw the centre screw from the body a few inches. Well lubricate the screw thread

and correctly locate the piston support adaptor.

2   Carefully slide the parallel sleeve with the groove end last onto the centre screw, up as far as the shoulder. Lubri-cate the gudgeon pin and its bores in the connecting rod and piston with Acheson's Colloids 'Oildag' graphite oil.

3   Fit the connecting rod and piston, side marked 'front' or '△' to the tool, with the connecting rod entered on the sleeve up to the groove. Fit the gudgeon pin into the piston bore up to the connecting rod. Next fit the remover/replacer bush flange end towards the gudgeon pin.

4   Screw the stop nut onto the centre screw and adjust the nut to give a 1/32 inch end play 'A' as shown in Fig. 1.16. Lock the nut securely with the lock screw. Ensure that the curved face of the adaptor is clean, and slide the piston on the tool so that it fits into the curved face of the adaptor with the pis-ton rings over the adaptor cut-away.

5   Screw the large nut up to the thrust race. Adjust the torque wrench to a setting of 12 lb ft. which will represent the minimum load for an acceptable fit. Use the torque wrench previously set on the large nut, and a ring spanner on the lock screw. Pull the gudgeon pin into the piston until the flange of the remover/replacer bush is 0.016 inch (for 1500 engines) or 0.005 inch (for 1750 engines) from the piston skirt. It is critically important that the flange is NOT allow-ed to contact the piston. Finally withdraw the BLMC service tool.

6   Should the torque wrench not 'break' throughout the pull, the fit of the gudgeon pin in the connecting rod is not within limits and the parts must be renewed.

7   Ensure that the piston pivots freely on the gudgeon pin and it is free to slide sideways. Should stiffness exist, wash the assembly in paraffin, lubricate the gudgeon pin with Acheson's Colloids 'Oildag' and recheck. Again if stiffness exists, dismantle the assembly and recheck for signs of in-grained dirt and positive damage.

47   Piston ring - replacement

1   Check that the piston ring grooves and oilways are thor-oughly clean and unblocked. Piston rings must always be fitted over the head of the piston and never from the bottom.

2   The easiest method to use when fitting rings is to wrap a long 0.020 inch feeler gauge round the top of the piston and place the rings one at a time, starting from the bottom oil control ring.

3   Fit the bottom rail of the oil control ring to the piston and position it below the bottom groove. Refit the oil control expander into the bottom groove and move the bottom oil con-trol ring rail up into the bottom groove. Fit the top oil con-trol rail into the bottom groove.

4   Ensure that the ends of the expander are butting, but not overlapping. Set the gaps of the rails and the expander at 90° to each other.

5   Refit the third and second tapered compression rings with the side marked TOP uppermost. NOTE: on 1750 en-gines the tapered compression ring is fitted into the second groove only.

6   Fit the chromium plated compression ring to the top groove.

48   Piston - replacement

The pistons complete with connecting rods, can be fitted to the cylinder bores in the following sequence:

1   With a wad of clean non-fluffy rag wipe the cylinder bores clean.

2   The pistons, complete with connecting rods, are fitted to their bores from above.

3   Set the piston ring gaps so that the gaps are equidistant around the circumference of the piston, (photo).

4   Well lubricate the top of the piston and fit a ring compressor or a jubilee clip of suitable diameter and shim steel.

5   As each piston is inserted into its bore ensure that it is the correct piston/connecting rod assembly for that particular bore; that the connecting rod is the right way round; and that the front of the piston is towards the front of the bore i. e., towards the chain chest of the engine. Lubricate the piston and bore well with Castrol GTX (photo).

6   The piston will slide into the bore only as far as the ring compressor. Gently tap the piston into the bore with a wooden or plastic hammer.

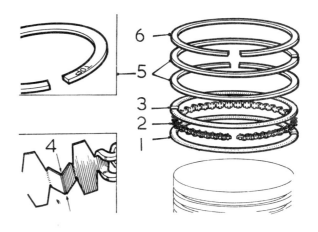

---

49   Connecting rod to crankshaft - refitting

1   Wipe clean the connecting rod half of the big end bearing cap and the underside of the shell bearing, and fit the shell bearing in position with its locating tongue engaged with the corresponding groove in the connecting rod.

2   If the old bearings are nearly new and are being refitted then ensure they are replaced in their correct locations in the correct rods.

3   Generously lubricate the crankpin journals with Castrol GTX and turn the crankshaft so that the crankpin is in the most advantageous position for the connecting rod to be drawn onto it.

4   Wipe clean the connecting rod bearing cap and back of the shell bearing and fit the shell bearing in position ensuring that the locating tongue at the back of the bearing engages with the locating groove in the connecting rod cap.

5   Generously lubricate the shell bearing and offer up the connecting rod cap to the connecting rod (photo).

6   Fit new multi-sided nuts to the connecting rod bolts and tighten to a torque wrench setting of 30 lb ft. (photo).

7   This photograph shows the big end cap and nuts in position and the connecting rod and big end cap identification marks.

8   Repeat the above described procedures for the three remaining piston/connecting rod assemblies.

---

50   Timing chain, crankshaft sprocket and tensioner - refitting

1   If the chain was removed for renewal, fit the new chain into the cylinder block.

2   Join the ends of the chain with a new link and position the link in the anvil of tool 18G1151 with the head of the pins towards the press. (See Fig. 1:11).

3   Fit the locating bridge with its legs centralising the link in the anvil.

4   Locate the plate of the link, chamfered side away from the chain on the bed of the press.

5   Press the plate fully onto the link pins, ensuring that the holes and pins are aligned.

6   Retract the press. Fit the rivet adaptor into the head of the press and tighten the press fully down onto the pins using hand pressure only on the press tommy bar.

7   Check that a slight side play exists on the link with no tight spots.

FIG. 1:26 PISTON RINGS

No.	Description	No.	Description
1	Bottom rail of oil control ring		ted together
2	Expander of oil control ring	5	Second and third taper rings
3	Top rail of oil control ring	6	Top chromium plated ring
4	Expander ends correctly but-		

49.5

49.6

49.7

8 Fit the second woodruff key to the crankshaft nose and locate the crankshaft sprocket on the crankshaft with the tapered face outwards. Drift into its final position with a piece of tube.

9 Engage the chain into mesh with the crankshaft sprocket.

10 Fit the adjustable guide into the chain chest making sure that the lower end engages in the adjuster. The adjustable guide is shown in Fig. 1.11.

11 NOTE. If the adjuster has been removed, check that it is correctly positioned so that the guide is not moved out of vertical alignment

12 Fit the fixed guide and lightly tighten the two securing bolts, spring and plain washers (photo).

13 This photo shows the adjuster screw with the locknut removed.

14 Tighten the adjuster screw until the guide is positioned vertically in the chain chamber and secure in position with the locknut (photo).

15 Fully tighten the two bolts securing the chain guides (photo).

16 Assemble the chain tensioner by inserting one end of the spring into the cylinder.

17 Compress the spring until the cylinder enters the plunger bore and ensure the peg in the plunger engages the helical slot. Insert and turn a 1/8 inch Allen key clockwise until the end of the cylinder is below the peg and the spring is held compressed (photo).

18 Insert the tensioner into the aperture at the front of the chain chamber and engage it into the adaptor. Screw in the adaptor (photo).

19 Clean the mating faces of the engine front cover and crankcase and fit a new gasket to the front cover.

20 Fit the cover in position and locate the long bolt shown in this photo so that it engages with the fixed chain guide.

21 Secure the front cover with the conventional bolt and dynamo adjustment link pivot, both using spring washers (photo).

51 Valve and valve spring - reassembly

To refit the valves and valve springs to the cylinder head, proceed as follows:

1 Rest the cylinder on its side and insert each valve and valve spring in turn, wiping down and lubricating each valve stem as it is inserted into the same valve guide from which it was removed (photo).

2 An oil seal is fitted between the cylinder head and valve spring on inlet valves only.

3 Fit the spring cups to the top of the valve springs and, with the base of the valve compressor on the valve head, compress the valve spring until the cotters can be slipped into place in the cotter grooves (photo).

4 Gently release the valve spring compressor.

5 Repeat this procedure until all eight valves and valve springs are fitted.

52 Cylinder head - replacement

After checking that both the cylinder block and cylinder head mating faces are perfectly clean, generously lubricate each cylinder with Castrol GTX.

1 Always use a new cylinder head gasket as the old gasket will be compressed and not capable of giving a good seal.

2 Never smear grease on either side of the gasket for when the engine heats up, the grease will melt and may allow compression leaks to develop.

3 Carefully lower the new cylinder head gasket into position. It is not possible to fit it the wrong way round (photo).

4 With the gasket in position carefully lower the cylinder head onto the cylinder block (photo).

5 With the cylinder head in position fit the cylinder head bolts and tighten finger tight.

6 When all are in position tighten in a diagonal and progressive manner to a final torque wrench setting of 60lb ft. (photo).

53 Camshaft and tappets - refitting

Unless new parts have been fitted to the cylinder head, camshaft, or camshaft housing, the chances are that the valve clearances will not have to be reset as the original shims will be refitted to the tappet buckets which will also be refitted in their original positions.

If new parts have been fitted, the camshaft and tappets must still be refitted and then the instructions followed as described in Section 54.

1 Smear the shims with petroleum jelly and then fit them into the tappets (photo).

2 Lubricate the camshaft bearings and carefully slide the camshaft into the housing.

3 Invert the camshaft housing and place the tappets in their respective bores in the order in which they were removed.

4 Place the fingers over the tappets as shown in this photograph and carefully refit the housing, taking care to seat the tappets onto the valve stems.

5 Temporarily refit the camshaft sprocket to the camshaft, and turn the camshaft until the sprocket and housing marks align (photo).

6 Fit the six housing securing bolts and tighten in a progressive and diagonal manner to a final torque wrench setting of 20lb ft. (photo).

7 Refer to Section 54 and check the tappet clearance. If adjustment is necessary, remove the camshaft housing and lift out the relevant tappets. Recover the shim inside the tappet and by calculation select the correct shim. Reassemble the tappet and camshaft housing again.

54 Tappet adjustment

It is not usual for the tappets to need re-adjustment throughout the life of the engine because of the lack of moving parts normally found with overhead valve installations. The reason for this is that the camshaft bears directly on the top of the tappet which in turn is in direct contact with the valve stem. Should new parts have been fitted then it will be necessary to check the clearances and adjust as necessary.

1 Obtain a 0 - 1 inch micrometer or very accurate vernier.

2 Open the bonnet and pull the breather hose from the cylinder head cover.

3 Pull the fuel feed pipe from the carburettor float chamber union and draw it through the thermostat housing clip.

4 Plug the end of the fuel pipe with a piece of tapered wood such as a pencil to stop fuel spurting out when the camshaft is rotated.

5 Pull off the ignition vacuum pipe from the manifold side of the carburettor body.

6 Undo and remove the six cylinder head cover securing bolts. Lift away the cover and the gasket.

7 Using a feeler gauge, check the clearance between the

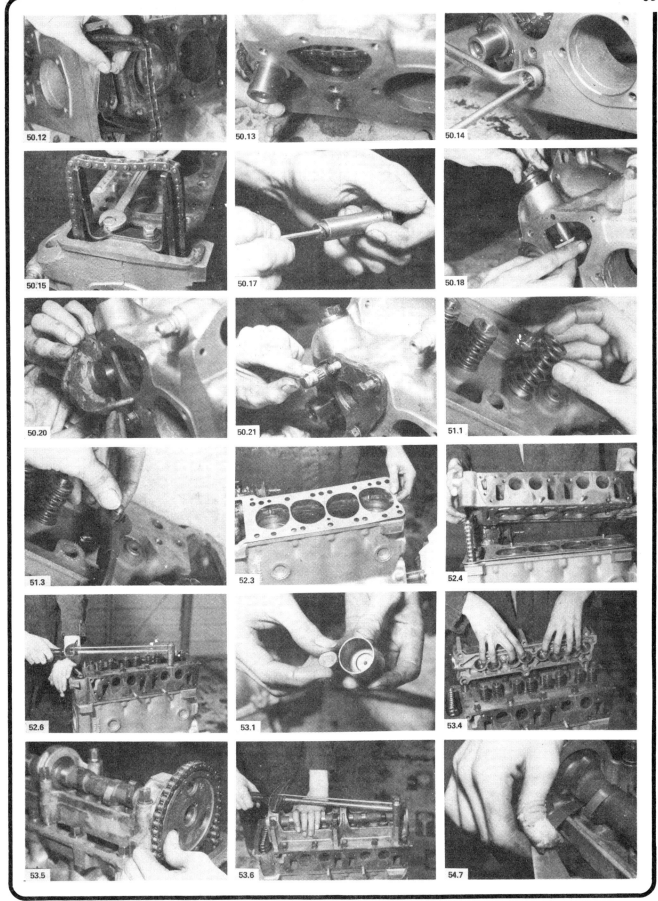

50.12

50.13

50.14

50.15

50.17

50.18

50.20

50.21

51.1

51.3

52.3

52.4

52.6

53.1

53.4

53.5

53.6

54.7

cam lobe and the tappet of each valve in the order given below (photo). Make a not of the results obtained.

8   The camshaft must only be turned in the normal direction of rotation. For this a mole wrench will make the job easier (photo).

Check No. 1 tappet with No. 8 valve fully open
Check No. 3 tappet with No. 6 valve fully open
Check No. 5 tappet with No. 4 valve fully open
Check No. 2 tappet with No. 7 valve fully open
Check No. 8 tappet with No. 1 valve fully open
Check No. 6 tappet with No. 3 valve fully open
Check No. 4 tappet with No. 5 valve fully open
Check No. 7 tappet with No. 2 valve fully open

9   Once the readings have been tabulated for all valves it should be noted that, when new parts have been fitted or the valve seats reground, adjustment of the valve tappet clearance to the standard setting of 0.016 to 0.018 inch (inlet) and 0.020 to 0.022 inch (exhaust) is only necessary if the clearance of either inlet or exhaust is less than 0.012 inch.

10   To adjust the clearance first undo and remove the two flywheel housing timing cover bolts and spring washers. Lift away the cover.

11   Turn the engine in the normal direction of rotation until the 1/4 TDC flywheel mark, with No. 1 cylinder about to commence the firing stroke, is in alignment with the pointer (photo).

12   Check that the camshaft sprocket and the housing marks align correctly.

13   Undo and remove the positive and then the negative terminal from the battery. Unscrew the battery clamp bar securing nuts and lift away the clamp bar and battery.

14   Undo and remove the four bolts and spring washers securing the combined top radiator stay and front lifting bracket. Lift away the bracket.

15   Undo and remove the two bolts and spring washers securing the engine steady and lifting bracket from the flywheel end of the cylinder head.

16   Remove the chain tensioner adaptor screw. Insert a 1/8 inch Allen key into the screw adaptor and turn it in a clockwise direction so as to retract the tensioner slipper (photo).

17   Undo and remove the bolt and spring washer securing the camshaft sprocket to the camshaft and withdraw the sprocket.

18   Undo and remove the six bolts which secure the camshaft housing to the cylinder head in a diagonal and progressive manner.

19   Carefully lift the camshaft housing sufficiently to allow the tappets to fall clear of the camshaft housing and remain in position on the valve stems. Draw the camshaft out of the housing from the flywheel end.

20   Remove the maladjusted tappet and recover the adjustment shim from within the tappet.

21   NOTE the thickness of the shim originally fitted (photo) and by using the following calculation determine the new thickness of shim required to give the correct inlet valve clearance of 0.016 to 0.018 inch and exhaust valve clearance of 0.020 to 0.022 inch.

Clearance as determined in paragraph 7 = A inch
Thickness of shim removed   = B inch
Correct clearance   = C inch
New shim thickness required = A + B - C inch

22   Shims are available in the following thicknesses:

0.097 inch, 2.47 mm	0.113 inch, 2.87 mm
0.099 inch, 2.52 mm	0.115 inch, 2.93 mm
0.101 inch, 2.56 mm	0.117 inch, 2.98 mm
0.103 inch, 2.62 mm	0.119 inch, 3.03 mm
0.105 inch, 2.67 mm	0.121 inch, 3.08 mm
0.107 inch, 2.72 mm	0.123 inch, 3.13 mm
0.109 inch, 2.77 mm	0.125 inch, 3.18 mm
0.111 inch, 2.83 mm	0.127 inch, 3.23 mm

23   Always check the shim thickness with a micrometer (photo).

24   If a range of shims is not available and the clearance is less than 0.012 inch it is possible to grind off a little metal from a shim using an oil stone, lubricated with paraffin, and a piece of soft wood as shown in the photo. Keep a check on the thickness of metal being removed, using the micrometer.

25   Smear the shims in petroleum jelly and fit them into the tappets.

26   Refit the tappets into their respective guides and insert the camshaft into the camshaft housing from the flywheel end.

27   The sequence for reassembly is now the reverse sequence to removal. Further information may be found in Section 53.

28   The radiator stay, lifting bracket securing bolts and spring washers should be tightened to a torque wrench setting of 30 lb ft.

29   The engine steady and flywheel end lifting bracket securing bolts and spring washers should be tightened to a torque wrench setting of 20 lb ft.

30   Tighten the camshaft sprocket securing bolt and spring washer to a torque wrench setting of 20 lb ft. (photo).

55   Engine - refitting to transmission unit

Full information will be found in Chapter 6/4.

56   Crankshaft pulley and vibration damper - refitting

1   Fit the pulley hub Woodruff key to the milled slot in the crankshaft (photo). This, and the operation in the next paragraph, can be done with the engine away from the transmission unit if considered more convenient.

2   Slide the oil slinger over the end of the crankshaft nose and push up against the crankshaft sprocket (photo).

3   With the engine bolted to the transmission unit, cut the protruding ends of the oil seals with a sharp knife. Take care they do not fall into the transmission casing (photo).

4   Lubricate the front seal and carefully push it into position. Note on some seals the word TOP is marked on the front face (photo).

5   Ease the crankshaft pulley and vibration damper over the nose of the crankshaft and engage the keyway with the Woodruff key previously positioned on the crankshaft (photo).

6   Refit the pulley securing bolt and a new tab washer (photo).

7   Tighten the pulley securing bolt to a torque wrench setting of between 60 to 70 lb ft. (photo).

8   To enable the previous operation to be carried out satisfactorily it will be necessary to lock the crankshaft using a screwdriver as shown in this photo.

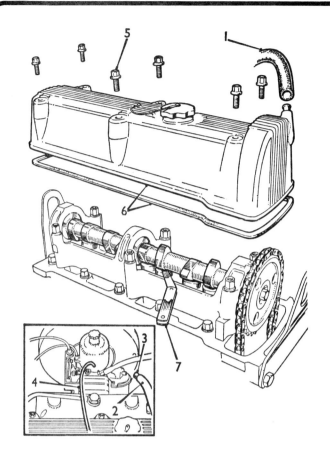

54.8

54.11

54.16

FIG. 1:27 CHECKING TAPPET ADJUSTMENT

No.	Description	No.	Description
1	Breather hose	4	Distributor vacuum pipe
2	Carburettor fuel pipe	5	Cylinder head cover bolts
3	Plug to stop fuel syphoning from pipe	6	Cylinder head cover and gasket
		7	Feeler gauge

54.21

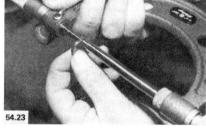

54.23

54.24

54.30

56.1

56.2

57 Engine - final assembly

1   Fit a new combined inlet and exhaust manifold gasket taking care it is fitted the correct way round (photo).

2   Carefully refit the combined inlet and exhaust manifold and carburettor installation to the side of the cylinder head and secure in position with the two nuts and spring washers and seven bolts. Tighten all fixings in a progressive and diagonal manner (photo).

3   Refit the oil pressure warning light switch to the right hand side of the cylinder block (photo).

4   Ease the starter motor drive into position. Make sure the main terminal is away from the cylinder block for inertia type starter motors (photo).

5   Secure the starter motor with the two bolts and spring washers (photo).

6   Refit the radiator top mounting to the top of the cylinder head and secure with the two bolts and spring washers, tightening to a torque wrench setting of 30 lb ft. (photo).

7   Refit the engine steady and lifting bracket to the flywheel end of the cylinder head. Secure with the two bolts and spring washers and tighten to a torque wrench setting of 30 lb ft. (photo).

8   Refit the radiator lower mounting and secure with the two bolts and spring washers, tightening to a torque wrench setting of 30 lb ft. (photo).

9   Slowly turn the crankshaft in the normal direction of rotation until the 1/4 TDC mark on the flywheel is aligned with the pointer. No 1 cylinder should be at the top of the compression stroke and just about to commence the power stroke.

10   Fit the distributor with the clamp plate and engage the driving dog into the distributor drive shaft. The rotor arm should now point to the segment in the distributor cap which leads to No 1 spark plug (the one nearest the fan).

11   Replace the two distributor clamp bolts and washers and lightly tighten. The ignition should be accurately set when the engine is back in the car as described in Chapter 4/10.

12   Slide the dynamo adjustment link over its mounting on the cylinder block (photo).

13   Thread the long dynamo mounting bolt through the cast web on the cylinder block and the front end bracket, and lightly secure with the spring washer and nyloc nut (photo).

14   Refit the rear mounting bolt, spring washer and nyloc nut.

15   Assemble the water pump pulley and fan and offer up to the water pump drive flange. Secure with the three bolts and spring washers (photo).

16   Refit the fan belt and adjust the position of the dynamo until there is $\frac{1}{2}$ inch of lateral movement at the mid point position of the belt run between the dynamo pulley and the water pump (photo).

17   Clean the mating faces of the thermostat housing and cylinder head and fit a new gasket to the thermostat housing. (photo).

18   Fit the housing to the cylinder head and tighten the three securing bolts to a torque wrench setting of 8 - 10 lb ft. (photo).

19   Fit the thermostat into the housing (photo).

20   Make sure the mating faces of the top hose elbow and thermostat housing are clean and fit a new gasket (photo).

21   Fit the three elbow securing bolts noting that one also retains the fuel pipe clip. Tighten the three bolts to a torque wrench setting of 8 - 10 lb ft. (photo).

22   Refit the dip stick guide tube union to the side of the transmission casing (photo).

23   Ease the fuel feed pipe onto the float chamber union (photo).

24   Refit the ignition coil mounting bracket and any radio suppressor capacitors to the side of the cylinder block and secure with the two bolts, plain and spring washers. (photo).

25   Ease the hose onto the water pump and move the clip so that it may be easily undone when the engine is back in the car (photo).

26   Refit the mounting to the power unit at the rear of the cylinder block near to the left hand end by the fan (photo). Secure with the nut, spring and plain washer.

27   Fit new spark plugs to the cylinder head. Do not forget to check the electrode gaps first (photo).

28   This photo shows the location of the enlarged portion of the radiator cowling through which the fan belt may be removed or refitted when the radiator is in position.

29   Refit the radiator to the upper and lower mounting brackets and secure with the four bolts and plain washers (photo).

30   Tighten the top and bottom radiator hose clips (photos).

31   Insert the fuel pump push rod, and then the fuel pump. Secure with the two bolts and spring washers (photos).

32   The cylinder head cover should not be fitted until the complete power unit is in place, as it is easily damaged.

58 Engine and transmission - refitting

Although the engine can be replaced by one man and a suitable winch, it is easier if two are present, one to control the winch and the other to guide the engine into position so it does not foul anything. Generally speaking replacement is a reversal of the procedures used when removing the unit, but the following points are of special note:

1   Ensure all the loose leads, cables etc, are tucked out of the way. If not, it is easy to trap one and so cause much additional work after the unit is replaced.

2   Carefully lower the engine whilst an assistant recouples the drive shafts to the final drive unit. When finally in position refit the following:

a)   Mounting nuts, bolts and washers.
b)   Speedometer drive cables.
c)   Clutch slave cylinder; check adjustment.
d)   Gear change linkage/cables.
e)   Wires to oil pressure switch, temperature gauge thermal transmitter, ignition coil, distributor and dynamo.
f)   Carburettor controls.
g)   Air cleaner and cylinder head cover.
h)   Exhaust system/down pipe to manifold.
i)   Earth and starter motor cables.
j)   Heater and servo hoses.
k)   Vacuum advance and retard pipe.
l)   Distributor cap and HT leads.
m)   Fuel pump.
n)   Battery.
o)   If applicable, bleed brake hydraulic system and pressurise hydrolastic suspension.

3   Check that the drain taps are closed and refill the cooling system with water. Full information will be found in Chapter 2.

4   Finally refill the power unit with Castrol GTX (photo).

59 Engine - initial start up after overhaul or major repair

1   Make sure that the battery is fully charged and that the oil, water and fuel are replenished.

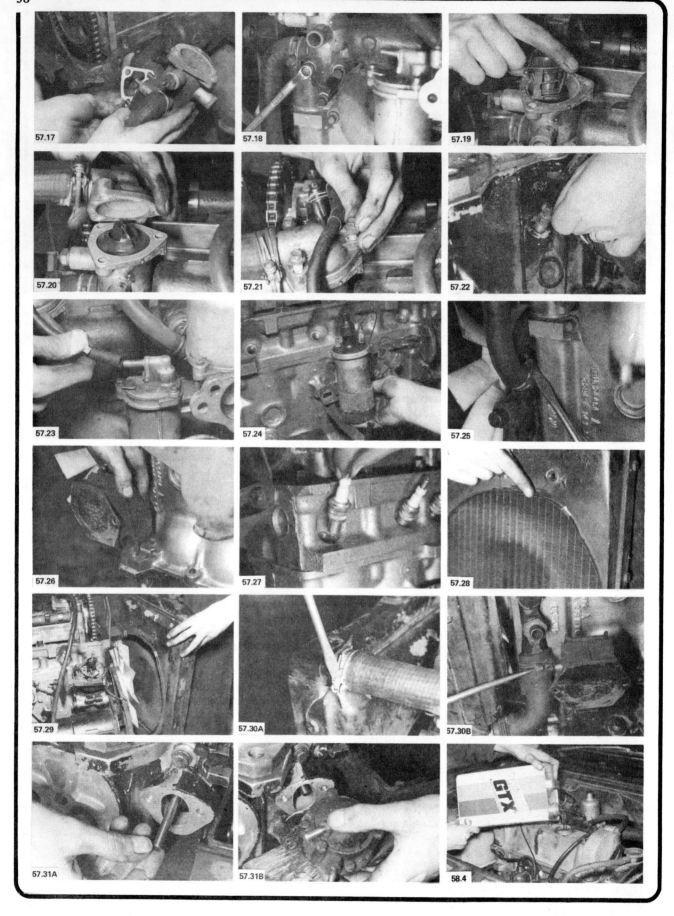

57.17

57.18

57.19

57.20

57.21

57.22

57.23

57.24

57.25

57.26

57.27

57.28

57.29

57.30A

57.30B

57.31A

57.31B

58.4

2   If the fuel system has been dismantled it will require several revolutions of the engine on the starter motor to get the petrol up to the carburettor. An initial prime by pouring petrol down the carburettor feed pipe will help the engine to fire quickly thus relieving the load on the battery.

3   As soon as the engine fires and runs, keep it going at a fast tickover only (not faster) and bring it up to normal working temperature.

4   As the engine warms up there will be odd smells and some smoke from parts getting hot and burning off oil deposits. The signs to look for are leaks of oil or water which will be obvious, if serious. Check also the clamp connections of the exhaust pipes to the manifolds as these do not always 'find' their exact gas tight position until the warmth and vibration have acted on them and it is almost certain that they will need tightening further. This should be done, of course, with the engine stopped.

5   When normal running temperature has been reached adjust the idling speed as described in Chapter 3.

6   Stop the engine and wait a few minutes to see if any lubricant or coolant is dripping out when the engine is stationary.

7   Road test the car to check that the timing is correct and giving the necessary smoothness and power. Do not race the engine - when new bearings and/or pistons and rings have been fitted it should be treated as a new engine and run in at reduced revolutions for the first 500 miles.

Fault Finding Chart - Engine

Cause	Trouble	Remedy
SYMPTOM: ENGINE FAILS TO TURN OVER WHEN STARTER BUTTON PULLED		
No current at starter motor	Flat or defective battery	Charge or replace battery. Push-start car.
	Loose battery leads	Tighten both terminals and earth ends of earth lead.
	Defective starter solenoid or switch or broken wiring	Run a wire direct from the battery to the starter motor or by-pass the solenoid.
	Engine earth strap disconnected	Check and retighten strap.
Current at starter motor	Jammed starter motor drive pinion	Place car in gear and rock from side to side. Alternatively, free exposed square end of shaft with spanner.
	Defective starter motor	Remove and recondition.
SYMPTOM: ENGINE TURNS OVER BUT WILL NOT START		
No spark at spark plug	Ignition system damp or wet	Wipe dry the distributor cap and ignition leads.
	Ignition leads to spark plugs loose	Check and tighten at both spark plug and distributor cap ends.
	Shorted or disconnected low tension leads	Check the wiring on the CB and SW terminals of the coil and to the distributor.
	Dirty, incorrectly set, or pitted contact breaker points.	Clean, file smooth, and adjust.
	Faulty condenser	Check contact breaker points for arcing, remove and fit new.
	Defective ignition switch	By-pass switch with wire.
	Ignition leads connected wrong way round	Remove and replace leads to spark plugs in correct order.
	Faulty coil	Remove and fit new coil.
	Contact breaker point spring earthed or broken	Check spring is not touching metal part of distributor. Check insulator washers are correctly placed. Renew points if the spring is broken.
No fuel at carburettor float chamber or at jets	No petrol in petrol tank	Refill tank!
	Vapour lock in fuel line (In hot conditions or at high altitude)	Blow into petrol tank, allow engine to cool, or apply a cold wet rag to the fuel line.
	Blocked float chamber needle valve	Remove, clean, and replace.
	Fuel pump filter blocked	Remove, clean, and replace.
	Choked or blocked carburettor jets	Dismantle and clean.
	Faulty fuel pump	Remove, overhaul, and replace.
Excess of petrol in cylinder or carburettor flooding	Too much choke allowing too rich a mixture to wet plugs	Remove and dry spark plugs or with wide open throttle, push-start the car.
	Float damaged or leaking or needle not seating	Remove, examine, clean and replace float and needle valve as necessary.
	Float lever incorrectly adjusted	Remove and adjust correctly.
SYMPTOM: ENGINE STALLS AND WILL NOT START		
No spark at spark plug	Ignition failure - sudden	Check over low and high tension circuits for

Cause	Trouble	Remedy
		breaks in wiring.
	Ignition failure - misfiring precludes total stoppage	Check contact breaker points, clean and adjust. Renew condenser if faulty.
	Ignition failure - In severe rain or after traversing water splash	Dry out ignition leads and distributor cap.
No fuel at jet	No petrol in petrol tank	Refill tank.
	Petrol tank breather choked	Remove petrol cap and clean out breather hole or pipe.
	Sudden obstruction in carburettor(s)	Check jet, filter, and needle valve in float chamber for blockage.
	Water in fuel system	Drain tank and blow out fuel lines.
Intermittent spark at spark plug	Ignition leads loose	Check and tighten as necessary at spark plug and distributor cap ends.
	Battery leads loose on terminals	Check and tighten terminal leads.
	Battery earth strap loose on body, attachment point	Check and tighten earth lead to body attachment point.

SYMPTOM: ENGINE MISFIRES OR IDLES UNEVENLY

Cause	Trouble	Remedy
Intermittent sparking at spark plug	Engine earth lead loose	Tighten lead.
	Low tension leads to SW and CB terminals on coil loose	Check and tighten leads if found loose.
	Low tension lead from CB terminal side to distributor loose	Check and tighten if found loose.
	Dirty, or incorrectly gapped plugs	Remove, clean, and regap.
	Dirty, incorrectly set, or pitted contact breaker points	Clean, file smooth, and adjust.
	Tracking across inside of distributor cover	Remove and fit new cover.
	Ignition too retarded	Check and adjust ignition timing.
	Faulty coil	Remove and fit new coil.
Fuel shortage at engine	Mixture too weak	Check jets, float chamber needle valve, and filters for obstruction. Clean as necessary. Carburettor incorrectly adjusted.
	Air leak in carburettor	Remove and overhaul carburettor.
	Air leak at inlet manifold to cylinder head, or inlet manifold to carburettor	Test by pouring oil along joints. Bubbles indicate leak. Renew manifold gasket as appropriate.
Mechanical wear	Incorrect valve clearances	Adjust to take up wear.
	Burnt out exhaust valves	Remove cylinder head and renew defective valves.
	Sticking or leaking valves	Remove cylinder head, clean, check and renew valves as necessary.
	Weak or broken valve springs	Check and renew as necessary.
	Worn valve guides or stems	Renew valve guides and valves.
	Worn pistons and piston rings	Dismantle engine, renew pistons and rings.

SYMPTOM: LACK OF POWER & POOR COMPRESSION

Cause	Trouble	Remedy
Fuel/air mixture leaking from cylinder	Burnt out exhaust valves	Remove cylinder head, renew defective valves.
	Sticking or leaking valves	Remove cylinder head, clean, check, and renew valves as necessary.
	Worn valve guides and stems	Remove cylinder head and renew valves and valve guides.
	Weak or broken valve springs	Remove cylinder head, renew defective springs.
	Blown cylinder head gasket (Accompanied by increase in noise)	Remove cylinder head and fit new gasket.
	Worn pistons and piston rings	Dismantle engine, renew pistons and rings.
	Worn or scored cylinder bores	Dismantle engine, rebore, renew pistons & rings.
Incorrect adjustments	Ignition timing wrongly set. To advanced or retarded	Check and reset ignition timing.
	Contact breaker points incorrectly	

Cause	Trouble	Remedy
Carburation and ignition faults	gapped	Check and reset contact breaker points.
	Incorrect valve clearances	Check and adjust
	Incorrectly set spark plugs	Remove, clean and regap.
	Carburation too rich or too weak	Tune carburettor for optimum performance.
	Dirty contact breaker points	Remove, clean, and replace.
	Fuel filters blocked causing to end fuel starvation	Dismantle, inspect, clean, and replace all fuel filters.
	Distributor automatic balance weights or vacuum advance and retard mechanisms not functioning correctly	Overhaul distributor.
	Faulty fuel pump giving top end fuel starvation	Remove, overhaul, or fit exchange reconditioned fuel pump.

SYMPTOM: EXCESSIVE OIL CONSUMPTION

Cause	Trouble	Remedy
Oil being burnt by engine	Badly worn perished or missing valve stem oil seals.	Remove, fit new oil seals to valve stems.
	Excessively worn valve stems and valve guides	Remove cylinder head and fit new valves and valve guides.
	Worn piston rings.	Fit oil control rings to existing pistons or purchase new pistons.
	Worn pistons and cylinder bores	Fit new pistons and rings, rebore cylinders.
	Excessive piston ring gap allowing blow-up	Fit new piston rings and set gap correctly.
	Piston oil return holes choked	Decarbonise engine and pistons.
Oil being lost due to leaks	Leaking oil filter gasket	Inspect and fit new gasket as necessary.
	Leaking tap cover gasket	Inspect and fit new gasket as necessary.
	Leaking tappet chest gasket	Inspect and fit new gasket as necessary.
	Leaking timing case gasket	Inspect and fit new gasket as necessary.
	Leaking sump gasket	Inspect and fit new gasket as necessary.
	Loose sump plug	Tighten, fit new gasket if necessary.

SYMPTOM: UNUSUAL NOISES FROM ENGINE

Cause	Trouble	Remedy
Excessive clearances due to mechanical wear	Worn valve gear (Noisy tapping from top cover)	Inspect and renew parts as necessary.
	Worn big end bearing (Regular heavy knocking)	Drop sump, if bearings broken up clean out oil pump and oilways, fit new bearings. If bearings not broken but worn fit bearing shells.
	Worn chain and gear (Rattling from front of engine)	Remove timing cover, fit new timing wheels and timing chain.
	Worn main bearings (Rumbling and vibration)	Remove crankshaft, if bearing worn but not broken up, renew. If broken up strip oil pump and clean out oilways.
	Worn crankshaft (Knocking, rumbling and vibration)	Regrind crankshaft, fit new main and big end bearings.

Chapter 2 Cooling system

Contents

Specifications

Type ... ...

Pressurised radiator. Thermo-siphon, pump assisted and fan cooled. Separate expansion tank.

Thermostat

Type	Non pressure sensitive - wax

Settings

Standard	82° C (180° F)
Hot climate	74° C (165° F)
Cold climate	88° C (190° F)

Blow off pressure of expansion tank cap ... ...   13 lb/sq in

Cooling system capacity ... ... $7\frac{1}{4}$ pints (9 1/8 pints with heater)

Torque wrench settings

	lb ft	kg m
Thermostat housing to cylinder head	8 to 10	1.1 to 1.4
Water outlet elbow (cover)	8 to 10	1.1 to 1.4
Water pump set screws	18 to 20	2.5 to 2.8
Plug - water pump body	35	4.8
Pulley	18	2.5
Dynamo mounting bolts	18 to 20	2.5 to 2.8

General description

The engine cooling water is circulated by a thermo-siphon, water pump assisted system. The coolant is pressurised. This is primarily to prevent premature boiling in adverse conditions and also to allow the engine to operate at its most efficient running temperature, this being just under the boiling point of water. The overflow pipe from the radiator is connected to an expansion chamber which makes topping up unnecessary. The coolant expands when hot, and instead of being forced down the overflow pipe and lost, it flows into the expansion chamber. As the engine cools the coolant contracts and because of the pressure differential flows back into the top tank of the radiator.

The cap on the expansion chamber is set to a pressure of 13 lb/sq inch which increases the boiling point of the coolant to 230° F. If the water temperature exceeds this figure and the water boils, the pressure in the system forces the internal valve of the cap off its seat thus opening the expansion tank overflow pipe along which the steam from the boiling water escapes and so relieves the pressure. It is, therefore, important to check that the expansion chamber cap is in good condition and that the spring behind the sealing washers has not weakened. Check that the rubber seal has not perished and its seating in the neck is clean, to ensure a good seal. Also check the radiator filler cap rubber seal and neck, to ensure a good seal. Most garages have a special tool which enables a radiator cap to be pressure tested.

The cooling system comprises the radiator, top and bottom hoses, heater hoses (if a heater/demister is fitted), the impeller water pump (mounted on the front of the engine, it carries the fan blades and is driven by the fan belt), the thermostat and the two drain taps.

The system functions in the following manner: Cold water from the bottom of the radiator circulates up the lower radiator hose to the water pump where it is pushed round the water passages in the cylinder clock, helping to keep the cylinder bores and pistons cool.

The water then travels up into the cylinder head and circulates round the combustion chambers and valve seats absorbing more heat. Then, when the engine is at its correct operating temperature, the water travels out of the cylinder head, past the open thermostat into the upper radiator hose, and so into the radiator header tank. The water travels down the radiator where it is rapidly cooled by the rush of cold air through the radiator core. As the radiator is mounted next to the wheel arch the fan PUSHES cold air through the radiator matrix. The water now cool, reaches the bottom of the radiator. The cycle is then repeated.

When the engine is cold the thermostat (a valve able to open and close according to the temperature) maintains the circulation of the water in the engine by returning it via the by-pass in the cylinder block. Only when the correct minimum operating temperature has been reached, as shown in the 'Specifications', does the thermostat begin to open, allowing water to return to the radiator.

2 Cooling system - draining

1   If the engine is cold, remove the filler cap from the radiator by turning the cap anticlockwise (See Fig. 2:1). If the engine is hot, then turn the filler cap very slightly until pressure in the system has had time to release. Use a rag over the cap to protect your hand from escaping steam. If, with the engine very hot the cap is released suddenly, the drop in pressure can result in the water boiling. With the pressure released the cap can be removed.
2   If antifreeze is used in the cooling system, drain it into a bowl having a capacity of at least 10 pints for re-use.
3   Remove the drain plug in the bottom of the radiator lower tank. If no drain tap is fitted, disconnect the lower radiator hose. When viewed from the side the plug is on the bottom lefthand side of the radiator as shown in Fig. 2:1. Also remove the engine drain plug which is located at the front lefthand side of the cylinder block half way down the casting.
4   When the water has finished running, probe the drain plug orifices with a short piece of wire to dislodge any particles of rust or sediment which may be causing a blockage.
5   It is important to note that neither the expansion tank nor the heater can be drained so during cold weather an antifreeze solution must be used. Always use an antifreeze with an ethylene glycol or glycerine base.

3 Cooling system - flushing

With time the cooling system will gradually lose its efficiency as the radiator becomes choked with rust, scale deposits from the water, and other sediment. To clean the system out, remove the radiator filler cap and drain plug and leave a hose running in the filler cap neck for ten to fifteen minutes.

In very bad cases the radiator should be reverse flushed. This can be done with the radiator in position The cylinder block plug is refitted and a hose with a suitable tapered adaptor placed in the drain plug hole, or the bottom hose union if no drain plug is fitted. Water under pressure is then forced through the radiator and out of the header tank filler cap neck.

It is recommended if the engine is cool, to place some polythene over the engine to stop water finding its way into the ignition system.

The hose should now be removed and placed in the radiator cap filler neck and the radiator washed out in the usual manner.

4 Cooling system - filling

1   Refit the cylinder block and radiator drain plug (or bottom hose if this was disconnected).
2   Fill the system slowly to ensure that no air locks develop. If a heater is fitted, check that the valve in the heater is open (control to HOT), otherwise an air lock may form in the heater. The best type of water to use in the cooling system is rain water, use this whenever possible.
3   Completely fill the radiator, replace the cap, remove the expansion chamber cap and check that it is half full of coolant.
4   Replace the expansion chamber cap and turn it firmly in a clockwise direction to lock it in position (Fig. 2:1).
5   Run the engine at a fast idle speed for approximately half a minute and remove the radiator filler cap slowly. Top up if necessary to the top of the filler neck and replace the cap.

5 Radiator - removal, inspection and cleaning

The radiator on all models is removed in the following manner:
1   Drain the cooling system as described in Section 2 of this Chapter.
2   Slacken the top radiator hose clip at the radiator end of the hose and carefully draw off the hose (2) (Fig. 2:2).
3   Unwind the clip (3) securing the spill hose to the filler neck and carefully draw off the spill hose.
4   Undo and remove the two radiator top fixing bracket bolts (4) and washers.
5   Slacken the radiator bottom hose clip at the radiator end and carefully draw off the bottom hose (5).
6   Undo and remove the two radiator lower fixing bracket bolts (6), plain washers and rubber bushes.
7   The radiator and cowling may now be carefully lifted away from its location. The fragile matrix must not be touched by the fan blades as it easily punctures.
8   With the radiator away from the car any leaks can be soldered or repaired with a suitable substance such as 'Cataloy'. Clean out the inside of the radiator by flushing as described earlier in this Chapter. When the radiator is out of the car it is advantageous to turn it upside down and reverse flush. Clean the exterior of the radiator by carefully using a compressed air jet or a strong jet of water to clear away road dirt, flies etc.
9   Inspect the radiator hoses for cracks, internal or external perishing and damage by overtightening of the securing clips. Replace the hoses if suspect. Examine the radiator hose and spill pipe clips and renew them if they are rusted or distorted.
10   The drain plug should be renewed if leaking or threads worn, but first ensure the leak is not caused by a faulty fibre washer.

6 Radiator - replacement

1   Refitting the radiator is the reverse sequence to removal. (See Section 5).
2   If new hoses are to be fitted they can be a little difficult

to fit onto the radiator, so lubricate them with a little soap.

3   Refill the cooling system as described in Section 4.

7   Thermostat - removal, testing and replacement

1   To remove the thermostat first partially drain the cooling system (usually 4 pints is enough), loosen the upper radiator hose clip at the thermostat cover elbow (1) (Fig. 2:3) and ease the hose from the elbow.

2   Unscrew the three bolts securing the top cover to the thermostat housing.

3   Lift away the thermostat top cover (2) and its gasket (3) from the thermostat housing.

4   The thermostat (4) may now be withdrawn from the housing.

5   Test the thermostat for correct functioning by suspending it on a string in a saucepan of cold water together with a thermometer. Heat the water and note the temperature at which the thermostat begins to open. This should be 82° C (180° F). It is advantageous in winter to fit a thermostat that does not open too early. Continue heating the water until the thermostat is fully open. Then let it cool down naturally.

6   If the thermostat does not fully open in boiling water, or does not close down as the water cools, then it must be discarded and a new one fitted. Should the thermostat be stuck open when cold this will be apparent when removing it from the housing.

7   Refitting the thermostat is the reverse sequence to removal. Always ensure that the thermostat housing and top cover mating faces are clean and flat. If the top cover is badly corroded and eaten away, fit a new cover. Always use a new paper joint.

8   If a new winter thermostat is fitted, provided the summer one is still functioning correctly, it can be placed on one side and refitted in the spring. Thermostats should last for two to three years, at least, before renewal.

8   Thermostat housing - removal and refitting

1   Partially drain the cooling system (usually 4 pints is enough) as described in Section 2.

2   Detach the Lucar connector from the thermal transmitter (2) (Fig. 2:6).

3   Slacken the hose clips securing the heater hose, radiator top hose and water pump hose to the thermostat housing and carefully ease the three hoses from the housing.

4   Undo and remove the three bolts (4) securing the thermostat housing to the cylinder head.

5   Carefully lift the thermostat housing away from the cylinder head. Recover the joint washer adhering to either the housing or cylinder head.

6   Refitting the housing is the reverse sequence to removal. Make sure the mating faces of the housing and cylinder head are free of old joint washer or jointing compound and always fit a new joint washer.

7   Refill the cooling system as described in Section 4.

9   Water pump - removal and refitting

1   Drain the cooling system as described in Section 2.

2   Refer to Section 5 and remove the radiator complete with its cowling.

3   Slacken the dynamo mounting bolts and remove the fan belt shown in Fig. 2:5.

4   Unscrew and remove the three bolts securing the fan and pulley to the water pump hub. Lift away the fan and pulley.

5   Slacken the hose clips and carefully detach the hoses from the water pump.

6   Undo the three bolts securing the water pump to the cylinder block front face. Lift away the water pump and its gasket.

7   Refitting the water pump is the reverse sequence to removal. The following additional points should however, be noted:

a)   Make sure the mating faces of the cylinder block and water pump are clean. Always use a new gasket.

b)   Tighten the water pump securing bolts to a torque wrench setting of 18 - 20 lb ft.

c)   Tighten the water pump fan and pulley bolts to a torque wrench setting of 18 lb ft.

10   Water pump - dismantling and overhaul

Before undertaking the dismantling of a water pump to effect a repair check that all parts are available. It may be quicker and more economic to replace the complete unit.

1   Refer to Fig. 2:4 and using a universal three legged puller carefully draw the hub (1) from the centre shaft.

2   With a pair of pointed pliers or a screwdriver, remove the bearing locating wire.

3   Using a soft faced hammer drive the spindle and bearing assembly (3) out towards the rear of the pump body.

4   It is possible to detach the impeller from the shaft on early 1500 models, but not on later 1500 and 1750 models. To remove the impeller (4) place the shaft vertically in between soft faces of a bench vice with the impeller resting on the top of the jaws and, with a soft metal drift, drive the shaft through the impeller.

5   Lift away the seal (5) noting which way round it is fitted.

6   Carefully inspect the condition of the spindle and bearing assembly and if they show signs of wear or corrosion, new parts should be obtained. Inspect the seal carbon ring which should have its contact face highly polished with no traces of pitting or scoring. If it was found that coolant was leaking from the pump, a new seal should be obtained.

7   With all parts clean and ready for reassembly, first press the bearing and shaft assembly into the bearing housing until the holes line up with the holes for the locating wire.

8   Next press the pulley hub onto the spindle until its face is flush with the end of the spindle as shown in Fig. 2:8. Should the pulley hub be a loose fit on the spindle, a new pulley hub must be fitted.

9   Refit the bearing locating wire (Early 1500 models only).

10   On later 1500 and 1750 models, carefully adjust the position of the spindle bearing assembly so that the distance between the rear face of the spindle bearing outer track and the seal housing shoulder is 0.596 to 0.606 inch (dimension B Fig. 2:9).

11   Fit a new seal to the spindle (later 1500 and 1750 models).

12   Carefully press or drift the impeller onto the spindle until a clearance of 0.020 to 0.030 inch exists between the impeller and the body at C.

11   Fan belt - removal and replacement

If the fan belt is worn or has stretched unduly, it should be renewed. The most usual reason for replacement is that

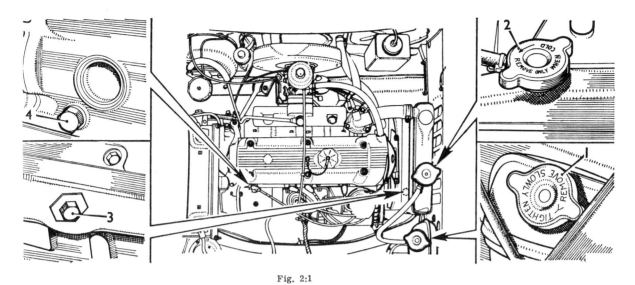

Fig. 2:1

No.	Description	No.	Description	No.	Description	No.	Description
1	Expansion tank pressure cap	2	Radiator filler cap	3	Radiator drain plug	4	Cylinder block drain plug

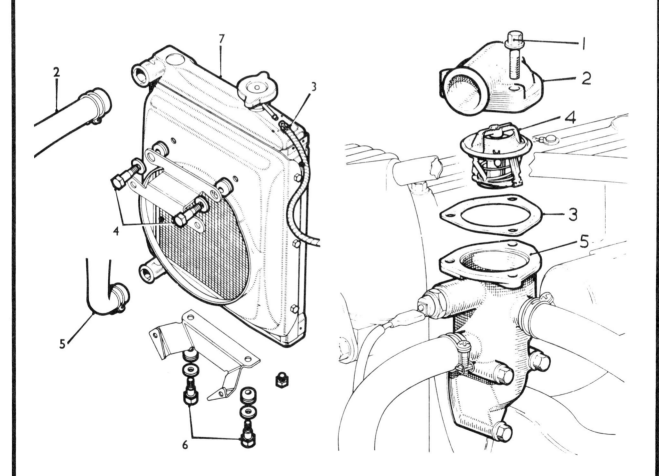

FIG. 2:2 RADIATOR AND MOUNTINGS

No.	Description	No.	Description
2	Radiator top hose	5	Radiator bottom hose
3	Spill hose	6	Bottom mounting fixing bolts
4	Top mounting fixing bolts	7	Radiator and cowling assembly

FIG. 2:3 THERMOSTAT HOUSING

No.	Description	No.	Description
1	Thermostat top cover securing bolt	3	Gasket
2	Thermostat top cover	4	Thermostat
		5	Thermostat housing

66

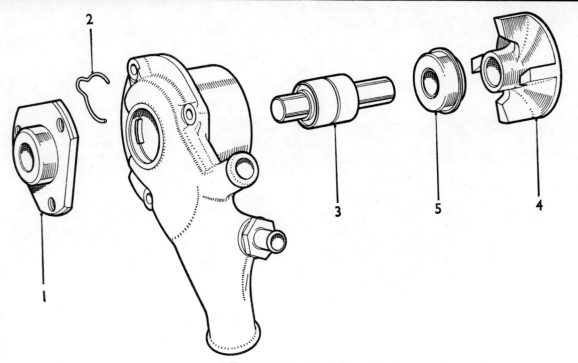

FIG. 2:4 WATER PUMP COMPONENTS

No.	Description	No.	Description	No.	Description	No.	Description
1	Fan and pulley hub	3	Bearing and shaft assembly	4	Pump impeller	5	Seal
2	Locating wire for bearing						

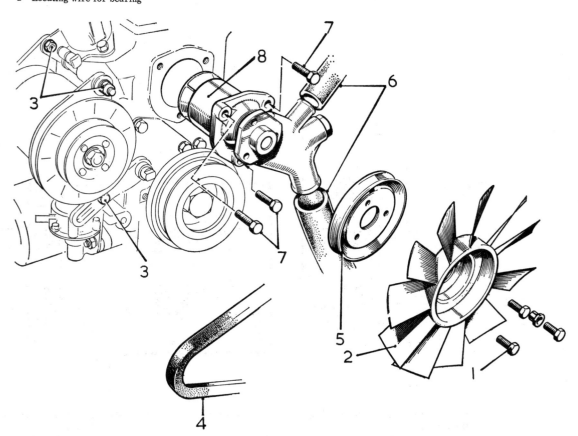

FIG. 2:5 WATER PUMP REMOVAL

No.	Description	No.	Description	No.	Description	No.	Description
1	Fan securing bolts	3	Generator mountings	5	Drive pulley	7	Water pump mounting bolts
2	Fan	4	Fan belt	6	Pump hose connections	8	Water pump

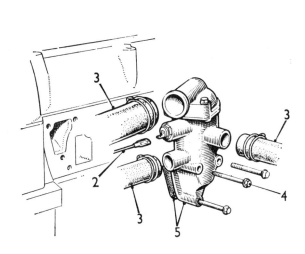

FIG. 2:6 THERMOSTAT HOUSING CONNECTIONS AND FIXINGS

No.	Description	No.	Description
2	Thermal transmitter cable		bolts
3	Hose and clips	5	Thermostat housing and
4	Thermostat housing securing		gasket.

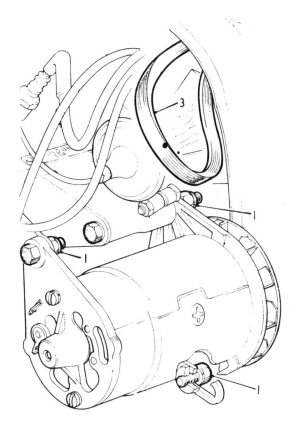

FIG. 2:7 FAN BELT REMOVAL

No.	Description	No.	Description
1	Generator mountings	3	Fan belt

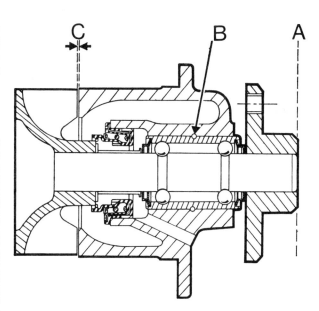

FIG. 2:8 CROSS SECTIONAL VIEW OF WATER PUMP (EARLY 1500 MODELS)

No.	Description	No.	Description
A	Spindle and hub face flush	C	0.020 - 0.030 inch clearance
B	Bearing wire		

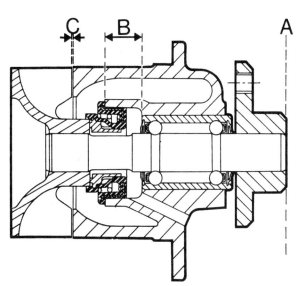

FIG. 2:9 CROSS SECTIONAL VIEW OF WATER PUMP (LATER 1500 AND 1750 MODELS)

No.	Description	No.	Description
A	Spindle and hub face flush	C	0.020 to 0.030 inch clearance.
B	0.596 to 0.606 inch		

the belt has broken in service. It is recommended that a spare belt is always carried in the car. Replacement is a reversal of the removal sequence, but as replacement due to breakage is the most usual operation it is detailed below:

1   Loosen the dynamo pivot and slotted link bolts and move the dynamo towards the engine.
2   Carefully manoeuvre the belt between each fan blade in turn, through the small gap at the top front side of the radiator.
3   Slip the belt over the crankshaft, water pump and dynamo pulleys.
4   Adjust the belt as detailed in the following Section and tighten the dynamo mounting bolts. NOTE: After fitting a new belt it will require adjustment 250 miles later.

12   Fan belt - adjustment

It is important to keep the fan belt correctly adjusted and it is considered that this should be a regular maintenance task every 6000 miles. If the belt is loose it will slip, wear rapidly and cause the dynamo and water pump to malfunction. If the belt is too tight the dynamo and water pump bearings will wear rapidly causing premature failure of these components.

The fan belt tension is correct when there is $\frac{1}{2}$ inch of lateral movement at the mid point position of the belt run between the dynamo pulley and the water pump.

To adjust the fan belt, slacken the dynamo securing bolts and move the dynamo in or out until the correct tension is obtained. It is easier if the dynamo bolts are only slackened a little so it requires some force to move the dynamo. In this way the tension of the belt can be arrived at more quickly than by making frequent adjustments. If difficulty is experienced in moving the dynamo away from the engine, a tyre lever placed behind the dynamo and resting against the block gives good control so that the dynamo can be held in position whilst the securing bolts are tightened.

13   Expansion tank

The radiator coolant expansion tank is mounted on the inner wing valance just in front of the radiator. Normally it should not require any maintenance. It is important that the expansion tank pressure filler cap is not removed whilst the engine is hot.

Should it be found necessary to remove the expansion tank, disconnect the radiator to expansion tank spill hose connection at the radiator filler neck, having first slackened the clip.

Undo and remove the expansion tank bracket securing screws and carefully lift away the tank together with its bracket and hose.

Refitting is the reverse sequence to removal. Add either water or antifreeze solution until it is half full.

14   Antifreeze mixture

1   In circumstances where it is likely that the temperature will drop below freezing it is essential that some of the water is drained and an adequate amount of ethylene glycol antifreeze such as Castrol Antifreeze is added to the cooling system.
2   If Castrol Antifreeze is not available, any antifreeze which conforms with specifications BS 3151 or BS 3152 can be used. Never use an antifreeze with an alcohol base as evaporation is too high.
3   Castrol Antifreeze with an anti-corrosion additive can be left in the cooling system for up to two years, but after six months it is advisable to have the specific gravity of the coolant checked at your local garage, and thereafter once every three months.
4   Add a 30% antifreeze solution ($\frac{1}{4}$ pint neat antifreeze) to the expansion tank to prevent freezing.
5   The table below gives the amount of antifreeze and the degree of protection.

Antifreeze	Commences to freeze		Frozen solid		Amount of antifreeze
%	°C	°F	°C	°F	Pints
25	−13	9	−26	−15	$2\frac{1}{4}$
$33\frac{1}{3}$	−19	−2	−36	−33	3
50	−36	−33	−48	−53	$4\frac{1}{2}$

6   Never use antifreeze in the windscreen washer reservoir as it will cause damage to the paintwork.

Cause	Trouble	Remedy
SYMPTOM: OVERHEATING Heat generated in cylinder not being successfully disposed of by radiator	Insufficient water in cooling system	Top up radiator.
	Fan belt slipping (Accompanied by a shrieking noise on rapid engine acceleration)	Tighten fan belt to recommended tension or replace if worn.
	Radiator core blocked or radiator grill restricted	Reverse flush radiator, remove obstructions
	Bottom water hose collapsed, impeding flow	Remove and fit new hose.
	Thermostat not opening properly	Remove and fit new thermostat.
	Ignition advance and retard incorrectly set (Accompanied by loss of power and perhaps, misfiring)	Check and reset ignition timing.
	Carburettor incorrectly adjusted (mixture too weak)	Tune carburettor.
	Exhaust system partially blocked	Check exhaust pipe for constrictive dents and blockages.
	Oil level in sump to low	Top up sump to full mark on dipstick.
	Blown cylinder head gasket(Water/steam being forced down the radiator overflow pipe under pressure)	Remove cylinder head, fit new gasket.
	Engine not yet run-in	Run-in slowly and carefully.
	Brakes binding	Check and adjust brakes if necessary.
SYMPTOM: UNDERHEATING Too much heat being dispersed by radiator	Thermostat jammed open	Remove and renew thermostat.
	Incorrect grade of thermostat fitted allowing premature opening of valve	Remove and replace with new thermostat which opens at a higher temperature.
	Thermostat missing	Check and fit correct thermostat.
SYMPTOM: LOSS OF COOLING WATER Leaks in system	Loose clips on water hoses	Check and tighten clips if necessary.
	Top or bottom water hoses perished and leaking.	Check and replace any faulty hoses.
	Radiator core leaking	Remove radiator and repair.
	Thermostat gasket leaking	Inspect and renew gasket.
	Pressure cap spring worn or seal ineffective	Renew pressure cap.
	Blown cylinder head gasket (Pressure in system forcing water/steam down overflow pipe	Remove cylinder head and fit new gasket.
	Cylinder wall or head cracked	Dismantle engine, dispatch to engineering works for repair.

Chapter 3 Fuel system and carburation

Contents

Specifications

Air cleaner

Type	Replaceable paper element

Carburettor

Type	SU HS6, horizontal	
Needle*	Size	Type
1500	KP (1969/70) or BAS (1971)	Fixed (KP). Springloaded (BAS)
1750 (Manual transmission)	BAR	Spring loaded
1750 (Automatic transmission)	BBH	Spring loaded
Jet size	0.100 in	
Piston spring	Red	

* Needle sizes may vary for ECE market models. Refer to operators handbook or contact BLMC dealer.

Fuel pump

Make and type	SU mechanical, AUF 702
Suction (minimum)	6 in Hg
Pressure (minimum)...	3 lb/sq in

Fuel tank

Type	Flat tank in rear floor. Vented by breather pipe
Capacity	9 gallons

Torque wrench settings	lb ft	Kg m
Manifold to cylinder head	18 to 20	2.5 to 2.8
Adaptor plugs	30	4.1
Carburettor studs	6 to 8	0.8 to 1.1
Petrol pump nuts	15 to 18	2.1 to 2.5
Petrol pump studs	6	0.8

1 General description

The fuel system comprises a fuel tank at the rear of the car, a mechanical fuel pump located on the bulkhead side of the crankcase next to the oil filter, and a single horizontally mounted SU carburettor. A renewable paper element air cleaner is fitted which must be renewed at the recommended mileages.

2 Fuel pump - general description

The mechanically operated fuel pump is located on the rear lefthand side of the crankcase and is operated by a separate lobe on the camshaft via a short pushrod. As the pushrod moves horizontally to and fro it actuates a rocker lever, one end of which is connected to the diaphragm operating rod. The operation is shown in Fig. 3.1. When the pushrod is moved outwards by the cam lobe, the diaphragm via the rocker arm moves downwards causing fuel to be drawn in through the filter, past the inlet valve flap and into the diaphragm chamber. As the cam lobe moves round, the diaphragm moves upwards under the action of a spring, and fuel flows via the large outlet valve to the carburettor float chamber.

When the float chamber has the requisite amount of fuel in it, the needle valve in the top of the chamber shuts off the fuel supply, causing pressure in the fuel delivery line to hold the diaphragm down against the action of the diaphragm spring until the needle valve opens to admit more fuel.

3 Fuel pump - removal and replacement

1 Apply handbrake, and raise front of car for access to fuel pump which is below the generator.
2 Remove the fuel inlet and outlet connections from the fuel pump. (Fig. 3.2).
3 Unscrew the two pump mounting flange nuts and remove

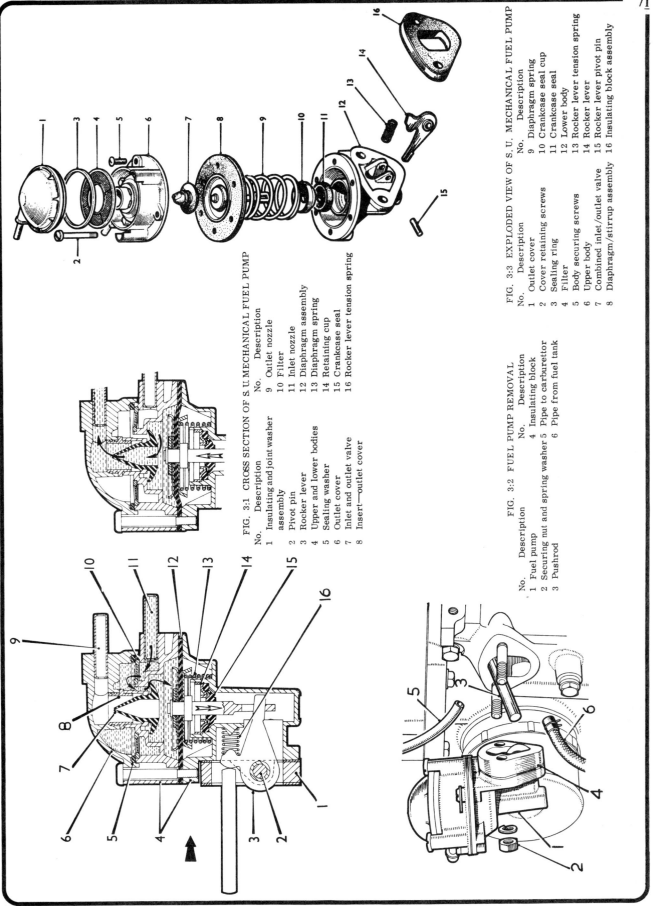

FIG. 3:1 CROSS SECTION OF S.U. MECHANICAL FUEL PUMP

No.	Description	No.	Description
1	Insulating and joint washer assembly	9	Outlet nozzle
2	Pivot pin	10	Filter
3	Rocker lever	11	Inlet nozzle
4	Upper and lower bodies	12	Diaphragm assembly
5	Sealing washer	13	Diaphragm spring
6	Outlet cover	14	Retaining cup
7	Inlet and outlet valve	15	Crankcase seal
8	Insert—outlet cover	16	Rocker lever tension spring

FIG. 3:2 FUEL PUMP REMOVAL

No.	Description	No.	Description
1	Fuel pump	4	Insulating block
2	Securing nut and spring washer	5	Pipe to carburettor
3	Pushrod	6	Pipe from fuel tank

FIG. 3:3 EXPLODED VIEW OF S.U. MECHANICAL FUEL PUMP

No.	Description	No.	Description
1	Outlet cover	9	Diaphragm spring
2	Cover retaining screws	10	Crankcase seal cup
3	Sealing ring	11	Crankcase seal
4	Filter	12	Lower body
5	Body securing screws	13	Rocker lever tension spring
6	Upper body	14	Rocker lever
7	Combined inlet/outlet valve	15	Rocker lever pivot pin
8	Diaphragm/stirrup assembly	16	Insulating block assembly

together with the two spring washers.

4   Carefully slide the pump off the two studs followed by the insulating block assembly and gaskets. Withdraw the pushrod from its location in the side of the cylinder block.

5   Replacement of the pump is a reversal of the above procedure. Remember to use new gaskets, but on no account alter the original total thickness of the insulating block and gaskets. Do not forget to insert the pushrod into the cylinder block.

4   Fuel pump - dismantling, inspection and reassembly

1   Thoroughly clean the outside of the pump in paraffin and dry. To ensure correct reassembly mark the upper and lower body flanges.

2   Remove the cover retaining screws, (2) (Fig. 3.3), lift away the cover followed by the sealing ring (3) and fuel filter (4).

3   Remove the six screws holding the upper body to the lower body making special note of the position of the three shorter screws. Separate the two halves (6, 12).

4   As the combined inlet and outlet valve is a press fit into the body, very carefully remove the valve (7) taking care not to damage the very fine edge of the inlet valve.

5   With the diaphragm (8) and rocker (14) held down against the action of the diaphragm spring (9) tap out the rocker lever pivot pin (15) using a parallel punch. Lift out the rocker lever (14) and spring (13).

6   Lift out the diaphragm (8) and spring (9) having first well lubricated the lower seal (11) to avoid damage as the spindle stirrup is drawn through.

7   It is recommended that unless the seal (11) is damaged it be left in position, as a special extractor is required for removal.

8   Carefully wash the filter gauge (4) in petrol and clean all traces of sediment from the upper body (6). Inspect the diaphragm (8) for signs of distortion, cracking or perishing and fit a new one if suspect.

9   Inspect the fine edge and lips of the combined inlet and outlet valve(7) and also check that it is a firm fit in the upper body. Finally inspect the outlet cover (1) for signs of corrosion, pitting or distortion and fit a new component if necessary.

10   To reassemble, first check that there are no sharp edges on the diaphragm spindle and stirrup and well lubricate the oil seal. Insert the stirrup and spindle into the spring (9) then through the oil seal (11) and position the stirrup ready for rocker lever engagement.

11   Fit the combined inlet/outlet valve (7) ensuring that the groove registers in the housing correctly. Check that the fine edge of the inlet valve contacts its seating correctly and evenly.

12   Match up the screw holes in the lower body and holes in the diaphragm and depress the rocker lever until the diaphragm lies flat. Fit the upper body (6) and hold in place by the three short screws (5), but do not tighten fully. Refit the filter (4), new sealing washer (3) and the outlet cover (1) suitably positioned to connect to the outlet hose to the carburettor. Replace the three long screws (2) and then tighten all screws firmly in a diagonal pattern.

13   Insert the rocker lever (14) and spring (13) into the crankcase and hold in position using the rocker lever pivot pin (15).

5   Fuel pump - testing

If the pump is suspect, or has been overhauled, it may be quickly dry tested holding a finger over the inlet nozzle and operating the rocker lever through three complete strokes. When the finger is released a suction noise should be heard. Next hold a finger over the outlet nozzle and press the rocker arm fully. The pressure generated should hold for a minimum of fifteen seconds.

6   SU Carburettor - description

1   The variable choke SU carburettor as shown in Fig. 3.4 is a relatively simple instrument and is basically the same irrespective of its size and type. It differs from most other carburettors in that instead of having a number of various sized fixed jets for different conditions, only one variable jet is fitted to deal with all possible conditions.

2   Air passing rapidly through the carburettor draws petrol from the jet so forming the petrol/air mixture. The amount of petrol drawn from the jet depends on the position of the tapered carburettor needle, which moves up and down the jet orifice according to the engine load and throttle opening, thus effectively altering the size of jet so that exactly the right amount of fuel is metered for the prevailing road conditions.

3   The position of the tapered needle in the jet is determined by engine vacuum. The shank of the needle is held at its top end in a piston which slides up and down the dashpot in response to the degree of manifold vacuum.

4   With the throttle fully open, the full effect of inlet manifold vacuum is felt by the piston which has an air bleed into the choke tube on the outside of the throttle. This causes the piston to rise fully, bringing the needle with it. With the accelerator partially closed, only slight inlet manifold vacuum is felt by the piston (although, of course, on the engine side of the throttle the vacuum is greater), and the piston only rises a little, blocking most of the jet orifice with the metering needle.

5   To prevent the piston fluttering and giving a richer mixture when the accelerator is suddenly depressed, an oil damper and light spring are fitted inside the dashpot.

6   The only portion of the piston assembly to come into contact with the piston chamber or dashpot is the actual central piston rod. All the other parts of the piston assembly, including the lower choke portion, have sufficient clearance to prevent any direct metal to metal contact which is essential if the carburettor is to function correctly.

7   The correct level of the petrol in the carburettor is determined by the level of the float chamber. When the level is correct the float rises and, by means of a lever resting on top of it, closes the needle valve in the cover of the float chamber. This closes off the supply of fuel from the pump. When the level in the float chamber drops as fuel is used in the carburettor, the float drops. As it does, the float needle is unseated so allowing more fuel to enter the float chamber and restore the correct level.

7   SU Carburettor - removal and replacement

1   Carefully detach the distributor vacuum unit vacuum pipe from the carburettor body. (Fig. 3.5).

2   Disconnect the engine breather pipe from the side of the carburettor body and the fuel feed pipe from the float chamber.

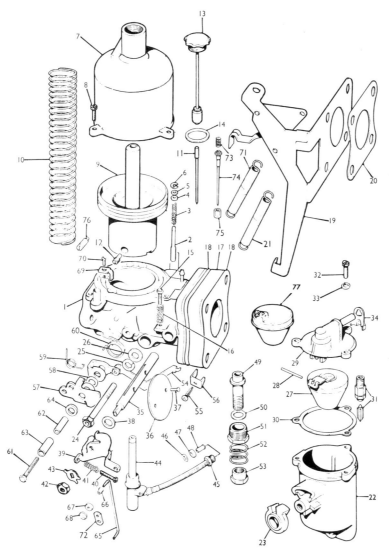

FIG. 3:4 EXPLODED VIEW OF S. U. CARBURETTOR

No.	Description	No.	Description	No.	Description	No.	Description
1	Body	21	Throttle return spring	40	Cam stop screw	59	Spring for cam lever
2	Piston lifting pin	22	Float - chamber	41	Spring for screw	60	Spring for pick - up lever
3	Spring for pin	23	Adaptor	42	Nut for spindle	61	Pivot bolt
4	Sealing washer	24	Bolt for float - chamber	43	Tab washer for nut (1500 only)	62	Pivot tube - inner
5	Plain washer	25	Spring washer	44	Jet assembly	63	Pivot tube - outer
6	Circlip	26	Plain washer	45	Nut	64	Distance washer
7	Piston chamber	27	Float (1500 only)	46	Washer	65	Throttle lever rod
8	Screw for chamber	28	Hinge pin for float	47	Gland	66	Bush
9	Piston	29	Lid for float - chamber	48	Ferrule	67	Washer (early 1500 units only)
10	Spring	30	Gasket	49	Jet bearing	68	Lock washer
11*	Needle	31	Needle and seat	50	Washer	69	Piston guide
12*	Needle locking screw	32	Screw for lid	51	Jet locking nut	70	Screw for guide
13	Piston damper	33	Spring washer	52	Spring	71	Tension spring
14	Sealing washer	34	Baffle plate	53	Jet adjusting nut	72	Anchor tag
15	Throttle adjusting screw	35	Throttle spindle	54	Pick up lever and link	73	Spring**
16	Spring for screw	36	Throttle disc	55	Screw for link	74	Needle**
17	Spacer	37	Screw for disc	56	Bracket for link	75	Support guide for needle**
18	Gasket	38	Washer for spindle	57	Cam lever	76	Support guide locking screw**
19	Progressive throttle linkage	39	Throttle return lever	58	Washer	77	Plastic float**
20	Gasket						

† *Used on fixed needle carburettors*
†* *Used on spring - loaded needle carburettors*

Plug the end to stop dirt ingress, with the tapered end of a pencil.

3   Release the speedometer cable clip from the air cleaner assembly intake tube and unscrew the centre nut. The air cleaner assembly may now be lifted away from the carburettor air intake.

4   Disconnect the choke control inner cable and outer cable from the carburettor.

5   Undo and remove the four nuts and washers securing the carburettor to the inlet manifold studs.

6   Carefully draw off the carburettor from the studs and recover the insulator gaskets and abutment bracket.

7   Refitting the carburettor is the reverse sequence to removal. The following additional points should, however, be noted:

a)   Refer to Section 18 and adjust the throttle cable.

b)   Refer to Section 19 and adjust the choke control cable.

8 SU Carburettor - dismantling and reassembling

1   All reference numbers relate to Fig. 3.4. Unscrew the piston damper (13) and lift away from the chamber and piston assembly (7, 9). Using a screwdriver or small file, scratch identification marks on the suction chamber and carburettor body (1) so that they may be fitted together in their original position. Remove the three suction chamber retaining screws (8) and lift the suction chamber from the carburettor body leaving the piston in situ.

2   Lift the piston spring (10) from the piston, noting which way round it is fitted, and remove the piston. Invert it and allow the oil in the damper bore to drain out. Place the piston in a safe place so that the needle will not be touched or the piston roll onto the floor. It is recommended that the piston be placed on the neck of a narrow jam jar with the needle inside, so acting as a stand.

3   Mark the position of the float chamber lid relative to the body, and unscrew the three screws (32) holding the float chamber lid (29) to the float chamber body (22). Remove the lid and withdraw the pin (28) thereby releasing the float and float lever (27). Using a spanner or socket remove the needle valve assembly (31).

4   Disconnect the jet link from the base of the jet and unscrew the nut (45) holding the flexible nylon tube into the base of the float chamber (22). Carefully withdraw the jet and nylon connection tube.

5   Unscrew the jet adjustment nut (53) and lift away together with its locking spring (52). Also unscrew the jet locknut (51) and lift away together with the brass washer (50) and jet bearing (49).

6   Remove the bolt (24) securing the float chamber to the carburettor body and separate the two parts.

7   To remove the throttle and actuating spindle, release the two screws (37) holding the throttle in position in the slot in the spindle (35), make a note of the tapered edges of the throttle (36) and slide it out of the spindle from the carburettor body.

8   Reassembly is a straight reversal of the dismantling sequence.

9 SU Carburettor - examination and repair

The SU carburettor generally speaking is most reliable, but even so it may develop one of several faults which may not be readily apparent unless a careful inspection is carried out. The common faults the carburettor is prone to are:
1   Piston sticking
2   Float needle sticking
3   Float chamber flooding
4   Water and dirt in the carburettor.

In addition the following parts are susceptible to wear after high mileages and as they vitally affect the economy of the engine they should be checked and renewed where necessary, every 24000 miles:

a)   The carburettor needle. If this has been incorrectly fitted at some time so that it is not centrally located in the jet orifice, then the metering needle will have a tiny ridge worn on it. If a ridge can be seen then the needle must be renewed. SU carburettor needles are made to very fine tolerances and, should a ridge be apparent, no attempt should be made to rub the needle down with fine emery paper. If it is wished to clean the needle, it can be polished lightly with metal polish.

b)   The carburettor jet. If the needle is worn it is likely that the rim of the jet will be damaged where the needle has been striking it. It should be renewed, as otherwise fuel consumption will suffer. The jet can also be badly worn or ridged on the outside from where it has been sliding up and down between the jet bearing every time the choke has been pulled out. Removal and renewal is the only answer.

c)   Check the edges of the throttle and the choke tube for wear. Renew if worn.

d)   The washers fitted to the base of the jet and under the float chamber lid may leak after a time and can cause a great deal of fuel wastage. It is wisest to renew them automatically when the carburettor is stripped down.

e)   After high mileages the float chamber needle and seat are bound to be ridged. They are not an expensive item to replace and must be renewed as a set. They should never be renewed separately.

10 SU Carburettor - piston sticking

1   The hardened piston rod which slides in the centre guide tube in the middle of the dashpot is the only part of the piston assembly (which comprises the jet needle, suction disc and piston choke) which should make contact with the dashpot. The piston rim and the choke periphery are machined to very fine tolerances so that they will not touch the dashpot or the choke tube walls.

2   After high mileages wear in the centre guide tube may allow the piston to touch the dashpot wall. This condition is known as sticking.

3   If piston sticking is suspected and it is wished to test for this condition, rotate the piston about the centre guide tube at the same time as sliding it up and down inside the dashpot. If any portion of the piston makes contact with the dashpot wall then that portion of the wall must be polished with a metal polish until clearance exists. In extreme cases, fine emery cloth can be used.

The greatest care should be taken to remove only the minimum amount of metal to provide the clearance, as too large a gap will cause air leakage and will upset the functioning of the carburettor. Clean down the walls of the dashpot and the piston rim and ensure that there is no oil on them. A trace of oil may be judiciously applied to the piston rod.

4   If the piston is sticking, under no circumstances try to clear it by trying to alter the tension of the light return spring.

11 SU Carburettor - float needle sticking

1   If the float needle sticks, the carburettor will soon run dry and the engine will stop, despite there being fuel in the tank.
   The easiest way to check a suspected sticking float needle is to remove the inlet pipe at the carburettor and, where a mechanical fuel pump is fitted, turn the engine over on the starter motor by pressing the solenoid rubber button. Where an electrical fuel pump is fitted, turn on the ignition but do not start the engine. If fuel spurts from the end of the pipe (direct it towards the ground, into a wad of cloth or into a jar) then the fault is almost certain to be a sticking float needle.
2   Remove the float chamber, dismantle the valve and clean the housing and float chamber out thoroughly.

12 SU Carburettor - float chamber flooding

   If fuel emerges from the small breather hole in the cover of the float chamber this is known as flooding. It is caused by the float chamber needle not seating properly in its housing; normally this is because a piece of dirt or foreign matter is jammed between the needle and the needle housing. Alternatively, the float may have developed a leak or be maladjusted so that it is holding open the float chamber needle valve even though the chamber is full of petrol. Remove the float chamber cover, clean the needle assembly, check the setting of the float as detailed later in this Chapter and shake the float to verify if any has leaked into it.

13 SU Carburettor - water or dirt in the carburettor

1   Because of the size of the jet orifice, water or dirt in the carburettor is normally easily cleaned. If dirt in the carburettor is suspected, lift the piston assembly and flood the float chamber. The normal level of the fuel should be about 1/16 inch below the top of the jet, so that on flooding the carburettor the fuel should flow out of the jet hole.
2   If little or no petrol appears, start the engine (the jet is never completely blocked) and with the throttle fully open, blank off the air intake. This will cause a partial vacuum in the choke tube and help suck out any foreign matter from the jet tube. Release the throttle as soon as the engine speed alters considerably. Repeat this procedure several times, stop the engine and then check the carburettor as detailed in the first paragraph of this Section.
3   If this failed to do the trick then there is no alternative but to remove and blow out the jet.

14 SU Carburettor - jet centering

1   This operation is always necessary if the carburettor has been dismantled; but to check if this is necessary on a carburettor in service, first screw up the jet adjusting nut as far as it will go without forcing it, and lift the piston and then let it fall under its own weight. It should fall onto the bridge making a soft metallic click. Now repeat the above procedure but this time with the adjusting nut screwed right down. If the soft metallic click is not audible in either of the two tests proceed as follows:

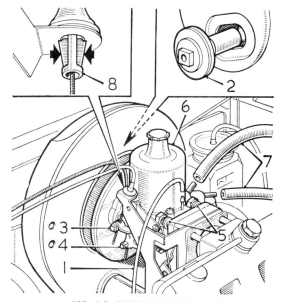

FIG. 3:5 CARBURETTOR REMOVAL

No.	Description	No.	Description
1	Distributor vacuum pipe		securing nuts and spring washers
2	Air cleaner securing bolt		
3	Throttle inner cable attachment	6	Carburettor
4	Choke inner cable attachment	7	Fuel supply pipe and engine breather pipe
5	Carburettor mounting flange	8	Throttle outer cable attachment

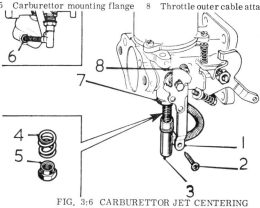

FIG. 3:6 CARBURETTOR JET CENTERING

No.	Description	No.	Description
1	Jet link	5	Adjusting nut
2	Jet link securing screw	6	Fuel feed pipe to jet
3	Jet	7	Jet locknut
4	Spring	8	Lifting pin

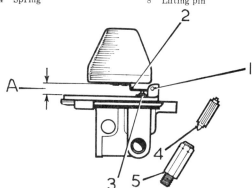

FIG. 3:7 FLOAT CHAMBER FUEL LEVEL ADJUSTMENT

No.	Description	No.	Description
1	Float lever pivot pin	4	Needle
2	Float lever	5	Valve body
3	Needle valve	A	Setting dimension - see Section 15

2   Disconnect the jet link (1), (Fig. 3.6) from the bottom of the jet, and the nylon flexible tube from the underside of the float chamber (6). Gently slide the jet and the nylon tube from the underside of the carburettor body. Next unscrew the jet adjusting nut (5) and lift away the nut and the locking spring. Refit the adjusting nut without the locking spring and screw it up as far as possible without forcing. Replace the jet and tube, but there is no need to reconnect the tube.

3   Slacken the jet locking nut (7) so that it may be rotated with the fingers only. Unscrew the piston damper and lift away the damper. Gently press the piston down onto the bridge and tighten the locknut (7). Lift the piston using the lifting pin (8) and check that it is able to fall freely under its own weight. Now lower the adjusting nut (5) and check once again. If this time there is a difference in the two metallic clicks, repeat the centering procedure until the sound is the same for both tests.

4   Gently remove the jet and unscrew the adjusting nut. Refit the locking spring and jet adjusting nut. Top up the damper with oil, if necessary, and replace the damper. Connect the nylon flexible tube to the underside of the float chamber and finally reconnect the jet link.

---

15   SU Carburettor - float chamber fuel level adjustment (float with metal lever)

---

1   It is essential that the fuel level in the float chamber is always correct as otherwise excessive fuel consumption may occur. On reassembly of the float chamber check the fuel level before replacing the float chamber cover in the following manner.
2   Invert the float chamber cover so that the needle valve is closed. It should be possible to place a round bar of 0.12 to 0.18 in (3.2 to 4.2 mm) diameter (A: Fig. 3.7) parallel to the float chamber cover without fouling the float, or if the float stands proud of the bar then it is necessary to bend the float lever slightly until the clearance is correct.
Note: A No 31 drill is 0.12 in and No 15 drill is 0.18 in.

---

16   SU Carburettor - needle replacement

---

1   Should it be found necessary to fit a new needle, first remove the piston and suction chamber assembly, marking the chamber for correct reassembly in its original position.
2   Slacken the needle or support guide locking screw and withdraw the needle or support guide/needle assembly from the piston.
3   Upon refitting a new needle it is important that the shoulder on the shank, or the lower edge of the guide is flush with the underside of the piston. Use a straight edge such as a metal rule for the adjustment. Refit the piston and suction chamber and check for freedom of piston movement. (Fig. 3.8).

---

17   SU Carburettor - adjustment and tuning

---

1   To adjust and tune the SU carburettor proceed in the following manner: Check the colour of the exhaust at idling speed with the choke fully in. If the exhaust tends to be black and the tailpipe interior is also black, it is a fair indication that the mixture is too rich. If the exhaust is colourless and the deposit in the exhaust pipe is very light grey it is likely that the mixture is too weak. This condition may also

be accompanied by intermittent misfiring, while too rich a mixture will be associated with 'hunting'. Ideally the exhaust should be colourless with a medium grey pipe deposit.
2   The exhaust pipe deposit should only be checked after a good run of at least 20 miles. Idling in city traffic and stop/start motoring is bound to produce excessively dark exhaust pipe deposit.
3   Once the engine has reached its normal operating temperature, detach the carburettor air intake cleaners.
4   Only two adjustments are provided on the SU carburettor. Idling speed is governed by the throttle adjusting screw (3) (Fig. 3.9) and the mixture strength by the jet adjusting nut (5). The SU carburettor is correctly adjusted for the whole of its engine revolution range when the idling mixture strength is correct.
5   Idling speed adjustment is effected by the idling adjusting screw (3). To adjust the mixture set the engine to run at about 1000 rpm by screwing in the idling screw.
6   Check the mixture strength by lifting the piston of the carburettor approximately 1/32 inch with the piston lifting pin (4) so as to disturb the air flow as little as possible. If:

a)   The speed of the engine increases appreciably, the mixture is too rich;
b)   The engine speed immediately decreases, the mixture is too weak;
c)   The engine speed increases very slightly, the mixture is correct.

To alter the mixture, rotate the adjusting nut, (which is at the bottom of the carburettor) in a clockwise direction (ie. downwards) to enrich the mixture, or anticlockwise (ie. upwards) to weaken the muxture. Only turn the adjusting nut a flat at a time and check the mixture strength between each turn. It is likely that there will be a slight increase or decrease in rpm after the mixture adjustment has been made, so the throttle idling adjusting screw should now be turned so that the engine idles the correct speed.

---

18   Throttle cable - removal, refitting and adjustment

---

1   Disconnect the inner cable from the carburettor throttle spindle, located as shown in Fig. 3.10.
2   Release the outer cable from the carburettor abutment bracket.
3   Release the inner cable from the accelerator pedal arm by drawing the nipple from its location in the top of the pedal arm and lifting the cable from the slot in the arm.
4   Detach the throttle cable from the servo pipe clip.
5   The inner and outer cable assembly can now be withdrawn from the servo mounting plate in a forwards direction from the front of the car.
6   Refitting the cable is the reverse sequence to removal. It will however be necessary to adjust the cable as described in the following paragraphs.
7   Refer to Fig. 3.10 and slacken the throttle cable trunnion bolt.
8   Carefully pull down on the inner cable until all free movement of the accelerator pedal has been removed.
9   Hold the inner cable so it takes up the line shown in Fig. 3.10 and then raise the cam operating lever until it just contacts the cam.

10   Move the trunnion up the cable until it contacts the operating lever. Tighten the trunnion bolt.

11   Depress the accelerator pedal and check that approximately 1/16 inch free movement takes place on the throttle cable before the cam operating lever begins to move.

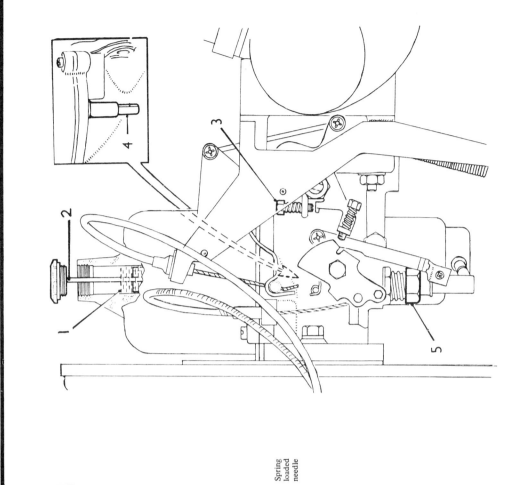

FIG. 3:9 CARBURETTOR ADJUSTMENT POINTS

No. Description   No. Description
1   Oil level in dashpot   4   Piston lifting pin
2   Damper   5   Jet adjusting nut
3   Idle speed adjustment screw

FIG. 3:8 NEEDLE FITTING INTO PISTON

1 Needle shoulder flush with   Fixed   3 Support guide locking screw
   bottom of piston   needle   4 Support guide flush with bottom of piston
2 Needle securing screw   5 Needle
                                Spring   6 Assembly of spring, support guide and needle
                                loaded
                                needle

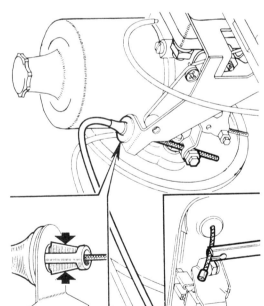

Fig. 3:10 Throttle cable fixing points

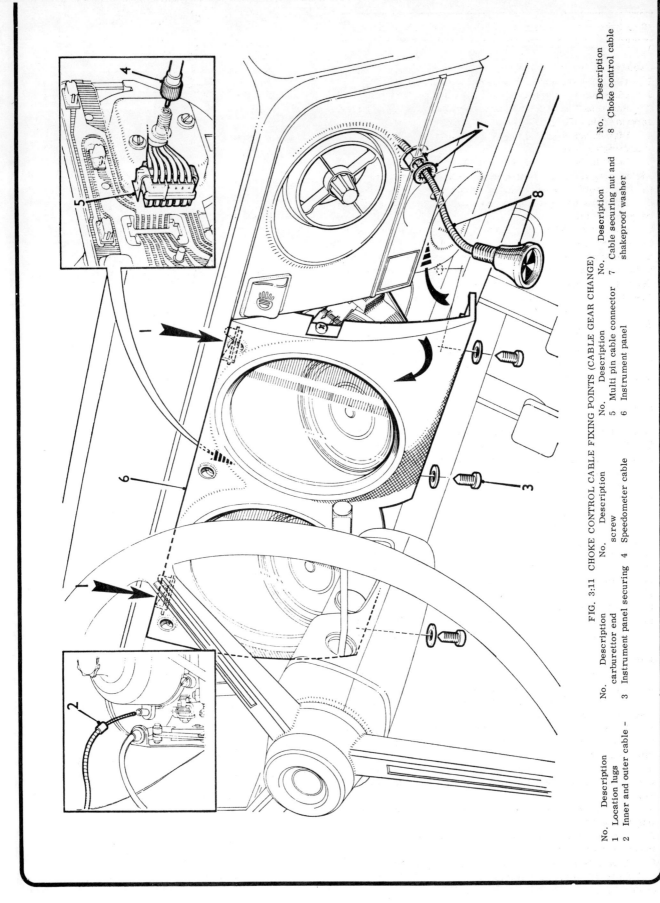

FIG. 3:11 CHOKE CONTROL CABLE FIXING POINTS (CABLE GEAR CHANGE)

No.	Description	No.	Description	No.	Description	No.	Description
1	Location lugs	3	Instrument panel securing screw	5	Multi pin cable connector	7	Cable securing nut and shakeproof washer
2	Inner and outer cable – carburettor end	4	Speedometer cable	6	Instrument panel	8	Choke control cable

19   Choke control - removal, refitting and adjustment

Cable gear change models
1   For safety reasons, disconnect the battery.
2   Disconnect the choke control from the carburettor.
3   Refer to Fig. 3.11 and undo and remove the securing screws from below the instrument panel.
4   Disconnect the speedometer cable from the rear of the speedometer head.
5   Refer to the righthand insert to Fig. 3.11 and detach the wiring plug from the rear of the instrument panel and draw the instrument panel away from the facia.
6   Undo the nut and shakeproof washer securing the outer cable to the facia panel.
7   The inner and outer cable assembly may now be withdrawn from the body grommet.
8   Refitting the cable is the reverse sequence to removal. It is important that the inner cable trunnion is connected to the lower of the two holes on the carburettor choke lever. The cable must be adjusted as described later in this Section.

Rod gear change models
1   For safety reasons disconnect the battery.
2   Disconnect the choke cable from the carburettor.
3   Undo and remove the screws securing the glovebox lid support to the facia located as shown in Fig. 3.12.
4   Undo and remove the screws and washers securing the glovebox lid striker.
5   Undo and remove the side and lower glovebox retaining screws and washers, and withdraw the glovebox.
6   Remove the grub screws securing the control knobs to the heater controls, and withdraw the knobs. (Fig. 3.13).
7   Carefully prise away the heater control masking plate using a knife or thin wide bladed screwdriver.
8   Undo and remove the two screws securing the heater controls to the facia panel.
9   Remove the nut and shakeproof washer securing the outer cable to the facia panel.
10   The inner and outer cable may now be withdrawn from the body grommet. Note that this cable uses the same grommet as the bonnet release cable.
11   Refitting is the reverse sequence to removal. Note that the inner cable trunnion is connected into the lower of the two holes on the carburettor choke lever. It will be necessary to adjust the cable as described later in this Section.

Adjustment
1   Refer to Fig. 3.14 and slacken the cable trunnion bolt.
2   Make sure that the choke control knob is pushed in fully.
3   Adjust the fast idle adjusting screw so that a small clearance exists between the end of the screw and the cam.
4   Adjust the position of the trunnion so as to give a free movement of the cable of 1/16 inch before the cam lever begins to move.
5   Pull out the choke control knob approximately ½ inch (see inset to Fig. 3.14) until the linkage is just about to move the jet.
6   Start the engine and allow to warm up to normal operating temperature.
7   Turn the fast idle screw to give an engine speed of between 1000 and 1100 rpm.
8   Return the choke control knob to its fully closed position and check that there is a small gap (Fig. 3.14), between the end of the fast idle adjusting screw and the cam.

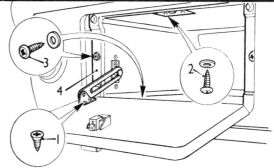

FIG. 3:12 GLOVE BOX COMPARTMENT FIXINGS

No.	Description	No.	Description
1	Glovebox lid support fixing screw	3	Compartment fixing screw
2	Striker fixing screw	4	Compartment

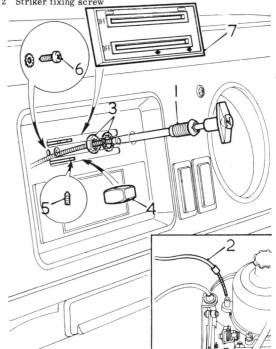

FIG. 3:13 CHOKE CONTROL CABLE FIXING POINTS (ROD GEAR CHANGE)

No.	Description	No.	Description
1	Choke control cable	4	Heater control knob
2	Inner and outer cable - carburettor end	5	Heater control knob grub screw
3	Cable fixing nut and shakeproof washer	6	Heater control unit securing screw
		7	Heater control masking plate

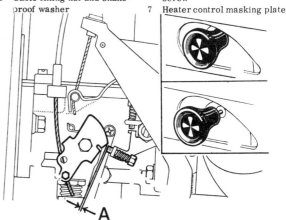

FIG. 3:14 CHOKE CONTROL ADJUSTMENT
A. Minimum gap 1/16 inch

20 Accelerator pedal - removal and refitting

1　Detach the throttle cable from the pedal arm by drawing the nipple from its location in the top of the pedal arm and lifting the cable from the slot in the arm.
2　Extract the split pin and lift away the washer from the pedal pivot, located as shown in Fig. 3.15.
3　Very carefully lever the pivot from the mounting bracket sufficiently for the pedal to be withdrawn.
4　Check the accelerator pedal arm and pivot for wear, and if evident, a new pedal assembly should be fitted.
5　Refitting is the reverse sequence to removal. Lubricate the pedal pivot with a little Castrol LM Grease.

21 Fuel tank - removal and refitting

1　For safety reasons, disconnect the battery.
2　Undo and remove the four self tapping screws securing the access panel from the floor of the boot. This panel is shown in Fig. 3.16.
3　Disconnect the fuel gauge sender unit cable and main fuel pipe from the sender unit. To do this, squeeze the clip ears with a pair of pliers.
4　Remove the petrol filler cap.
5　Detach the breather pipe from the clip on the tank flange and push the pipe back through the body grommet.
6　Undo and remove the tank securing bolts, spring and plain washers, and lift away the tank taking care to disengage the filler pipe neck from the body grommet.
7　Refitting the fuel tank is the reverse procedure to removal. It will be necessary to pass the breather pipe through

the body grommet as the tank is raised into position.

22 Fuel tank - cleaning

With time it is likely that sediment will collect in the bottom of the fuel tank. Condensation, resulting in rust and other impurities, is sometimes found in the fuel tank of a car more than three or four years old.
When the tank is removed, it should be vigorously flushed out and turned upside down and, if facilities are available, steam cleaned.

23 Fuel tank sender unit - removal and refitting

1　For safety reasons disconnect the battery.
2　Undo and remove the four self tapping screws securing the access panel from the floor of the boot. This panel is shown in Fig. 3.16.
3　Disconnect the fuel gauge sender unit cable.
4　Detach the main fuel pipe from the sender unit by squeezing the ears of the clip with a pair of pliers and pulling off the cable.
5　Using two crossed screwdrivers, remove the fuel gauge tank unit by turning through approximately 30°, and lift away from the tank. Take great care not to bend the float wire.
6　If the sender unit is suspect, check the circuit, gauge and sender unit as described in Chapter 10.
7　Refitting is the reverse sequence to removal. Always fit a new sealing washer located between the fuel gauge tank unit and the tank itself.

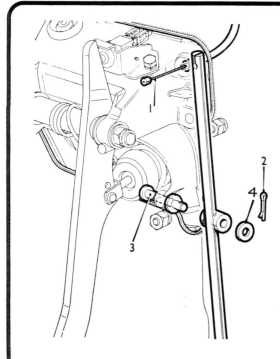

FIG. 3:15 ACCELERATOR PEDAL ASSEMBLY

No.	Description	No.	Description
1	Inner cable	3	Pedal pivot
2	Split pin	4	Spacer washer

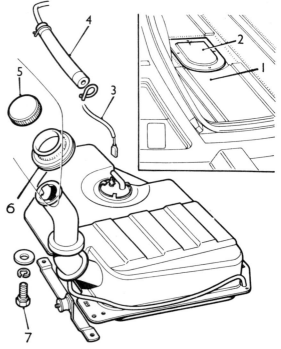

FIG. 3:16 FUEL TANK ASSEMBLY

No.	Description	No.	Description
1	Boot floor	5	Filler cap
2	Access panel	6	Filler neck body grommet
3	Sender unit electric cable	7	Fuel tank fixing bolt
4	Main fuel pipe		

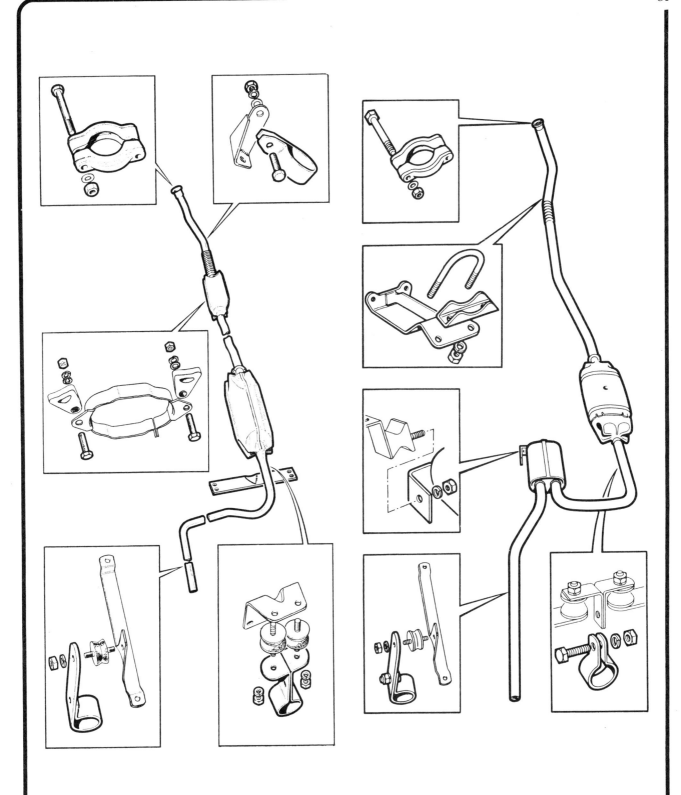

Fig. 3:17 Exhaust system (cable operated gear change)   Fig. 3:18 Exhaust system (rod operated gear change)

Cause	Trouble	Remedy
SYMPTOM: FUEL CONSUMPTION EXCESSIVE		
Carburation and ignition faults	Air cleaner choked and dirty giving rich mixture	Remove, clean and replace air cleaner.
	Fuel leaking from carburettor, fuel pumps, or fuel lines	Check for and eliminate all fuel leaks. Tighten fuel line union nuts.
	Float chamber flooding	Check and adjust float level.
	Generally worn carburettor	Remove, overhaul and replace.
	Distributor condenser faulty	Remove, and fit new unit.
	Balance weights or vacuum advance mechanism is distributor faulty	Remove, and overhaul distributor.
Incorrect adjustment	Carburettor incorrectly adjusted mixture too rich	Tune and adjust carburettor.
	Idling speed too high	Adjust idling speed.
	Contact breaker gap incorrect	Check and reset gap.
	Valve clearances incorrect	Check clearances and adjust as necessary
	Incorrectly set spark plugs	Remove, clean, and regap.
	Tyres under-inflated	Check tyre pressures and inflate if necessary.
	Wrong spark plugs fitted	Remove and replace with correct units.
	Brakes dragging	Check and adjust brakes.
SYMPTOM: INSUFFICIENT FUEL DELIVERY OR WEAK MIXTURE DUE TO AIR LEAKS		
Dirt in system	Petrol tank air vent restricted	Remove petrol cap and clean out air vent
	Partially clogged filters in pump and carburettor.	Remove and clean filters.
	Dirt lodged in float chamber needle housing	Remove and clean out float chamber and needle valve assembly.
	Incorrectly seating valves in fuel pump	Remove, dismantle, and clean out fuel pump.
	Fuel pump diaphragm leaking or damaged	Remove, and overhaul fuel pump.
	Gasket in fuel pump damaged	Remove, and overhaul fuel pump.
	Fuel pump valves sticking due to petrol gumming	Remove, and thoroughly clean fuel pump.
Air leaks	Too little fuel in fuel tank (Prevalent when climbing steep hills)	Refill fuel tank.
	Union joints on pipe connections loose	Tighten joints and check for air leaks.
	Split in fuel pipe on suction side of fuel pump	Examine, locate, and repair.
	Inlet manifold to block or inlet manifold to carburettor gasket leaking	Test by pouring oil along joints – bubbles indicate leak. Renew gasket as appropriate

Chapter 4 Ignition system

Contents

Specifications

Spark plugs

Make	Champion
Type	N9Y
Size	14 mm
Gap	0. 024 to 0. 026 inch (0. 36 mm to 0. 41 mm)
Firing order	1 3 4 2

Coil

Type	Lucas 11C 12 or 16C 6
Primary resistance at 20⁰ C (68⁰ F)	3.0 to 3.4 ohms (11C 12). 1.43 to 1.48 ohms (16C 6)
Consumption	
Ignition switched on	3.5 to 4.0 amps (11C 12. 4.5 to 5 amp (16C 6)
at 2000 rpm	1 amp

Distributor

Type	Lucas 25D4 or 45DA
Serial number	41246 or 41418
Rotational direction of rotor	Anticlockwise
Contact breaker points gap	0. 014 to 0. 016 in
Dwell angle...	60⁰ ± 3⁰ (25D4) or 51 ± 5% (45D4)
Condenser capacity	0. 18 to 0. 24 mF
Automatic advance	Vacuum and centrifugal
Centrifugal advance:	
Deceleration (vacuum pipe disconnected)	20⁰ - 24⁰ at 6000 rpm
	14⁰ - 18⁰ at 4000 rpm
	8⁰ - 12⁰ at 2000 rpm
	6⁰ - 10⁰ at 1500 rpm
	0⁰ - 1⁰ at 900 rpm
	800 rpm - no advance

Vacuum advance

Starts	6 in Hg
Finishes	14 in Hg at 16⁰

Ignition timing

Marks location	Marks on camshaft sprocket boss and housing in conjunction with flywheel
1500 (1969/70 models)	12⁰ BTDC at 1000 rpm (stroboscopic vacuum pipe disconnected)
1500 (1971) and 1750	13⁰ BTDC at 1000 rpm (stroboscopic vacuum pipe disconnected)

Torque wrench setting

	lb ft	Kg m
Distributor to plate	2. 5	0. 35
Distributor clamp bolt	3. 0	0. 41
Spark plug	14	1. 9

General description

In order that the engine may run correctly it is necessary for an electrical spark to ignite the fuel/air mixture in the combustion chamber at exactly the right moment in relation to engine speed and load. The ignition system is based on supplying low tension voltage from the battery to the ignition coil, where it is converted to high tension voltage. The high tension voltage is powerful enough to jump the spark plug gap in the cylinders many times a second under high compression pressure, providing that the ignition system is in good working order and that all adjustments are correct.

The ignition system comprises two individual circuits known as the low tension circuit and the high tension circuit.

The low tension circuit (sometimes known as the primary circuit) comprises the battery, lead to control box, lead to the ignition switch, to the low tension or primary coil windings (terminal SW) and the lead from the low tension coil windings (coil terminal CB) to the contact breaker points and condenser in the distributor.

The high tension circuit (sometimes known as the secondary circuit) comprises the high tension or secondary coil winding, the heavily insulated ignition lead from the centre of the coil to the centre of the distributor cap, the rotor arm, the spark plug leads and the spark plugs.

The complete ignition system operation is as follows: low tension voltage from the battery is changed within the ignition coil to high tension voltage by the opening and closing of the contact breaker points in the low tension circuit. High tension voltage is then fed via the carbon brush in the centre of the distributor cap to the rotor arm of the distributor. The rotor arm revolves inside the distributor cap, and each time it comes in line with one of the four metal segments in the cap, these being connected to the spark plug leads, the opening and closing of the contact breaker points causes the high tension voltage to build up, jump the gap from the rotor arm to the appropriate metal segment and so, via the spark plug lead, to the spark plug where it finally jumps the gap between the two spark plug electrodes, one being connected to the earth system.

The ignition timing is advanced and retarded automatically to ensure the spark occurs at just the right instant for the particular load at the prevailing engine speed.

The ignition advance is controlled both mechanically and by a vacuum operated system. The mechanical governor mechanism comprises two lead weights which move out under centrifugal force from the central distributor shaft as the engine speed rises. As they move outwards they rotate the cams relative to the distributor shaft, and so advance the spark. The weights are held in position by two light springs, and it is the tension of the springs which is largely responsible for correct spark advancement.

The vacuum control comprises a diaphragm, one side of which is connected via a small bore tube to the carburettor, and the other side to the contact breaker plate. Depression in the induction manifold and carburettor, which varies with engine speed and throttle opening, causes the diaphragm to move, so moving the contact breaker plate and advancing or retarding the spark. A fine degree of control is achieved by a spring in the vacuum assembly.

2   Contact breaker points - adjustment

1   To adjust the contact breaker points so that the correct gap is obtained, first release the two clips securing the distributor cap to the distributor body, and lift away the cap. Clean the inside and outside of the cap with a dry cloth. It is unlikely that the four segments will be badly burned or scored, but if they are the cap must be renewed. If only a small deposit is on the segments it may be scraped away using a small screwdriver.

2   Push in the carbon brush, located in the top of the cap, several times to ensure that it moves freely. The brush should protrude by at least $\frac{1}{4}$ inch.

3   Gently prise the contact breaker points open to examine the condition of their faces. If they are rough, pitted or dirty, it will be necessary to remove them for resurfacing, or for replacement points to be fitted.

4   Presuming the points are satisfactory, or that they have been cleaned or replaced, measure the gap between the points by turning the engine over until the contact breaker arm is on the peak of one of the four cam lobes. A 0.015 inch feeler gauge should now just fit between the points.

5   If the gap varies from this amount, slacken the contact plate securing screw and adjust the contact gap by inserting a screwdriver in the notched hole at the end of the plate, turning clockwise to decrease, and anticlockwise to increase, the gap. Tighten the securing screw and check the gap again.

6   Replace the rotor arm and distributor cap and clip the

spring blade retainers into position.

3   Contact breaker points - removal and replacement

1   If the contact breaker points are burned, pitted or badly worn, they must be removed and either replaced or their faces must be filed smooth.

2   To remove the points, unscrew the terminal nut (4) (Fig. 4.1) and remove it together with the washer under its head. Remove the flanged nylon bush, the condenser lead and the low tension lead from the terminal pin. Lift off the contact breaker arm and remove the large fibre washer from the terminal pin.

3   The adjustable contact breaker plate is removed by unscrewing one holding down screw (2) and removing it, complete with spring and flat washer.

4   To reface the points, rub the faces on a fine carborundum stone, or on fine emery paper. It is important that the faces are rubbed flat and parallel to each other so that there will be complete face to face contact when the points are closed. One of the points will be pitted and the other will have deposits on it.

5   It is necessary to remove completely the built up deposits, but unnecessary to rub the pitted point right to the stage where all the pitting has disappeared, though obviously if this is done it will prolong the time before the operation of refacing the points has to be repeated.

6   To replace the points, first position the adjustable contact breaker plate, and secure it with its screw, spring and flat washer. Fit the fibre washer to the terminal pin and fit the contact breaker arm over it. Insert the flanged nylon bush with the condenser lead immediately under its head, and the low tension lead under that, over the terminal pin. Fit the steel washer and screw on the securing nut.

7   The points are now reassembled and the gap should be set as detailed in the previous Section.

4   Condenser - removal, testing and replacement

1   The purpose of the condenser (sometimes known as a capacitor) is to ensure that when the contact breaker points open there is no sparking across them which would waste voltage and cause wear.

2   The condenser is fitted in parallel with the contact breaker points. If it develops a short circuit, it will cause ignition failure, as the points will be prevented from interrupting the low tension circuit.

3   If the engine becomes very difficult to start, or begins to miss after several miles running, and the breaker points show signs of excessive burning, then the condition of the condenser must be suspect. A further test can be made by separating the points by hand with the ignition switched on. If this is accompanied by a flash it is indicative that the condenser has failed.

4   Without special test equipment, the only sure way to diagnose condenser trouble is to replace a suspected unit with a new one and note if there is any improvement.

5   To remove the condenser from the distributor, remove the distributor cap and the rotor arm. Unscrew the contact breaker arm terminal nut, remove the nut, washer and flanged nylon bush and release the condenser. Replacement of the condenser is simply a reversal of the removal process. Take particular care that the condenser lead does not short circuit against any portion of the breaker plate.

5   Distributor - lubrication

1   It is important that the distributor cam is lubricated with petroleum jelly at the specified mileages, and that the breaker arm, governor weights and cam spindle are lubricated with engine oil once every 6000 miles. In practice it will be found that lubrication every 3000 miles is preferable although this is not recommended by the manufacturers.

2   Great care should be taken not to use too much lubricant, as any excess that might find its way onto the contact breaker points could cause burning and misfiring.

3   To gain access to the cam spindle, lift away the rotor arm. Drop no more than two drops of engine oil onto the screw head. This will run down the spindle when the engine is hot and lubricate the bearings. No more than ONE drop of oil should be applied to the pivot post. (Fig. 4. 2).

6   Distributor - removal and replacement

1   Prior to removing the distributor, remove the flywheel housing cover. Determine which spark plug lead is attached to No 1 spark plug. This is the one nearest to the fan.

2   Release the clips securing the distributor cap to the body and lift away the distributor cap.

3   Slowly turn the crankshaft in the normal direction of rotation until the 1/4 TDC mark with No 1 cylinder on the power stroke is aligned with the housing pointer as shown in the insert to Fig. 4.3.

4   Release the low tension cable connector from the side of the distributor.

5   Unscrew the high tension lead retaining cap from the coil and remove the spark plug leads. The distributor cap can now be completely removed.

6   Remove the vacuum tube connector at the distributor vacuum unit housing.

7   Remove the two distributor body clamp bolts and washers securing the clamp plate to the cylinder block. The distributor may now be lifted up with the clamp plate still attached.

8   If it is not wished to disturb the ignition timing, then under no circumstances should the clamp pinch bolt, which secures the distributor in its relative position in the clamp, be loosened. Providing the distributor is removed without the clamp being loosened from the distributor, and the engine is not turned, the ignition timing will not be lost.

9   Replacement is a reversal of the above sequence. If the engine has been turned, it will be necessary to retime the ignition. This will also be necessary if the clamp pinch bolt has been loosened.

7   Distributor - dismantling

1   With the distributor removed from the car and on the bench, remove the distributor cap and lift off the rotor arm (1) (Fig. 4.4). If very tight, lever it off gently with a screwdriver.

2   Remove the contact breaker points as described in Section 3.

3   Remove the condenser (6) from the contact plate by releasing its securing screw and washer.

4   Unlock the vacuum unit spring from its mounting pin on the moving contact plate.

5   Lift out the contact plate.

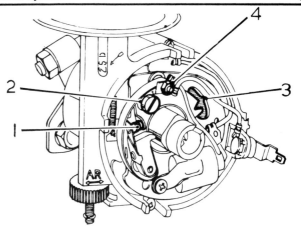

FIG. 4:1 CONTACT BREAKER POINT ADJUSTMENT

No.	Description	No.	Description
1	Contact breaker points	4	Moving contact spring and ter-
2	Contact plate securing screw		minals securing nut.
3	Screwdriver slot		

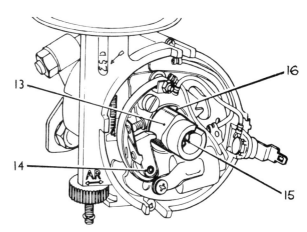

FIG. 4:2 LUBRICATION POINTS FOR DISTRIBUTOR.

No.	Description	No.	Description
13	Contact breaker cam		screw
14	Contact breaker pivot	16	Centrifugal mechanism lubrica-
15	Cam spindle and centre		tion point.

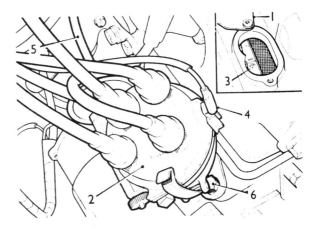

FIG. 4:3 DISTRIBUTOR REMOVAL

No.	Description	No.	Description
1	Flywheel housing cover plate	4	L T lead connector
2	Distributor cap	5	H T leads
3	Timing marks on flywheel	6	Distributor clamp plate securing screw

6   Unscrew and remove the two screws and washer (7) which hold the contact breaker base plate (7) in position and remove the earth lead from the relevant screw. Remember to replace this lead on reassembly.

7   Lift out the contact breaker base plate.

8   Note the position of the slot in the rotor arm drive in relation to the offset drive dog at the opposite end of the distributor. It is essential that this is reassembled correctly as otherwise the timing may be 180° out.

9   Unscrew the cam spindle retaining screw (8) which is located in the centre of the rotor arm drive shaft cam (9) and remove the cam spindle.

10   Lift out the centrifugal weights (21) together with their springs (20).

11   To remove the vacuum unit (14), spring off the small circlip securing the advance adjustment knurled nut (19) which should then be unscrewed. With the micrometer adjusting nut removed, release the spring (19) and the micrometer adjusting nut lock spring clip (23). This is the clip that is responsible for the 'clicks' when the micrometer adjuster nut (14) is turned and it is small and easily lost, as is the circlip, so put them in a safe place. Do not forget to replace the lock spring clip on reassembly.

12   It is necessary to remove the distributor drive shaft or spindle only if it is thought to be excessively worn. With a thin parallel pin punch drive out the retaining pin (11) from the driving tongue collar (12) on the bottom end of the distributor drive shaft. The shaft can then be removed. Recover the thrust washers (12).

13   The distributor is now ready for inspection.

8   Distributor - inspection and repair

1   Thoroughly wash all mechanical parts in petrol and wipe dry using a clean non-fluffy rag.

2   Check the points that have already been described previously. Check the distributor cap for signs of tracking, indicated by a thin black line between the segments. Replace the cap if any signs of tracking are found.

3   If the metal portion of the rotor arm is badly burned or loose, renew the arm. If slightly burnt, clean the arm with a fine file. Check that the carbon brush moves freely in the centre of the distributor cover.

4   Examine the fit of the breaker plate on the bearing plate and also check the breaker arm pivot for looseness, or wear, and renew as necessary.

5   Examine the balance weights and pivot pins for wear, and renew the weights or cam assembly if a degree of wear is found.

6   Examine the shaft and the fit of the cam assembly on the shaft. If the clearance is excessive compare the items with new units and renew either, or both, if they show excessive wear.

7   If the shaft is a loose fit in the distributor bushes and can be seen to be worn, it will be necessary to fit a new shaft and bushes. The old bushes in the early distributor, or the single bush in the later ones, are simply pressed out. NOTE: Before inserting new bushes they should be stood in engine oil for 24 hours.

8   Examine the length of the balance weight springs and compare them with a new spring. If they have stretched they should be renewed.

9   Distributor - reassembly

1   Reassembly is a straight reversal of the dismantling process, but there are several points which should be noted in addition to those already given in the Section on dismantling.

2   Lubricate the balance weights and other parts of the mechanical advance mechanism, the distributor shaft, and the portion of the shaft on which the cam bears, with SAE 20 engine oil, during reassembly. Do not oil excessively but ensure these parts are adequately lubricated.

3   On reassembling the cam driving pins with the centrifugal weights, check that they are in correct position so that when viewed from above, the rotor arm should be at the six o'clock position, and the small offset on the driving dog must be on the right.

4   Check the action of the weights in the fully advanced and fully retarded positions and ensure they are not binding.

5   Tighten the micrometer adjusting nut to the middle position on the timing scale.

6   If the oil seal (18) (Fig. 4.4) has stretched or is damaged, obtain and fit a new one.

7   Finally, set the contact breaker gap to the correct clearance of 0.015 inch.

10   Ignition - timing

1   If the clamp plate pinch bolt has been loosened on the distributor and the static timing lost, or if for any other reason it is wished to set the ignition timing, proceed as follows:

2   Refer to Section 2 and check the contact breaker points. Reset as necessary.

3   Assemble the clamp plate to the distributor body but do not tighten the pinch bolt fully. Where the distributor has a knurled micrometer adjustment nut, set this to approximately the mid position of its travel range.

4   Slowly turn the crankshaft in the normal direction of rotation with the 1/4 TDC mark on the flywheel aligned with the pointer as shown in the insert to Fig. 4.3. No 1 cylinder should be at the top of the compression stroke and just about to commence the power stroke.

5   Fit the distributor and engage the driving dog into the distributor drive shaft. Provided the distributor drive shaft has not been disturbed or has been refitted correctly, the rotor arm should now point to the segment in the distributor cap which leads to No 1 spark plug (the one nearest the fan).

6   Replace the two distributor clamp bolts and washers but do not tighten fully yet.

7   Now rotate the crankshaft anti-clockwise approximately 20° then turn it clockwise again until the timing pointer indicates 11° BTDC (1969/70 models) or 12° BTDC (other models). (This is slightly lower than the stroboscopic timing given in the Specifications which allows for approximately 1° of centrifugal advance at 1000 rpm).

8   Rotate the distributor body anti-clockwise a little, then rotate it slowly clockwise until the points just commence to open. Now tighten the clamp bolts. Difficulty is sometimes experienced in determining exactly when the contact breaker points open. This can be ascertained most accurately by connecting a 12 volt bulb in parallel with the contact breaker points (one lead to earth and the other from the distributor low tension terminal). Switch on the ignition, and turn the advance and retard adjuster until the bulb lights up, indicating that the points have just opened.

9   Replace the distributor cap and reconnect the spark plug leads. Do not forget the HT lead to the centre of the ignition coil.

10   If it was not found possible to align the rotor arm correctly,

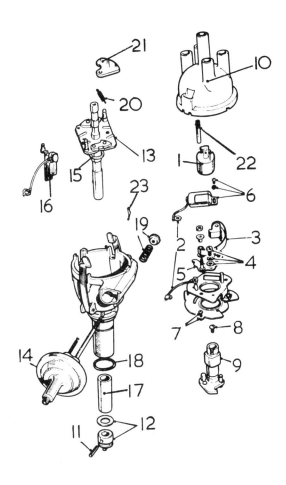

FIG. 4:4 DISTRIBUTOR COMPONENT PARTS

No.	Description	No.	Description
1	Rotor arm	12	Drive dog and thrust washer
2	Capacitor and action plate	13	Action plate
3	Moving contact breaker	14	Vacuum timing control unit
4	Fixed contact plate secur-	15	Distance collar
	ing screw and washer	16	L T terminal
5	Fixed contact plate	17	Bearing bush
6	Condenser, securing screw	18	Oil seal
	and washer	19	Micrometer adjustment nut and
7	Contact breaker base plate		spring
	and retaining screws	20	Timing control weight spring
8	Cam securing screw	21	Timing control weight
9	Cam spindle	22	Carbon brush and spring
10	Distributor cap	23	Spring for micrometer adjust-
11	Drive dog securing pin		ment nut

one or two things is wrong: either the distributor drive shaft has been incorrectly refitted, in which case it must be removed and replaced as described in Chapter 1, or the distributor has been dismantled and the distributor cam spindle refitted 180º out. To rectify, it will be necessary to partially dismantle the distributor, lift the camshaft pins from the centrifugal weight holes and turn the camshaft through 180º. Refit the pins into the weights and reassemble.

11   It should be noted that the adjustment which has been made is nominal and the final adjustment should be made under running conditions.

12   First start the engine and allow to warm up to normal running temperature, and then accelerate in top gear from 30 to 50 mph, listening for heavy pinking of the engine. If this occurs, the ignition needs to be retarded slightly until just the faintest trace of pinking can be heard under these operating conditions. If the distributor has a micrometer adjuster, this can be used, but where there is no adjuster, the distributor will have to be rotated slightly anti-clockwise.

13   Since the ignition advance adjustment enables the firing point to be related correctly to the grade of fuel used, the fullest advantage of any change of fuel will only be obtained by re-adjustment of the ignition settings.

11   Spark plugs and leads

1   The correct functioning of the spark plugs is vital for the proper running and efficiency of the engine.

2   At intervals of 6000 miles the plugs should be removed, examined, cleaned, and if worn excessively, replaced. The condition of the spark plug will also tell much about the general condition of the engine.

3   If the insulator nose of the spark plug is clean and white, with no deposits, this is indicative of a weak mixture, or too hot a plug (a hot plug transfers heat away from the electrode slowly - a cold plug transfers heat away quickly).

4   The plugs fitted as standard are the Champion N9Y 14 mm type. If the top and insulator nose is covered with hard black looking deposits, then this is indicative that the mixture is too rich. Should the plug be black and oily, then it is likely that the engine is fairly worn, as well as the mixture being too rich.

5   If the insulator nose is covered with light tan to greyish brown deposits, then the mixture is correct, and it is likely that the engine is in good condition.

6   If there are any traces of long brown tapering stains on the outside of the white portion of the plug, then the plug will have to be renewed, as this shows that there is a faulty joint between the plug body and the insulator, and compression is being allowed to leak away.

7   Plugs should be cleaned by a sand blasting machine, which will free them from carbon more than by cleaning by hand. The machine will also test the condition of the plugs under compression. Any plug that fails to spark at the re-commended pressure should be renewed.

8   The spark plug gap is of considerable importance, as, if it is too large or too small the size of the spark and its efficiency will be seriously impaired. The spark plug gap should be set to 0.025 inch for the best results.

9   To set it, measure the gap with a feeler gauge, and then bend open, or close, the outer plug electrode until the correct gap is achieved. (Fig. 4.5). The centre electrode should never be bent as this may crack the insulation and cause plug failure, if nothing worse.

10   When replacing the plugs, remember to use new washers and replace the leads from the distributor in the correct firing order which is 1 3 4 2, cylinder No 1 being nearest the fan.

11 The plug leads require no routine maintenance other than being kept clean and wiped over regularly. At intervals of 6000 miles, however, pull each lead off the plug in turn and remove them from the distributor by slackening the screws located as shown in Fig. 4.3. Water can seep down these joints giving rise to a white corrosive deposit which must be carefully removed from the end of each cable.

12 Ignition system - fault symptoms

There are two main symptoms indicating ignition faults. Either the engine will not start or fire, or the engine is difficult to start and misfires. If it is a regular misfire, ie the engine is only running on two or three cylinders, the fault is almost sure to be in the secondary, or high tension, circuit. If the misfiring is intermittent, the fault could be in either the high or low tension circuits. If the engine stops suddenly, or will not start at all, it is likely that the fault is in the low tension circuit. Loss of power and overheating, apart from faulty carburation settings, are normally due to faults in the distributor, or incorrect ignition timing.

13 Fault diagnosis - engine fails to start

1 If the engine fails to start and it was running normally when it was last used, first check that there is fuel in the petrol tank. If the engine turns over normally on the starter motor and the battery is evidently well charged, then the fault may be in either the high or low tension circuits. First check the HT circuit. NOTE: If the battery is known to be fully charged, the ignition comes on, and the starter motor fails to turn the engine, CHECK THE TIGHTNESS OF THE LEADS ON THE BATTERY TERMINALS and also the secureness of the earth lead to its CONNECTION TO THE BODY. It is quite common for the leads to have worked loose, even if they look and feel secure. If one of the battery terminal posts gets very hot when trying to work the starter motor this is a sure indication of a faulty connection to that terminal.

2 One of the commonest reasons for bad starting is wet or damp spark plug leads and distributor. Remove the distributor cap. If condensation is visible, internally dry the cap with a rag and also wipe over the leads. Replace the cap.

3 If the engine still fails to start, check that current is reaching the plugs by disconnecting each plug lead in turn at the spark plug end, and holding the end of the cable about 3/16 inch away from the cylinder block. Spin the engine on the starter motor by pressing the rubber button on the starter motor solenoid switch (under the bonnet).

4 Sparking between the end of the cable and the block should be fairly strong with a regular blue spark (hold the lead with rubber to avoid electric shocks). If current is reaching the plugs, then remove them and clean and regap them to 0.025 inch. The engine should now start.

5 Spin the engine as before, when a rapid succession of blue sparks between the end of the lead and the block indicate that the coil is in order, and that either the distributor cap is cracked; the carbon brush is stuck or worn; the rotor arm is faulty; or the contact points are burnt, pitted or dirty. If the points are in bad shape, clean and reset them as described in Section 11.

6 If there are no sparks from the end of the lead from the coil, then check the connections of the lead to the coil and distributor head, and if they are in order, check out the low tension circuit starting with the battery.

7 Switch on the ignition and turn the crankshaft so the contact breaker points have fully opened. Then, with either a 20 volt voltmeter or bulb and length of wire, check that current from the battery is reaching the starter solenoid switch. No reading indicates that there is a fault in the cable to the switch or in the connections at the switch or at the battery terminals. Alternatively, the battery earth lead may not be properly earthed to the body.

8 If in order, check that current is reaching terminal A (the one with the brown lead) in the control box, by connecting the voltmeter between A and an earth. If there is no reading, this indicates a faulty cable or loose connections between the solenoid switch and the A terminal. Remedy and the car will start.

9 Check with the voltmeter between the control box terminal A1 and earth. No reading means a fault in the control box. Fit a new control box and start the car.

10 If in order, then check that current is reaching the ignition switch by connecting the voltmeter to the ignition switch input terminal (the one connected to the brown/blue lead) and earth. No reading indicates a break in the wire or a faulty connection at the switch or A1 terminals.

11 If the correct reading (approx 12 volts) is obtained check the output terminal on the ignition switch (the terminal connected to the white lead). No reading means that the ignition switch is broken. Replace with a new unit and start the car.

12 If current is reaching the ignition switch output terminal, then check the A3 terminal on the fuse unit with the voltmeter. No reading indicates a break in the wire or loose connections between the ignition and the A3 terminal. Even if the A3 - A4 fuse is broken, current should still be reaching the coil as it does not pass through the fuse. Remedy and the car should now start.

13 Check the switch terminal on the coil (it is marked SW and the lead from the switch connects to it). No reading indicates loose connections or a broken wire from the A3 terminal on the fuse unit. If this proves to be the fault, remedy and start the car.

14 Check the contact breaker terminal on the coil (it is marked CB) and if no reading is recorded on the voltmeter then the coil is broken and must be replaced. The car should start when a new coil has been fitted.

15 If a reading is obtained at the CB terminal then check the wire from the coil for loose connections etc. The final check on the low tension circuit is across the breaker points. No reading means a broken condenser, which when replaced will enable the car to finally start.

14 Fault diagnosis - engine misfires

1 If the engine misfires regularly, run it at a fast idling speed, and short out each of the plugs in turn by placing a short screwdriver across from the plug terminal to the cylinder. Ensure that the screwdriver has a wooden or plastic insulated handle.

2 No difference in engine running will be noticed when the plug in the defective cylinder is short circuited. Short circuiting the working plugs will accentuate the misfire.

3 Remove the plug lead from the end of the defective plug and hold it about 3/16 inch away from the block. Restart the engine. If the sparking is fairly strong and regular the fault must lie in the spark plug.

4 The plug may be loose, the insulation may be cracked

Measuring plug gap. A feeler gauge of the correct size (see ignition system specifications) should have a slight 'drag' when slid between the electrodes. Adjust gap if necessary

Adjusting plug gap. The plug gap is adjusted by bending the earth electrode inwards, or outwards, as necessary until the correct clearance is obtained. Note the use of the correct tool

Normal. Grey-brown deposits lightly coated core nose. Gap increasing by around 0.001 in (0.025 mm) per 1000 miles (1600 km). Plugs ideally suited to engine and engine in good condition

Carbon fouling. Dry, black, sooty deposits. Will cause weak spark and eventually misfire. Fault: over-rich fuel mixture. Check: carburettor mixture settings, float level and jet sizes; choke operation and cleanliness of air filter. Plugs can be re-used after cleaning

Oil fouling. Wet, oily deposits. Will cause weak spark and eventually misfire. Fault: worn bores/piston rings or valve guides; sometimes occurs (temporarily) during running-in period. Plugs can be re-used after thorough cleaning

Overheating. Electrodes have glazed appearance, core nose very white - few deposits. Fault: plug overheating. Check: plug value, ignition timing, fuel octane rating (too low) and fuel mixture (too weak). Discard plugs and cure fault immediately

Electrode damage. Electrodes burned away; core nose has burned, glazed appearance. Fault: initial pre-ignition. Check: for 'Overheating' but may be more severe. Discard plugs and remedy fault before piston or valve damage occurs

Split core nose (may appear initially as a crack). Damage is self-evident, but cracks will only show after cleaning. Fault: pre-ignition or wrong gap-setting technique. Check: ignition timing, cooling system, fuel octane rating (too low) and fuel mixture (too weak). Discard plugs, rectify fault immediately

or the points may have burnt away giving too wide a gap for the spark to jump. Worse still, one of the points may have broken off. Either renew the plug, or clean it, reset the gap, and then test it.

5   If there is no spark at the end of the plug lead, or if it is weak and intermittent, check the ignition lead from the distributor to the plug. If the insulation is cracked or perished, renew the lead. Check the connections at the distributor cap.

6   If there is still no spark, examine the distributor cap carefully for tracking. This can be recognised by a very thin black line running between two or more electrodes, or between an electrode and some other part of the distributor.

These lines are paths which now conduct electricity across the cap thus letting it run to earth. The only answer is a new distributor cap.

7   Apart from the ignition timing being incorrect, other causes of misfiring have already been dealt with under the Section dealing with failure of the engine to start.

8   If the ignition timing is too far retarded, it should be noted that the engine will tend to overheat, and there will be a quite noticeable drop in power. If the engine is overheating and the power is down, and the ignition timing is correct, then the carburettor should be checked, as it is likely that this is where the fault lies. See Chapter 3 for details.

Chapter 5 Clutch and actuating mechanism

Contents

Specifications

Make ... ...   Borg and Beck

Type ... ...   Diaphragm spring

Clutch plate diameter ... ...   7.75 in (197 mm)

Facing material
   1500 ... ...   Ferodo RYZ or Mintex H26 or Raybestos WR7 or Small and Parkes DSW8

   1750 ... ...   Thermoid 11046

	1500	1750
Number of damper springs	6	6
Damper spring colour	2 natural	2 natural
	2 red/grey	2 white/blue
	1 yellow/grey	1 yellow/grey
	1 blue/grey	1 blue/grey

Clutch release bearing ... ...   Ball journal

Clutch fluid ... ...   Castrol Girling Brake Fluid

Torque wrench settings	lb ft	kg m
Clutch cover	15 to 18	2.1 to 2.5
Clutch to pressure plate	35 to 38	4.8 to 5.2
Clutch thrust plate screw	8 to 10	1.1 to 1.4
Slave cylinder bolts	18 to 20	2.5 to 2.8
Flywheel bolts	60	8.3

1 General description

The main parts of the clutch assembly are: the clutch drive plate assembly, the flywheel/pressure plate assembly, and the release bearing assembly. When the clutch is in use, the driven plate assembly, being splined to the primary gear, is under pressure from the diaphragm spring and the friction linings are hard against the flywheel and pressure plate. The driven plate is, therefore, rotated with the flywheel, and drive is transmitted to the splined primary gear and to the transmission unit input gear via a little idler gear.

When the driver depresses the clutch pedal, hydraulic fluid passes from the clutch master cylinder under pressure to the clutch slave cylinder. The piston, within the slave cylinder, moves the operating lever in such a manner that the release bearing is depressed. The diaphragm spring pressure is released from the driven plate and, therefore, the drive line is broken and engine torque is no longer transmitted to

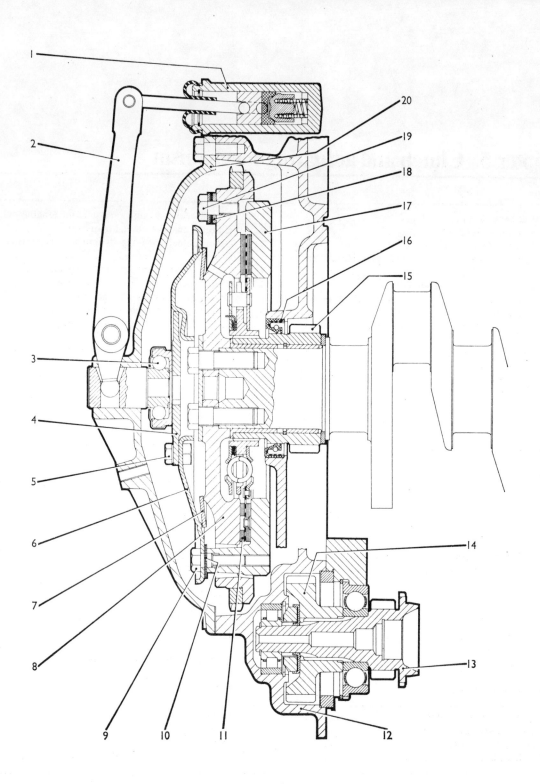

FIG. 5:1 CROSS SECTIONAL VIEW THROUGH CLUTCH

No.	Description	No.	Description	No.	Description	No.	Description
1	Slave cylinder	6	Diaphragm	11	Driven plate	16	Oil seal
2	Operating lever	7	Diaphragm spring	12	Flywheel housing	17	Pressure plate
3	Release bearing	8	Flywheel	13	First motion shaft	18	Drive strap
4	Thrust plate	9	Drive strap bolt	14	Input gear	19	Drive strap bolt
5	Thrust plate bolt	10	Drive strap	15	Primary gear	20	Clutch cover

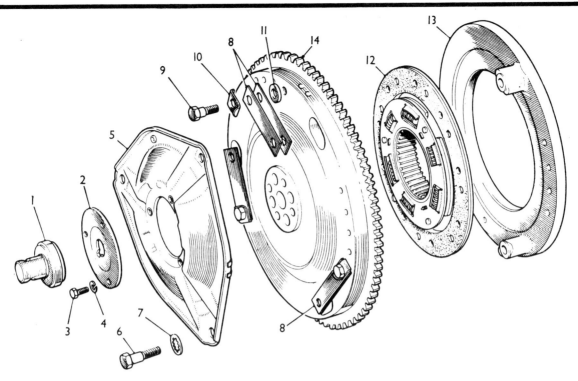

FIG. 5:2 CLUTCH COMPONENTS

No.	Description	No.	Description	No.	Description	No.	Description
1	Thrust bearing and shaft assembly	4	Spring washer	8	Drive strap	12	Driven plate
2	Thrust plate	5	Diaphragm assembly	9	Drive strap dowel bolt	13	Pressure plate
3	Thrust plate bolt	6	Diaphragm dowel bolt	10	Lock washer for bolt	14	Flywheel
		7	Shakeproof washer	11	Spacer		

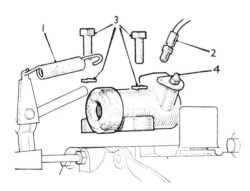

FIG. 5:3 CLUTCH SLAVE CYLINDER FIXINGS

No.	Description	No.	Description
1	Return spring	3	Bolts and spring washers
2	Pipe to master cylinder	4	Bleed nipple

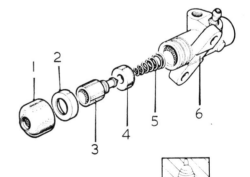

FIG. 5:4 CLUTCH SLAVE CYLINDER COMPONENTS AND CROSS SECTIONAL VIEW

No.	Description	No.	Description
1	Dust cover	4	Seal
2	Retaiher cap	5	Spring
3	Piston	6	Body

the transmission unit.

It will be seen from Fig. 5. 1 that the primary gear also forms part of the hub from the driven plate. This hub and gear assembly is able to remain stationary, or rotate relative to the crankshaft. It is, therefore, possible for the crankshaft to rotate while the driven plate and gears within the transmission unit remain still.

As the friction linings on the clutch driven plate wear, the pressure plate automatically moves closer to the driven plate to compensate. This makes the centre of the diaphragm spring nearer to the release bearing, so decreasing the release bearing clearance but not the clutch free pedal travel, as, unless the master cylinder has been disturbed, this is automatically compensated for.

2   Clutch system - bleeding

Whenever the clutch hydraulic system has been overhauled, a part renewed, or the level in the reservoir is too low, air will have entered the system necessitating its bleeding. During this operation the level of hydraulic fluid in the reservoir should not be allowed to fall below half full, otherwise air will be drawn in again.

1   Obtain a clean and dry jam jar, plastic tubing at least 12 inches long and able to fit tightly over the bleed screw of the slave cylinder, a supply of Castrol Girling Brake Fluid and an assistant.
2   Check that the master cylinder reservoir is full and if not, fill it. Cover the bottom inch of the jar with hydraulic fluid.
3   Remove the rubber dust cap (if fitted) from the bleed screw on the slave cylinder and, with a suitable spanner, open the bleed screw one turn.
4   Place one end of the tube securely over the end of the bleed screw and insert the other end in the jar so that the tube end is below the level of the fluid.
5   The assistant should now pump the clutch pedal up and down quite quickly until the air bubbles cease to emerge from the end of the tubing. He should also check the reservoir frequently to ensure that the hydraulic fluid does not drop too far so letting air into the system.
6   When no more air bubbles appear, tighten the bleed screw on the next pedal downstroke.
7   Replace the rubber dust cap over the bleed nipple. NOTE: Never re-use the fluid bled from the hydraulic system.

3   Clutch slave cylinder - removal and refitting

1   It is not necessary to drain the clutch master cylinder when removing the slave cylinder. If fluid is to be left in the master cylinder, however it is necessary to seal the vent hole in the reservoir cap. Wipe the top of the reservoir and unscrew the cap. Place a piece of thick polythene over the top of the reservoir and refit the cap.
2   Wipe the hydraulic pipe union at its connection on the slave cylinder with a clean non-fluffy rag. Unscrew the union nut with an open ended spanner and wrap the exposed end in a piece of clean non-fluffy rag to prevent dirt ingress. (Fig. 5:3)
3   Note how the clutch lever return spring is fitted and then detach it from the slave cylinder. Undo and remove the two bolts with spring washers that secure the slave cylinder to the clutch housing. Carefully withdraw the slave cylinder leaving the pushrod attached to the clutch operating lever.

4   Refitting is the reverse procedure to removal. Bleed the hydraulic system as described in Section 2.

4   Clutch slave cylinder - dismantling, examination and reassembly

1   Clean the exterior of the slave cylinder using a dry non-fluffy rag.
2   Carefully ease back the dust cover (1) (Fig. 5. 4) from the body and lift away. Also remove the piston stop end cap (2) which is held in place by two crimped slots in the side of the cap.
3   Remove the piston assembly and spring, by carefully shaking out these components. Remove the piston seal (4) using your fingers. Do not use a screwdriver as this could scratch the piston.
4   Inspect the inside of the cylinder for score marks caused by impurities in the hydraulic fluid. If any are found a new slave cylinder will be necessary.
5   If the cylinder is sound, thoroughly clean it out with fresh hydraulic fluid.
6   The old rubber seal (4) will probably be swollen and visibly worn. Smear the new rubber seal with hydraulic fluid and refit it to the stem of the piston ensuring that the smaller periphery, or back of the seal, is against the piston (3).
7   Place the small end of the spring (5) onto the piston stem. Thoroughly wet the seal and cylinder bore with clean hydraulic fluid and insert the piston assembly into the bore of the cylinder. Gently ease the edge of the seal into the bore so that it does not roll over. Refit the end cap (2) into place and, using a pair of engineer's pliers, crimp the slots to retain it in position. Fit a new dust cover (1) to the end of the cylinder.

5   Clutch master cylinder - removal and refitting

1   Drain the hydraulic fluid from the clutch hydraulic system by attaching a length of suitable size plastic tubing to the bleed screw on the slave cylinder. Place the other end in a clean jam jar. Open the bleed screw, with an open ended spanner, one complete turn and depress the clutch pedal. Tighten the bleed screw and allow the pedal to return. Repeat this procedure until the system has been drained.
2   Using a pair of pliers, extract the brake pedal to pushrod clevis pin split pin and lift away the plain washer. Withdraw the clevis pin from the pushrod yoke. (Fig. 5.5).
3   Slacken the clip and disconnect the righthand demister tube from the heater unit.
4   Using an open ended spanner, undo the flexible hydraulic pipe connection at the slave cylinder.
5   Undo and remove the two nuts and spring washers securing the master cylinder and carefully withdraw it together with the flexible hydraulic pipe.
6   Using an open ended spanner, undo the flexible hydraulic pipe connection at the master cylinder.
7   The master cylinder refitting procedure is the reverse to removal, but care must be taken when offering up to the bulkhead that the pushrod is in line with clutch pedal. Once connections have been made the hydraulic system must be bled as described in Section 2.

6   Clutch master cylinder - dismantling, examination and reassembly

1   The numbers in the text refer to Fig. 5. 6. Pull off the

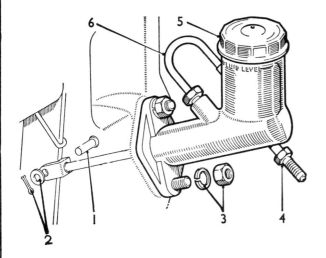

FIG. 5:5 CLUTCH MASTER CYLINDER FIXINGS

No.	Description	No.	Description
1	Clevis pin	4	Union to slave cylinder
2	Split pin and plain washer	5	Reservoir cap
3	Nut and spring washer	6	Pipe to slave cylinder

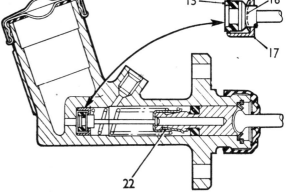

FIG. 5:7 CLUTCH MASTER CYLINDER FULLY ASSEMBLED.
NOTE THE CORRECT FITTING OF VALVE AND THIMBLE

No.	Description	No.	Description
15	Valve seal	17	Valve spacer
16	Curved washer	22	Thimble

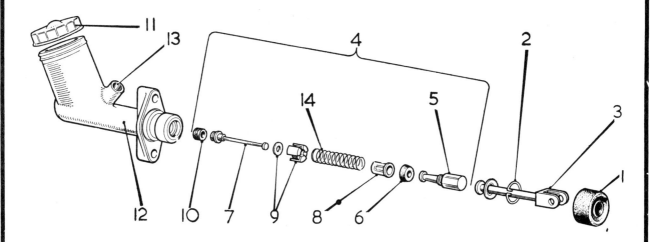

FIG. 5:6 CLUTCH MASTER CYLINDER COMPONENTS

No.	Description	No.	Description	No.	Description	No.	Description
1	Dust cover	5	Piston	9	Curved washer and spacer	12	Master cylinder body
2	Circlip – pushrod	6	Piston seal	10	Valve seal	13	Outlet pipe union bore
3	Pushrod	7	Valve stem	11	Master cylinder cap	14	Spring
4	Piston and valve assembly	8	Spring retainer				

rubber dust cover (1) which exposes the circlip (2). This must be removed so the pushrod, complete with metal retaining washer, can be pulled out of the master cylinder.

2   Pull the piston (5) and valve assembly as one unit from the master cylinder.

3   The next step is to separate the piston and valve assemblies. With the aid of a s m a l l screwdriver, prise up the inner leg of the piston return spring retainer (8) which engages under a shoulder in the front of the piston (5) and holds the retainer (8) in place.

4   The retainer (8), spring (14) and valve assembly can then be separated from the piston.

5   To dismantle the valve assembly, compress the spring (14) and move the retainer (8) which has an offset hole to one side in order to release the valve stem (7) from the retainer (8).

6   With the seat spacer (9) and curved valve seal washer (9) removed, the rubber seals can be removed using the fingers or a non-metal pointed rod such as a knitting needle.

7   Clean and carefully examine all parts, especially the piston cup and rubber washers, for signs of distortion, swelling, splitting or other wear and check the piston and cylinder for wear and scoring. Renew any parts that are suspect. It is recommended that, whenever a master cylinder is dismantled, new rubber seals are always fitted.

8   Rebuild the piston and valve assembly in the following sequence ensuring that all parts are thoroughly wetted with clean brake fluid.

a)   Fit the piston seal (6) to the piston (5) so that the larger circumference of the lip will enter the cylinder bore first.

b)   Fit the valve seal (10) to the valve (7) in the same manner as in (a) above.

c)   Place the valve spring seal washer (9) so that its convex face abuts against the valve stem flange (7) and then fit the seat spacer (9) and spring (14).

d)   Fit the spring retainer (8) to the spring (14) which must then be compressed so the valve stem (7) can be re-inserted into the retainer (8).

e)   Replace the front of the piston (5) in the retainer (8) and then press down the r e t a i n i n g leg so it locates under the shoulder at the front of the piston.

f)   With the valve assembly well lubricated with clean hydraulic fluid, carefully insert it in the master cylinder bore taking care that the rubber seal (6) is not damaged or the lip reversed as it is pushed into the bore.

g)   Fit the pushrod (3) and washer in place and secure with the circlip (2). Smear the sealing areas of the dust cover with Girling Rubber Grease and also pack the c o v e r with rubber grease to act as a dust trap, and fit to the master cylinder body. The master cylinder is now ready for refitting to the car.

---

7   Clutch - removal and replacement (engine in car)

The sequence for removing the clutch when the engine is in the car differs slightly when the later type rod gear change system is utilised instead of cables. These differences are fully described where applicable.

1   Open the bonnet and disconnect the two battery terminals. Release the battery clamp bar securing nuts and ease back the clamp. Lift away the battery and battery tray from the engine compartment.

2   Undo and remove the nut securing the heavy duty cable to the rear of the starter motor and withdraw the cable from the terminal. On pre-engaged starter motors make a note of

the electrical cable connections at the rear of the solenoid and disconnect the three cables.

3   Undo and remove the two bolts and spring washers securing the starter motor to the flywheel housing. Carefully draw the starter motor out of engagement of the flywheel and lift away from the engine.

4   Place a piece of soft wood on the saddle of a gauge hydraulic jack and located on the underside of the transmission case. Raise the jack until the weight of the complete power unit is just taken from the mountings.

5   Cable gear change models only.

a)   Undo and remove the nut and large d i a m e t e r washer securing the engine rear mounting centre bolt to the mounting.

b)   Undo and remove the three bolts with spring washers that secure the engine rear mounting bracket to the clutch housing cover. Lift away the engine rear mounting bracket.

6   Rod gear change models only.

a)   Slacken the bolts that secure the engine rear mounting to the sub frame bracket.

b)   Undo and remove the three bolts and spring washers that secure the engine rear mounting bracket to the sub-frame.

c)   Undo and remove the two nuts and spring washers that secure the engine rear mounting to the bracket on the clutch housing cover. The engine rear mounting assembly may now be lifted away.

7   Both models.

Make a note of which way round the clutch return spring is fitted and disconnect the spring from both the slave cylinder and release arm.

8   Undo and remove the ten bolts and spring washers that secure the clutch housing cover to the flywheel housing. Lift away the clutch housing cover having first carefully withdrawn the pushrod from the slave cylinder.

9   With a scriber or file, mark the position of the clutch thrust plate relative to the diaphragm so that it may be refitted in its o r i g i n a l position. Undo and remove the three bolts and spring washers securing the clutch thrust plate to the diaphragm.

10   Undo and remove the four bolts that secure the flywheel to the end of the crankshaft. These can be tight so, to stop the crankshaft rotating, chock the front wheels and select top gear.

11   Move the gear change lever back to neutral and, turning the flywheel a quarter of a turn at a time, drift the flywheel from the dowels in the end of the crankshaft with a hard wood block and hammer, or a large diameter soft metal drift. Take care that the flywheel does not drop, by having an assistant ready to catch it.

12   Mark the relative positions of the diaphragm, flywheel and pressure plate so they may be refitted in their original positions upon reassembly. Then undo and remove the three shaped diaphragm retaining bolts and star washers.

13   Lift away the diaphragm and flywheel from the pressure plate.

14   Note which way round the driven plate is fitted and lift from the pressure plate.

15   The clutch and flywheel assembly is now ready for inspection as described in Section 9.

16   Whilst the c l u t c h is away from the engine, check the crankshaft primary gear end float. Full information on this check will be found in Chapter 1/44.

17   To reassemble the clutch, first lay the pressure plate on a flat surface with the three securing lugs facing upwards.

18   Place the driven plate on the pressure plate with the larger damper spring boss uppermost. This is identified by the

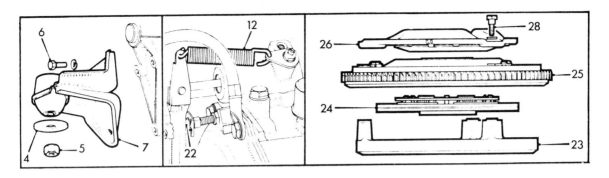

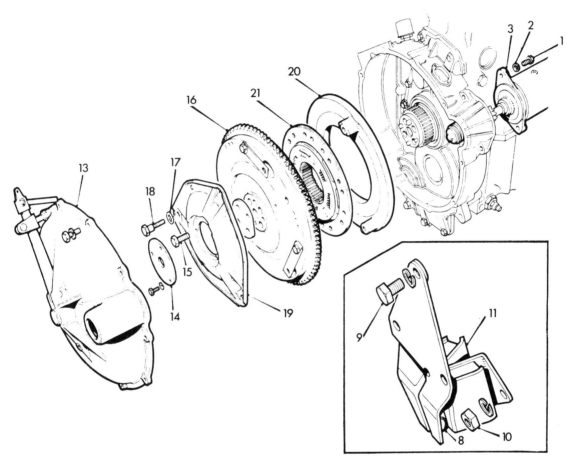

FIG. 5:8 CLUTCH REMOVAL SEQUENCE GUIDE

No.	Description	No.	Description	No.	Description
1	Starter motor securing bolt		securing bolt	15	Flywheel bolts
2	Spring washer	9	Engine rear mounting securing bolt	16	Flywheel
3	Starter motor	10	Engine rear mounting securing nut	17	Shakeproof washer
4	Washer	11	Engine rear mounting (rod gear	18	Diaphragm securing bolts and
5	Engine rear mounting nut		change)		shakeproof washer
6	Engine rear mounting securing bolt	12	Clutch lever return spring	19	Diaphragm
7	Engine rear mounting (cable	13	Clutch housing cover	20	Pressure plate
	gear change)	14	Clutch thrust plate	21	Driven plate
8	Engine rear mounting to subframe				

Inset: Top Centre
22 Clutch operating lever and stop clearance

Inset: Top Right

23 Pressure plate	25 Flywheel	27 Diaphragm spring securing	
24 Driven plate	26 Diaphragm	bolt and shakeproof washer	

two words 'Flywheel Side'. (photos).

19 Lower the flywheel over the pressure plate and driven plate, making sure that the previously made marks on the pressure plate are aligned. There are letters 'A' stamped on these two parts which will also assist refitting correctly. (photo).

20 Refit the diaphragm aligning the previously made marks. Replace the three shaped bolts and star washers but do not tighten fully. (photo).

21 Note the location of the larger dowel in the end of the crankshaft and its mating hole in the flywheel. Line up the dowel with the hole and fit the flywheel and clutch assembly to the flywheel.

22 Replace the four bolts securing the flywheel to the crankshaft and tighten in a diagonal and progressive manner to a torque wrench setting of 60 lb ft.

23 The three diaphragm securing bolts may now be tightened to a torque wrench setting of 15 to 18 lb ft.

24 Fit the clutch thrust bearing plate to the diaphragm aligning the previously made marks and secure with the three bolts and spring washers.

25 The clutch housing cover may now be refitted. Secure in position with the ten bolts and spring washers. Tighten them in a diagonal manner to a torque wrench setting of 15 to 18 lb ft.

26 Refit the clutch return spring to the clutch slave cylinder and clutch lever, the same way round as was noted on removal.

27 Rod gear change models only.

a) Fit the engine rear mounting to the bracket on the clutch housing cover and secure with the two nuts and spring washers.

b) Fit the engine rear mounting bracket to the sub frame and secure in position with the three bolts and spring washers.

c) Tighten the bolts that secure the engine rear mounting to the sub frame bracket.

28 Cable gear change models only.

a) Carefully engage the engine rear mounting to its centre bolt.

b) Refit and tighten the three bolts with spring washers that secure the engine rear mounting to the clutch housing cover.

c) Finally replace the nut and large plain washer to the engine rear mounting centre bolt. Tighten the nut fully.

29 Remove the garage hydraulic jack supporting the weight of the complete power unit.

30 Refit the starter motor, battery tray and battery, remaking the necessary electrical connections.

31 It is now necessary to adjust the clearance between the clutch withdrawal lever and its stop. Pull on the clutch release lever to overcome the action of the spring and check the clearance using feeler gauges. The correct clearance is 0.052 inch. If adjustment is necessary, slacken the locknut and, with an open ended spanner, turn the squared shank of the stop in an anticlockwise direction to decrease the clearance, or clockwise direction to increase it. Retighten the locknut.

8   Clutch - removal and replacement (engine out of the car)

The procedure is basically identical to that for working with the engine in the car, with the exceptions of the initial preparatory work and release of the engine rear mounting. Follow the instructions given in Section 7, paragraphs 3, 7 to 26, 30 and 31.

9   Clutch - inspection and overhaul

1 Thoroughly clean all parts by wiping with a rag to remove any dust.

2 Examine the clutch disc friction linings for wear, loose or broken springs and rivets. The linings must be proud of the rivets and light in appearance with the material structure visible. If it is dark in appearance, further investigation is necessary as it is a sign of oil contamination caused by oil leaking past the crankshaft rear seal.

3 Check the machined faces of the flywheel and pressure plate for signs of grooving. If evident, new parts should be fitted. Inspect the pressure plate for signs of hair line cracks usually caused by overheating due to clutch slip.

4 Inspect the three driving straps and, if they show signs of distortion, overheating or looseness, fit a complete set and not individually.

5 Carefully fit the clutch disc to the crankshaft primary drive gear and check for wear of the splines. If evident a new disc should be tried to ensure the wear is on the disc splines and not on the primary drive gear. Should the latter splines also be worn a new gear must be fitted and the end float adjusted by means of a selective fit thrust washer. Full information will be found in Chapter 1.

6 Carefully inspect the diaphragm for signs of overheating or cracking. If evident, a new diaphragm must be obtained.

7 Check the clutch release bearing for wear or roughness when the inner track is held and the outer track rotated. If it is blue in colour, it is an indication that it has overheated due to incorrect clutch adjustment. Obtain a new bearing and fit as described in Section 10.

10 Clutch release bearing - removal, inspection and refitting

1 Refer to Section 7 or 8, depending on whether the engine is in or out of the car, and follow the instructions up to and including the removal of the clutch housing cover.

2 Using a pair of pliers remove the clutch lever pivot pin split pin and withdraw the lever pivot pin noting which way round the pin head is fitted. Also note which way round the clutch lever is fitted. (Fig. 5.9).

3 Pull the clutch lever out of engagement of the release bearing shaft and lift away from the clutch housing cover.

4 Remove the bearing and shaft assembly from the clutch housing cover.

5 Check the clutch release bearing for wear or roughness when the inner track is held and the outer track rotated. If it is blue in colour, it is an indication that it has overheated due to incorrect clutch adjustment.

6 To remove the release bearing, using a bench vice and suitable metal packing, press the old bearing from the shaft.

7 Refitting and reassembling the release bearing is the reverse sequence to removal. Take care that the clutch lever is fitted the correct way round. Finally, adjust the clutch clearance between the withdrawal lever and stop as described in Section 7:31.

11 Clutch pedal - removal and refitting

1 Removal and refitting of the clutch pedal is basically similar to that for the brake pedal with the exception of the following

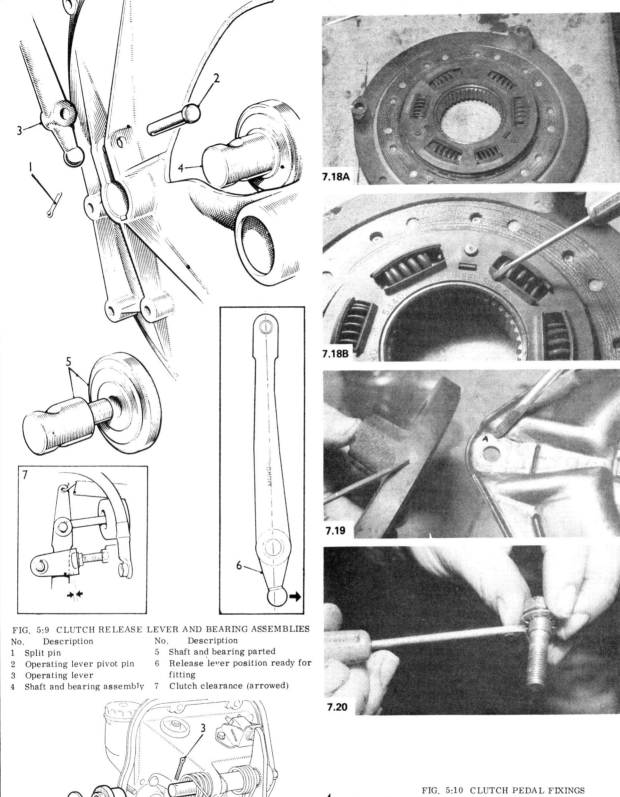

FIG. 5:9 CLUTCH RELEASE LEVER AND BEARING ASSEMBLIES

No.	Description	No.	Description
1	Split pin	5	Shaft and bearing parted
2	Operating lever pivot pin	6	Release lever position ready for fitting
3	Operating lever		
4	Shaft and bearing assembly	7	Clutch clearance (arrowed)

7.18A

7.18B

7.19

7.20

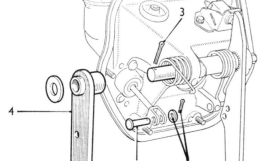

FIG. 5:10 CLUTCH PEDAL FIXINGS

No.	Description	No.	Description
1	Split pin and plain washer	3	Split pin
2	Clevis pin	4	Clutch pedal

sequence. (Full information of removal of the pedal and bracket assembly will be found in Chapter 9/23.)
2   With the pedal and bracket assembly away from the car,
using a pair of pliers, extract the split pin from the clutch
pedal clevis pin. Lift away the plain washer and withdraw
the clevis pin. Note which way round the head is fitted.
3   Extract the split pin from the clutch pedal pivot, disengage the return spring from the pedal and slide off the pedal.
4   Refitting the pedal to the pedal bracket is the reverse
sequence to removal.

12 Clutch squeal - diagnosis and cure

1   If on taking up the drive, or when changing gear, the
clutch squeals, this is a sure indication of a badly worn clutch
release bearing. As well as regular wear due to normal use,
wear of the clutch release bearing is much accentuated if the
clutch is ridden, or held down for long periods in gear, with
the engine running. To minimise wear of this component the
car should always be taken out of gear at traffic lights and
for similar hold ups.
2   The clutch release bearing is not an expensive item.

13 Clutch slip - diagnosis and cure

1   Clutch slip is a self evident condition which occurs when
the clutch friction plate is badly worn; the release arm free
travel is insufficient; oil or grease have got onto the flywheel
or pressure plate faces; or the pressure plate itself is faulty.
2   The reason for clutch slip is that, due to one of the faults
listed above, there is either insufficient pressure from the
pressure plate, or insufficient friction from the friction plate,
to ensure solid drive.
3   If small amounts of oil get onto the clutch, they will be
burnt off under the heat of clutch engagement, in the process
gradually darkening the linings. Excessive oil on the clutch
will burn off leaving a carbon deposit which can cause quite
bad slip, or fierceness, spin and judder.
4   If clutch slip is suspected, and confirmation of this condition is required, there are several tests which can be made:
a)   With the engine is second or third gear and pulling lightly
up a moderate incline, sudden depression of the accelerator
pedal may cause the engine to increase its speed without any
increase in road speed. Easing off on the accelerator will
then give a definite drop in engine speed without the car
slowing.
b)   Drive the car at a steady speed in top gear and, braking
with the left leg, try and maintain the same speed by pressing

down on the accelerator. Providing the same speed is maintained, a change in the speed of the engine confirms that slip
is taking place.
c)   In extreme cases of clutch slip the engine will race under normal acceleration conditions.
   If slip is due to oil or grease on the linings a temporary
cure can sometimes be effected by squirting carbon tetro-
chloride into the clutch. The permanent cure, of course, is
to renew the clutch driven plate, and trace and rectify the
oil leak.

14 Clutch spin - diagnosis and cure

1   Clutch spin is a condition which occurs when there is a
leak in the clutch hydraulic actuating mechanism; the release arm free travel is excessive; there is an obstruction
in the clutch either on the primary gear splines, or in the
operating lever itself; or the oil may have partially burnt
off the clutch linings and have left a resinous deposit which
is causing the clutch disc to stick to the pressure plate or
flywheel.
2   The reason for clutch spin is that due to any, or a combination of, the faults just listed, the clutch pressure plate is
not completely freeing from the centre plate even with the
clutch pedal fully depressed.
3   If clutch spin is suspected, the condition can be confir-
med by extreme difficulty in engaging first gear from rest,
difficulty in changing gear, and very sudden take-up of the
clutch drive at the fully depressed end of the clutch pedal travel as the clutch is released.
4   Check the clutch master and slave cylinders and the connecting hydraulic pipe for leaks. Fluid in one of the rubber
boots fitted over the end of either the master or slave cylinders is a sure signs of a leaking piston seal.
5   If these points are checked and found to be in order then
the fault lies internally in the clutch, and it will be necessary
to remove it for examination.

15 Clutch judder - diagnosis and cure

1   Clutch judder is a self evident condition which occurs
when the power unit mountings are loose or too flexible;
when there is oil on the faces of the clutch friction plate; or
when the clutch has been assembled incorrectly.
2   The reason for clutch judder is that due to one of the
faults just listed, the clutch pressure plate is not freeing
smoothly from the friction disc, and is snatching.
3   Clutch judder normally occurs when the clutch pedal is
released in first or reverse gears, and the whole car shud-
ders as it moves backwards or forwards.

Chapter 6 Transmission

Contents

Specifications

Type	Manual, cable or rod remote control	
No. of forward speeds	5	
Synchromesh	All forward speeds	
Ratios:	1500	1750
Fifth	0.80:1	0.87:1
Fourth...	1.00:1	1.00:1
Third	1.37:1	1.37:1
Second...	2.00:1	2.00:1
First	3.20:1	3.20:1
Reverse	3.47:1	3.47:1
Overall ratios:		
Fifth	3.34:1	3.38:1
Fourth...	4.2 :1	3.89:1
Third	5.76:1	5.33:1
Second...	8.42:1	7.79:1
First	13.54:1	12.45:1
Reverse	14.56:1	13.49:1
Road speed at 1,000 rpm		
Fifth ratio	19.61 mph (31.6 KmPH)	19.4 mph (31 KmPH)
Fourth ratio	15.6 mph (25.1 KmPH)	16.85 mph (27.1 KmPH)
Speed gear ratio	15/6	14/6
Primary drive ratio	1.066:1	1.066:1

Torque Wrench Settings

Flywheel bolts	60	8.3
Clutch cover	15 to 18	2.1 to 2.5
Clutch to pressure plate	35 to 38	4.8 to 5.2
Clutch thrust plate screw...	8 to 10	1.1 to 1.4
Drain plug - magnetic	40 to 50	5.5 to 6.9
Flywheel housing - studs	6	0.8
nuts	17 to 19	2.4 to 2.6
set screws...	17 to 19	2.4 to 2.6
Transmission case to block 5/16 inch bolts	20 to 25	2.8 to 3.4
3/8 inch bolts	30	4.1

Specifications

Detent plug - small	15 to 20	2.1 to 2.8
large	35 to 40	4.8 to 5.5
Access plug - 3-4 fork (cable gear change)	55 to 60	7.6 to 8.3
First motion shaft nut	120	16.6
Layshaft nuts	120	16.6
Third motion shaft nut	150	20.7
Bell-crank levers pivot nut (rod gear change) ...	25	3.4
Remote control steady rod nuts (see text)		
'C' and 'D'	25	3.4
'B'	35	4.8
Differential cover - 5/16 inch nuts	17 to 19	2.4 to 2.6
3/8 inch nuts	24 to 26	3 to 3.6
studs...	6	0.8
Differential end cover set screws	18	2.5

1   General description

The transmission unit has five forward speeds and a reverse. Synchromesh is incorporated on all five forward speeds. Fourth gear is a direct drive ratio and fifth a 'gearing-up' ratio to provide high speed cruising at reduced engine revolutions.

The component parts of the transmission unit are shown in Fig. 6:1. All numbers in brackets refer to this illustration. The individual parts operate in the following manner:

Engine torque at the rear of the crankshaft is transmitted to the first motion shaft gear (3) by primary gears located on the engine side of the flywheel housing. The first motion shaft is supported in two bearings (4, 5) and has inside the inner end a needle roller bearing (6) into which is located the left hand end of the third motion shaft (34). The first motion shaft inner gear is in constant mesh with the largest gear of the layshaft cluster (42). This means that whenever the first motion shaft is rotating, the first four forward speed and the reverse speed laygears also rotate. The synchroniser for the fifth speed gear (51) is splined to the right hand end of the layshaft (43). This fifth speed gear is free to rotate on the layshaft and is mounted on needle roller bearings instead of bushes.

When the gear change lever is moved from fourth to fifth position, the outer sleeve of the synchroniser is moved to the left and dogs are meshed so as to provide transmission of power from the layshaft to the fifth speed gear and then on to the final drive pinion (31).

The first (24), second (16) and third (15) speed gears are free to rotate on the third motion shaft and yet are in constant mesh with their matching gears on the layshaft. This means that whenever the first motion shaft is rotated these gears also rotate on the third motion shaft.

When one of these gears is selected, one at the inner end of the first motion shaft meshes with the third motion shaft; this brings into action one of two synchromesh assemblies (11, 20). Movement of the outer synchromesh sleeves and dogs to either the left or right will select the required gear.

Reverse gear may be engaged between the straight toothed gear on the sleeve of the synchroniser (20) and the small straight toothed gear in the centre of the layshaft.

The synchroniser sleeves are splined to hubs, which are also splined to the shafts, so that when the dogs on the sleeve are engaged with any required gear, that selected gear is then coupled to the shaft.

Cone clutches in the form of baulk rings (12, 19, 21) enable the speeds of the dogs on the gears and sleeves to synchronise to ensure easy and quiet gear changing.

The remote control system is connected to the gear selectors by either cables (early models) or rods (later models).

As with usual BLMC transverse power units the transmission unit, final drive and engine share a common lubrication system.

Whenever the transmission unit or engine is being worked upon it will be necessary to use information contained in both this Chapter and Chapter 1. For any major work to be carried out on the transmission unit or flywheel housing the unit must be removed from the car and then separated into the two major assemblies.

2   Crankshaft primary gear end float - adjustment

It is possible to adjust the crankshaft primary gear end float with the power unit either in or out of the car. Both methods are given.

Engine in car
1   Refer to Chapter 5/7 and remove the clutch and flywheel assembly.
2   Using a vernier depth gauge, or sets of feeler gauges, measure the depth of the crankshaft recess in the flywheel (Fig. 6.2).
3   Fit the existing thrust washer and gear to the end of the crankshaft if they have been removed previously.
4   With the fingers, push the gear firmly towards the engine as far as possible and again using either a vernier depth gauge or sets of feeler gauges, measure the length of crankshaft boss protruding from the gear.
5   Select a new thrust washer so that the measurement obtained in paragraph 4 gives a reading of 0.003 to 0.005 inch more than that obtained in paragraph 2.
6   Thrust washers are available in the following thicknesses:
    0.153 to 0.155 inch (3.89 to 3.94 mm)
    0.156 to 0.158 inch (3.96 to 4.01 mm)
    0.159 to 0.161 inch (4.04 to 4.09 mm)
    0.162 to 0.164 inch (4.11 to 4.17 mm)
7   Reassembly is the reverse sequence to dismantling.

Engine out of car
1   Refer to Chapters 5/8 and remove the clutch and flywheel assembly.

103

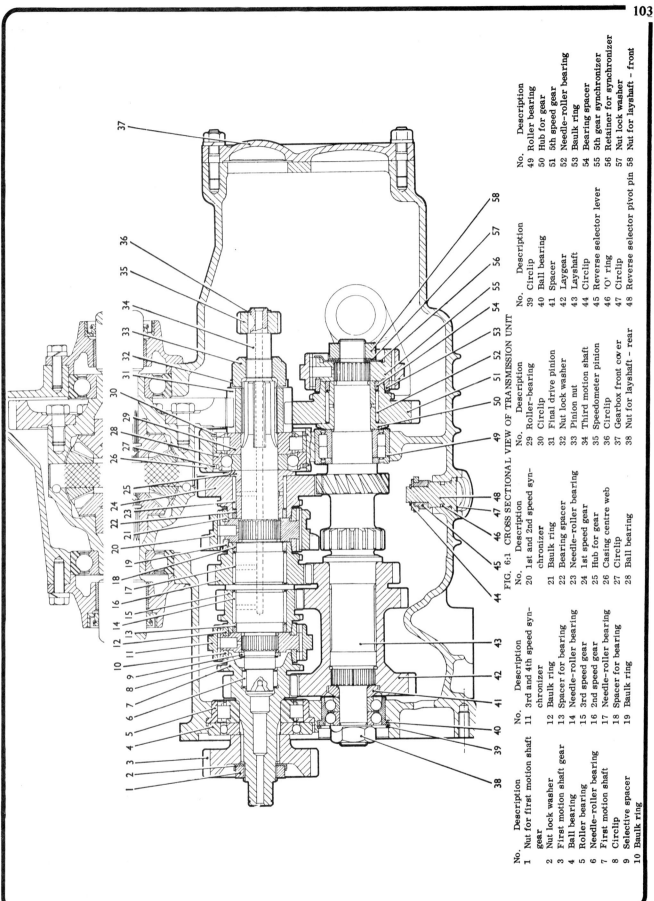

FIG. 6:1 CROSS SECTIONAL VIEW OF TRANSMISSION UNIT

No.	Description
1	Nut for first motion shaft gear
2	Nut lock washer
3	First motion shaft gear
4	Ball bearing
5	Roller bearing
6	Needle-roller bearing
7	First motion shaft
8	Circlip
9	Selective spacer
10	Baulk ring

No.	Description
11	3rd and 4th speed synchronizer
12	Baulk ring
13	Spacer for bearing
14	Needle-roller bearing
15	3rd speed gear
16	2nd speed gear
17	Needle-roller bearing
18	Spacer for bearing
19	Baulk ring

No.	Description
20	1st and 2nd speed synchronizer
21	Baulk ring
22	Bearing spacer
23	Needle-roller bearing
24	1st speed gear
25	Hub for gear
26	Casing centre web
27	Circlip
28	Ball bearing

No.	Description
29	Roller-bearing
30	Circlip
31	Final drive pinion
32	Nut lock washer
33	Pinion nut
34	Third motion shaft
35	Speedometer pinion
36	Gearbox front cover
37	Nut for layshaft - rear
38	Nut for layshaft - rear

No.	Description
39	Circlip
40	Ball bearing
41	Spacer
42	Laygear
43	Layshaft
44	Circlip
45	Reverse selector lever
46	'O' ring
47	Circlip
48	Reverse selector pivot pin

No.	Description
49	Roller bearing
50	Hub for gear
51	5th speed gear
52	Needle-roller bearing
53	Baulk ring
54	Bearing spacer
55	5th gear synchronizer
56	Retainer for synchronizer
57	Nut lock washer
58	Nut for layshaft - front

2   Bend back the locking tabs on the four shaped tab washers and then undo and remove the seventeen housing retaining bolts and nuts from inside and outside the clutch housing
3   Wrap some sellotape around the splines of the primary gear to prevent damage to the oil seal and carefully draw the flywheel housing from the rear of the engine and transmission unit.
4   Fit the existing thrust washer and gear to the end of the crankshaft if they have been previously removed.
5   Refit the flywheel to the end of the crankshaft and secure with the four bolts which should be tightened to a torque wrench setting of 60 lb ft.
6   Using feeler gauges determine the clearance 'A' between the boss face of the crankshaft and the rear face of the primary gear (Fig. 6:3).
7   Select a thrust washer to give the correct clearance of 0.003 to 0.005 inch.
8   Thrust washers are available in the sizes given in paragraph 6 of the 'Engine in car' section earlier.
9   Reassembly is the reverse sequence to dismantling.

3   Crankshaft primary gear oil seal - removal and refitting

It is possible to remove and refit the oil seal with the power unit in the car although it is far easier to do if the power unit is out of the car. Both methods are given.

Engine in car
1   Refer to Chapter 5/7 and remove the clutch and flywheel assembly.
2   Using a small three legged universal puller with thin feet, locate the feet behind the splines of the primary drive gear and very carefully draw the primary drive gear and oil seal from the end of the crankshaft.
3   Well lubricate the new seal.
4   Wrap some sellotape around the splines of the primary gear to prevent damage to the oil seal and enter the oil seal onto the primary gear, lip facing innermost.
5   Using a small soft metal drift very carefully tap the new seal into position.
6   Refer to Section 2 and check the primary gear end float. Adjust as necessary.
7   Reassembly is now the reverse sequence to dismantling.

Engine out of car.
1   With the power unit out of the car, refer to Section 2 paragraphs 1 to 4 inclusive and remove the clutch and flywheel assembly and the flywheel housing.
2   Using a screwdriver carefully remove the old seal noting which way round it is fitted.
3   Well lubricate the new seal and fit to the flywheel housing using a suitable diameter tube.
4   Refer to Section 2 and check the primary gear end float. Adjust as necessary.
5   Reassembly is now the reverse sequence to dismantling.

4   Transmission - separation from engine

Before commencing work, clean the exterior of the engine and transmission unit thoroughly using a grease solvent such as paraffin or 'Gunk'. After the solvent has been applied and allowed to stand for a time, a vigorous jet of water will wash off the solvent together with all grease and dirt. If the dirt is thick and deeply embedded, work the solvent into it

with a wire brush. Finally wipe down the exterior of the unit with a dry non-fluffy rag. The transmission unit may be separated from the engine as follows:
1   Unscrew the union securing the dipstick guide tube to the side of the transmission casing. Lift away the guide tube and dipstick (Fig. 6:4).
2   Undo and remove the two bolts securing the distributor body clamp to the cylinder block and carefully lift away the distributor. Withdraw the oil pump drive shaft.
3   Undo and remove the two bolts and spring washers securing the starter motor to the flywheel housing. Lift away the starter motor.
4   Undo the centre bolt securing the oil filter to the side of the transmission casing and lift away the oil filter. Be prepared to catch oil which will seep from the filter when it is withdrawn.
5   Undo and remove the two nuts and spring washers that secure the fuel pump to the side of the transmission casing. Withdraw the pump and insulator block from the two mounting studs and then recover the operating push rod (photo).
6   The eight bolts and spring washers securing the clutch housing cover to the flywheel housing may next be removed. Lift away the clutch housing cover.
7   Unscrew the three bolts securing the thrust plate and lift away the thrust plate.
8   Remove the two bolts and spring washers securing the flywheel housing cover to the housing and lift away the cover.
9   Using a screwdriver, lock the flywheel, then undo and remove the four bolts securing the flywheel to the end of the crankshaft.
10   Working through the starter motor aperture drift the flywheel from the dowels in the inside of the end of the crankshaft using a soft metal drift or hard wood block.
11   Bend back the flywheel housing securing bolt lock tabs and undo and remove the seventeen nuts and bolts from inside and outside the housing (photo).
12   Wrap some sellotape around the splines on the primary drive gear to prevent damage to the oil seal and carefully remove the flywheel housing (photo).
13   Undo and remove the eleven bolts and spring washers that secure the transmission casing to the mounting flange of the crankcase (photo).
14   Drift the locating dowels accurately mating the transmission casing to the crankcase.
15   Carefully lift the engine from the transmission casing (photo).

5   Transmission (cable gear change) - dismantling

With the transmission unit separated from the engine and placed on a clean work bench, dismantle the transmission unit in the following manner:
1   If the splash shield has not already been removed, bend back the locking tab washer and undo the securing bolt. Lift away the splash shield, bolt and tab washer.
2   Undo and remove the two nuts and spring washers securing the front mounting to the front cover securing studs. Lift away the front mounting.
3   Undo and remove the further one nut and spring washer and then the five bolts and spring washers securing the front cover to the transmission case. Lift away the front cover and its gasket.
4   Remove the old gasket from the front cover and traces of any jointing compound.
5   Unscrew and remove the two long bolts with plain and

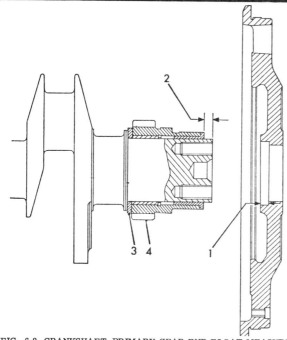 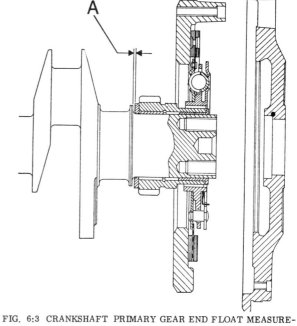

FIG. 6:2 CRANKSHAFT PRIMARY GEAR END FLOAT MEASURE-
MENTS (ENGINE IN CAR)

No.	Description	No.	Description
1	Depth of crankshaft recess in flywheel	3	Selective thrust washer
2	Crankshaft boss protrusion	4	Crankshaft primary gear

FIG. 6:3 CRANKSHAFT PRIMARY GEAR END FLOAT MEASURE-
MENTS (ENGINE OUT OF CAR)

A - clearance between crankshaft boss face and rear face of primary gear

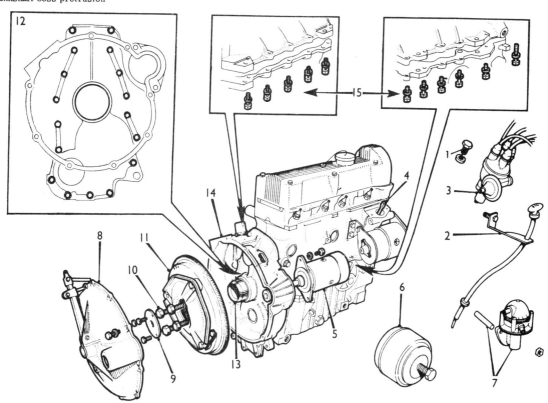

FIG. 6:4 SEPARATION OF ENGINE AND TRANSMISSION UNIT

No.	Description	No.	Description	No.	Description	No.	Description
1	Distributor clamp bolt	6	Oil filter	10	Flywheel bolts		mary drive gear splines
2	Dipstick and guide tube	7	Fuel pump and pushrod	11	Flywheel	14.	Flywheel housing
3	Distributor	8	Clutch housing cover	12	Flywheel housing fixings	15	Transmission to engine
4	Oil pump drive shaft	9	Clutch thrust plate	13	Tape wrapped around pri-		securing bolts and spring washers.
5	Starter motor						

4.5

4.11

4.12

4.13

4.15

spring washers that secure the oil pump to the transmission casing.

6   Using a piece of metal shaped as shown in Section 8, photo 8:102 and gripped with a mole wrench, undo and remove the pump outlet.

7   Unscrew the magnetic drain plug from the bottom of the front face of the transmission casing.

8   Using a large socket unscrew the speedometer drive gear housing and lift away from the transmission unit (Fig. 6:7).

9   Undo the two nuts and spring washers that secure the bracket to the differential casing. Lift away the bracket.

10   Refer to Chapter 8 / 2 and remove the differential unit from the transmission casing.

11   Using a pair of circlip pliers, remove the circlip that retains the speedometer pinion on the end of the third motion shaft.

12   Ease the speedometer drive pinion from the end of the third motion shaft using a screwdriver. Take care not to damage the gear teeth.

13   Extract the Woodruff key from the keyway in the end of the third motion shaft.

14   Using a pair of circlip pliers, remove the outer bearing retaining circlip located on the end of the first motion shaft.

15   Ease the spigot bearing from the end of the first motion shaft using a screwdriver. Take care not to damage the bearing.

16   Again using a pair of circlip pliers, remove the circlip in front of the gear on the first motion shaft, this being exposed once the spigot bearing has been removed.

17   Withdraw the idler gear and shaft from the transmission case. It may be necessary to ease it out of its fitted position with a screwdriver (Fig. 6:8).

18   Recover the inner thrust washer from the back of the idler gear.

19   Using a pair of circlip pliers, remove the idler gear bearing inner and outer retaining circlips.

20   To remove the idler gear bearing, carefully drift out using a soft metal drift and driving it out from within the transmission unit. This will, of course, only be necessary if the bearing is to be renewed.

21   Using a chisel, bend back the lock washer ears locking the nut on the end of the first motion shaft.

22   It will now be necessary to lock two gears together by moving two synchromesh collars into mesh with a screwdriver.

23   Using a socket or large ring spanner unscrew the nut on the end of the first motion shaft. Note this nut has a left hand thread.

24   Remove the lock washer exposed once the nut has been removed.

25   Using two screwdrivers, or small tyre levers, carefully draw the first motion shaft gear from the first motion shaft.

26   Bend back the lockwasher securing the nut on the rear end of the layshaft and, with a socket, unscrew the nut. Note this nut has a left hand thread.

27   Using a socket and extension bar, undo the nut on the front end of the layshaft.

28   Bend back the lockwasher securing the nut on the end of the third motion shaft and, using a large socket, undo and remove the nut followed by the lock washer.

29   Unscrew and remove the plug retaining the first and second speed detent plunger and spring in the transmission case. Recover the spring and plunger. Note this plug has three washers under its head (Fig. 6:11).

30   Release the locknut and unscrew the taper bolt securing

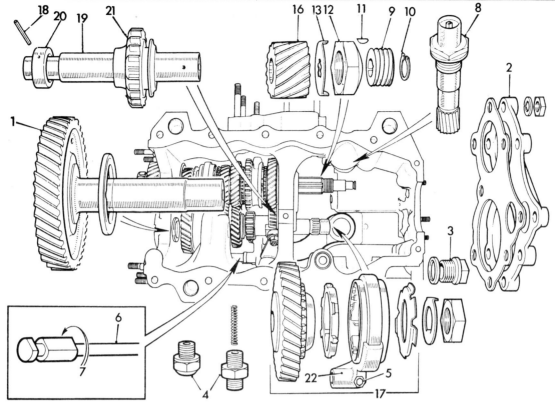

FIG. 6:7 FRONT COVER, REVERSE IDLER AND FIFTH SPEED ASSEMBLIES

No.	Description	No.	Description	No.	Description
1	Idler gear	8	Speedometer pinion assembly	16	Final drive pinion
2	Front cover	9	Speedometer drive gear	17	Fifth speed synchronizer assembly
3	Fifth/reverse selector rod plug	10	Circlip	18	Spring pin
4	Fifth/reverse selector detent plug	11	Woodruff key	19	Reverse idler shaft
5	Fifth speed selector fork screw	12	Final drive pinion nut	20	Collar
6	Selector rod	13	Lockwasher	21	Reverse idler gear
7	Removal of selector rod by rotating through 180°	14	Layshaft front nut	22	Fifth speed selector fork
		15	Lockwasher		

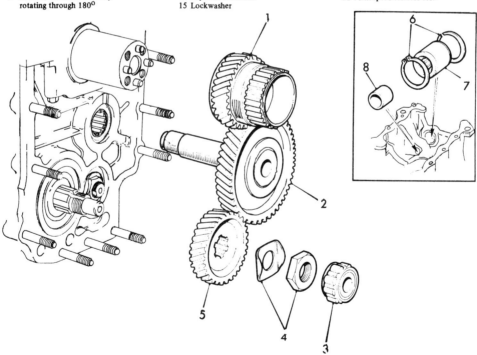

FIG. 6:8 THE THREE PRIMARY GEARS AND BEARINGS

No.	Description	No.	Description	No.	Description	No.	Description
1	Crankshaft primary gear	3	First motion shaft spigot bearing	5	First motion shaft gear	7	Idler gear needle roller bearing
2	Idler gear	4	Nut and lockwasher	6	Circlips	8	Idler gear cleeve bearing

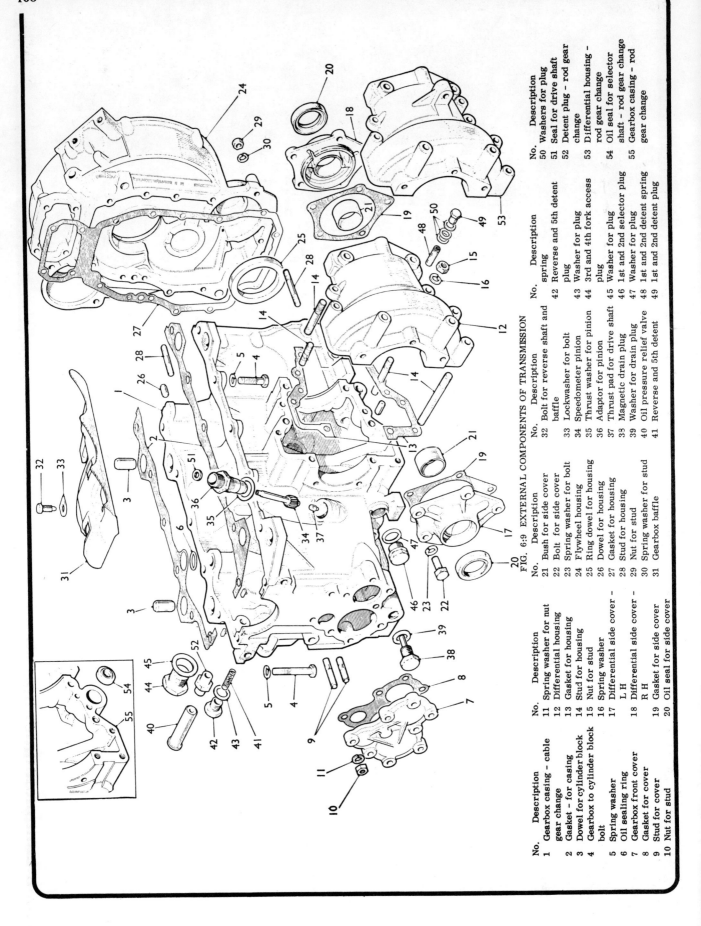

FIG. 6:9 EXTERNAL COMPONENTS OF TRANSMISSION

No.	Description	No.	Description	No.	Description	No.	Description	No.	Description
1	Gearbox casing – cable gear change	11	Spring washer for nut	21	Bush for side cover	32	Bolt for reverse shaft and baffle	42	Reverse and 5th detent plug	50	Washers for plug
2	Gasket – for casing	12	Differential housing	22	Bolt for side cover	33	Lockwasher for bolt	43	Washer for plug	51	Seal for drive shaft
3	Dowel for cylinder block	13	Gasket for casing	23	Spring washer for bolt	34	Speedometer pinion	44	3rd and 4th fork access plug	52	Detent plug – rod gear change
4	Gearbox to cylinder block bolt	14	Stud for housing	24	Flywheel housing	35	Thrust washer for pinion	45	Washer for plug	53	Differential housing – rod gear change
5	Spring washer	15	Nut for stud	25	Ring dowel for housing	36	Adaptor for pinion	46	1st and 2nd selector plug	54	Oil seal for selector shaft – rod gear change
6	Oil sealing ring	16	Spring washer	26	Dowel for housing	37	Thrust pad for drive shaft	47	Washer for plug	55	Gearbox casing – rod gear change
7	Gearbox front cover	17	Differential side cover – L H	27	Gasket for housing	38	Magnetic drain plug	48	1st and 2nd detent spring		
8	Gasket for cover	18	Differential side cover – R H	28	Stud for housing	39	Washer for drain plug	49	1st and 2nd detent plug		
9	Stud for cover	19	Gasket for side cover	29	Nut for stud	40	Oil pressure relief valve				
10	Nut for stud	20	Oil seal for side cover	30	Spring washer for stud	41	Reverse and 5th detent				
				31	Gearbox baffle						

FIG. 6:10 INTERNAL COMPONENTS OF TRANSMISSION (CABLE GEAR CHANGE)

1 Primary gear – crankshaft
2 Thrust washer for gear
3 Idler gear
4 Thrust washer for idler gear – outer
5 Thrust washer for idler gear – inner
6 Bearing for idler gear – outer
7 Circlip for bearing – outer
8 Circlip for bearing – inner
9 Bearing for idler gear – inner
10 First motion shaft gear (input)
11 First motion shaft
12 Bearing for shaft – spigot
13 Circlip for bearing outer track
14 Circlip for bearing inner track
15 Nut for first motion shaft
16 Lock washer for nut
17 Ball bearing for shaft
18 Roller bearing for shaft
19 Needle roller bearing for shaft
20 Synchronizer
21 Circlip for synchronizer
22 Spacer for synchronizer (selective)
23 Baulk ring
24 Synchronizer collar
25 Plunger for synchronizer
26 Spring for plunger
27 Key
28 1st and 2nd speed selector fork
29 Bolt for fork
30 Locknut
31 Washer for locknut
32 1st and 2nd speed selector rod
33 3rd speed gear
34 Bearing for gear
35 Spacer for bearing
36 Third motion shaft
37 2nd speed gear
38 Bearing for gear
39 Spacer for bearing
40 Synchronizer hub
41 Plunger for synchronizer
42 Spring for plunger
43 Key
44 Synchronizer collar/reverse mainshaft gear
45 Baulk ring
46 First speed gear
47 Bearing for gear
48 Spacer for bearing
49 Hub for gear
50 Ball bearing for 3rd motion shaft
51 Roller bearing for 3rd motion shaft
52 Circlip for roller bearing
53 Circlip for ball bearing
54 Final drive pinion
55 Nut for pinion
56 Lock washer for nut
57 Speedometer pinion
58 Key for pinion
59 Circlip for pinion
60 3rd and 4th speed selector fork
61 3rd and 4th speed selector rod
62 5th and reverse speed selector fork
63 5th and reverse speed selector rod
64 Detent plunger for selector rod
65 Laygear
66 Bearing for layshaft – rear
67 Circlip for bearing
68 Nut for layshaft – rear
69 Lockwasher for nut
70 Bearing for layshaft – front
71 Laygear
72 Spacer for laygear
73 5th speed gear
74 Bearing for gear
75 Hub for gear
76 Spacer for bearing
77 Synchronizer hub
78 Synchronizer collar
79 Baulk ring
80 Plunger for synchronizer
81 Spring for plunger
82 Key
83 Retainer for synchronizer
84 Nut for layshaft – front
85 Lock washer for nut
86 Reverse idler gear
87 Shaft for gear
88 Collar for shaft
89 Roll pin for collar
90 Reverse selector lever
91 Pivot pin for lever
92 'O' ring for pin
93 Circlip for pin – outer
94 Washer for pin
95 Circlip for pin – inner
96 Reverse selector fork
97 Washer
98 Nut
99 Reverse selector interlock
100 Plunger for interlock
101 Ball for interlock
102 Spring for ball
103 Reverse interlock plate
104 Bolt for plate
105 Lock washer

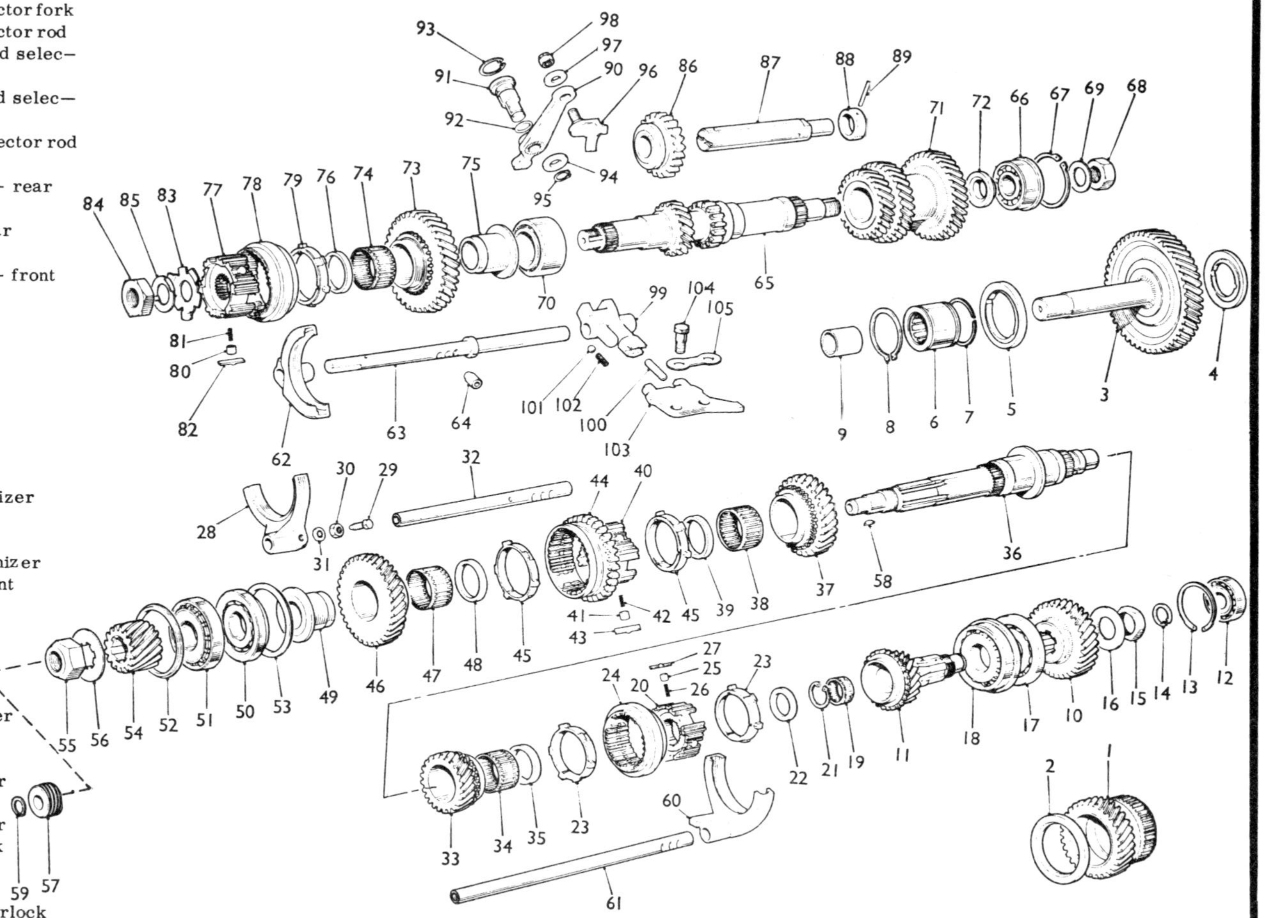

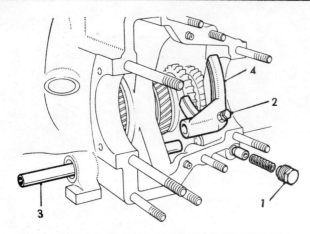

FIG. 6:11 FIRST/SECOND SPEED SELECTOR FORK AND PLUN-
GER ASSEMBLY

No.	Description	No.	Description
1	First/second speed detent plug	3	First/second speed selector rod
2	First/second speed selector fork retaining screw	4	First/second speed selector fork

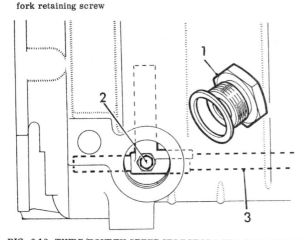

FIG. 6:12 THIRD/FOURTH SPEED SELECTOR FORK AND ACCESS
PLUG

No.	Description	No.	Description
1	Third/fourth speed selector fork access plug		fork retaining screw
2	Third/fourth speed selector	3	Third/fourth speed selector rod

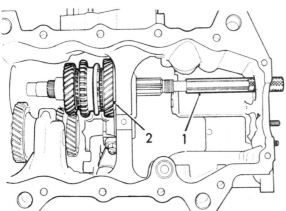

FIG. 6:13 MAINSHAFT REMOVAL

No.	Description	No.	Description
1	Metal drift		nizer and gears
2	First/second speed synchro-		

the third and fourth speed selector fork to the selector rod
(Fig. 6:12).

31 Disengage the two synchromesh collars previously locked
and carefully withdraw the third and fourth speed selector
rod. It will be of assistance to screw a bolt into the exposed
end and pull out using a mole wrench.

32 Undo and remove the reverse and fifth speed detent plunger and spring retaining cap nut and lift away the spring and
detent plunger. Note this cap nut has a fibre washer under its
head.

33 Bend back the fifth and reverse speed retainer nut lock
washer and unscrew the nut. Lift away the lock washer.

34 The retainer may now be lifted out of the centre of the
fifth and reverse speed synchromesh unit.

35 Using a screwdriver, carefully ease the final drive pinion
from the end of the third motion shaft.

36 Release the locknut and unscrew the taper bolt securing
the fifth and reverse speed selector fork to the selector rod.

37 Screw a bolt into the threaded end of the fifth and reverse
speed selector rod and draw the selector rod from the transmission casing. Gripping the bolt with a mole wrench will
make this job easier.

38 Lift away the fifth and reverse speed selector fork from
the synchromesh unit collar.

39 Lift the fifth speed synchromesh hub and collar assembly from the end of the layshaft. Recover the fifth speed
baulk ring from the cone on the front of the fifth speed gear.

40 Using a small diameter parallel pin punch, carefully drift
out the spring pin securing the reverse idler shaft collar to
the idler shaft.

41 Using a soft metal drift as well as a screwdriver, carefully remove the idler shaft and recover the collar and reverse idler.

42 Lift the baulk ring from the fifth speed gear hub.

43 Using a screwdriver, carefully lift the bearing spacer
from the layshaft.

44 Lift the fifth speed from the bearing on the layshaft.

45 Slide the fifth speed gear bearing and hub from the layshaft.

46 Using a suitable diameter drift and soft faced hammer,
tap the layshaft out of the transmission casing.

47 By carefully using a narrow soft metal drift, tap the layshaft front bearing from its housing in the centre web of the
transmission casing.

48 Using a soft metal drift, release the bearing assembly
retaining ring from its location on the front of the first motion shaft bearing assembly.

49 Working from the inside of the transmission casing, carefully drift out the first motion shaft complete with the ball and
roller bearing assemblies.

50 Remove the ball and roller bearings from the first motion shaft using a universal three legged puller and suitable
thrust pad. This operation will only be necessary if the bearings are to be renewed (see Section 7).

51 Lift away the baulk ring from the synchroniser collar
exposed when the first motion shaft has been removed.

52 Undo and remove the third and fourth selector fork locking nut and taper bolt securing it to the selector rod.

53 Undo and remove the third and fourth selector rod detent
plunger retaining plug, noting that there are two washers located under the head.

54 Lift away the spring and plunger.

55 Carefully withdraw the third and fourth selector rod from
the transmission casing.

56 Using a pair of circlip pliers, remove the third and fourth
speed synchronizer spacer retaining circlip from the end of

the third motion shaft.

57 Slide the spacer from the third motion shaft.

58 Carefully remove the third and fourth speed synchronizer assembly from the third motion shaft. It will be necessary to release the collar from the selector fork.

59 Remove the baulk ring located on the cone at the front of the third speed gear.

60 Using a screwdriver, ease out and remove the bearing spacer from within the hub of the third speed gear.

61 Slide the third speed gear and bearing from the third motion shaft.

62 Using a suitable diameter drift, carefully drift the third motion shaft from the transmission casing.

63 Lift out the third and fourth speed selector fork from the transmission casing.

64 Lift out the remaining first and second speed gear cluster from the transmission casing. Note the way the gears are fitted together so that on reassembly they are replaced the correct way round first time.

65 Lift the second speed gear assembly from the synchronizer hub and first speed gear assembly.

66 Remove the bearing, spacer and baulk ring from the second speed gear.

67 Lift the synchronizer hub assembly from the first speed gear and recover the baulk ring.

68 Lift out the bearing spacer from the hub of the first speed gear.

69 Separate the hub, bearing and baulk ring from the first speed gear.

70 Using a pair of circlip pliers, remove the circlip that retains the twin track ball race in the outer end of the transmission case.

71 Using a thin soft metal drift, tap out the twin track ball race sufficiently to position two screwdrivers behind the outer track flange whereupon the bearing can be levered out of its housing.

72 Using a screwdriver, carefully ease out the circlip that is located in front of the roller race situated in the centre web of the transmission casing.

73 With a narrow soft metal drift, carefully tap out the roller and ball bearing races from the centre web of the transmission casing. Note which way round the races are fitted.

74 Lift out the laygear from the transmission casing.

75 Recover the spacer from the end of the laygear.

76 Bend back the tabs locking the two reverse interlock securing bolts and then undo and remove the two bolts.

77 Carefully lift away the interlock selector and plate, taking care to recover the ball bearing, spring and plunger.

78 Lift out the oil pump pick up pipe from the bottom of the transmission casing.

---

6   Transmission (rod gear change) - dismantling

The procedure for dismantling this later type of transmission assembly is basically identical to that described for the cable gear change type with the exception of the selector assemblies. When these are being removed compare them and their locations with those illustrated in Fig. 6:16 so that they are refitted correctly on reassembly.

---

7   Transmission components - examination and renovation

---

1   Carefully clean and then examine all the component parts starting with the baulk ring synchronizers, for general wear,

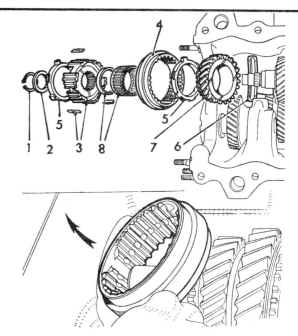

FIG. 6:14 THIRD/FOURTH SPEED ASSEMBLY

No.	Description	No.	Description
1	Circlip	5	Baulk ring
2	Spacer	6	Third/fourth selector fork
3	Synchronizer hub and keys	7	Third speed gear
4	Synchronizer collar	8	Spacer and bearing

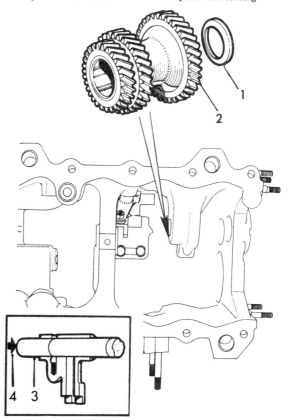

FIG. 6:15 LAYGEAR AND FIFTH/REVERSE SELECTOR ROD ASSEMBLIES

No	Description	No.	Description
1	Spacer		spring
2	Laygear	4	Push in metal rod so removing
3	Metal rod to retain ball and		selector rod

FIG. 6:16 INTERNAL COMPONENTS OF TRANSMISSION (ROD GEAR CHANGE)

No.	Description	No.	Description
1.	Primary gear-crankshaft.	60.	5th and reverse speed selector fork.
2.	Thrust washer for gear.	61.	Locknut for gear.
3.	Idler gear.	62.	Locknut for bolt.
4.	Thrust washer for idler gear-outer.	63.	Bolt for fork.
5.	Thrust washer for idler gear-inner.	64.	5th and reverse speed selector rod.
6.	Bearing for idler gear-outer.	65.	Layshaft.
7.	Circlip for bearing-outer.	66.	Bearing for layshaft-rear.
8.	Circlip for bearing-inner.	67.	Circlip for bearing.
9.	Bearing for idler gear-inner.	68.	Nut for layshaft-rear.
10.	First motion shaft gear (input).	69.	Lock washer for nut.
11.	First motion shaft.	70.	Bearing for layshaft-front.
12.	Bearing for shaft-spigot.	71.	Laygear.
13.	Circlip for bearing outer track.	72.	Spacer for laygear.
14.	Circlip for bearing inner track.	73.	5th speed gear.
15.	Nut for first motion shaft.	74.	Bearing for gear.
16.	Lock washer for nut.	75.	Hub for gear.
17.	Ball bearing for shaft.	76.	Spacer for bearing.
18.	Roller bearing for shaft.	77.	Synchronizer hub.
19.	Needle roller bearing for shaft.	78.	Synchronizer collar.
20.	Synchronizer hub.	79.	Baulk ring.
21.	Circlip for synchronizer.	80.	Plunger for synchronizer.
22.	Spacer for synchronizer (selective).	81.	Spring for plunger.
23.	Baulk ring.	82.	Key.
24.	Synchronizer collar.	83.	Retainer for synchronizer.
25.	Plunger for synchronizer.	84.	Nut for layshaft-front.
26.	Spring for plunger.	85.	Lock washer for nut.
27.	Key.	86.	Reverse idler gear.
28.	Baulk ring.	87.	Shaft for gear.
29.	Slotted spring pin.	88.	Collar for shaft.
30.	1st to 4th speed selector rod.	89.	Roll pin for collar.
31.	1st and 2nd speed fork.	90.	Reverse selector lever.
32.	3rd and 4th speed selector fork.	91.	Pivot pin for lever.
33.	3rd speed gear.	92.	'O' ring for pin.
34.	Bearing for gear.	93.	Circlip for pin-outer.
35.	Spacer for bearing.	94.	Washer for pin.
36.	Third motion shaft.	95.	Circlip for pin-inner.
37.	2nd speed gear.	96.	Reverse selector fork.
38.	Spacer for bearing.	97.	Washer.
39.	Bearing for gear.	98.	Nut.
40.	Synchronizer hub.	99.	Reverse selector interlock.
41.	Plunger for synchronizer.	100.	Plunger for interlock.
42.	Spring for plunger.	101.	Ball for interlock.
43.	Key.	102.	Spring for ball.
44.	Synchronizer collar/reverse main-shaft gear.	103.	Reverse interlock plate.
		104.	Reverse operating lever.
45.	Baulk ring.	105.	Circlip for reverse operating lever.
46.	First speed gear.	106.	Bolt for plate.
47.	Bearing for gear.	107.	Lock washer for bolt.
48.	Spacer for bearing.	108.	Selector shaft.
49.	Hub for gear.	109.	Interlock spool.
50.	Ball bearing for 3rd motion shaft.	110.	Torsion spring.
51.	Roller bearing for 3rd motion shaft.	111.	Circlip for interlock spool.
52.	Circlip for roller bearing.	112.	Retaining collar for interlock spool.
53.	Circlip for ball bearing.	113.	Pin.
54.	Final drive pinion.	114.	Pivot post.
55.	Nut for pinion.	115.	'O' ring seal.
56.	Lock washer for nut.	116.	Bush for bell-crank levers.
57.	Speedometer pinion.	117.	Washer.
58.	Key for pinion.	118.	Nut.
59.	Circlip for pinion.	119.	Spacer for bell-crank levers.
		120.	Lower bell-crank lever.
		121.	Centre bell-crank lever.
		122.	Upper bell-crank lever.

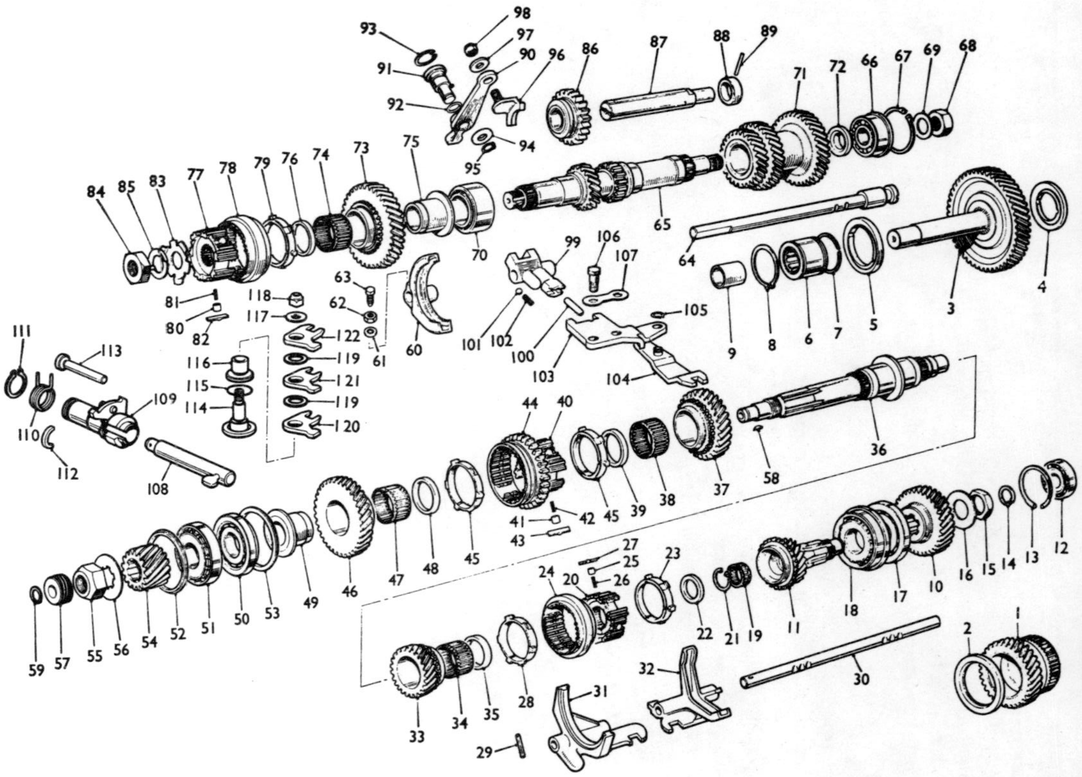

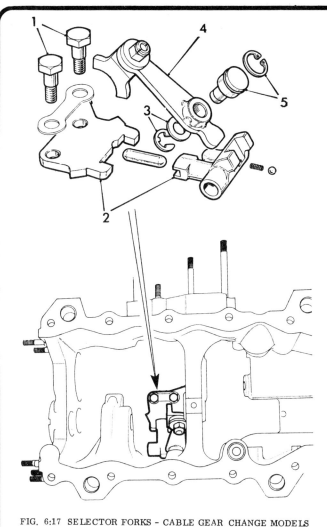

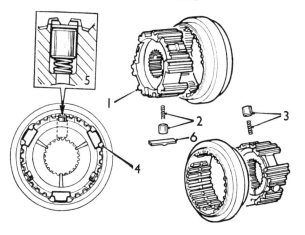

FIG. 6:17 SELECTOR FORKS - CABLE GEAR CHANGE MODELS

No.	Description	No.	Description
1	Selector assembly securing bolts	3	Circlip and washer
2	Interlock plate and interlock assembly	4	Reverse selector lever and fork
		5	Selector pivot and retaining circlip

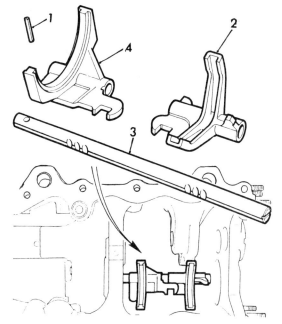

FIG. 6:19 SELECTOR FORKS - ROD GEAR CHANGE MODELS
(Part 1)

No.	Description	No.	Description
1	Spring pin	3	First/second selector rod
2	Third/fourth speed selector fork	4	First/second speed selector fork

FIG. 6:18 SYNCHRONIZER ASSEMBLY

No.	Description	No.	Description
1	Hub		cutaway in hub
2	Plunger and spring	5	Cross section with plunger and spring assembled
3	Plunger and spring		
4	Cutaway in collar aligned with	6	Key

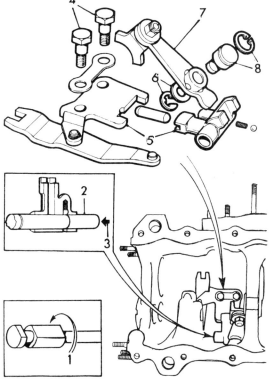

FIG. 6:20 SELECTOR FORKS - ROD GEAR CHANGE MODELS
(Part II)

No.	Description	No.	Description
1	Rotate fifth/reverse selector rod 180°	5	Interlock plate and interlock assembly
2	Metal rod to retain ball and spring in interlock assembly	6	'C' clip and washer
3	Push retainer into interlock	7	Selector lever and fork
4	Selector assembly securing bolts	8	Selector pivot and retaining circlip

distortion and damage to machined faces and threads.

2   Examine the gear wheels for excessive wear and chipping of the teeth and renew them as necessary. It is advisable to renew the mating gear as well.

3   Examine the condition of all ball and roller races used. If there is looseness between the inner and outer races, the bearings must be renewed.

4   Ensure that the ball and roller races are a good fit in their housings.

5   Inspect the baulk rings and test them with their mating tapers on the gears. If they slip before they contact the edge of the dog teeth on the gear, the hub and baulk ring must be renewed. Check all synchromesh unit plungers to ensure they are not pitted or worn.

6   Check the locking detent plungers are not pitted or worn and that the springs when compared with a new one (if available) have not weakened.

7   Even if there have been no signs of oil leaks, new seals and gaskets must be fitted.

8   Examine all bushes for wear and, if suspect, fit new ones.

9   Inspect the transmission case very carefully for signs of cracking or damage, especially on the underside, as well as at all mating surfaces, bearing housings and stud or bolt holes.

10   Once the synchromesh units have been dismantled for inspection they should be reassembled as follows:

a)   Fit the springs and plungers into the hub pockets.

b)   Align the cut-aways in the collar with those of the hub and then fit the hub to the collar.

c)   Press the keys into their slots with the raised ridge towards the collar.

d)   Note that the third/fourth and fifth speed synchronizer keys are shorter than those fitted to the first/second speed synchronizer and must not be interchanged. The third/fourth speed synchronizer keys are identical to those fitted to the fifth speed and may be interchanged.

When new, the baulk rings for all synchronizers are identical.

---

8   Transmission (cable gear change) - reassembly

---

1   Always use new washers, gaskets and joint washers throughout reassembly. Generously lubricate all the gears, brushes and bearings with oil as they are being assembled.

2   Check that all oil ways are clear. Also ensure that the interior of the casing is clean and that there are no burrs on studs or bolt holes in the bearing housings.

3   Place the oil pump pick-up pipe in the bottom of the transmission casing (photo).

4   Position the reverse interlock plate in the bottom of the transmission casing followed by the two hole tab washer and the two securing bolts. Do not tighten the bolts fully yet (photo).

5   Fit the spring and ball bearing into the reverse selector interlock and retain with a piece of metal rod or radio interference suppressor. Fit the interlock plunger into the reverse interlock and locate in position on the interlock plate. Tighten the two interlock plate securing screws and bend up the two locking tabs (photos).

6   Fit the spacer into the end of the laygear (photo).

7   Carefully lower the laygear into approximate position in the transmission case (photo).

8   Using a pair of circlip pliers, fit the ball bearing race retaining circlip into the centre web of the transmission case.

insert the ball race with the lettering towards the main part of the transmission case body (photo).

9   Fit the roller bearing next to the ball bearing race the correct way round as shown in this photo.

10   Using a suitable soft metal drift, carefully tap the roller race into its final position so that it will be possible to fit the roller race retaining circlip into the web groove (photo).

11   Fit the roller race retaining circlip making sure that it seats correctly in its groove (photo).

12   Fit the twin track ball race to the outer end of the transmission case (photo).

13   Using a piece of soft wood, carefully drift the twin track ball race into position so that it will be possible to fit the race retaining circlip into its groove in the transmission case (photo).

14   Using a pair of circlip pliers, contact the twin track ball race retaining circlip and fit it into its groove, making sure that it is seating correctly and that the step of the circlip faces away from the bearing (photo). If new bearings have been fitted it will be necessary to select a new circlip so as to eliminate end float on the bearing (Fig. 6:21). Circlips of the following thicknesses are available:

Spacer thickness	Identification colour
0.0635 to 0.0645 inch (1.62 to 1.65 mm)	orange
0.065 to 0.066 inch (1.66 to 1.69 mm)	blue
0.0665 to 0.0675 inch (1.70 to 1.72 mm)	self finish
0.068 to 0.069 inch (1.74 to 1.76 mm)	green

15   Assemble the first speed gear bearing, hub and baulk ring to the first speed gear (photo).

16   Fit the bearing spacer into the baulk ring end of the first speed gear (photo).

17   Fit the synchronizer hub assembly to the baulk ring on the first speed gear (photo).

18   Assemble the second speed gear bearing, spacer and baulk ring to the second speed gear (photo).

19   Fit the second speed gear assembly to the synchronizer hub and first speed gear assembly (photo).

20   Insert the third motion shaft through the previously assembled gear cluster and then fit on the third speed gear. This will give an idea of how the assembled gear cluster will look when assembled into the transmission case. Remove the third motion shaft again (photo).

21   Carefully lower the first and second speed gear cluster into the transmission case (photo).

22   Fit the securing bolt and locknut to the third and fourth speed selector fork (photo).

23   Place the third and fourth speed selector fork into the bottom of the transmission case.

24   Carefully insert the third motion shaft into the first and second speed gear assemblies (photos).

25   It will probably be necessary to use a piece of wood and hammer to finally position the third motion shaft (photo).

26   This photograph shows what the assembled gears and third motion shaft should look like at this stage.

27   Lock the end of the third motion shaft with a screwdriver or piece of metal bar, in preparation for the next operation (photo).

28   Using a soft metal drift, carefully drive the inner roller race of the third motion shaft onto the third motion shaft (photo).

29   Fit the third speed gear and bearing onto the third motion shaft (photo).

30   Locate the bearing spacer in the hub of the third speed gear (photo).

31   Carefully manipulate the synchronizer collar onto the end of the third motion shaft (photo).

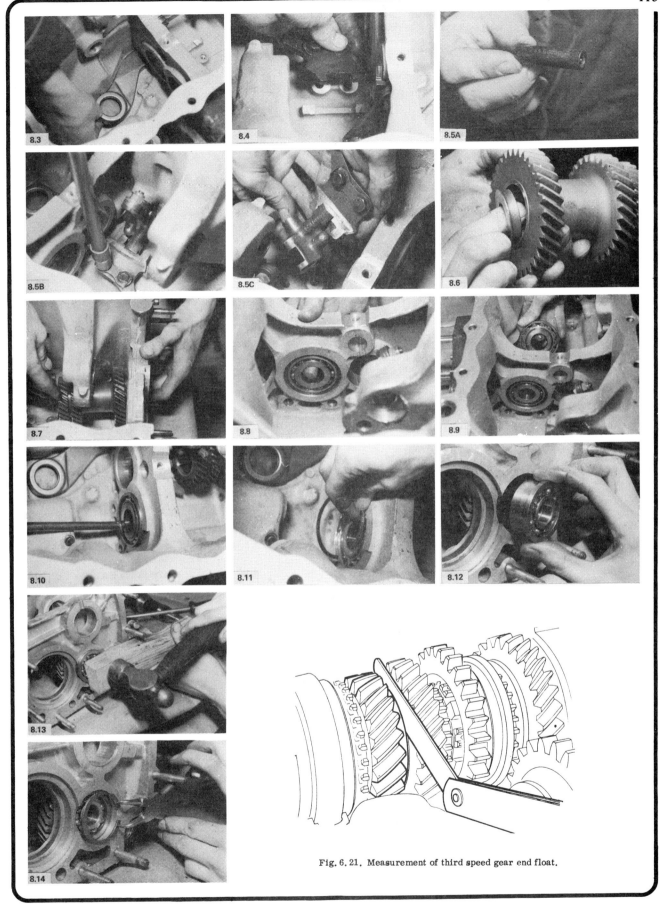

Fig. 6.21. Measurement of third speed gear end float.

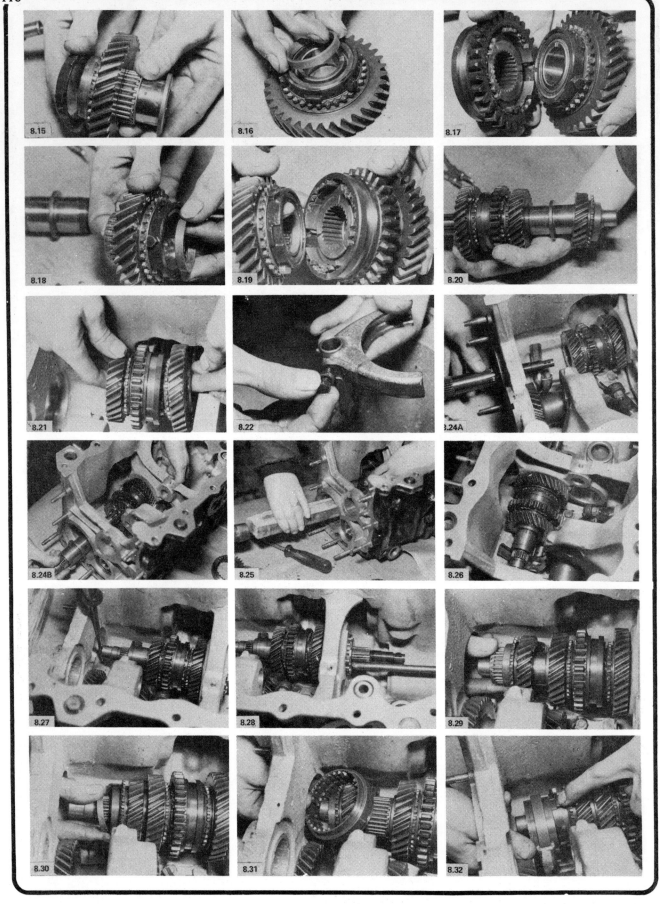

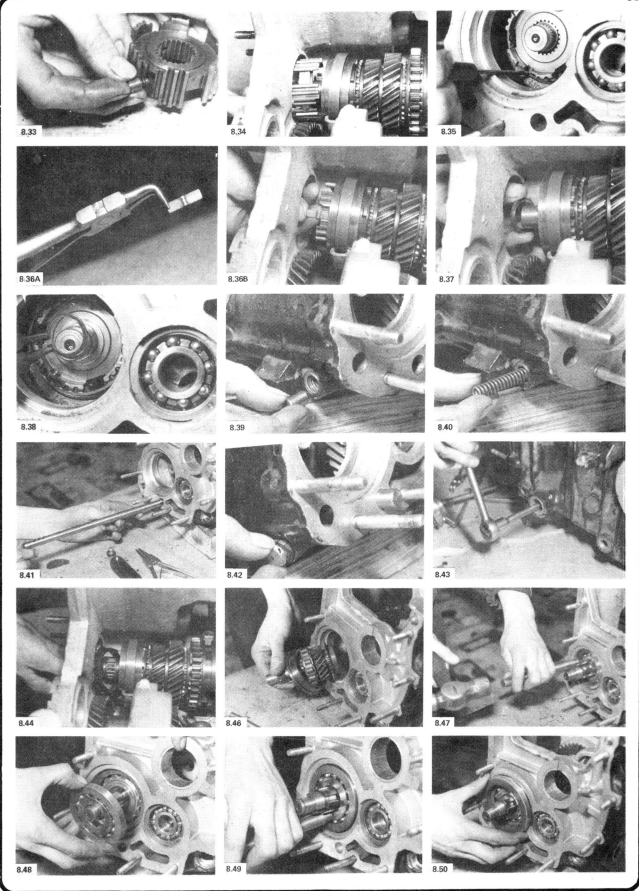

8.33 8.34 8.35 8.36A 8.36B 8.37 8.38 8.39 8.40 8.41 8.42 8.43 8.44 8.46 8.47 8.48 8.49 8.50

32 Slide the baulk ring through the synchronizer collar and then engage the collar with the third/fourth speed selector fork and push the collar up into mesh with the dog teeth on the third speed gear (photo). Note the boss on the baulk ring which locates in the grooves in the synchronizer collar.

33 Place the plungers and springs in the bores of the synchronizer hub (photo).

34 Slide the synchronizer hub half way onto the third motion shaft (photo) aligning the cutaways with the bosses on the baulk ring as shown in photograph 8:32.

35 It will be necessary to depress the spring loaded plungers for them to pass into synchronizer collar (photo).

36 Insert each of the three synchromesh unit keys into the cutaways of the synchronizer hub. The r a i s e d part must face outwards (photos).

37 Place the selective spacer for the synchronizer onto the third m o t i o n shaft (photo). The spacer is to stop any end float of the synchromesh unit and is available in five different thicknesses:

Spacer thickness	Identification colour
0.093 to 0.094 inch (2.36 to 2.38mm)	yellow
0.095 to 0.096 inch (2.41 to 2.43mm)	self finish
0.097 to 0.098 inch (2.45 to 2.48mm)	black
0.099 to 0.100 inch (2.51 to 2.53mm)	orange
0.101 to 0.102 inch (2.56 to 2.58mm)	blue
0.103 to 0.104 inch (2.61 to 2.63mm)	green

38 Fit the spacer retaining circlip making sure it is seating correctly (photo).

39 Insert the detent plunger, tapered end first, into its bore in the transmission case (photo).

40 Refit the detent plunger spring (photo).

41 Carefully insert the third and fourth selector rod into the transmission case, engaging the selector fork with the selector rod (photo).

42 Refit the plunger and spring retaining plug noting that two washers are fitted under the head. Tighten to a torque wrench setting of 15 to 20 lb ft (photo).

43 Tighten the selector fork to rod securing tapered bolt making sure the taper enters the hole in the selector rod. Lock by tightening the locknut (photo).

44 Fit the baulk ring to the synchronizer collar (photo).

45 Using a suitable diameter tube, carefully drift the plain roller bearing onto the first motion shaft.

46 Insert the first motion shaft into the transmission casing, taking care to engage it with the end of the third motion shaft (photo).

47 Using a soft metal drift, carefully tap the bearing outer track into position (photo).

48 Fit the outer ball bearing race to the first motion shaft. (photo).

49 Carefully tap the ball bearing inner track into position using a soft metal drift (photo).

50 Fit the bearing assembly retaining r i n g, if necessary tapping it into its final position with a soft faced hammer (photo). If a new, or reconditioned, transmission assembly, transmission case or flywheel housing is to be fitted, the bearing assembly retaining ring must be checked as follows:

a) Double check that the first motion s h a f t bearings are firmly pressed home in their housing.

b) Refer to Fig. 6:22 and measure the depth of the bearing housing from the face of the bearing to the outer face of the casing (A).

c) Measure the depth of the ring recess in the first motion shaft gear pocket of the flywheel housing (B).

d) Add 0.007 inch to the sum of the measurements made in paragraphs (b) and (c). This is the compressed thickness of a new gasket.

e) Select a ring equal in thickness to the dimension calculated in (d).

f) Rings are available in the following thicknesses:
0.337 to 0.339 inch (8.56 to 8.61 mm)
0.339 to 0.341 inch (8.61 to 8.66 mm)
0.341 to 0.343 inch (8.66 to 8.71 mm)
0.343 to 0.345 inch (8.71 to 8.76 mm)
0.345 to 0.347 inch (8.76 to 8.81 mm)

51 Support the weight of the laygear and carefully insert the layshaft into the transmission casing (photo).

52 Using a suitable diameter tube, drift the front layshaft bearing into the transmission casing web. (photo).

53 Fit the fifth speed gear hub onto the layshaft so that the large diameter is next to the bearing (photo).

54 Slide the fifth speed gear bearing onto the hub (photo).

55 Fit the fifth speed gear to the bearing (photo).

56 Push the b e a r i n g fully home and then fit the bearing spacer to the layshaft (photos).

57 Place the baulk ring onto the fifth speed gear hub (photo).

58 Place the reverse idler gear in the transmission case and hold it in its approximate f i t t e d position with the selector fork guide facing the centre web (photo).

59 Fit the reverse selector to the idler fork guide and insert the reverse idler gear shaft so that the locking taper bolt hole will line up with the threaded hole in the centre web (photo). Fit the taper bolt and lock washer.

60 Fit the reverse idler shaft collar to the shaft (photo).

61 With a small parallel pin punch, or screwdriver, position the idler shaft collar so that its locking pin hole aligns with the hole in the shaft (photo).

62 Carefully insert the shaft collar locking pin and tap home fully with a suitable diameter drift (photo).

63 Fit the fifth speed baulk ring to the gear and then slide the synchromesh hub and collar assembly onto the end of the layshaft (photo).

64 Place the fifth and reverse gear selector fork onto the synchromesh unit collar (photo).

65 The fifth and reverse s p e e d selector rod may now be fitted to the transmission case. The correct way round is shown in this photo.

66 Carefully insert the fifth and reverse speed selector rod, taking care to engage it with the reverse selector interlock and the fifth and reverse selector fork. The interlock ball and spring retainer previously placed in the reverse selector interlock must be recovered, as the selector rod is inserted into the reverse selector interlock (photo).

67 Screw a suitable threaded bolt into t h e end of the fifth and reverse speed selector rod and tap the head of the bolt to assist in final location (photo).

68 Line up the selector fork securing bolt hole with the hole in the fifth and reverse speed selector rod using a screwdriver, and then carefully fit the bolt and locknut. Tighten these fixings securely (photo).

69 Slide the final drive pinion onto the end of the third motion shaft (photo).

70 Fit a new lockwasher and replace the large securing nut (photo).

71 Place the fifth and reverse speed synchromesh unit retainer to the layshaft, the correct way round, as shown in this photograph.

72 Fit the retainer lock washer and nut to the end of the layshaft (photo).

73 Insert the reverse and fifth speed detent plunger into the transmission case (photo).

74 Follow the detent plunger with the spring and secure in

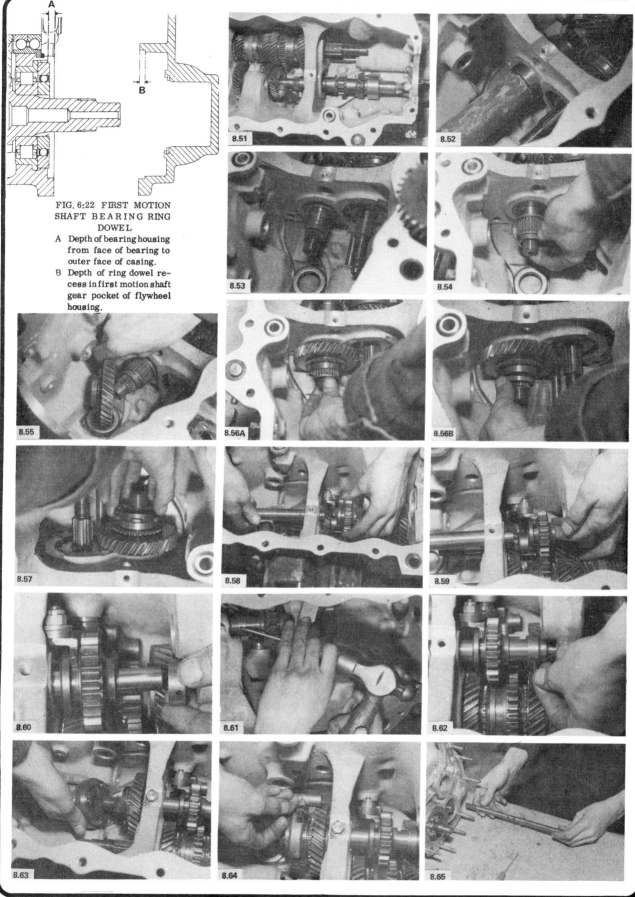

FIG. 6:22 FIRST MOTION
SHAFT BEARING RING
DOWEL

A Depth of bearing housing
from face of bearing to
outer face of casing.

B Depth of ring dowel recess in first motion shaft
gear pocket of flywheel
housing.

8.51

8.52

8.53

8.54

8.55

8.56A

8.56B

8.57

8.58

8.59

8.60

8.61

8.62

8.63

8.64

8.65

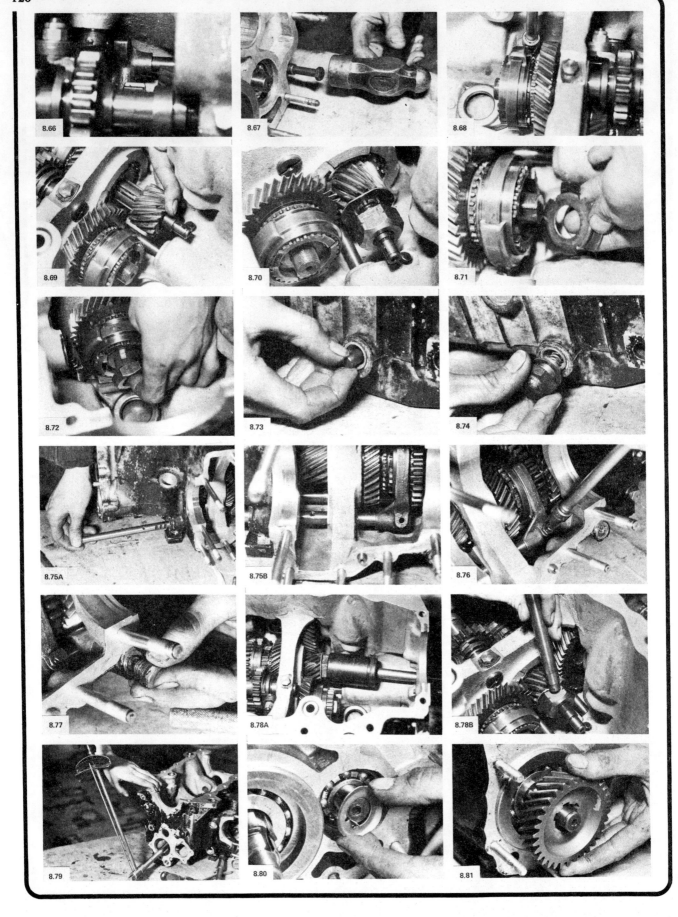

8.66

8.67

8.68

8.69

8.70

8.71

8.72

8.73

8.74

8.75A

8.75B

8.76

8.77

8.78A

8.78B

8.79

8.80

8.81

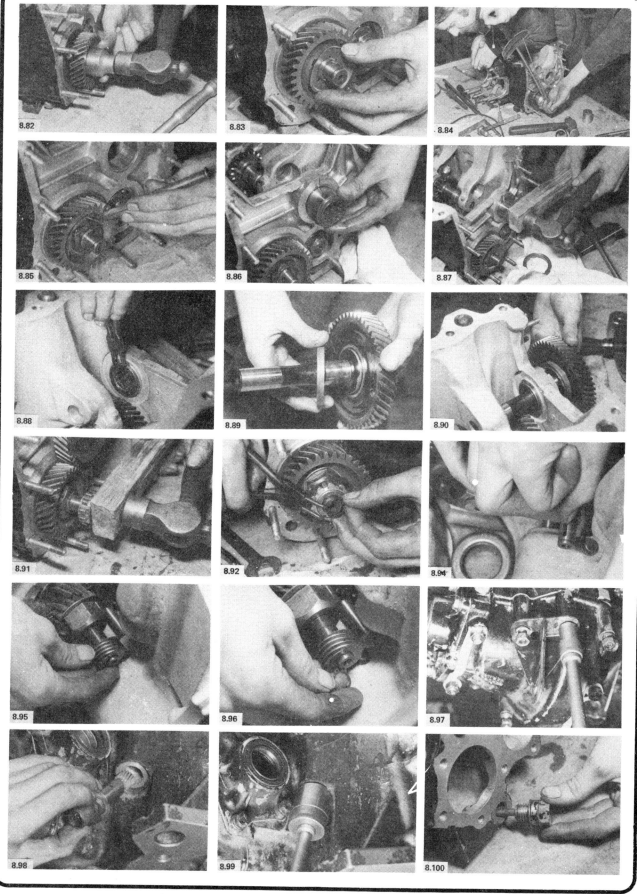

position with the cap nut and fibre washer (photo).

75 Fit the third and fourth speed selector rod to the transmission case, taking care to line up the securing bolt holes in the selector fork and selector rod (photos).

76 Fit the taper bolt and locknut to the selector fork; carefully tighten the securing bolt and lock the locknut (photo).

77 Insert the first and second speed detent plunger and spring into the bore in the transmission case and secure in position with the plug and three washers (photo).

78 The pinion securing nut should now be tightened as firmly as possible using either a ring spanner, a soft metal drift or socket as shown in this photograph (A). Lock by bending over the lockwasher (photo B).

79 Tighten the front nut on the end of the layshaft to a torque wrench setting of 120 lb ft (photo).

80 Fit the layshaft rear nut lockwasher and nut to the end of the layshaft and tighten to a torque wrench setting of 120 lb ft. Bend over the lockwasher (photo). Note this nut has a left hand thread.

81 Place the first motion shaft gear onto the first motion shaft, the correct way round, as shown in this photograph.

82 Using a suitable size socket, drift the first motion shaft gear into its final position on the first motion shaft (photo).

83 Place the lockwasher onto the end of the first motion shaft with the ears facing outwards (photo).

84 Refit the nut and tighten to a torque wrench setting of 120 lb ft. It will be necessary to lock two gears together by moving two synchromesh collars into mesh with a screwdriver (photo). Note: This nut has a left hand thread.

85 Using a chisel bend over the lock washer ears (photo).

86 Fit the idler gear bearing to the transmission casing (photo).

87 Tap the bearing into its final position with a piece of soft wood (photo).

88 Fit the idler gear bearing inner and outer retaining circlip (photo).

89 Slide the inner thrust washer onto the idler gear (photo).

90 Fit the idler gear and shaft into the transmission case, carefully meshing it with the first motion shaft gear (photo).

91 Refit the inner bearing circlip onto the end of the first motion shaft and then, using a piece of soft wood, drift on the spigot bearing (photo).

92 Fit the outer bearing circlip to the outermost end of the first motion shaft (photo).

93 Refer to Chapter 8/2 and fit the differential unit to the transmission casing.

94 Fit the Woodruff key to the end of the third motion shaft (photo).

95 Slide the speedometer pinion onto the end of the third motion shaft (photo).

96 Fit the speedometer pinion retaining circlip (photo).

97 Fit the bracket to the differential housing, if this has not already been done (photo).

98 Carefully insert the speedometer cable drive gear and housing into the transmission casing screw into the housing (photo).

99 Tighten the drive gear housing using a socket (photo).

100 Clean the magnetic drain plug and screw into the transmission casing (photo).

101 Replace the oil pump and screw in the pump outlet connection (photo).

102 Using a piece of metal, shaped as shown in this photo and gripped with a mole wrench, tighten the pump outlet connection (photo).

103 Secure the oil pump with the two long bolts with plain and spring washers (photo).

104 Fit a new gasket to the front cover and slide into position over the two studs (photo).

105 Refit the front mounting, and secure the front cover and mounting with the five bolts and spring washers and two nuts and spring washers (photo).

106 The transmission unit is now ready to have the splash shield refitted and then for refitting to the engine as described in Section 10 (photo).

---

9   Transmission (rod gear change) - reassembly

The procedure for reassembling this type of transmission assembly is basically identical to that described for the cable gear change type, with the exception of the selector assemblies. These differences will have been noted during the dismantling procedure and, therefore, during reassembly, if this sequence is reversed no problems will arise.
Comparison of Fig. 6:10 and Fig. 6:16 will show the differences between the two transmission units and the location of the revised parts.

---

10   Transmission - refitting to engine

---

1   Refit a new oil sealing ring to the transmission casing (photo).

2   Locate new sealing strips into the slots on either side of the front oil seal location (photo).

3   Fit the splash shield and secure in position with the bolt and tab washer (photo).

4   Bend up the tab washer, so locking the splash shield securing bolt (photo).

5   Smear a little grease onto the mating faces of the transmission casing and carefully locate new joint washer halves to the mating face (photo).

6   With the help of an assistant, carefully lift the engine and then place on the transmission casing (photo).

7   Refit the crankshaft primary gear to the end of the crankshaft (photo).

8   Refit the idler gear outer thrust washer and retain in position with a dab of grease (photo).

9   Smear a little grease onto the flywheel housing-to-engine and transmission case mating face and fit a new joint washer (photo).

10   Lubricate the end of the crankshaft ready for the primary gear to be fitted (photo).

11   Wrap some sellotape around the primary gear splines to prevent damage to the oil seal, and smear on a little grease. Slide on the primary gear (photo). Refer to Section 2 and check the end float.

12   If a new flywheel housing oil seal is to be fitted this should be done as described in Section 3.

13   Carefully fit the flywheel housing to the engine and transmission casing (photo).

14   Using a sharp knife, cut away the sellotape from the splines on the primary gear (photo).

15   Replace the seventeen flywheel housing securing nuts, bolts and tab washers, but do not tighten fully yet.

16   Replace the eleven transmission casing to crankcase securing bolts and spring washers, but do not tighten fully yet.

17   Carefully tap the dowels up, so accurately locating the transmission casing and crankcase mating flanges.

18   Tighten the eleven bolts and spring washers to the correct torque wrench setting: 3/8 inch bolts - 30 lb ft; 5/16 inch bolts - 20 to 25 lb ft.

8.101

8.102

8.103

8.104

8.105

8.106

.10.1

10.2

10.3

10.4

10.5

10.6

10.7

10.8

10.9

10.10

10.11

10.13

10.14

10.19

10.20

10.21

10.22

19   Tighten the seventeen bolts and nuts securing the flywheel housing to the engine/transmission case to a torque wrench setting of 18 lb ft. Bend over the lock washer tabs (photo).
20   Before refitting the clutch/flywheel assembly, note that there is a master dowel in the end of the crankshaft. This has a larger diameter than the other three (photo).
21   Refit the clutch/flywheel assembly to the crankshaft and, with a suitable drift, drive the flywheel fully home (photo).
22   Locate the spacer plate on the inside of the clutch and replace the four securing bolts (photo).
23   Tighten the flywheel retaining bolts to a torque wrench setting of 60 lb ft (photo).
24   Refit the clutch thrust plate and secure with the three bolts and spring washers (photo). Tighten these bolts to a torque wrench setting of 8 to 10 lb ft.
25   Replace the clutch housing cover and secure with the eight bolts and spring washers. Tighten the bolts to a torque wrench setting of 15 to 18 lb ft (photo).
26   Insert the fuel pump operating push rod and replace the fuel pump and insulator block. Secure with the two nuts and spring washers. Tighten the nuts to a torque wrench setting of 15 to 18 lb ft.
27   Refit the oil filter and secure with the centre bolt which should be tightened to a torque wrench setting of 20 lb ft.
28   Replace the starter motor and secure in position with the two bolts and spring washers which should be tightened to a torque wrench setting of 30 lb ft.
29   Insert the oil pump drive shaft and refit the distributor. Secure the distributor clamp plate with the two bolts and spring washers which should be tightened to a torque wrench setting of 8 to 10 lb ft.
30   Replace the dipstick guide tube and secure in position with the union nut.

11 Remote control (cable gear change) - removal and refitting

1   Place a container having a capacity of at least ten pints under the engine/transmission unit drain plug. Unscrew and remove the drain plug and allow all the oil to drain out.
2   Unscrew the cable locking nut from each of the cables at the transmission unit end (Fig. 6:23).
3   Unscrew the outer cable gland nut from each of the cables.
4   Carefully pull out the fifth speed/reverse outer cable from the transmission.
5   Unscrew the inner cable gland nut and detach the cable from the transmission.
6   Repeat the operations in paragraphs 4 and 5 but for the first and second speed cable.
7   Screw a long bolt into the end of the first and second speed selector rod and push the rod into the neutral position.
8   Repeat the operations in paragraphs 4 and 5 but for the third and fourth speed cable.
9   Unscrew and remove the nut and spring washer that secures the heat shield front mounting.
10   Undo and remove the four nuts and spring washers that secure the silencer mounting brackets to the body.
11   Undo and remove the four bolts and spring washers that secure the change speed control to the heat shield.
12   Pull off the Lucar connectors from the two terminals on the reverse light switch.
13   Unscrew the knob from the gear change lever.
14   Move the carpeting from around the gear change lever area and then undo and remove the six screws and washers

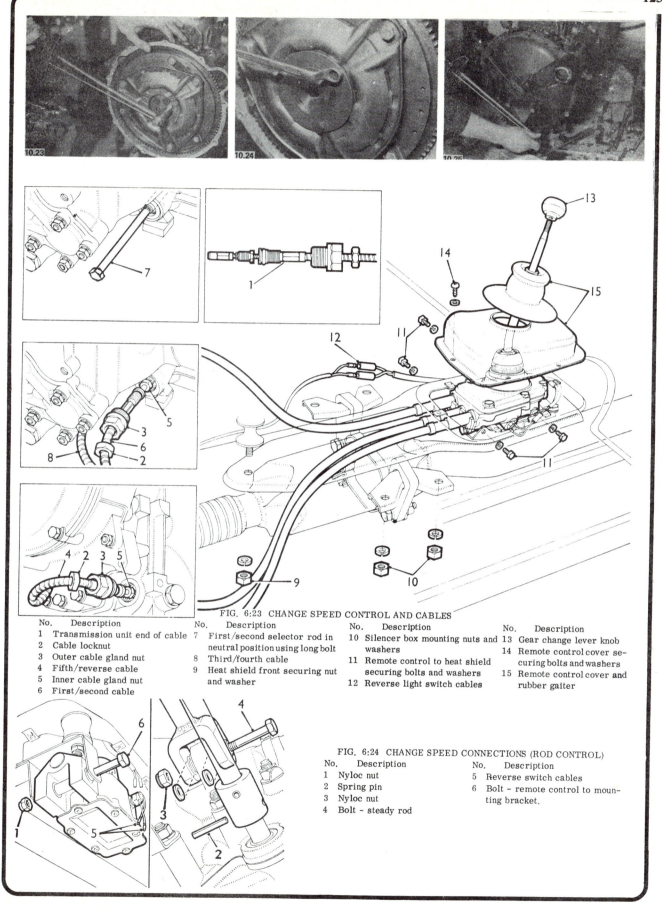

FIG. 6:23 CHANGE SPEED CONTROL AND CABLES

No.	Description
1	Transmission unit end of cable
2	Cable locknut
3	Outer cable gland nut
4	Fifth/reverse cable
5	Inner cable gland nut
6	First/second cable
7	First/second selector rod in neutral position using long bolt
8	Third/fourth cable
9	Heat shield front securing nut and washer
10	Silencer box mounting nuts and washers
11	Remote control to heat shield securing bolts and washers
12	Reverse light switch cables
13	Gear change lever knob
14	Remote control cover securing bolts and washers
15	Remote control cover and rubber gaiter

FIG. 6:24 CHANGE SPEED CONNECTIONS (ROD CONTROL)

No.	Description
1	Nyloc nut
2	Spring pin
3	Nyloc nut
4	Bolt – steady rod
5	Reverse switch cables
6	Bolt – remote control to mounting bracket.

125

that secure the change speed lever control.

15   Lift away the cover and rubber gaiter from over the top of the gear change lever.

16   The complete change speed remote control assembly and cables may now be lifted away from the car.

17   Refitting the assembly is the reverse sequence to removal but it will be necessary to pull out the selector rods before the inner cables can be reconnected.

18   The cables must be adjusted as described in Section 15.

19   Finally refill the engine/transmission unit with oil.

12   Remote control (rod gear change) - removal and refitting

1   Unscrew the gear change lever knob.

2   Using a small diameter parallel pin punch remove the spring pin that retains the extension rod to the selector shaft.

3   Undo and remove the nyloc nut and long bolt that secures the steady rod to the transmission casing. Recover the two plain washers located either side of the transmission casing boss.

4   Pull off the Lucar connectors from the two terminals on the reverse light switch.

5   Undo and remove the nyloc nut and long bolt that secures the remote control to the mounting bracket.

6   Lift away the remote control from the car.

7   Refitting is the reverse sequence to removal but the following additional points should be noted:

8   Always use a new spring pin when securing the selector extension rod to the selector shaft.

9   Adjust the reverse switch as described in Section 17.

10   The remote control must be adjusted as described in Section 16.

13   Remote control (cable gear change) - dismantling and reassembly

1   Undo and remove the six bolts and spring washers that secure the control unit cover to the body. Lift away the cover (Fig. 6:25).

2   Slide off the plain washer and spring from the gear change lever.

3   Lift off the interlock and its pivot from the control unit body.

4   Disengage the gear change lever from the interlock.

5   Undo and remove the two bolts and spring washers that secure the cable retaining plate to the body of the control unit.

6   Unscrew and remove the inner nuts and lockwashers securing the cables to the selector jaws.

7   Remove the cables from the control unit body.

8   Release the reverse light switch locknut and unscrew the reverse light switch.

9   Lift away the selector shaft retaining plate.

10   Carefully withdraw the three selector shafts taking precautions to collect the ball bearings and springs as they are released.

11   Lift away the three selector jaws.

12   Undo and remove the reverse selector stop retaining bolt and spring washer.

13   Lift away the reverse stop and its dowel.

14   Reassembly is the reverse sequence to dismantling but the following additional points should be noted;

a)   Apply a non-hardening sealer to the cable retaining plate

before it is refitted to the body.

b)   Lubricate the jaws, shafts and lever with a graphite base grease once these parts have been refitted to the body.

14   Remote control (rod gear change) - dismantling and reassembly

1   Rotate the gear change lever retaining dome from the body in an anti-clockwise direction so to release the bayonet fitting (Fig. 6:26).

2   Lift away the gear change lever assembly.

3   Undo and remove the six bolts securing the bottom cover to the remote control body.

4   Undo and remove the nyloc nut securing the steady rod to the body and lift away the steady rod.

5   Release the reverse light switch locknut and unscrew the reverse light switch.

6   Move the extension rod eye rearwards and remove the spring pin that retains the extension rod to the extension rod eye, using a small diameter parallel pin punch.

7   Now move the extension rod eye forwards and, again using a small diameter parallel pin punch, drift out the second spring pin.

8   The extension rod may now be withdrawn from the body

9   Using a screwdriver, ease out the end plug from the rear end of the body.

10   Withdraw the support rod and remove the extension rod eye.

11   Using a pair of circlip pliers, or a small screwdriver, remove the circlip from the extension rod eye.

12   Lift away the ball-end bearing seat and then separate the bearing from the seat.

13   Reassembly is the reverse sequence to dismantling, but the following two additional points should be noted:

a)   Always use new spring pins to retain the extension rod and support rod.

b)   The bottom cover should be fitted so that the reverse stop is towards the front of the remote control body.

15   Remote control change speed cables - adjustment

If difficulty is being experienced in selecting or changing gears, the cables must be checked for correct adjustment otherwise damage can be caused to the gears and synchronizers.

Also, if the cables have been detached from the transmission or remote control, they must be checked and reset as necessary.

1   Move the gear change lever to the neutral position (Fig. 6:27).

2   Unscrew the knob from the end of the gear change lever.

3   Move the carpeting away from the floor around the base of the gear change lever.

4   Undo and remove the six bolts and washers that secure the cover to the floor panel.

5   Ease the cover and rubber up the gear change lever and lift away.

6   Undo and remove the six bolts and spring washers that secure the control unit cover to the body. Lift away the cover.

7   Remove the plain washer and spring from the gear change lever.

8   Disengage the gear change lever from the interlock.

9   Using a spanner, slacken the cable adjustment nuts on each cable.

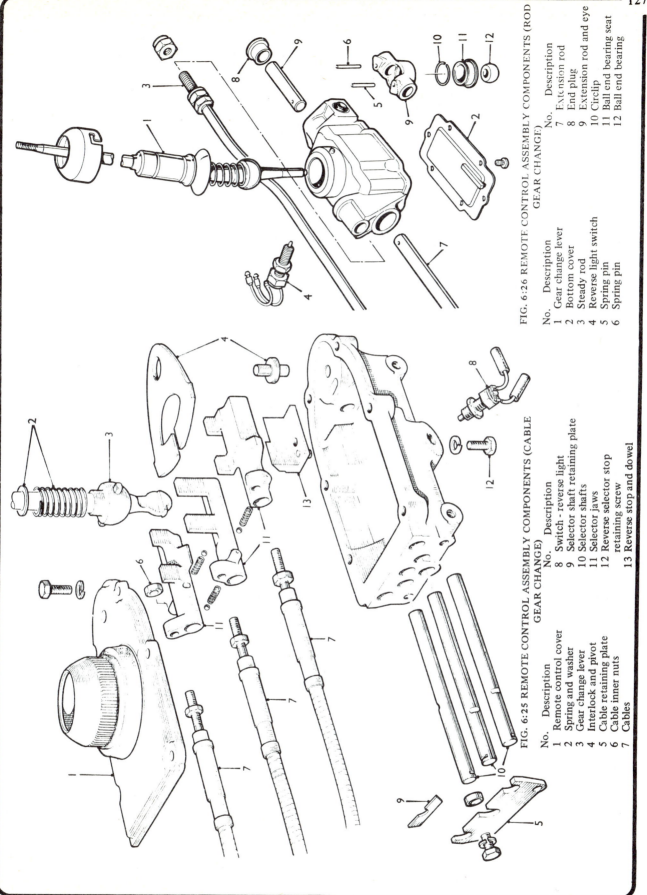

FIG. 6:26 REMOTE CONTROL ASSEMBLY COMPONENTS (ROD GEAR CHANGE)

No.	Description	No.	Description
1	Gear change lever	7	Extension rod
2	Bottom cover	8	End plug
3	Steady rod	9	Extension rod and eye
4	Reverse light switch	10	Circlip
5	Spring pin	11	Ball end bearing seat
6	Spring pin	12	Ball end bearing

FIG. 6:25 REMOTE CONTROL ASSEMBLY COMPONENTS (CABLE GEAR CHANGE)

No.	Description	No.	Description
1	Remote control cover	8	Switch - reverse light
2	Spring and washer	9	Selector shaft retaining plate
3	Gear change lever	10	Selector shafts
4	Interlock and pivot	11	Selector jaws
5	Cable retaining plate	12	Reverse selector stop retaining screw
6	Cable inner nuts	13	Reverse stop and dowel
7	Cables		

10   Remove the transmission unit detent plugs, springs and plungers for each of the selector rods.   These may be seen in Fig. 6:7.

11   Place each selector rod so that the neutral (centre) detent groove is exactly central in the end of the plunger bore. For this a powerful torch and a mirror is useful.

12   Fit the plungers back in their respective bores.

13   Make up three metal rods 1/4 inch diameter and 1. 2 inches long and fit one into each bore.

14   Remove the sealing washers from each detent plug. Note that three washers are used under the head of the first/second speed detent plug when it is finally refitted.

15   Screw in each plug into its respective bore finger tight so making sure that the selector rods are retained in their neutral positions.

16   Use the adjustment nuts attached to the cables in such a manner that the selector jaws align in the neutral position and also the interlock passes freely through the jaws with an equal clearance at each side.

17   Remove the detent plugs, recover the metal rods and refit the springs and plugs using the correct washers.

18   Reassemble the gear change lever and top cover to the body, refit the floor cover, carpeting, and finally the gear change lever knob.

---

16   Remote control (rod gear change) - adjustment

---

1   Release the connectors from the reverse light switch.

2   Slacken the reverse light switch locknut.

3   Move the gear change lever to the neutral position between the fifth gear and reverse positions.

4   Ascertain the free movement of the gear change lever by gently pulling the knob rearwards ie, towards the reverse gear position, until the reverse stop is felt.

5   Refer to Fig. 6:28. The free movement at 'A' should be 0.030 inch which is equivalent to a gear change lever knob movement of between 3/4 to 1/2 inch.

6   Slacken the three s t e a d y rod securing nuts and either increase the effective rod length to reduce gear lever free movement, or reduce the effective rod length to increase gear lever free movement.

7   Tighten the two innermost steady rod securing nuts 'C' and 'D' Fig. 6:28 preferably to a torque w r e n c h setting of 24 lb ft.

8   Tigthen the one remaining nut 'B' preferably to a torque wrench setting of 5 lb ft.   Note: It is important that the rear locknut 'C' is held firmly with a spanner to take the torque reaction whilst the nut 'B' is finally tightened.

9   The reverse light switch must now be adjusted as described in Section 17.

---

17   Reverse light switch - adjustment

---

1   Move the gear change lever to the reverse gear position.

2   Disconnect the two wires from the reverse light switch connectors (Fig. 6:28 inset).

3   Slacken the reverse light switch locknut.   Screw in the reverse light switch as far as possible and then unscrew it two complete turns.

4   Reconnect the w i r i n g to the reverse light switch, and switch on the ignition.

5   Slowly screw in the reverse light switch until the reverse lights come on. Screw in the switch one more complete turn.

6   Tighten the reverse light switch locknut, switch off the ignition and move the gear change lever to the neutral position.

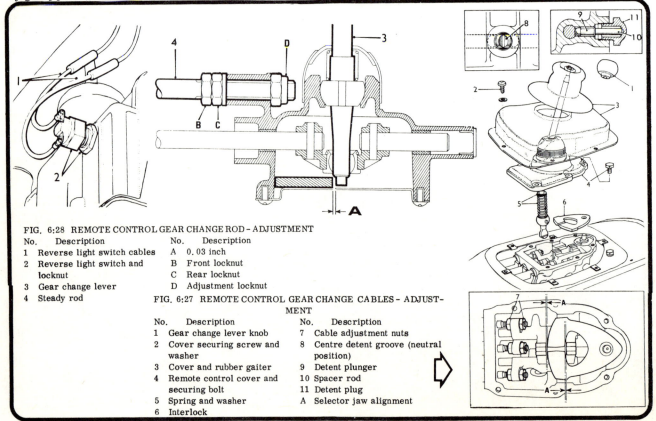

FIG. 6:28 REMOTE CONTROL GEAR CHANGE ROD - ADJUSTMENT

No.	Description	No.	Description
1	Reverse light switch cables	A	0. 03 inch
2	Reverse light switch and locknut	B	Front locknut
		C	Rear locknut
3	Gear change lever	D	Adjustment locknut
4	Steady rod		

FIG. 6:27 REMOTE CONTROL GEAR CHANGE CABLES - ADJUSTMENT

No.	Description	No.	Description
1	Gear change lever knob	7	Cable adjustment nuts
2	Cover securing screw and washer	8	Centre detent groove (neutral position)
3	Cover and rubber gaiter	9	Detent plunger
4	Remote control cover and securing bolt	10	Spacer rod
5	Spring and washer	11	Detent plug
6	Interlock	A	Selector jaw alignment

Cause	Trouble	Remedy
SYMPTOM: WEAK OR INEFFECTIVE SYNCHROMESH		
General wear	Synchronising cones worn, split or damaged	Dismantle and overhaul transmission unit. Fit new gear wheels and synchronsing cones
	Synchromesh dogs worn, or damaged	Dismantle and overhaul transmission unit. Fit new synchromesh unit.
SYMPTOM: JUMPS OUT OF GEAR		
General wear or damage	Broken gearchange fork rod spring	Dismantle and replace spring.
	Transmission unit coupling dogs badly worn	Dismantle transmission unit. Fit new coupling dogs.
	Selector fork rod groove badly worn	Fit new selector fork rod.
	Selector fork rod securing screw and locknut loose	Tighten securing screw and locknut.
SYMPTOM: EXCESSIVE NOISE		
Lack of maintenance	Incorrect grade of oil in transmission unit or oil level too low	Drain, refill, or top up transmission unit with correct grade of oil.
General wear	Bush or needle roller bearings worn or damaged	Dismantle and overhaul transmission unit Renew bearings.
	Gearteeth excessively worn or damaged	Dismantle, overhaul transmission unit. Renew gearwheels.
	Laygear thrust washers worn allowing excessive end play	Dismantle and overhaul transmission unit Renew thrust washers.
SYMPTOM: EXCESSIVE DIFFICULTY IN ENGAGING GEAR		
Clutch not fully disengaging	Clutch pedal adjustment incorrect	Adjust clutch pedal correctly.

Chapter 7 Drive shafts and universal joints

1   General description

Drive is transmitted from the differential unit to the front wheels by means of two drive shafts. Fitted at either end of each shaft are universal joints which allow for vertical movement of the front wheels.

The outer universal joints are of the Hardy Spicer Birfield constant velocity joint type. The drive shaft fits inside the circular outer constant velocity joint which is also on the driven shaft. Drive is transmitted from the drive shaft to the driven shaft by six steel balls. These are located in curved grooves, machined in line with the axis of the shaft on the inside of the driven shaft and outside of the drive shaft, which keeps them together. The constant velocity joint is packed with a special grease and enclosed in a rubber boot.

The inner universal joint comprises a pair of needle roller bearings located in bearing caps which are housed within a tubular 'pot' housing. Like the outer joint, it is packed with a special grease and sealed by a rubber boot.

2   Hub and drive shaft - removal and refitting

1   Chock the rear wheels, apply the handbrake, remove the front wheel trims, and slacken the wheel nuts.
2   Jack up the front of the car and support on firmly based axle stands located under the main longitudinal members. Remove the wheel nuts and lift away the road wheel.
3   Extract the split pin locking the hub nut. Undo and remove the hub nut.
4   Using a jack, or other suitable means, support the weight of the lower suspension arm.
5   Undo and remove the two upper swivel ball joint securing bolts. Disengage the brake hydraulic pipe bracket (Fig. 7:2).
6   Undo and remove the two bolts and washers securing the brake caliper unit, lift it clear and, using some string or wire, support its weight away from the disc so that the flexible hose is not strained.
7   Using a large universal puller and suitable thrust pad, pull the disc and driving flange assembly from the hub.
8   Undo and remove the nut securing the steering arm swivel ball joint and, using a universal ball joint separator, detach the ball joint from the steering arm (Fig. 7:3).
9   Undo and remove the lower suspension arm ball joint securing bolts.
10   Using the universal puller again and suitable thrust pad, carefully pull the hub assembly from the drive shaft.

11   Refer to Fig. 7:4 and, using a metal lever as shown, carefully detach the drive shaft from the differential and lift away the complete drive shaft assembly.
12   Refitting the hub and drive shaft is the reverse sequence to removal but the content of the following paragraphs should be noted.
13   Make sure that the chamfers on the end of the shaft and the shaft splines are free from damage or burrs before entering the shaft into the differential unit.
14   Should any difficulty be found in engaging the shaft pulley into the differential circlip, try fitting a $3\frac{1}{2}$ inch diameter jubilee clip round the pot joint housing and applying an even and sustained pressure by hand onto the shaft. Use a drift located on the jubilee clip to drive the shaft into its full engagement position.
15   A special tool (part No 18G1104A) is normally required to pull the drive shaft through the hub bearing as shown in Fig. 7:6 but it should be possible to make up something like it using two long threaded nuts, high tensile steel bolt, a piece of tube and a selection of washers.
16   Any torque wrench settings necessary will be found in Chapter 11.

3   Outer universal joint - dismantling, inspection and overhaul

There is little point in dismantling the outer constant velocity joints if they are known to be badly worn. In this case it is better to remove the old joint from the shaft and fit a new unit. To remove and then dismantle the joint proceed as follows:
1   Remove the drive shaft from the car and separate it from the front hub as described in Section 2 of this Chapter. Wire the drive shaft and pot housing to stop joint separating.
2   Thoroughly clean the exterior of the drive shaft and rubber gaiter, preferably not using a liquid cleaner.
3   Mount the drive shaft vertically in between soft faces in a vice with the joint facing outwards.
     Using a screwdriver, prise off the large diameter aluminium gaiter retaining ring towards the stub axle. Also prise off the small diameter aluminium ring, again using a screwdriver. Turn back the gaiter and, if it is to be renewed, it is recommended that the gaiter be cut off and thrown away.
4   Before the joint can be dismantled it must be removed from the drive shaft. This is easily done by firmly tapping the outer edge of the constant velocity joint with a hide or

131

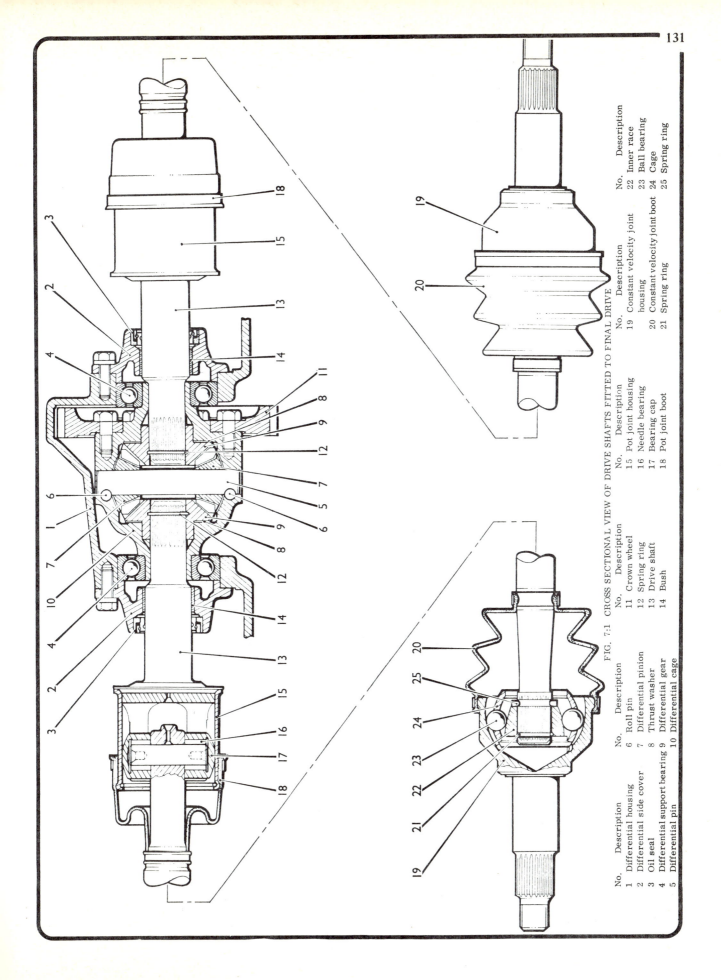

FIG. 7.1 CROSS SECTIONAL VIEW OF DRIVE SHAFTS FITTED TO FINAL DRIVE

No.	Description	No.	Description	No.	Description
1	Differential housing	6	Roll pin	11	Crown wheel	15	Pot joint housing	19	Constant velocity joint	22	Inner race
2	Differential side cover	7	Differential pinion	12	Spring ring	16	Needle bearing		housing	23	Ball bearing
3	Oil seal	8	Thrust washer	13	Drive shaft	17	Bearing cap	20	Constant velocity joint boot	24	Cage
4	Differential support bearing	9	Differential gear	14	Bush	18	Pot joint boot	21	Spring ring	25	Spring ring
5	Differential pin	10	Differential cage								

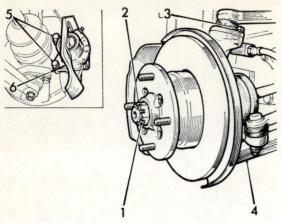

FIG. 7:2 HUB REMOVAL

No.	Description	No.	Description
1	Split pin	4	Lower suspension arm
2	Hub nut	5	Brake caliper securing bolts
3	Upper ball joint securing bolts	6	Brake caliper

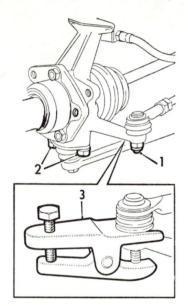

FIG. 7:3 STEERING ARM AND LOWER SUSPENSION ARM

No.	Description	No.	Description
1	Ball joint securing nut	3	Universal ball joint separators
2	Lower suspension arm ball joint securing bolts		

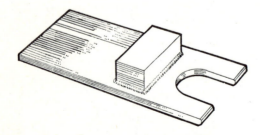

Fig. 7:4 Shaped metal lever to separate drive shaft from differential housing

plastic headed hammer. Alternatively, use a copper drift located on the inner member as shown in Fig. 7:8 and give the drift a sharp blow. Whichever method is used, the inner spring ring will be contracted so releasing the joint from the shaft.

5   Ease off the round section spring ring and, when reassembling, use the new one supplied in the service kit.

6   Mark the position of the inner and outer races with a dab of paint so that upon reassembly the mated parts can be correctly replaced.

7   Refer to Fig. 7:9 and tilt the inner race until one ball bearing is released. Repeat this operation easing out each ball bearing in turn, using a small screwdriver.

8   Manipulate the cage until the special elongated slot coincides with the lands of the bell housing. Drop one of the lands into the slot and lift out the cage and race assembly (Fig. 7:10).

9   Turn the inner race at right angles to the cage and in line with the elongated slot. Drop one land into the slot and withdraw the inner race as shown in Fig. 7:11.

10   Thoroughly clean all component parts of the joint by washing in paraffin.

11   Examine each ball bearing in turn for cracks, flat spots or signs of the surface pitting. Check the inner and outer tracks for widening which will cause the ball bearings to be a loose fit. This, together with excessive wear in the ball cage, will lead to the characteristic 'knocking' on full lock. The cage, which fits between the inner and outer races, must be examined for wear in the ball cage windows and for cracks which are likely to develop across the narrower portions between the outer rims and the holes for the ball bearings. If wear is excessive then all parts must be renewed as a matched set.

12   To reassemble, first ensure that all parts are very clean and then lubricate with Duckhams Bentone Grease, No Q5795-2 which is supplied under part number ARF 1457. Do not, under any circumstances, use any other grease. Provided that all parts have been cleaned and well lubricated they should fit together easily without force.

13   Refit the inner race into the cage by manipulating one of the lands into the elongated slot in the cage. Insert the cage and inner race assembly into the ball joint by fitting one of the elongated slots over one of the lands in the outer race. Rotate the inner race to line up with the bell housing in its original previously marked position.

14   Taking care not to lose the position, tilt the cage until one ball bearing can be inserted into a slot. Repeat this procedure until all six ball bearings are in their correct positions. Ensure that the inner race moves freely in the bell housing throughout its movement range, taking care that the ball bearings do not fall out.

15   Using the remainder of the special grease, pack the joint evenly. Smear the inside of a new rubber boot with the special grease (Duckhams Bentone Grease, Number Q5795 supplied under part number AKF 1457) and fit the rubber boot and a new circlip to the end of the shaft.

16   Hold the shaft in a vice and locate the inner race on the splines. By pressing the constant velocity joint against the circlip, position the ring centrally and contract it in the chamber in the inner race leading edge with two screwdrivers. Using a soft faced hammer, sharply tap the end of the stub shaft to compress the ring and then tap the complete assembly onto the drive shaft. Double check that the shaft is fully engaged and the circlip fully locked against the inner race.

17   Ease the rubber boot over the constant velocity joint and

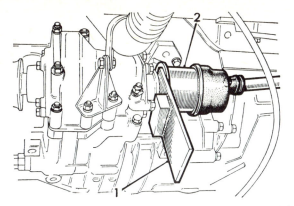

FIG. 7:5 DETACHING DRIVE SHAFT FROM DIFFERENTIAL

No.	Description	No.	Description
1	Metal lever	2	Pot joint housing

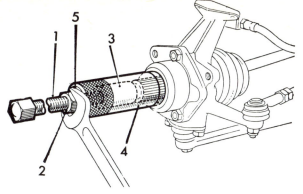

FIG. 7:6 PULLING DRIVE SHAFT THROUGH HUB BEARING

No.	Description	No.	Description
1	Long bolt	4	Metal tube
2	Nut	5	Packing washers
3	Long nut		

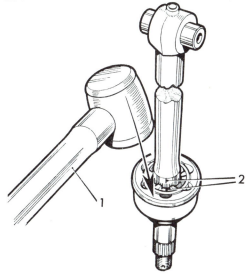

FIG. 7:7 FREEING DRIVE SHAFT FROM RETAINER RING

No.	Description	No.	Description
1	Soft faced hammer		shaft and joint to ensure cor
2	Identification marks on drive		rect refitting

Fig. 7:8 Using soft metal drift to remove constant velocity joint from drive shaft

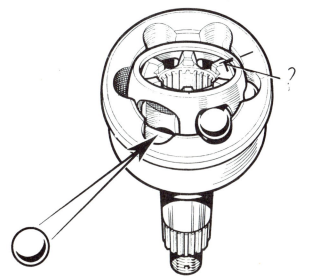

FIG. 7:9 MOVEMENT OF CAGE AND INNER RACE TO REMOVE
THE BALL BEARINGS
Arrow shows identification marks for correct reassembly

Fig. 7:10 Positioning of cage in preparation for removal

Fig. 7:11 Positioning of inner track so it may be removed

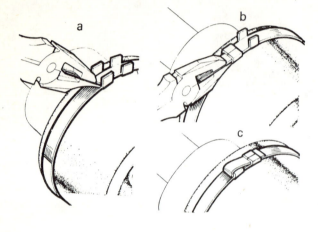

Fig. 7:12 Correct fitment of rubber boot clips

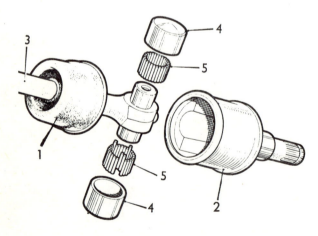

FIG. 7:13 COMPONENT PARTS OF POT JOINT

No.	Description	No.	Description
1	Rubber boot	4	Bearing cap
2	Pot joint housing	5	Bearing needles
3	Drive shaft		

ensure the moulded edges of the boot are seating correctly in the retaining groove of the shaft and bell housing. Secure in position with the large and small clips. Check that the tab of the large clip is pulled away from the direction of rotation as shown in Fig. 7:12. Do not use wire as this cuts into the rubber boot.

4   Inner universal joint – dismantling, inspection and overhaul

1   Carefully remove the wire or clip that secures the pot joint rubber boot and roll back the rubber boot.
2   With a scriber or file, mark the shaft and pot housing so that they may be refitted in their original positions, and draw the shaft from the pot housing.
3   Lift away the bearing caps from the drive shaft cross piece and lift away the needle bearings.
4   If the rubber boot is to be renewed it may be cut off the shaft, otherwise, leave it where it is.
5   Wash all parts in paraffin and wipe dry with a clean non-fluffy rag.
6   Examine the bearings and bearing surfaces of the pot joint for damage, grooving or excessive wear. If evident, new parts must be obtained.
7   Inspect the rubber boot for signs of cuts, splits or perishing. If evident, a new rubber boot must be obtained as if dirt finds its way into the joint, wear will rapidly occur.
8   Reassembly is the reverse sequence to removal. All components must be smeared with Shell Tivellor 'A' grease, pack number AKF 1910 which contains the correct quantity of 100 cc for smearing the parts and packing of one joint.
9   Position the rubber boot over the joint with the ribs registering in the groove of the shaft and over the ridge of the joint housing.

5   Constant velocity joint gaiter – removal and refitting

1   At regular intervals the rubber boots which protect the outer universal joints should be inspected for damage. If they are torn, split or damaged they must be renewed as soon as possible as they are open to road dust, grit and water which would lead to rapid deterioration of the ball bearings in the joint.
2   Should a new rubber boot be necessary, it requires the removal of the outer drive shaft and front hub assembly as described in Section 2.
3   Mount the outer drive shaft centrally in a bench vice fitted with soft jaws.
4   Using a screwdriver prise off the larger diameter aluminium gaiter retaining ring towards the stub axle.
5   Prise off the small diameter aluminium ring again using a screwdriver. Turn back the gaiter and, if it is to be renewed, it is recommended that the gaiter be cut off and then thrown away.
6   Before a new rubber gaiter may be fitted the joint must be separated from the drive shaft. This is easily done by firmly tapping the outer edge of the constant velocity joint with a hide or plastic headed hammer. Alternatively, use a copper drift located on the inner member as shown in Fig. 7:8 and give the drift a sharp blow. Whichever method is used, the inner spring ring will be contracted so releasing the joint from the shaft.
7   Ease off the round section spring ring and, when reassembling use the new one supplied in the service kit.

8   Wipe the splines clean with a non-fluffy rag and smear with some Duckhams Bentone Grease, Number Q5795 which is supplied under part number AKF 1457. Do not use any other grease.

9   Slide the new gaiter small end first, onto the shaft taking care not to nick it on the circlips. Push it down the shaft clear of the joint.

10   The constant velocity joint must contain 1 ounce of Duckhams Bentone Grease so, if it has not been dismantled and has not lost any through a damaged gaiter, add a little through the central splined hole. If the joint has lost grease the full quantity must be inserted.

11   Mount the joint assembly vertically in a bench vice fitted with soft jaws.

12   By pressing the constant velocity joint against the circlip, position the ring centrally and contract it in the chamber in the inner race leading edge with two screwdrivers. Using a soft faced hammer, sharply tap the end of the stub shaft to compress the ring and then tap the complete assembly onto the drive shaft. Double check that the shaft is fully engaged and the circlip fully locked against the inner race.

13   Ease the rubber boot over the constant velocity joint and ensure the moulded edges of the boot are seating correctly in the retaining groove of the shaft and bell housing. Secure in position with the large and small clips. Check that the tab of the large clip is pulled away from the direction of rotation as shown in Fig. 7:12. Do not use wire as this cuts into the rubber boot.

Chapter 8 Final drive

Contents

Specifications

Type	Helical gears and differential	
Ratio		
1500	3.94:1 (16/63)	
1750	3.65:1 (17/62)	
Torque wrench settings	lb ft	Kg m
Differential cover 5/16 in nuts	17 to 19	2.4 to 2.6
3/8 in nuts	24 to 26	3.0 to 3.6
Studs	6	0.8
Differential end cover set screws	18	2.5
Final drive pinion nut	150	20.7
Crownwheel bolts	40 to 50	5.5 to 7

1 General description

The differential unit is located on the bulkhead side of the combined engine and transmission unit. It is held in place by nuts and studs. The crownwheel, or drive gear, together with the differential gears, are mounted in the differential unit. The drive pinion is mounted on the third motion shaft.

All repairs can be carried out to the component parts of the differential unit only after the engine/transmission unit has been removed from the car. If it is wished to attend to the pinion, it will be necessary to separate the transmission casing from the engine.

The differential housing and gearbox casing are machined as a matched pair when assembled so that they can only be replaced as a pair, not separately. Also the final drive gear and pinion are mated and must be changed as a pair and not as individual gears.

2 Differential unit - removal and refitting

1 Remove the engine and transmission assembly as described in Chapter 1.
2 Remove the bolts and spring washers holding the differential side covers in position on the transmission and differential housing. Mark the side covers so that they may be refitted in their original positions and then remove them (photo). Recover any shims fitted under the left hand side cover (Fig. 8:2).
3 Bend back the differential housing securing nut locking tabs and remove the eight nuts and tab washers.
4 Using a soft faced hammer, carefully tap the differential

housing from the securing studs. Lift away the housing (photo)
5 Remove the collar retaining the interlock spool (rod gear change only) and withdraw the complete differential assembly (photo).
6 If the side covers were showing signs of oil leaks, the oil seals should be drifted out and new ones fitted with the lips facing inwards. Lubricate the new seals before refitting.
7 Remove the selector shaft oil seal from the differential housing if it shows signs of leaking, lubricate the new seal with oil and drift it in (rod gear change only).
8 To refit, first fit the locating collar into the groove of the interlock spool (rod gear change models only).
9 Place the differential assembly into the transmission casing with the assembly positioned slightly towards the righthand side.
10 Replace the differential housing, fit new tab washers and tighten the nuts sufficiently tight to hold the bearings firmly, yet not so tight as to prevent the differential from being moved laterally when the righthand cover is refitted.
11 Fit a new right hand cover gasket and then replace the cover. Tighten the five securing bolts and spring washers to a torque wrench setting of 18 lb ft (photo).
12 Using a soft metal drift located on the outer track of the lefthand bearing, tap the differential to ensure the righthand bearing is in full contact with the righthand side cover (Fig. 8:3).
13 Fit the lefthand side cover, leaving out the gasket, and tighten the cover bolts progressively in a diagonal manner to ensure full contact of the cover spigot with the bearing, yet not applying any pre-load.
14 Using a feeler gauge accurately determine the gap between the cover flange and the differential housing at not less

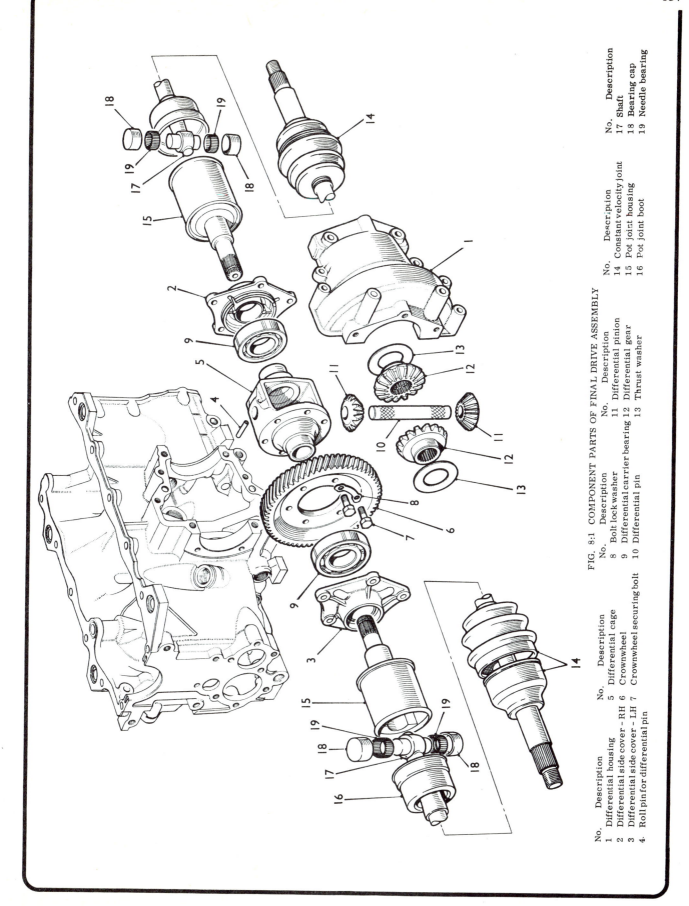

FIG. 8:1 COMPONENT PARTS OF FINAL DRIVE ASSEMBLY

No.	Description	No.	Description	No.	Description	No.	Description
1	Differential housing	5	Differential cage	8	Bolt lockwasher	11	Differential pinion	14	Constant velocity joint	17	Shaft
2	Differential side cover – RH	6	Crownwheel	9	Differential carrier bearing	12	Differential gear	15	Pot joint housing	18	Bearing cap
3	Differential side cover – LH	7	Crownwheel securing bolt	10	Differential pin	13	Thrust washer	16	Pot joint boot	19	Needle bearing
4	Roll pin for differential pin										

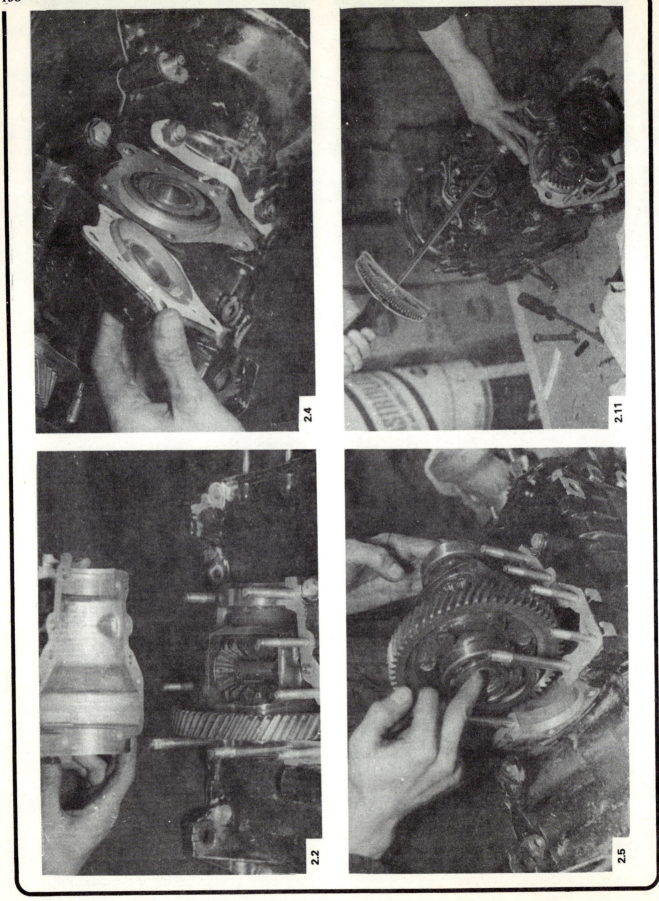

2.4

2.11

2.2

2.5

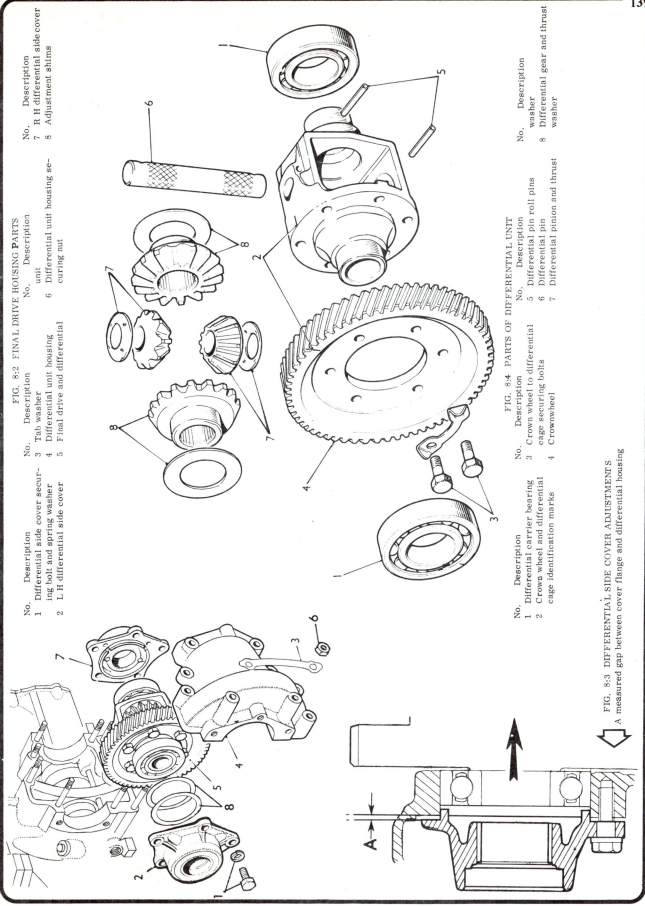

FIG. 8:2 FINAL DRIVE HOUSING PARTS

No.	Description
1	Differential side cover securing bolt and spring washer
2	L H differential side cover
3	Tab washer
4	Differential unit housing
5	Final drive and differential
6	Differential unit housing securing nut
7	R H differential side cover
8	Adjustment shims

FIG. 8:4 PARTS OF DIFFERENTIAL UNIT

No.	Description
1	Differential carrier bearing
2	Crown wheel and differential cage identification marks
3	Crown wheel to differential cage securing bolts
4	Crownwheel
5	Differential pin roll pins
6	Differential pin
7	Differential pinion and thrust washer
8	Differential gear and thrust washer

FIG. 8:3 DIFFERENTIAL SIDE COVER ADJUSTMENTS

A measured gap between cover flange and differential housing

than three points to ensure even tightness of the cover bolts.
15   If uneven readings are obtained in the tested positions, adjust the tightness of the bolts until the same reading is obtained. This will eliminate any distortion in the cover flange.
16   Should a condition arise whereby there is no gap between the flange and the casing, remove the cover and add a known thickness of shims between the cover and bearing to produce a clearance. The thickness of shims must, of course, be included in the calculation of the pre-load shim requirement.
17   The compressed thickness of the new side cover gasket is 0.008 inch and the required pre-load is 0.001 to 0.002 inch. The clearance between the cover flange and casing must be adjusted with shims to 0.009 to 0.010 inch.

To act as a g u i d e the following sample calculation is given:

Measured clearance	0.007 inch
Gasket compressed thickness	0.008 inch
Required pre-load	0.001 to 0.002 inch
Shim thickness required	0.002 inch

Note: Shims are available in 0.002 and 0.003 inch thicknesses.
18   Tighten the differential housing nuts, 5/16 inch 18 lb ft, and 3/8 inch 25 lb ft. Lock the nuts by bending over the lock tabs.

---

3   Differential unit - dismantling and reassembly

---

1   Using a good quality three legged puller and suitable thrust block, draw each differential carrier bearing from the differential carrier. This is only n e c e s s a r y, of course, if the bearings are worn and require renewal.
2   With a scriber, or file, mark the crown wheel and differential cage so that they can be refitted in their original positions (Fig. 8:4).
3   Release the lock washer tabs and undo and remove the eight crownwheel securing bolts. Lift away the crownwheel.
4   Using a small diameter pin punch, carefully tap out the two roll pins that retain the differential pinion pin.
5   With a soft metal drift, remove the pinion pin from the differential carrier.
6   Push the differential pinions and concave thrust washers around and remove from the case.
7   Ease the two side gears and thrust washers towards the centre of the differential case and lift away through the openings in the case.
8   Clean all the removed parts in paraffin and dry. Examine the gears for wear and chipped or damaged teeth, the thrust washers for wear or cracking, and the pinion pin for wear or loose fit in the differential housing.
9   If there was excessive noise in the drive or overun conditions, this may be caused by excessive backlash between the differential pinions and differential gears. Fit new pinions and/or differential gear thrust washers.
10   Check the bearings for side play and general wear. Inspect the inner tracks for signs of movement on their mounting, or the outer tracks rotating in their housing, and if either of the conditions exists, fit new parts.
11   If new gears are to be fitted, carefully drift in new circlips using a piece of suitable diameter rod.
12   Reassembly is the reverse sequence to dismantling. It should be noted that the larger diameter carrier bearing is fitted to the crownwheel side of the differential assembly.

Chapter 9 Braking system

Contents

Specifications

Make	Girling	
Footbrake	Hydraulic servo assisted on all four wheels	
Handbrake	Mechanical on rear wheels only	
Type of brakes:		
Front	Disc - Self adjusting	
Rear	Drum	
Front		
Disc diameter	9.68in. (246 mm)	
Pad area (total)	16sq in. (103 sq cm)	
Swept area (total)	182 sq in. (1174 sq cm)	
Lining material	Ferodo 2430 F	
Rear		
Drum diameter	8 inch (203 mm)	
Lining dimensions	1.5 x 6.25 in (38 x 158.7 mm)	
Swept area (total)	76 sq in (490 sq cm)	
Lining material	Mintex M79	
Wheel cylinder diameter	0.75 in (19 mm)	
Hydraulic fluid	Castrol Girling Brake Fluid	
Vacuum servo unit	Girling 'Super Vac'	

Torque wrench settings	lb ft	Kg m
Brake caliper to hub	40 to 50	5.5 to 6.9
Disc to driving flange	38 to 45	5.2 to 6.2
Shield to swivel hub	17 to 25	2.3 to 3.4
Bleed screw	4 to 6	0.5 to 0.8
Brake adjuster nut	4 to 6	0.5 to 0.8
Master cylinder to servo	17	2.3
Tandem master cylinder - tipping valve securing nut	35 to 45	4.8 to 6.2
Pressure reducing valve - end plug...	25 to 35	3.5 to 4.8
Pressure reducing valve - piston locknut ...	3 to 4	0.4 to 0.55
P D W A valve - electrical switch	2 to 2.5	0.28 to 0.35

Specifications

Torque wrench settings	lb ft	Kg m
P D W A valve - end plugs	16 to 20	2. 2 to 2. 8
Road wheel nuts	50	6. 9
Hub nut - Front	150	20. 7
Hub nut - Rear	60	8. 3

1   General description

Disc brakes are fitted to the front wheels, and drum brakes to the rear. All are operated u n d e r servo assistance
from the brake pedal, this being connected t o the master
cylinder and servo assembly mounted on the bulkhead.

The front brakes are of rotating d i s c and semi - rigid
mounted caliper design, whilst the rear brakes are of the internal expanding single l e a d i n g shoe type and operated by
either the hand or foot brake.

The front brake disc is secured to the driving flange of
the hub, and the c a l i p e r mounted on the steering swivel.
From Fig. 9:12 it will be seen that on the inner disc face side
of the caliper is a single hydraulic cylinder in which are placed two outward facing pistons. One piston is in contact with
a friction pad which, in turn, is in contact with one face of the
disc, and the second piston presses on a yoke which transmits
the pressure to a second pad in contact with the outer face of
the disc. Hydraulic fluid is able to pass to the cavity between the two pistons.

The rear brakes have one cylinder operating two shoes.
Attached to each of the rear wheel operating cylinders is a
mechanical expander, operated by the handbrake lever through
a cable which runs from the brake lever to the backplate brake
levers. This provides an independent means of rear brake
application.

Drum brakes have to be adjusted periodically to compensate for wear in the linings, whereas the front disc brakes
are adjusted automatically. It is not normal to have to adjust the handbrake system, as its efficiency is largely depen-
dent on the condition of the brake linings and the adjustment
of the brake shoes. The handbrake can, h o w e v e r, be adjusted separately to the footbrake operated hydraulic system.

The hydraulic brake functions in the following manner:
On application of the brake pedal, hydraulic fluid under pressure is pushed from the master cylinder to the brake operating cylinders at each wheel by means of a four-way union,
steel pipes and flexible hoses.

A pressure regulating valve, located next to one of the
radius arms, is fitted into the pipe line leading to the rear
brakes so that, under normal light brake action, the valve does
not operate and brake fluid passes freely to the rear brake
wheel cylinders. Under heavy braking action, the valve comes
into operation and limits the pressure to the rear brakes so
minimizing the possibility of rear wheel lock.

The mechanically operated stop light switch is secured
to the pedal mounting plate inside the car and is operated by
an extension of the brake pedal arm.

2   Drum brake adjustment

1   Jack up the rear of the car and place on firmly based
stands. Also check the front wheels to ensure that the car
cannot roll backwards or forwards.
2   Release the handbrake and, working under the car, locate
the adjuster as shown in Fig. 9:1. The brakes are adjusted

by turning the square headed adjuster in a clockwise or anti-
clockwise direction. Always use a square headed brake adjuster spanner as the edges of the adjuster are easily burred
if an adjustable wrench or open ended spanner is used.
3   Turn the adjuster in a clockwise direction, when viewed
from the c e n t r e of the car, until the brake shoes lock the
wheel. Turn the adjuster back until the wheel is free to rotate without the shoes rubbing.
4   Spin the wheel and apply the brakes hard to centralise
the shoes. Re-check that it is not possible to turn the adjusting screw further without locking the wheel.
5   NOTE: A rubbing noise when the wheel is spun is usually
due to dust on the brake drum and shoe lining. If there is no
obvious slowing down of the wheel due to brake binding there
is no need to slacken off the adjusters until the noise disap-
pears. It is better to remove the drum and clean, taking
care not to inhale any dust.
6   Repeat this process for the other brake drum. A good
tip is to paint the head of the adjusting screws white which
will facilitate future adjusting by making the adjuster heads
easier to see. Also a little graphite penetrating oil on the
adjuster threads will check any p o s s i b i l i t y of seizure by
rusting.

3   Bleeding the hydraulic system

Whenever the brake hydraulic s y s t e m has been overhauled, a part renewed, or the level in the reservoir becomes
too low, air will have entered the system necessitating its
bleeding. During the operation, the level of hydraulic fluid
in the reservoir should not be allowed to fall below half full,
otherwise air will be drawn in again.
1   Obtain a clean and dry glass jam jar, plastic tubing a t
least fifteen inches long and of suitable diameter to fit tightly
over the bleed screw, and a supply of Castrol Girling Brake
Fluid.
2   Check that on each rear brake backplate the wheel cylinder is free to slide within its locating slot. Ensure that all
connections are tight and all bleed screws closed. Chock the
wheels and release the handbrake.
3   Fill the master cylinder reservoir and the bottom inch
of the jam jar with hydraulic fluid. Take extreme care that
no fluid is allowed to come into contact with the paintwork as
it acts as a solvent and will damage the finish.
4   NOTE: The front disc brake should be bled first EXCEPT
where a tandem master cylinder is f i t t e d, when the rear
brakes must be bled first. Remove the rubber dust cap (if
fitted) from the end of the bleed screw and attach the bleed
tube to the bleed screw on the front caliper which is furthest
away from the master cylinder. Insert the other end of the
bleed tube in the jar containing one inch of hydraulic f l u i d.
Use a suitable sized open ended spanner and unscrew the bleed
screw about half a turn.
5   An assistant should now pump the brake pedal by first
depressing it o n e full stroke f o l l o w e d by three s h o r t
but rapid strokes and a l l o w i n g the pedal to return of its

own accord. Check the fluid level in the reservoir. Carefully watch the flow of fluid into the glass jar and, when air bubbles cease to emerge with the fluid during the next down stroke, tighten the bleed screw. Remove the plastic bleed tube and tighten the bleed screw, do not overtighten. Replace the rubber dust cap. Top up the fluid in the reservoir.

6 Repeat operations in paragraphs 4 and 5 for the second front brake caliper as applicable.

7 The rear brakes should be bled in the same manner as the front, except that each brake pedal stroke should be slow with a pause of three or four seconds between each stroke. This is to ensure that the valve fitted into the rear brake line does not operate.

8 Sometimes is may be found that the bleed operation for one or more cylinders is taking a considerable time. The cause is probably air being drawn past the bleed screw threads when the screw is loose. To counteract this condition, it is recommended that at the end of each downward stroke the bleed screw be tightened to stop air being drawn past the threads.

9 If after the bleed operation has been completed, the brake pedal operation still feels spongy, this is an indication that there is still air in the system, or that the master cylinder is faulty.

10 When a tandem master cylinder is fitted a slightly different technique is required. Attach two bleed tubes to right hand front and righthand rear brakes and bleed both at the same time, in the same manner as for a single master cylinder except that the brake pedal must not be fully depressed at any time except when the complete system has been fully bled.

11 Repeat the previous operation for the lefthand front and lefthand rear brakes.

12 Should it be noticed that during the bleed operation and with the ignition switched on the warning light glows, the bleed operation must be continued until all traces of air are removed. Ascertain which brake caused the light to glow and then attach a bleed tube to the bleed screw at the opposite end of the car and open the bleed screw. Slowly depress the brake pedal and, when the light goes out, release the pedal and tighten the bleed screw.

13 Check and top up the reservoir fluid level with fresh hydraulic fluid. Never re-use old brake fluid.

---

4 Drum brake shoes - inspection, removal and refitting

After high mileages, it will be necessary to fit replacement shoes with new linings. Refitting new brake linings to shoes is not considered economic, or possible, without the use of special equipment. However, if the services of a local garage or workshop having brake re-lining equipment are available then there is no reason why the original shoes should not be successfully relined. Ensure that the correct specification linings are fitted to the shoes.

1 Chock the front wheels, jack up the rear of the car and place on firmly based axle stands. Remove the road wheel.

2 Release the handbrake and back off the brake shoe adjuster by turning in an anticlockwise direction, when viewed from the centre of the car.

3 Using a wide bladed screwdriver, carefully prise off the hub dust cap located as shown in Fig. 9:2.

4 With a pair of pliers, straighten the ears of the hub nut split pin and then withdraw the split pin.

5 With a suitable sized spanner, undo and remove the hub nut. Note that the lefthand hub has a lefthand thread, and the

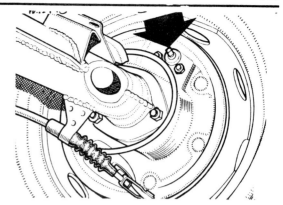
Fig. 9:1 Rear brake adjuster (arrowed)

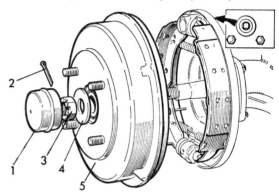
FIG. 9:2 REAR BRAKE DRUM REMOVAL

No.	Description	No.	Description
1	Dust cap	4	Plain washer
2	Split pin	5	Brake drum
3	Castellated nut		

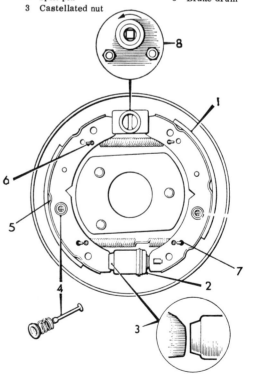
FIG. 9:3 REAR BRAKE COMPONENTS

No.	Description	No.	Description
1	Leading shoe	5	Trailing shoe
2	Wheel cylinder	6	Return spring (plain)
3	Abutment for trailing shoe	7	Return spring (shaped)
4	Anti rattle spring assembly	8	Adjuster

righthand hub has a righthand thread. Lift away the plain spacing washer.

6   Remove the brake drum and hub. If it is tight, use a soft faced hammer and tap outwards on the circumference, rotating the drum whilst completing this operation.

7   The brake linings should be renewed if they are so worn that the rivet heads are flush with the surface of the lining. If bonded linings are fitted, they must be renewed when the lining material has worn down to $1/16$ in, at its thinnest point.

8   Using a pair of pliers, release the trailing brake shoe anti-rattle springs by rotating through 90°. Lift away the steady pin, spring and cup washer (Fig. 9:3).

9   Disengage the trailing shoe from the wheel cylinder abutment and then the abutment link in the adjuster link.

10   Repeat the operation in paragraph 8 for the leading shoe.

11   Carefully remove both brake shoes complete with springs, at the same time easing the handbrake operating lever from the leading shoe. Take care that the links in the adjuster housing do not fall out, and retain them with an elastic band around the adjuster assembly.

12   If the shoes are to be left off for a while, do not depress the brake pedal otherwise the piston will be ejected from the cylinder causing unnecessary work.

13   Thoroughly clean all traces of dust from the shoes, backplates and brake drums using a stiff brush. It is recommended that compressed air is NOT used as it blows up dust which should not be inhaled. Brake dust can cause judder or squeal and, therefore, it is important to clean out as described.

14   Check that the piston is free in its cylinder, that the rubber dust covers are undamaged and in position, and that there are no hydraulic fluid leaks. Ensure the handbrake lever assembly is free and the brake adjuster operates correctly. Lubricate the threads on the adjusting wedge with a graphite based penetrating oil.

15   Prior to reassembly, smear a trace of Castrol PH Brake Grease to the steady platforms, both ends of the brake shoes and the adjuster links. Do not allow any grease to come into contact with the linings or rubber parts. Refit the shoes in the reverse sequence to removal, taking care that the adjuster links are correctly positioned in the adjuster housing with the angle of the link registering against the adjuster wedge. The two pull off springs should preferably be renewed every time new shoes are fitted, and must be refitted in their original web holes. Position them between the web and backplate.

16   Back off the adjuster and replace the brake drum and hub assembly. Refit the plain washer and castellated nut tightening the latter to a torque wrench setting of 60 lb ft. Align to the next split pin hole and lock with a new split pin. Do not pack the dust cap with grease. Replace the road wheel.

17   Adjust the rear brake as described in Section 2 and then lower the car to the ground. Check correct adjustment of the handbrake and finally road test.

---

5   Rear brake wheel cylinder - removal, inspection and overhaul

---

If hydraulic fluid is leaking from the brake wheel cylinder, it may be necessary to dismantle it and replace the seal. Should brake fluid be found running down the side of the wheel or if it is noticed that a pool of liquid forms alongside one wheel and the level in the master cylinder has dropped, it is indicative of failed seals.

1   Remove the brake drum/hub assembly and brake shoes

as described in Section 4. Clean down the rear of the backplate using a stiff brush. Place a quantity of rag under the backplate to catch any hydraulic fluid that may issue from the open pipe or wheel cylinder.

2   Wipe the top of the brake master cylinder reservoir and unscrew the cap. Place a piece of thick polythene over the top of the reservoir and replace the cap. This is to stop hydraulic fluid syphoning out.

3   Using an open ended spanner, carefully unscrew the hydraulic pipe connection union to the rear of the wheel cylinder.

4   Extract the split pin and lift away the washer and clevis pin connecting the handbrake cable yoke to the wheel cylinder operating lever (Fig. 9:4).

5   Ease off the rubber boot from the rear of the wheel cylinder.

6   Using a screwdriver, carefully draw off the retaining plate and spring plate from the rear of the wheel cylinder (Fig. 9:5).

7   The wheel cylinder may now be lifted away from the brake backplate. Detach the handbrake lever from the wheel cylinder.

8   To dismantle the wheel cylinder, first ease off the rubber dust cover retaining ring with a screwdriver, and the rubber dust cover itself. Withdraw the piston from the wheel cylinder body and, with the fingers, remove the piston seal from the piston noting which way round it is fitted. (Do not use a metal screwdriver as this could scratch the piston) (Fig. 9:6).

9   Inspect the inside of the cylinder for score marks caused by impurities in the hydraulic fluid. If any are found, the cylinder and piston will require renewal. NOTE: If the wheel cylinder requires renewal always ensure that the replacement is exactly similar to the one removed.

10   If the cylinder is sound, thoroughly clean it out with fresh hydraulic fluid.

11   The old rubber seal will probably be swollen and visibly worn. Smear the new rubber seal with hydraulic fluid and reassemble into the cylinder. Fit a new dust seal and retaining clip.

12   Using Castrol PH Brake Grease, smear the backplate where the wheel cylinder slides, and refit the handbrake lever on the wheel cylinder ensuring that it is the correct way round. The spindles of the lever must engage in the recess on the cylinder arms.

13   The handbrake lever may now be fed through the slot in the backplate until the neck of the wheel cylinder is correctly located in the slot.

14   Slide the spring plate between the wheel cylinder and backplate. The retaining plate may now be inserted between the spring plate and wheel cylinder, taking care the pips of the spring plate engage in the holes of the retaining plate.

15   Replace the rubber boot and reconnect the handbrake cable yoke to the handbrake lever. Insert the clevis pin, head upwards, and plain washer. Lock with a new split pin.

16   Reassembling the brake shoes and drum/hub assembly is the reverse sequence to removal. Finally bleed the hydraulic system as described in Section 3.

---

6   Brake shoe adjuster - removal and refitting

---

1   Should it be necessary to remove the brake adjuster, first remove the road wheel, brake drum/hub assembly and brake shoes as described in Section 4.

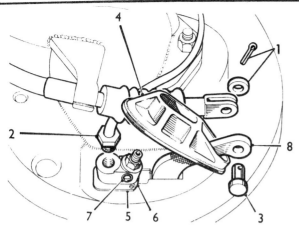

FIG. 9:4 WHEEL CYLINDER ATTACHMENTS

No.	Description	No.	Description
1	Split pin and washer	5	Retaining plate
2	Brake hydraulic pipe	6	Spring plate
3	Clevis pin	7	Wheel cylinder
4	Rubber boot	8	Handbrake lever

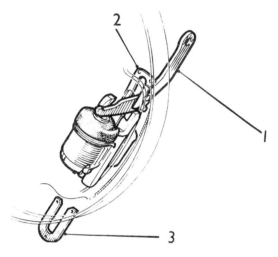

FIG. 9:5 WHEEL CYLINDER TO BACKPLATE FIXINGS

No.	Description	No.	Description
1	Handbrake lever	3	Retaining plate
2	Spring plate		

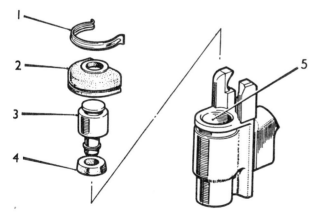

FIG. 9:6 WHEEL CYLINDER COMPONENTS

No.	Description	No.	Description
1	Retaining ring	4	Piston seal
2	Rubber dust cover	5	Cylinder bore
3	Piston		

2   Release the two adjuster retaining nuts and lift away, together with the spring washers. The adjuster can now be lifted away from the backplate.

3   Check that the screw can be screwed both in and out to its fullest extent without showing signs of tightness.

4   Lift away the two adjuster links and thoroughly clean the adjuster assembly. Inspect the adjuster body and two links for signs of excessive wear, and fit new parts as necessary.

5   Lightly smear the adjuster links with Castrol PH Grease and reassemble. Double check correct operation by holding the two links between the fingers and rotating the adjuster screw whereupon the links should move out together.

7   Drum brake backplate - removal and refitting

1   To remove the backplate, refer to Section 4, paragraphs 1 to 6 inclusive and remove the drum/hub assembly.

2   Extract the split pin and lift away the plain washer locking the clevis pin, securing the handbrake cable yoke to the wheel cylinder handbrake lever. Lift away the clevis pin (Fig. 9:7).

3   Wipe the top of the brake master cylinder reservoir and unscrew the cap. Place a piece of thick polythene over the reservoir and refit the cap. This is to stop the hydraulic fluid syphoning out.

4   Using an open ended spanner, carefully unscrew the hydraulic pipe connection union to the rear of the wheel cylinder.

5   Undo and remove the three nuts with spring washers securing the hub axle and backplate to the radius arm.

6   Using a tapered soft metal drift, carefully drive the hub axle and backplate from the radius arm, and separate the hub axle from the backplate.

7   Refitting is the reverse sequence to removal. It will be necessary to bleed the brake hydraulic system as described in Section 3.

8   Handbrake - adjustment

It is usual when the rear brakes are adjusted that any excessive free movement of the handbrake will automatically be taken up. However, in time, the handbrake cables will stretch and it will be necessary to take up the free play by shortening the cables at the point where they are attached to the handbrake lever.

Never try to adjust the handbrake to compensate for wear on the rear brake linings. It is usually badly worn brake linings that lead to the excessive handbrake travel. If upon inspection the rear brake linings are in good condition, or they have been renewed recently and the handbrake reaches the end of its ratchet travel before the brakes operate, adjust the cables as follows:

1   Refer to Section 2 and ensure the rear brakes are correctly adjusted.

2   Release the handbrake lever and then pull it on until the third notch position on the ratchet is reached.

3   Adjust the nuts at the handbrake lever end of the two cables until the rear wheels can just be turned by heavy hand pressure (Fig. 9:8).

4   Release the handbrake lever and check that the rear brakes are not binding.

9   Handbrake cable – removal and refitting

1   Chock the front wheels, jack up the rear of the car and support on firmly based axle stands.
2   Release the handbrake lever. Undo and remove the respective handbrake cable adjustment nut followed by the outer cable adjustment nut (Fig. 9:9).
3   Detach the inner cable from the handbrake lever and lift away the long spring and plain washer.
4   Release the outer cable to body clips from the underside of the floor panels.
5   Extract the split pin and lift away the washer and clevis pin connecting the handbrake cable yoke to the wheel cylinder operating yoke.
6   Detach the rubber boot from the outer cable rear abutment and then disengage the outer cable from the radius arm clips.
7   Withdraw the complete handbrake cable assembly rearwards from the large body rubber grommet.
8   Refitting is the reverse sequence to removal. It will be necessary to adjust the cable as described in Section 8.

10   Front disc brake pad – removal, inspection and refitting

1   Apply the handbrake, jack up the front of the car and place on firmly based axle stands. Remove the road wheel.
2   Using a pair of pliers, withdraw the two pad retaining pin locking wire clips and withdraw the retaining pins. The two pads may now be lifted out of the caliper. (Fig. 9:10).
3   Inspect the thickness of the lining material and, if it is less than 1/8 inch it is recommended that the pads be renewed. If one of the pads is slightly more worn than the other, it is permissible to change these round. Always fit new pads of the manufacturer's recommended specification.
4   To refit the pads, it is first necessary to extract a little brake fluid from the system. To do this, fit a plastic bleed tube to the bleed screw and immerse the free end in 1 inch of hydraulic fluid in a jar. Slacken off the bleed screw one complete turn and press back the indirect piston. Next, push the yoke towards the disc until the new indirect pad can be inserted. Press back the direct piston into the bore and then tighten the bleed screw. Fit the new direct pad.
5   Insert the retaining pins with their heads furthermost from the caliper pistons and secure with wire clips.
6   Wipe the top of the hydraulic fluid reservoir and remove the cap. Top up and depress the brake pedal several times to settle the pads, and then recheck the hydraulic fluid level.

11   Front disc brake caliper – removal, overhaul and refitting

1   Chock the rear wheels, apply the handbrake, remove the front wheel trim and slacken the wheel nuts. Jack up the front of the car and support on firmly based stands. Remove the road wheel.
2   Wipe the top of the brake master cylinder reservoir and unscrew the cap. Place a piece of thick polythene over the top and refit the cap. This is to prevent hydraulic fluid syphoning out.
3   Using an open ended spanner, undo the union nut securing the brake hydraulic pipe to the caliper (Fig. 9:11).
4   Undo and remove the two bolts and spring washers which

secure the caliper to the steering swivel assembly and carefully lift away the caliper from the disc.
5   Using a pair of pliers, withdraw the two pad retaining pin wire clips and remove the two retaining pins. Lift away the pads (Fig. 9:10).
6   Place the yoke of the caliper between soft faces in a bench vice and tighten sufficiently to hold the caliper.
7   Using the fingers, press the indirect piston fully into its bore in the caliper and then press the cylinder body down (Fig. 9:12).
8   Make a note of the position of the yoke spring relative to the yoke, and then lift away the spring.
9   Very carefully remove the retaining rings and dust covers from the cylinder, if necessary using a small screwdriver. The bore or piston must not be scratched.
10   Lift out the special bias ring from the indirect piston.
11   Using a compressed air jet, or foot pump, applied to the hydraulic pipe connection bore, eject the two pistons, taking suitable precautions not to allow them to fly out.
12   The seals may be removed from the cylinder using a non-metal rod, or the fingers.
13   Finally remove the bleed screw. It is important that the adjustment screw within the cylinder body is not disturbed.
14   Thoroughly clean the internal parts of the caliper using only Castrol Girling Cleaning Fluid or methylated spirits.
15   Carefully inspect the fine finish of the bore and pistons and if signs of scoring or corrosion is evident, a new caliper assembly must be obtained. Before commencing to reassemble, obtain a new seal set and also a new bias spring.
16   To reassemble the caliper, first fit the new bias spring into the indirect piston in such a manner that the radius end enters the piston first.
17   Apply a little clean hydraulic fluid to the pistons and seals, but not to the cylinder grooves or sliding edges of the yoke.
18   Very carefully fit the previous wetted seals into the cylinder grooves and then fit the pistons into the cylinder. The indirect piston with the bias ring must be fitted in the opposite end of the cylinder to the pads.
19   Refit the dust cover and retaining rings, making sure that the widest retaining ring secures the dust cover furthermost from the pads.
20   The yoke spring is next refitted to the yoke, and this must be positioned as was noted during dismantling.
21   Fit the cylinder to the yoke, engaging the tongue of the yoke into the slot of the bias ring fitted into the indirect piston.
22   With a small screwdriver, locate the legs of the yoke spring into the sliding grooves on the cylinder. The angled leg of the spring must engage in the groove on the cylinder opposite to the bleed screw. Refit the bleed screw.
23   The pads may now be refitted, this being the reverse sequence to removal.
24   Refitting the caliper is the reverse sequence to removal. It will be necessary to bleed the hydraulic system, full details of which may be found in Section 3.

12   Front brake disc – removal, renovation and refitting

1   Chock the rear wheels, apply the handbrake, jack up the front of the car and support on firmly based axle stands. Remove the road wheel.
2   Using a pair of pliers, bend straight the ears of the hub nut locking split pin and withdraw the split pin (Fig. 9:13).

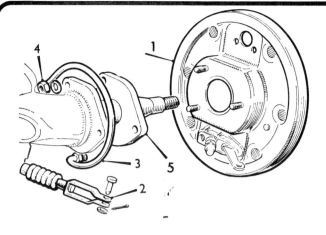

FIG. 9:7 DRUM BRAKE BACKPLATE REMOVAL FROM RADIUS ARM

No.	Description	No.	Description
1	Backplate	4	Backplate securing nut
2	Handbrake cable yoke	5	Radius arm mounting flange
3	Brake hydraulic pipe		

FIG. 9:8 HANDBRAKE CABLE ADJUSTMENT

No.	Description	No.	Description
1	Cables	3	Cable adjustment nuts
2	Handbrake lever		

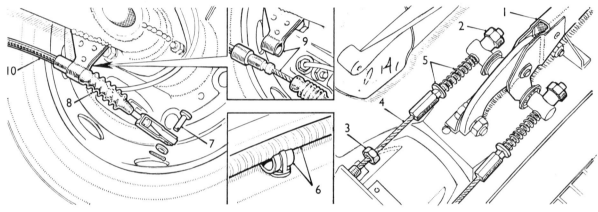

FIG. 9:9 HANDBRAKE CABLE REMOVAL

No.	Description	No.	Description	No.	Description	No.	Description
1	Handbrake lever	4	Inner cable	7	Clevis pin	9	Backplate end securing clip
2	Cable adjustment nut	5	Tension spring and washer	8	Rubber boot	10	Outer cable assembly
3	Outer cable securing nut	6	Cable and body mounting clip				

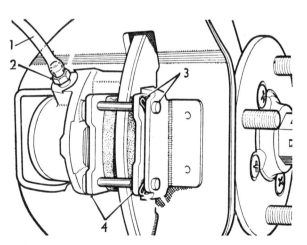

FIG. 9:10 DISC BRAKE PAD REMOVAL

No.	Description	No.	Description
1	Bleed tube	3	Wire clip and retaining pin
2	Bleed screw	4	Brake pads

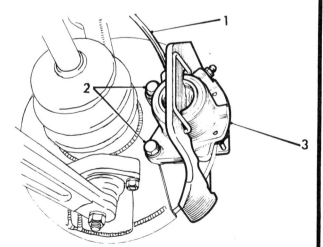

FIG. 9:11 DISC BRAKE CALIPER REMOVAL

No.	Description	No.	Description
1	Hydraulic pipe	3	Caliper unit
2	Caliper securing bolts		

3   Undo and remove the hub nut using a suitable socket or ring spanner, as this nut is very tight.

4   Support the weight of the lower suspension arm with a small jack or suitable packing.

5   Undo and remove the upper swivel ball joint two securing bolts and spring washers. Detach the brake pipe support bracket.

6   Undo and remove the two bolts and spring washers that secure the caliper to the steering swivel. Hang the caliper on wire or string so as not to strain the flexible pipe.

7   Using a universal three legged puller, with the feet located behind the wheel mounting flange (drive plate), and a suitable thrust pad, carefully draw the disc and drive plate assembly from the hub.

8   Mark the relative positions of the disc and drive plate so that they may be refitted in their original positions, and separate the two parts.

9   Thoroughly clean the disc and inspect for signs of deep scoring or excessive corrosion. If these are evident, the disc may be re-ground, but no more than a maximum total of 0.060 inch may be removed. It is, however, desirable to fit a new disc if at all possible.

10   Refitting the disc is the reverse sequence to removal. The hub nut must be tightened to a torque wrench setting of 150 lb ft.

11   Measure the run out at the outer periphery of the disc by means of feeler gauges positioned between the inside of the caliper and the disc. If the run out of the friction faces exceeds 0.009 inch, remove the disc and reposition it on the drive plate. Should the run-out be really bad, the disc is probably distorted due to overheating and a new one must be fitted.

13   Brake master cylinder (single) - removal and refitting

1   Apply the handbrake and chock the front wheels. Drain the fluid from the master cylinder reservoir and master cylinder by attaching a plastic bleed tube to one of the brake bleed screws, undo the screw one turn and then pump the fluid out into a clean glass container by means of the brake pedal. Hold the brake pedal against the floor at the end of each stroke and tighten the bleed nipple. When the pedal has returned to its normal position, loosen the bleed nipple and repeat the process until the master cylinder reservoir is empty.

2   Wipe the area around the four way hydraulic pipe union and, with an open ended spanner, disconnect the hydraulic pipe to the master cylinder at the four-way union. (Fig. 9:14).

3   Undo and remove the two nuts and spring washer securing the brake master cylinder to the rear of the servo unit, and lift away the master cylinder and hydraulic pipe.

4   Refitting is the reverse sequence to removal. Always start the union nut at the end of the short hydraulic pipe before finally tightening the master cylinder retaining nuts. It will be necessary to bleed the hydraulic system and full details will be found in Section 3.

14   Brake master cylinder (single) - dismantling and re-assembly

If a replacement master cylinder is to be fitted, it will be necessary to lubricate the seals before fitting to the car as they have a protective coating when originally assembled. Remove the blanking plug from the hydraulic pipe union seating. Ease back and remove the plunger dust cover. Inject clean hydraulic fluid into the master cylinder and operate the

piston several times so the fluid will spread over all the internal working surfaces.

If the master cylinder is to be dismantled after removal proceed as follows:

1   Carefully withdraw the complete plunger assembly from the bore. The assembly is separated by lifting the thimble leaf over the shouldered end of the plunger. The plunger seal may now be eased off using the fingers only (Fig. 9:15).

2   Depress the plunger return spring, allowing the valve stem to slide through the keyhole in the thimble thus releasing the tension in the spring.

3   Detach the valve spacer, taking care of the spacer spring washer which will be found located under the valve head.

4   Examine the bore of the cylinder carefully for any signs of scores or ridges. If this is found to be smooth all over, new seals can be fitted. If, however, there is any doubt of the condition of the bore, then a new master cylinder must be fitted.

5   If examination of the seals shows them to be apparently oversize or swollen, or very loose in the plunger, suspect oil contamination in the system. Ordinary lubricating oil will swell these rubber seals, and if one is found to be swollen, it is reasonable to assume that all seals in the braking system will need attention.

6   Thoroughly clean all parts in either Girling Cleaning Fluid or Industrial Methylated Spirits. Ensure that the by-pass ports are clear.

7   All components should be assembled wet by dipping in clean brake fluid. Fit a new valve seal the correct way round as shown in the inset to Fig. 9:15, so that the flat side is correctly seating on the valve head. Place the dished washer with the dome against the underside of the valve head. Hold it in position with the valve spacer, ensuring that the legs face towards the valve seal.

8   Replace the plunger return spring centrally on the spacer, insert the thimble into the spring, and depress until the valve stem engages in the keyhole in the thimble.

9   Ensure that the spring is central on the spacer before fitting a new plunger seal onto the plunger, with the flat face against the face of the plunger.

10   Insert the reduced end of the plunger into the thimble until the thimble engages under the shoulder of the plunger, and press home the thimble leaf.

11   Check that the master cylinder bore is clean and smear with clean brake fluid. With the plunger suitably wetted with brake fluid, carefully insert the assembly into the bore with the valve end first. Ease the lips of the plunger seal carefully into the bore.

12   The master cylinder is now ready for refitting to the car.

15   Brake master cylinder (tandem) - removal and refitting

1   Drain the tandem master cylinder and reservoir in a similar manner to that described for the single master cylinder. Full information will be found in Section 13:1.

2   Using an open ended spanner, undo the union connecting the master cylinder fluid pipe from the P D W A valve. This is the union on the top lefthand side when looking at the valve from the front of the car.

3   Undo and remove the two hydraulic pipe union nuts on the side of the tandem master cylinder.

4   Undo and remove the two nuts and spring washers securing the brake master cylinder to the rear of the servo unit and lift away the master cylinder.

5   Refitting is the reverse sequence to removal. Always

149

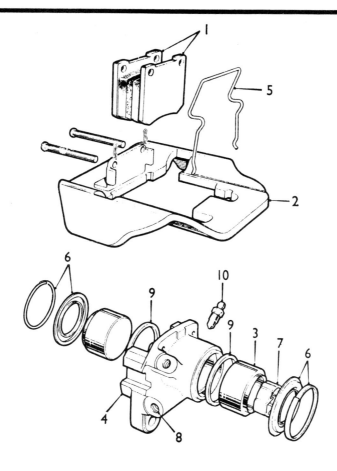

FIG. 9:12 DISC BRAKE CALIPER COMPONENTS

No.	Description	No.	Description	No.	Description	No.	Description
1	Brake pads	4	Cylinder body		cover	9	Piston seal
2	Yoke	5	Yoke spring	7	Bias spring	10	Bleed screw
3	Indirect piston	6	Dust cover retaining ring and	8	Hydraulic fluid inlet		

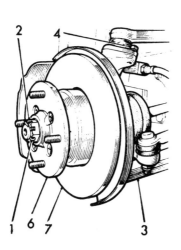
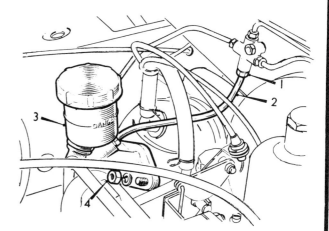

FIG. 9:13 FRONT BRAKE DISC REMOVAL

No.	Description	No.	Description
1	Split pin		curing bolts
2	Hub nut	5	Caliper securing bolts
3	Lower suspension arm	6	Drive plate
4	Upper swivel ball joint se-	7	Disc

FIG. 9:14 BRAKE MASTER CYLINDER REMOVAL

No.	Description	No.	Description
1	Union nut	3	Master cylinder and reservoir
2	Hydraulic pipe	4	Master cylinder fixing nut

start the union nuts before finally tightening the master cylinder retaining nuts. It will be necessary to bleed the hydraulic system and full details will be found in Section 3.

16 Brake master cylinder (tandem) - dismantling and reassembly

1   Refer to the introduction to Section 14 with regard to replacement master cylinders.
2   Undo and remove the two screws holding the reservoir to the master cylinder body. Lift away the reservoir. Using a suitable sized Allen key, or wrench, unscrew the tipping valve nut and lift away the seal. Using a suitable diameter rod, push the primary plunger down the bore, this operation enabling the tipping valve to be withdrawn (Fig. 9:16).
3   Using a compressed air jet, very carefully applied to the rear outlet pipe connection, blow out all the master cylinder internal components. Alternatively, shake out the parts. Take care that adequate precautions are taken to ensure all parts are caught as they emerge.
4   Separate the primary and secondary plungers from the intermediate spring. Use the fingers to remove the gland seal from the primary plunger.
5   The secondary plunger assembly should be separated by lifting the thimble leaf over the shouldered end of the plunger. Using the fingers, remove the seal from the secondary plunger.
6   Depress the secondary spring, allowing the valve stem to slide through the keyhole in the thimble, thus releasing the tension on the spring.
7   Detach the valve spacer, taking care of the spring washer which will be found located under the valve head.
8   Examine the bore of the cylinder carefully for any signs of scores or ridges. If this is found to be smooth all over new seals can be fitted. If, however, there is any doubt of the condition of the bore, then a new cylinder must be fitted.
9   If examination of the seals shows them to be apparently oversize, or swollen, or very loose on the plungers, suspect oil contamination in the system. Oil will swell these rubber seals, and if one is found to be swollen, it is reasonable to assume that all seals in the braking system will need attention.
10   Thoroughly clean all parts in either Girling Cleaning Fluid or Methylated Spirits. Ensure that the by-pass ports are clear.
11   All components should be assembled wet by dipping in clean brake fluid. Using fingers only, fit new seals to the primary and secondary plungers ensuring that they are the correct way round. Place the dished washer with the dome against the underside of the valve seat. Hold it in position with the valve spacer ensuring that the legs face towards the valve seal.
12   Replace the plunger return spring centrally on the spacer, insert the thimble into the spring and depress until the valve stem engages in the keyhole of the thimble.
13   Insert the reduced end of the plunger into the thimble, until the thimble engages under the shoulder of the plunger, and press home the thimble leaf. Replace the intermediate spring between the primary and secondary plungers.
14   Check that the master cylinder bore is clean and smear with clean brake fluid. With the complete assembly suitably wetted with brake fluid, carefully insert the assembly into the bore. Ease the lips of the plunger seals carefully into the bore. Push the assembly fully home.
15   Refit the tipping valve assembly, and seal, to the cylinder

bore and tighten the securing nut to a torque wrench setting of 35 to 45 lb ft. Replace the hydraulic fluid reservoir and tighten the two retaining screws.
16   The master cylinder is now ready for refitting to the servo unit. Bleed the complete hydraulic system and road test the car.

17 Vacuum servo unit - description

A vacuum servo unit is fitted into the brake hydraulic circuit in series with the master cylinder, to provide assistance to the driver when the brake pedal is depressed. This reduces the effort required by the driver to operate the brakes under all braking conditions.

The unit operates by vacuum obtained from the induction manifold and comprises basically a booster diaphragm, control valve, slave cylinder and a non-return valve.

The servo unit and hydraulic master cylinder are connected together so that the servo unit piston rod acts as the master cylinder pushrod. The driver's braking effort is transmitted through another pushrod to the servo unit piston and its built-in control system. The servo unit piston does not fit tightly into the cylinder, but has a strong diaphragm to keep its edges in constant contact with the cylinder wall, so assuring an air tight seal between the two pads. The forward chamber is held under vacuum conditions created in the inlet manifold of the engine and, during periods when the brake pedal is not in use, the controls open a passage to the rear chamber so placing it under vacuum conditions as well. When the brake pedal is depressed, the vacuum passage to the rear chamber is cut off and the chamber opened to atmospheric pressure. The consequent rush of air pushes the servo piston forward in the vacuum chamber and operates the main push rod to the master cylinder.

The controls are designed so that assistance is given under all conditions and, when the brakes are not required, vacuum in the rear chamber is established when the brake pedal is released. All air from the atmosphere entering the rear chamber is passed through a small air filter.

Under normal operating conditions the vacuum servo unit is very reliable and does not require overhaul except at very high mileages. In this case it is far better to obtain a service exchange unit, rather than repair the original unit.

18 Vacuum servo unit - removal and refitting

1   Wipe the area around the four way connector and then disconnect the hydraulic fluid pipe using an open ended spanner on the union nut (Fig. 9:17).
2   Slacken the clip securing the vacuum hose to the servo unit. Carefully draw the hose from its union.
3   Undo and remove the parcel shelf securing screws and then lift the parcel shelf sufficiently to give access to the brake pedal mountings.
4   Using a pair of pliers, extract the split pin in the end of the brake pedal to push rod clevis pin. Lift away the plain washer and withdraw the clevis pin.
5   Move the position of the accelerator pedal, so giving better access to the servo unit securing nuts. Undo and remove the four nuts and spring washers which hold the servo unit to the bulkhead.
6   The servo unit, complete with master cylinder, can now be lifted away from the engine compartment.

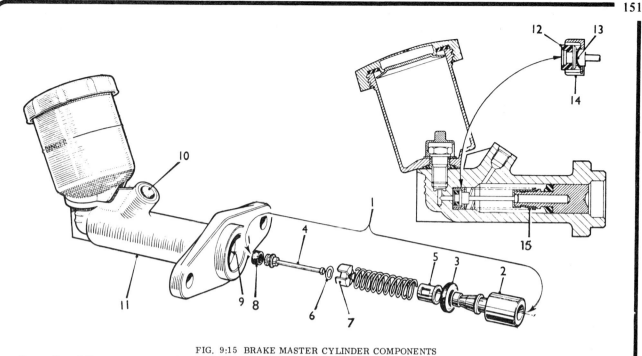

FIG. 9:15 BRAKE MASTER CYLINDER COMPONENTS

No.	Description	No.	Description	No.	Description	No.	Description
1	Piston assembly	6	Curved washer	10	Outlet port	13	Curved washer fitted in spacer
2	Piston	7	Spacer	11	Master cylinder body	14	Spacer
3	Piston seal	8	Valve seal	12	Valve seal correctly fitted on valve head	15	Thimble leaf depressed
4	Valve stem	9	Master cylinder bore				
5	Thimble						

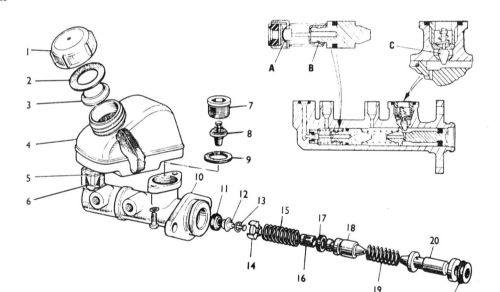

FIG. 9:16 BRAKE TANDEM MASTER CYLINDER COMPONENTS

No.	Description	No.	Description	No.	Description	No.	Description
1	Filler cap)	7	Securing nut	12	Valve stem	17	Seal
2	Gasket) assembly	8	Tipping valve	13	Spring washer - curved	18	Secondary plunger
3	Baffle)	9	Face seal	14	Valve spacer	19	Intermediate spring (black)
4	Reservoir - dual	10	Cylinder body	15	Secondary spring	20	Primary plunger
5	Circlip - internal	11	Valve seal	16	Spring retainer	21	Gland seal
6	Seal						

A Correct assembly of spring washer in centre valve

B Leaf of spring retainer

C As the brakes are applied the primary plunger moves down the cylinder and allows the tipping valve (C) to close the primary supply port. The assembly shows the unit in the off position.

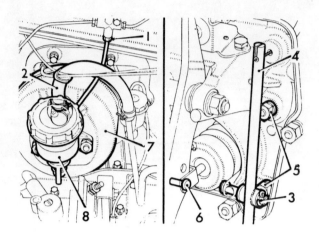

FIG. 9:17 VACUUM SERVO UNIT MOUNTING POINTS

No.	Description	No.	Description
1	Hydraulic pipe connected to four way connector	4	Accelerator pedal
2	Vacuum pipe	5	Servo unit mounting nuts
3	Split pin and washer - accelerator pedal	6	Brake pedal - clevis pin
		7	Servo unit
		8	Master cylinder

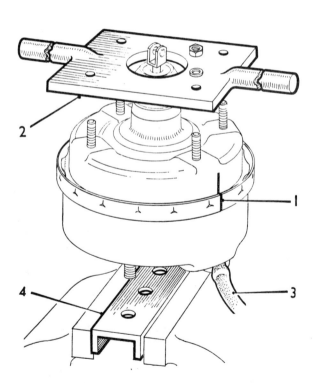

FIG. 9:18 SPECIAL TOOLS REQUIRED TO DISMANTLE GIRLING 'SUPER VAC' SERVO UNIT

No.	Description	No.	Description
1	Scribe marks	3	Vacuum applied
2	Lever	4	Base plate

7   Undo and remove the two nuts and spring washers securing the master cylinder to the servo unit and separate the two parts. Take care that the internal parts of the master cylinder do not fall out and also that no hydraulic fluid is spilled from the reservoir.

19 Girling 'Super-Vac' - dismantling, inspection and reassembly

Thoroughly clean the outside of the unit using a stiff brush and wipe with a non-fluffy rag. It cannot be too strongly emphasised that cleanliness is important when working on the servo. Before any attempt be made to dismantle, refer to Fig. 9:18 where it will be seen that two items of equipment are required. Firstly, a base plate must be made to enable the unit to be safely held in a vice. Secondly, a lever must be made similar to the form shown. Without these items it is impossible to dismantle satisfactorily.

To dismantle the unit proceed as follows:

1   Refer to Fig. 9:18 and, using a file or scriber, mark a line across the two halves of the unit to act as a datum for alignment.

2   Fit the previously made base plate into a firm vice and attach the unit to the plate using the master cylinder studs.

3   Fit the lever to the four studs on the rear shell as shown in Fig. 9:18.

4   Use a piece of long rubber hose and connect one end to the adaptor on the engine inlet manifold and the other end to the non-return valve. Start the engine and this will create a vacuum in the unit so drawing the two halves together.

5   Rotate the lever in an anticlockwise direction until the front shell indentations are in line with the recesses in the rim of the rear shell. Then press the lever assembly down firmly whilst an assistant stops the engine and quickly removes the vacuum pipe from the inlet manifold connector. Depress the operating rod so as to release the vacuum, whereupon the front (1) (Fig. 9:19) and rear halves should part. If necessary, use a soft faced hammer and lightly tap the front half to break the bond.

6   Lift away the rear shell followed by the diaphragm return spring (5), the dust cover, end cap and the filter. Also withdraw the diaphragm (9). Press down the valve rod (17) and shake out the valve retaining plate (21). Then separate the valve rod assembly from the diaphragm plate.

7   Gently ease the spring washer from the diaphragm plate and withdraw the pushrod (4) and reaction disc (22).

8   The seal and plate assembly in the end of the front shell are a press fit. It is recommended that, unless the seal is to be renewed, they be left in situ.

9   Thoroughly clean all parts in Girling Cleaning Fluid and wipe dry using a non-fluffy rag. Inspect all parts for signs of damage, stripped threads etc, and obtain new parts as necessary. All seals should be renewed and for this a 'Major Repair Kit' should be purchased. This kit will also contain two separate greases which must be used as directed, and not interchanged.

10   To reassemble first smear the seal (12) and bearing with grease numbered 64949008 and refit the rear shell (8) positioning it such that the flat face of the seal is towards the bearing. Press into position and refit the retainer (19).

11   Lightly smear the disc and hydraulic pushrod (4) with grease number 64949008. Refit the reaction disc (22) and pushrod (4) to the diaphragm plate (10) and press in the large spring washer. The small spring washer supplied in the 'Major Repair Kit' is not required. It is important that the

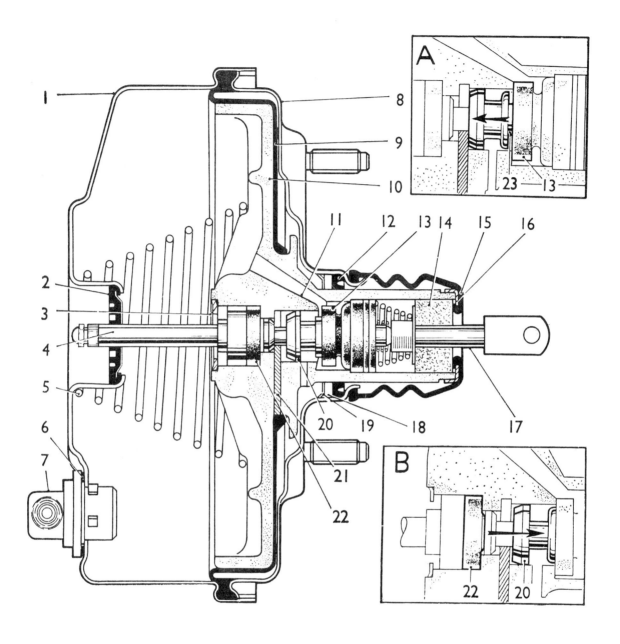

FIG. 9:19 GIRLING 'SUPER VAC' SERVO UNIT COMPONENT PARTS

No.	Description	No.	Description	No.	Description	No.	Description
1	Front shell	7	Non-return valve	13	Control valve	19	Retainer
2	Seal and plate assembly	8	Rear shell	14	Filter	20	Control piston
3	Retainer (sprag washer)	9	Diaphragm	15	Dust cover	21	Valve retaining plate
4	Push-rod – hydraulic	10	Diaphragm plate	16	End cap	22	Reaction disc
5	Diaphragm return spring	11	Vacuum port	17	Valve operating rod assembly	23	Atmospheric port
6	'O' ring	12	Seal	18	Bearing		

length of the pushrod (4) is not altered in any way and any attempt to move the adjustment bolt will strip the threads. If a new hydraulic pushrod has been required, the length will have to be reset. Details of this operation are given at the end of this Section.

12   Lightly smear the outer diameter of the diaphragm plate neck and the bearing surfaces of the valve plunger with grease number 64949008. Carefully fit the valve rod assembly into the neck of the diaphragm and fix with the retaining plate.

13   Fit the diaphragm into position and also the non-return valve (7) to the front shell (1). Next smear the seal and plate assembly with grease numbered 64949008 and press into the front shell (1) with the plate facing inwards.

14   Fit the front shell to the base plate and the lever to the rear shell. Reconnect the vacuum hose to the non-return valve and the adaptor on the engine inlet manifold. Position the diaphragm return spring in the front shell. Lightly smear the outer head of the diaphragm with grease numbered 64949009 and locate the diaphragm assembly in the rear shell. Position the rear shell assembly on the return spring and line up the previously made scribe marks.

15   The assistant should start the engine. Watching one's fingers very carefully, press the two halves of the unit together and, using the lever tool, turn clockwise to lock the two halves together. Stop the engine and disconnect the hose.

16   Press a new filter into the neck of the diaphragm plate, refit the end cap and position the dust cover onto the special lugs of the rear shell.

17   Hydraulic pushrod adjustment only applies if a new pushrod has been fitted. It will be seen from Fig. 9:20 that there is a bolt screwed into the end of the push rod. The amount of protrustion has to be adjusted in the following manner: remove the bolt and coat the threaded portion with Loctite Grade B. Reconnect the vacuum hose to the adaptor on the inlet valve and non-return valve. Start the engine and screw the prepared bolt into the end of the pushrod. Adjust the position of the bolt head so that it is 0.011 to 0.061 inch below the face of the front shell as shown by dimension 'A' in Fig. 9:20. Leave the unit for a minimum of 24 hours to allow the Loctite to set hard.

18   Refit the servo unit to the car as described in the previous Section. To test the servo unit for correct operation after overhaul, first start the engine and run for a minimum period of two minutes and then switch off. Wait for ten minutes and apply the footbrake very carefully, listening to hear the rush of air into the servo unit. This will indicate that vacuum was retained and, therefore, operating correctly.

---

20   Pressure differential warning actuator valve - removal, overhaul and refitting

---

1   Wipe the top of the brake hydraulic fluid reservoir and unscrew the cap. Place a piece of polythene over the top and refit the cap. This is to prevent hydraulic fluid syphoning out. For safety reasons disconnect the battery.

2   Detach the cable connector at the top of the pressure differential warning actuator valve (PDWA) switch (Fig. 9:21).

3   Wipe the area around the P D W A valve assembly and, using an open ended spanner, unscrew the union nut securing the rear brake fluid pipe to the valve, followed by the master cylinder to valve rear brake pipe, front brake fluid pipe and finally the master cylinder to valve front brake pipe.

4   Undo the P D W A valve securing bolt and lift away the

bolt, spring washer and the valve itself.

5   Wipe down the outside of the valve and then unscrew the switch from the top of the body. Tip the valve upside down and recover the ball bearing located under the switch (Fig.9:22)

6   Unscrew and remove the small end plug and copper gasket. The gasket should not be re-used but a new one must be obtained.

7   Carefully shake out the large piston assembly.

8   Unscrew and remove the large end plug and copper gasket. The gasket should not be re-used but a new one must be obtained.

9   Carefully shake out the small piston assembly.

10   Using the fingers, or a piece of non-metal tapered rod such as a knitting needle, remove the seals from the pistons.

11   Examine the bore of the valve carefully for any signs of scores, ridges of corrosion. If this is found to be smooth all over, new seals can be fitted. If there is any doubt of the condition of the bore, a new valve must be obtained.

12   If examination of the two seals shows them to be apparently oversize or swollen, or very loose on the pistons, suspect oil contamination in the system. Oil will swell these rubber seals, and if one is found to be swollen, it is reasonable to assume that all seals in the braking system will need attention.

13   Thoroughly clean all parts in either Girling Cleaning Fluid or Industrial Methylated spirits.

14   All parts must be assembled wet by dipping in clean brake fluid. Fit new seals to the pistons with the larger diameter of the seals facing towards the small diameter end of the pistons.

15   Insert the long piston into the bore until the radial groove is opposite the electrical switch aperture. The piston must not be pushed down too far so that the seal passes the switch and ball bearing aperture, otherwise the seal will be damaged and a further new one will have to be fitted.

16   Drop the ball bearing into place and move the piston slightly, if necessary, until the ball bearing is seating in the radial groove. Refit the electric switch and tighten to a torque wrench setting of 2 to 2.5 lb ft.

17   Screw in the small end plug, fitted with a new copper gasket, and tighten to a torque wrench setting of 16 to 20 lb ft.

18   Carefully insert the short piston into the bore and finally screw in the large end plug with a new copper gasket. Tighten the end plug to a torque wrench setting of 16 to 20 lb ft.

19   Refitting is the reverse sequence to removal. It will be necessary to bleed the complete hydraulic system and full information will be found in Section 3.

---

21   Pressure reducing valve - removal, overhaul and refitting

---

1   Wipe the top of the brake hydraulic fluid reservoir and unscrew the cap. Place a piece of polythene over the top and refit the cap. This is to prevent hydraulic fluid syphoning out.

2   Wipe the area around the valve located as shown in Fig. 9:23 and using an open ended spanner detach the two brake pipes from the valve.

3   Undo and remove the valve securing bolt and spring washer.

4   Carefully disconnect the flexible hose from the connector on the radius arm as described in Section 22.

5   The valve and flexible hose may now be lifted away from under the car.

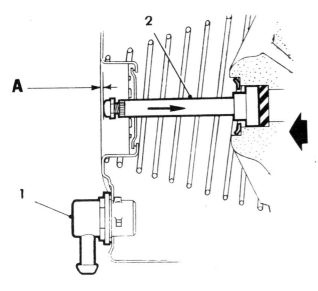

FIG. 9:20 THE CORRECT HYDRAULIC PUSH-ROD SETTING

No.	Description	No.	Description
A	Push-rod setting 0.011 to 0.016 inch below face	1	Vacuum applied
		2	Push-rod against reaction disc

FIG. 9:21 PRESSURE DIFFERENTIAL WARNING ACTUATOR VALVE

No.	Description	No.	Description
1	P D W A valve	5	Master cylinder to P D W A valve front brake fluid pipe
2	Lucar connector	6	Front brake fluid pipe
3	Master cylinder to P D W A valve rear brake fluid pipe	7	Valve securing bolt
4	Rear brake fluid pipe		

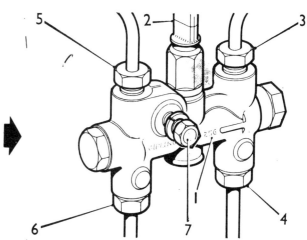

FIG. 9:22 PRESSURE DIFFERENTIAL WARNING ACTUATOR VALVE. COMPONENT PARTS

No.	Description	No.	Description
1	Electrical switch and operating ball	4	Large end plug and copper gasket
2	Small end plug and copper gasket	5	Small piston
3	Large piston	6	Piston seals

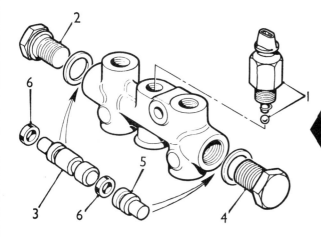

FIG. 9:23 BRAKE PRESSURE REDUCING VALVE

No.	Description	No.	Description
1	Brake pipes to valve		bracket on radius arm
2	Valve mounting bolt	4	Valve
3	Flexible hose connection to		

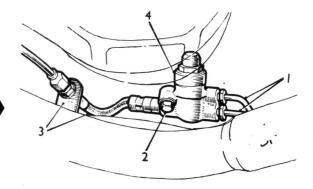

6   Wipe the outside of the valve and then hold the valve securely between soft faces in a vice. Unscrew and remove the end plug and lift out the tapered spring (Fig. 9:24).

7   Lift away the piston assembly from the bore of the valve followed by the spring seat and light spring.

8   Carefully hold the piston in a vice, again using the soft faces, in such a manner that the sleeve end is uppermost.

9   Unscrew and remove the valve sleeve securing nut and then withdraw the valve sleeve from the piston and shake out the valve plate.

10   Using the fingers, or a piece of non-metal rod such as a knitting needle, remove the seals from the piston, sleeve and end plug.

11   Slide off the valve bias clip from the valve sleeve and recover the ball bearing from the sleeve.

12   Remove the seal spacer, gland seal and rod guide from the end plug.

13   Refer to Section 20, paragraphs 11 to 13 and examine the parts as described.

14   All parts must be assembled wet by dipping in clean brake fluid. First fit the rod guide to the end plug with the large diameter of the rod guide uppermost.

15   Next fit the gland seal to the end plug making sure that the small diameter of the seal registers against the rod guide.

16   Fit the seal spacer onto the gland seal so that the flat face of the spacer is uppermost.

17   Carefully fit the new seals to the end plug, piston and valve sleeve.

18   Place the valve plate in the valve sleeve with the tapered edge of the valve plate facing upwards. Holding the valve plate in position, insert the threaded end of the piston into the opposite end of the sleeve and through the hole in the valve plate. Screw in the locknut and tighten to a torque wrench setting of 3 to 4 lb ft.

19   Drop the ball bearing into the port in the valve sleeve and retain in position by sliding the valve bias clip onto the sleeve and over the ball bearing.

20   Carefully insert the piston assembly into the bore of the reducing valve. Insert the light spring into the sleeve and position the spring seat on the spring.

21   Ease the reduced end of the tapered spring over the projecting piston and slide down until it registers in the spring seat. Refit the end plug and tighten to a torque wrench setting of 25 to 35 lb ft.

22   Refitting the reducing valve is the reverse sequence to removal. It will be necessary to bleed the complete hydraulic system and full details will be found in Section 3.

---

22   Flexible hose - inspection, removal and refitting

Inspect the condition of the flexible hydraulic hoses leading from the brake and clutch metal pipes. If any are swollen, damaged, cut or chafed, they must be renewed.

1   Unscrew the metal pipe union nut from its connection to the flexible hose, and then, holding the hexagon on the hose with a spanner, unscrew the attachment nut and washer (Fig. 9:25).

2   The end of the flexible hose can now be withdrawn from the mounting bracket and will be quite free.

3   Disconnect the flexible hose from the slave or wheel cylinder by unscrewing it, using a spanner.

4   Refitting is the reverse sequence to removal.

FIG. 9:25 FLEXIBLE HOSE REMOVAL

No.	Description	No.	Description
1	Union nut	4	Mounting bracket
2	Flexible hose locknut	5	Flexible hose
3	Shakeproof washer		

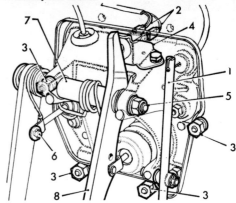

FIG. 9:26 BRAKE PEDAL REMOVAL - PART I

No.	Description	No.	Description
1	Accelerator pedal	4	Brake light switch
2	Brake light switch Lucar terminals	5	Pedal pivot nut
3	Pedal mounting bracket mounting nuts	6	Clutch pedal clevis pin
		7	Pedal pivot
		8	Brake pedal

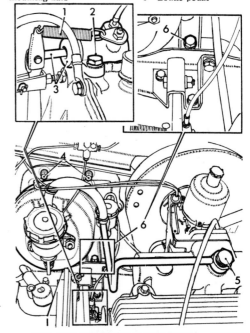

FIG. 9:27 BRAKE PEDAL REMOVAL - PART II

No.	Description	No.	Description
1	Clutch return spring	4	Mounting bracket top bolts
2	Clutch slave cylinder securing bolt	5	Servo unit vacuum pipe connection to manifold
3	Clutch slave cylinder and push rod	6	Mounting bracket to subframe securing bolt

23 Brake pedal – removal and refitting

1   Refer to Section 18 and remove the servo unit and brake master cylinder from the bulkhead.

2   Refer to Chapter 3/20 and remove the accelerator pedal.

3   Working under the dashboard, release the speedometer cable from the rear of the speedometer head.

4   Detach the two cable connectors to the brake light switch located at the top of the pedal arm (Fig. 9.26).

5   Undo and remove the four nuts and spring washers that secure the pedal mounting bracket to the bulkhead.

6   Slacken the clip securing the servo vacuum hose to the inlet manifold adaptor and remove the vacuum hose (Fig. 9:27).

7   Note which way round the clutch lever return spring is fitted and detach the spring from the clutch slave cylinder.

8   Undo and remove the two bolts securing the clutch slave cylinder to the clutch housing. Carefully withdraw the slave cylinder from the pushrod and tie back out of the way.

9   Undo and remove the two top mounting bracket retaining bolts and spring washers.

10   Undo and remove the mounting bracket to the sub-frame.

11   Release the speedometer cable from the transmission casing.

12   Carefully manipulate the pedal mounting bracket from the body aperture.

13   To release the brake pedal, undo and remove the nut and washer from the pedal pivot shaft.

14   Extract the split pin and remove the plain washer and clevis pin from the clutch pedal to pushrod yoke.

15   Using a suitable diameter soft metal drift, drive the pivot shaft and clutch pedal from the mounting bracket. The brake pedal may now be lifted away.

16   Refitting is the reverse sequence to removal. Lubricate the clutch, brake and accelerator pedal pivots with a little Castrol LM Grease. It will be necessary to bleed the brake hydraulic system and full information will be found in Section 3.

24 Brake stop light switch – removal and refitting

1   For safety reasons disconnect the battery terminals.

2   Disconnect the two cable connectors from the brake light switch located at the top of the brake pedal.

3   Undo and remove the two bolts with spring washers securing the switch mounting bracket to the pedal mounting bracket. Lift away the bracket, complete with switch.

4   To separate the switch from the bracket first, using a pair of pliers, withdraw the long switch locking split pin. Finally unscrew the switch from the bracket.

5   To refit the switch, screw it into the bracket until one complete thread of the switch housing is visible on the pedal side of the mounting bracket. Thereafter, refitting is the reverse sequence to removal.

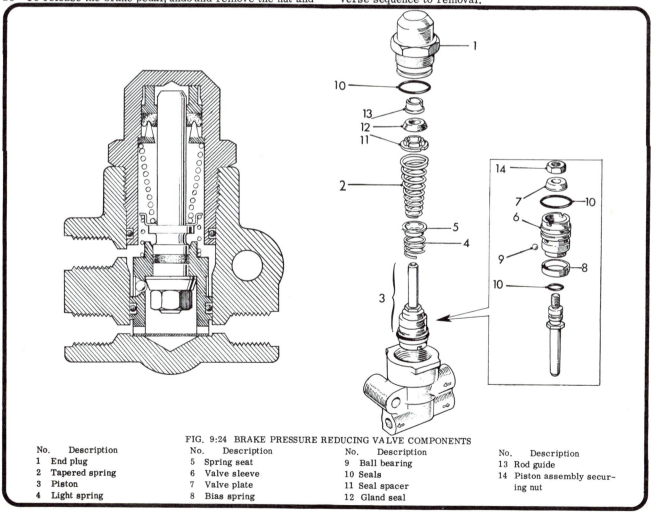

FIG. 9:24 BRAKE PRESSURE REDUCING VALVE COMPONENTS

No.	Description	No.	Description	No.	Description	No.	Description
1	End plug	5	Spring seat	9	Ball bearing	13	Rod guide
2	Tapered spring	6	Valve sleeve	10	Seals	14	Piston assembly securing nut
3	Piston	7	Valve plate	11	Seal spacer		
4	Light spring	8	Bias spring	12	Gland seal		

Cause	Trouble	Remedy
SYMPTOM: PEDAL TRAVELS ALMOST TO FLOORBOARDS BEFORE BRAKES OPERATE		
Leaks and air bubbles in hydraulic system	Brake fluid level too low	Top up master cylinder reservoir. Check for leaks.
	Wheel cylinder or caliper leaking	Dismantle wheel cylinder or caliper, clean fit new rubbers and bleed brakes.
	Master cylinder leaking (Bubbles in master cylinder fluid)	Dismantle master cylinder, clean, and fit new rubbers. Bleed brakes.
	Brake flexible hose leaking	Examine and fit new hose if old hose leaking Bleed brakes.
	Brake line fractured	Replace with new brake pipe. Bleed brakes.
	Brake system unions loose	Check all unions in brake system and tighten as necessary. Bleed brakes.
Normal wear	Linings over 75% worn	Fit replacement shoes and brake linings.
Incorrect adjustment	Drum brakes badly out of adjustment	Jack up car and adjust rear brakes.
	Master cylinder push rod out or adjustment causing too much pedal free movement	Reset to manufacturer's specifications.
SYMPTOM: BRAKE PEDAL FEELS SPRINGY		
Brake lining renewal	New linings not yet bedded-in	Use brakes gently until springy pedal feeling leaves.
	Brake drums or discs badly worn and weak or cracked	Fit new brake drums or discs.
Lack of maintenance	Master cylinder securing nuts loose	Tighten master cylinder securing nuts. Ensure spring washers are fitted.
SYMPTOM: BRAKE PEDAL FEELS SPONGY & SOGGY		
Leaks or bubbles in hydraulic system	Wheel cylinder or caliper leaking	Dismantle wheel cylinder or caliper, clean, fit new rubbers, and bleed brakes.
	Master cylinder leaking (Bubbles in master cylinder reservoir)	Dismantle master cylinder, clean, and fit new rubbers and bleed brakes. Replace cylinder if internal walls scored.
	Brake pipe line or flexible hose leaking	Fit new pipeline or hose.
	Unions in brake system loose	Examine for leaks, tighten as necessary.
SYMPTOM: BRAKES UNEVEN & PULLING TO ONE SIDE		
Oil or grease leaks	Linings and brake drums or discs contaminated with oil, grease, or hydraulic fluid.	Ascertain and rectify source of leak, clean brake drums, fit new linings.
Lack of maintenance	Tyre pressures unequal	Check and inflate as necessary.
	Radial ply tyres fitted at one end of car only	Fit radial ply tyres of the same make to all four wheels.
	Brake backplate caliper or disc loose	Tighten backplate caliper or disc securing nuts and bolts.
	Brake shoes or pads fitted incorrectly	Remove and fit shoes or pads correct way round.
	Different type of linings fitted at each wheel	Fit the linings specified by the manufacturer's all round.
	Anchorages for front or rear suspension loose	Tighten front and rear suspension pick-up points including spring locations.
	Brake drums or discs badly worn, cracked or distorted	Fit new brake drums or discs.
SYMPTOM: BRAKES TEND TO BIND, DRAG, OR LOCK-ON		
Incorrect adjustment	Brake shoes adjusted too tightly	Slacken off rear brake shoe adjusters two clicks.
	Handbrake cable over-tightened	Slacken off handbrake cable adjustment.
	Master cylinder push rod out of adjustment giving too little brake pedal free movement	Reset to manufacturer's specifications.

Fault Finding Chart - Braking system

Cause	Trouble	Remedy
Wear or dirt in hydraulic system or incorrect fluid	Reservoir vent hole in cap blocked with dirt	Clean and blow through hole.
	Master cylinder by-pass port restricted - brakes seize in 'on' position	Dismantle, clean, and overhaul master cylinder. Bleed brakes.
	Wheel cylinder seizes in 'on' position	Dismantle, clean and overhaul wheel cylinder. Bleed brakes.
Mechanical wear	Rear brake shoe pull off springs broken, stretched or loose	Examine springs and replace if worn or loose.
Incorrect brake assembly	Rear brake shoe pull off springs fitted wrong way round, omitted, or wrong type used	Examine, and rectify as appropriate.
Neglect	Handbrake system rusted or seized in the 'on' position	Apply 'Plus Gas' to free, clean and lubricate.

Chapter 10   Electrical system

Contents

Specifications

System	12 volt, negative earth
Fuses	17 amp (3.5 amp blow rating)

Battery

Type...	Lucas D9/DZ9, A9/AZ9, or A11/AZ11	
Capacity at 20 hr rate	40 amp - hr. or 50 amp - hr	
	A9/AZ9	A11/AZ11
Charge rate	3.5 amps	5 amps
Maximum charge	3.6 amps	4.5 amps
Initial charge	2.5 amps	3 amps
Electrolyte to fill battery	0.72 pint	0.9 pint

Dynamo

Type...	Lucas C40/1
Maximum output	22 ± 1 amps
Cut-in speed	1,581 rpm at 13.5 volts
Minimum brush length	$9/32$ in (7.14mm).

Starter motor

Type:

Early cars	Lucas M35G
Later cars - 1500...	Lucas M35J
1750	Lucas M35J pre-engaged

Cold countries:

1500	Lucas 35J pre-engaged
1750	Lucas 2M100 pre-engaged

Lucas M35G:

Brush spring tension	15 to 25 oz (425 to 709 gm)
Minimum brush length	5/16 in (7.9 mm)

Light running:

Speed	9500 to 11000 rpm
Current...	45 amps
Voltage	8.8 to 9.2 volts
Lock Torque...	11 lb ft (1.38 Kgm)
Current...	420 to 440 amps
Voltage	7.8 to 7.4 volts

Lucas M35J

Brush spring tension	28 oz (0.8 Kg)
Minimum brush length	3/8 in (9.5 mm)
Minimum commutator thickness	0.08 in (2.05 mm)
Lock torque	7 lb ft (0.97 Kgm) with 350-375 amps
Torque at 1000 rpm	4.4 lb ft (0.61 Kgm) with 260 to 275 amps
Light running current	65 amps at 8000 to 10000 rpm

Lucas M35J - Pre-engaged

Brush spring tension	28 oz (0.8 Kg)
Minimum brush length	3/8 in (9.5 mm)
Minimum commutator thickness	0.08 in (2.05 mm)
Lock torque	7 lb ft (0.97 Kgm) with 350 to 375 amps
Torque at 1000 rpm	4.4 lb ft (0.61 Kgm) with 260 to 275 amps
Light running current	65 amp at 8000 to 10000 rpm
Maximum armature end-float	0.010 in (0.25 mm)

Solenoid:

Closing (series) winding resistance	0.21 to 0.025 ohms
Hold-on (shunt) winding resistance	0.9 to 1.1 ohms

Lucas 2M100 - Pre-engaged:

Brush spring tension	36 oz (1.02 Kg)
Minimum brush length	0.375 in (9.5 mm)
Minimum commutator thickness	0.140 in (3.5 mm)
Lock torque	14.4 lb ft (2.02 Kgm) with 463 amps
Torque at 1000 rpm	7.3 lb ft (1.02 Kgm) with 300 amps
Light running current	40 amp at 6000 rpm (approx)
Maximum armature end-float	0.010 in (0.25 mm)

Solenoid:

Closing (series) winding resistance	0.25 to 0.27 ohm
Field resistance	6.0 ohms at 20°C (68°F)
Brush spring tension	20 to 34 oz (567 to 964 gms)
Brush - minimum length	$\frac{1}{4}$ inch (6.5 mm)
Pulley ratio	1.2 : 1

Control unit

System	Current - voltage control
Type...	Lucas RB 340
Setting at 20°C (68°F) 3000 RPM dynamo	(14.5 to 15.5 volts) (14.7 to 15.3 volts)
Cut-in voltage...	12.7 to 13.3 volts
Drop-off voltage	9.5 to 11.5 volts

Air gap settings:

	Prior to 37563	37563 onwards
Voltage and current regulator	0.054 ± 0.002 in (1.37 ± 0.05 mm)	0.022 ± 0.003 in (0.559 ± 0.08 mm)
Cut-out relay	0.040 ± 0.005 in (1.02 ± 0.13 mm)	0.030 ± 0.005 in (0.76 ± 0.13 mm)

Hold on (shunt) winding resistance   ... ...   0.76 to 0.80 ohm

Wiper motor:

Type...	Lucas 14W two speed, self switching
Armature end-float...	0.004 to 0.008 in (0.1 to 0.2 mm)
Running current-light	1.5 amps at 13.5 volts
Resistance: Armature winding	0.27 to 0.35 ohm at 16° C (60°F)
Brush length (minimum)...	3/16 in (4.8 mm)
Brush spring tension	5 to 7 oz (150 to 210 gm)
Arm pressure on spring...	11 to 13 oz (310 to 370 gm)

Horns

Type...	Lucas 9H or 6H
Maximum current consumption:	
9H	4 amps
6H	3 amps

Bulbs

	BLMC Part Number	Watts
Headlamp (LHD - except France and North America)	GLB 410	45/40
Headlamp LHD - France - vertical dip - yellow	GLB 411	45/40
Sealed beam headlamp unit (RHD left dip)	GLV 101	60/45
Sidelamp and flasher repeater	GLB 989	6
Direction indicator...	GLB 382	21
Tail and stop lamps	GLB 380	6/21
Rear number plate lamp...	GLB 207	6
Reverse lamp	BFS 273	21
Interior lamp	GLB 254	6
Panel and warning lamp...	37H 2139	2.2

1   General description

The electrical system is of the 12 volt negative earth type and the major components comprise a 12 volt battery of which the negative terminal is earthed; a voltage regulator and cut-out; a Lucas dynamo which is fitted to the front grille side of the engine and is driven from the crankshaft pulley; and a starter motor which is mounted on the same side of the engine as the dynamo.

The battery supplies a steady amount of current for the ignition, lighting and other electrical circuits and provides a reserve of electricity when the current consumed by the electrical equipment exceeds that being produced by the dynamo.

The dynamo is of the two brush type and works in conjunction with the voltage regulator and cut-out. The dynamo is cooled by a multi-bladed fan mounted behind the dynamo pulley which blows air through cooling holes in the dynamo end brackets. The output from the dynamo is controlled by the regulator which ensures a high output if the battery is in a low state of charge or the demands from the electrical equipment high, and a low output if the battery is fully charged and there is little demand from the electrical equipment.

When fitting electrical accessories to cars with a negative earth system it is important, if they contain Silicone Diodes or Transistors, that they are connected correctly, otherwise serious damage may result to the components concerned. Items such as radios, tape recorders, electronic ignition systems, electronic tachometer, automatic dipping, etc should all be checked for correct polarity.

It is important that the battery positive lead is always disconnected if the battery is to be boost charged or if body repairs are to be carried out using electric arc welding equipment, otherwise serious damage can be caused to the more delicate instruments.

2   Battery - removal and replacement

1   The battery is in a special carrier fitted on the right hand wing valance of the engine compartment. It should be removed once every three months for cleaning and testing. Disconnect the positive then the negative leads from the battery terminals by slackening the clamp retaining nuts and bolts or by unscrewing the retaining screws if terminal caps are fitted instead of clamps (Fig. 10:1).

2   Unscrew the clamp bar retaining nuts and lower to the side of the battery. Carefully lift the battery out of its compartment and hold it vertically to ensure that none of the electrolyte is spilled.

3   Replacement is a direct reversal of this procedure. NOTE: Replace the negative lead before the positive lead and smear the terminals with vaseline to prevent corrosion. NEVER use an ordinary grease.

3   Battery - maintenance and inspection

1   Normal weekly battery maintenance consists of checking the electrolyte level of each cell to ensure that the separators are covered by $\frac{1}{4}$ inch of electrolyte. If the level has fallen, top up the battery using distilled water only. Do not overfill. If the battery is overfilled or any electrolyte spilled, immediately wipe away the excess as electrolyte attacks and corrodes any metal it comes into contact with very rapidly.

2   If the battery is of the "Pacemaker" design (Types A9, AZ9, A11, AZ11) a special topping up procedure is necessary as follows:

a)   The electrolyte levels are visible through the translucent battery case or may be checked by fully raising the vent cover and tilting it to one side. The electrolyte level in each cell must be kept such that the separator plates are just covered. To avoid flooding, the battery must not be topped up within half an hour of it having been charged from any source other than from the generating system fitted to the car.

b) To top up the levels in each cell, raise the vent cover and pour distilled water into the trough until all the rectangular filling slots are full of distilled water and the bottom of the trough is just covered. Wipe the cover seating grooves dry and press the cover firmly into position. The correct quantity of distilled water will automatically be distributed to each cell.

c) The vent must be kept closed at all times except when being topped up.

3   As well as keeping the terminals clean and covered with vaseline, the top of the battery and especially the top of the cells should be kept clean and dry. This helps to prevent corrosion and ensures that the battery does not become partially discharged by leakage through dampness and dirt.

4   Once every three months remove the battery and inspect the battery securing nuts, battery clamp, tray and battery leads, for corrosion. (White fluffy deposit on the metal which is brittle to touch). If any corrosion is found, clean off the deposit with ammonia and paint over the clean metal with an anti-rust, anti-acid paint.

5   At the same time inspect the battery case for cracks. If a crack is found, clean and plug it with one of the proprietary compounds made for this purpose. If leakage through the crack has been excessive then it will be necessary to refill the appropriate cell with fresh electrolyte as described below. Cracks are frequently caused at the top of the battery case by pouring in distilled water in the middle of winter, AFTER instead of BEFORE a run. This gives the water no chance to mix with the electrolyte and so the former freezes and splits the battery case.

6   If topping up the battery becomes excessive and the case has been inspected for cracks that could cause leakage, but none are found, the battery is being overcharged and the voltage regulator will have to be checked and reset.

7   With the battery on the bench at the three monthly interval check, measure the specific gravity with a hydrometer to determine the state of charge and condition of the electrolyte. There should be very little variation between the different cells and if a variation in excess of 0.025 is present it will be due to either:

a)   Loss of electrolyte from the battery at some time caused by spilling or a leak, resulting in a drop in the specific gravity of the electrolyte when the deficiency was replaced with distilled water instead of fresh electrolyte.

b)   An internal short circuit caused by buckling of the plates or similar malady pointing to the likelihood of total battery failure in the near future.

8   The specific gravity of the electrolyte for fully charged conditions at the electrolyte temperatures indicated, is listed in Table A. The specific gravity of a fully discharged battery at different temperatures of the electrolyte is given in Table B.

Table A
Specific gravity - battery fully charged

1.268 at	100°F or 38°C	electrolyte temperature	
1.272 at	90°F or 32°C	"	"
1.276 at	80°F or 27°C	"	"
1.280 at	70°F or 21°C	"	"
1.284 at	60°F or 16°C	"	"
1.288 at	50°F or 10°C	"	"
1.292 at	40°F or 4°C	"	"
1.296 at	30°F or -1.5°C	"	"

Table B
Specific gravity - battery fully discharged

1.098 at	100°F or 38°C	electrolyte temperature	
1.102 at	90°F or 32°C	"	"
1.106 at	80°F or 27°C	"	"
1.110 at	70°F or 21°C	"	"
1.114 at	60°F or 16°C	"	"
1.118 at	50°F or 10°C	"	"
1.122 at	40°F or 4°C	"	"
1.126 at	30°F or -1.5°C	"	"

4   Battery - electrolyte replenishment

1   If the battery is in a fully charged state and one of the cells maintains a specific gravity reading which is 0.025 or more lower than the others and a check of each cell has been made with a special cadmium rod type voltmeter to check for short circuits, then it is likely that electrolyte has been lost from the cell with the low reading at some time.

2   Top up the cell with a solution of 1 part sulphuric acid to 2.5 parts of water. If the cell is already fully topped up draw some electrolyte out with a pipette.

3   When mixing the sulphuric acid and water NEVER ADD WATER TO SULPHURIC ACID - always pour the acid slowly onto the water in a glass container. IF WATER IS ADDED TO SULPHURIC ACID IT WILL EXPLODE.

4   Continue to top up the cell with the freshly made electrolyte and then recharge the battery and check the hydrometer readings.

5   Battery charging

1   When heavy demand is placed upon the battery, such as when starting from cold, and much electrical equipment is continually in use, it is a good idea occasionally to have the battery fully charged from an external source at the rate of 3.5 to 4 amps.

2   Continue to charge the battery at this rate until no further rise in specific gravity is noted over a four hour period.

3   Alternatively, a trickle charger, charging at the rate of 1.5 amps can be safely used overnight.

4   Except for topping up, the vent on "Pacemaker" type batteries must be kept closed. The electrolyte will flood over if the cover is raised while the battery is being trickle or fast charged.

5   Fast charging must only be undertaken in extreme circumstances and must not exceed 40 amps for A9 or AZ9 batteries, or 50 amps for A11 or AZ11 batteries, for a maximum period of one hour.

6   When checking or testing a "Pacemaker" type battery, a single cell heavy duty discharge tester cannot be used.

7   Whilst charging a battery, the temperature of the electrolyte should never exceed 100°F.

6   Dynamo - maintenance

1   Routine maintenance consists of checking the tension of the fan belt, and lubricating the dynamo rear bearing once every 6,000 miles.

2   The fan belt should be tight enough to ensure no slip between the belt and the dynamo pulley. If a shrieking noise comes from the engine when the unit is accelerated rapidly, it is likely that it is the fan belt slipping. On the other hand,

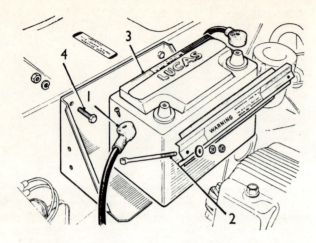

FIG. 10:1 BATTERY AND TRAY REMOVAL AND REFITTING

No.	Description	No.	Description
1	Battery terminals	3	Battery
2	Battery retaining bracket securing bolts	4	Battery tray securing bolts

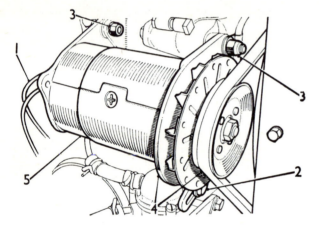

FIG. 10:2 DYNAMO MOUNTING POINTS

No.	Description	No.	Description
1	Electric cables to rear of dynamo		tings
2	Adjustment link securing bolt	4	Dynamo front cover and fan belt
3	Upper front and rear moun-	5	Dynamo

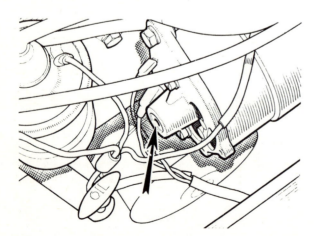

Fig. 10:3 Dynamo rear bearing lubrication

the belt must not be too taut or the bearings will wear rapidly and cause dynamo failure or bearing seizure. Ideally $\frac{1}{2}$ inch of total free movement should be available at the fan belt midway between the fan and the dynamo.

3   To adjust the fan belt tension, slightly slacken the three dynamo retaining bolts, and swing the dynamo on the upper two bolts outwards to increase the tension, and inwards to lower it (Fig. 10:2).

4   It is best to leave the bolts fairly tight so that considerable effort has to be used to move the dynamo, otherwise it is difficult to get the correct setting. If the dynamo is being moved outwards to increase the tension and the bolts have only been slackened a little, a long spanner acting as a lever, placed behind the dynamo with the lower end resting against the block, works very well in moving the dynamo outwards. Re-tighten the dynamo bolts and check that the dynamo pulley is correctly aligned with the fan belt.

5   Lubrication on the dynamo consists of inserting three drops of engine oil in the small oil hole in the centre of the commutator end bracket. This lubricates the rear bearing (Fig. 10:3). The front bearing is pre-packed with grease and requires no attention.

7   Dynamo testing in position

1   If, with the engine running, no charge comes from the dynamo, or the charge is very low, first check that the fan belt is in place and is not slipping. Then check that the leads from the control box to the dynamo are firmly attached and that one has not come loose from its terminal.

2   The lead from the 'D' terminal on the dynamo should be connected to the 'D' terminal on the control box, and similarly the 'F' terminals on the dynamo and control box should also be connected together. Check that this is so and that the leads have not been incorrectly fitted.

3   Make sure none of the electrical equipment such as the lights or radio, is on, and then pull the leads off the dynamo terminals marked 'D' and 'F'. Join the terminals together with a short length of wire.

4   Attach to the centre of this length of wire the negative clip of a 0-20 volts voltmeter and run the other clip to earth on the dynamo yoke. Start the engine and allow it to idle at approximately 750 rpm. At this speed the dynamo should give a reading of about 15 volts on the voltmeter. There is no point in raising the engine speed above a fast idle as the reading will then be inaccurate.

5   If no reading is recorded then check the brushes and brush connections. If a very low reading of approximately 1 volt is observed then the field winding may be suspect.

6   If a reading of between 4 to 6 volts is recorded it is likely that the armature winding is at fault.

7   With the Lucas C40-1 windowless yoke dynamo, it must be removed and dismantled before the brushes and commutator can be attended to.

8   If the voltmeter shows a good reading, then with the temporary link still in position, connect both leads from the control box to 'D' and 'F' on the dynamo ('D' to 'D' and 'F' to 'F'). Release the lead from the 'D' terminal at the control box end and clip one lead from the voltmeter to the end of the cable. and the other lead to a good earth. With the engine running at the same speed as previously, an identical voltage to that recorded at the dynamo should be noted on the voltmeter. If no voltage is recorded there is a break in the wire. If the voltage is the same as recorded at the dynamo then check the 'F' lead in a similar fashion. If both readings are the same

as at the dynamo then it will be necessary to test the control box.

8   Dynamo - removal and replacement

1   Undo and remove the bolt from the adjustment link.
2   Slacken the two mounting bolts and nuts and push the dynamo towards the engine. Lift the fan belt from the pulley.
3   Remove the mounting nuts and bolts and lift away the dynamo.
4   Replacement is a reversal of the above procedure. Do not finally tighten the retaining bolts and adjustment link bolt until the fan belt has been tensioned correctly.

9   Dynamo - dismantling and inspection

1   Mount the dynamo in a vice and unscrew and remove the two through bolts from the c o m m u t a t o r end bracket (see photo).
2   Mark the commutator end bracket and the dynamo casing so the end bracket can be replaced in its original position. Pull the end bracket off the armature shaft. NOTE: Some versions of the dynamo may have a raised pip on the edge of the casing. If so, marking the end bracket and casing is unnecessary. A pip may also be found on the drive end bracket at the opposite end of the casing (see photo).
3   Lift the two brush springs and draw the brushes out of the brush holders (arrowed in photo).
4   Measure the brushes and if worn down to $\frac{1}{4}$ inch or less, unscrew the screws holding the brush leads to the end bracket. Take off the brushes complete with leads. Old and new brushes are compared in the photograph.
5   If no locating pip can be found, mark the drive end bracket and the dynamo casing so that the drive end bracket can be replaced in its original position. Then pull the drive end bracket, complete with armature, out of the casing (photo).
6   Check the condition of the ball bearing in the drive end plate by firmly holding the plate and noting if there is visible side movement of the armature shaft in relation to the end plate. If play is present, the armature assembly must be separated from the end plate. If the bearing is sound there is no need to carry out the work described in the following two paragraphs.
7   Hold the armature in one hand (mount it carefully in a vice if preferred) and undo the nut holding the pulley wheel and fan in place. Pull off the pulley wheel and fan.
8   Next move the woodruff key (arrowed in photo) from its slot in the armature shaft and also the bearing locating ring.
9   Place the drive end bracket across the open jaws of a vice with the armature downwards and gently tap the armature shaft from the bearing in the end plate with the aid of a suitable drift (photo).
10   Carefully inspect the armature and check it for open or short circuited windings. It is a good indication of an open circuited armature when the commutator segments are burnt. If the armature has short circuited, the commutator segments will be very badly burnt, and the overheated armature windings badly discoloured. If open or short circuits are suspected then test by substituting the suspect armature for a new one (photo).
11   Check the resistance of the field coils. To do this, connect an ohmmeter between the field terminals and the yoke and note the reading on the ohmmeter which should be about 6 ohms.

9.1

9.2

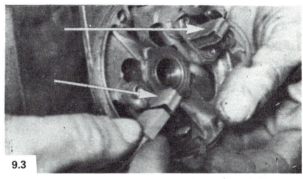

9.3

9.4

9.5

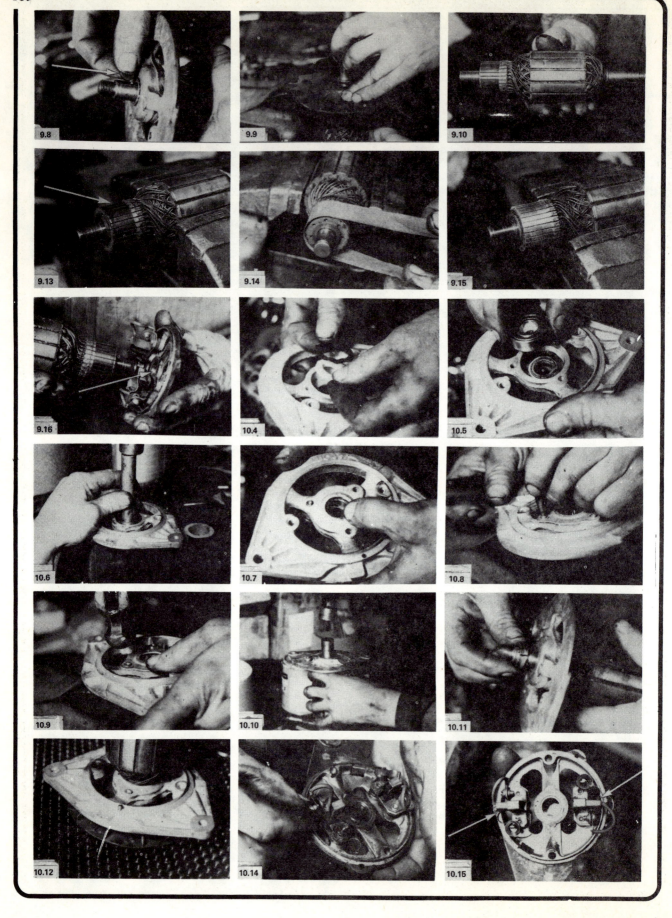

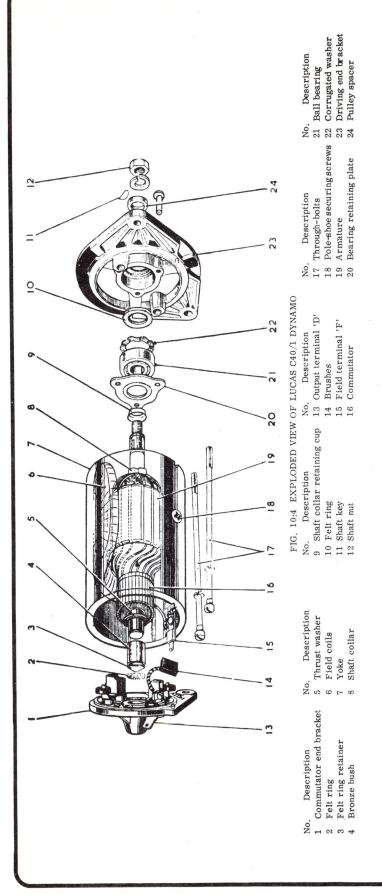

FIG. 10:4 EXPLODED VIEW OF LUCAS C40/1 DYNAMO

No.	Description	No.	Description	No.	Description
1	Commutator end bracket	9	Shaft collar retaining cup	17	Through-bolts
2	Felt ring	10	Felt ring	18	Pole-shoe securing screws
3	Felt ring retainer	11	Shaft key	19	Armature
4	Bronze bush	12	Shaft nut	20	Bearing retaining plate
5	Thrust washer	13	Output terminal 'D'	21	Ball bearing
6	Field coils	14	Brushes	22	Corrugated washer
7	Yoke	15	Field terminal 'F'	23	Driving end bracket
8	Shaft collar	16	Commutator	24	Pulley spacer

FIG. 10:5 THE DYNAMO COMMUTATOR

No.	Description	No.	Description
A	Fabricated type	1	Metal roll-over
B	Moulded type	2	Insulating cone

FIG. 10:6 CORRECT METHOD OF UNDERCUTTING THE COM-
MUTATOR

No.	Description	No.	Description
A	Correct way	2	Segments
B	Incorrect way	3	Insulator
1	Insulator		

If the ohmmeter reading is infinity this indicates an open circuit in the field winding. If the ohmmeter reading is below 5 ohms this indicates that one of the field coils is faulty and must be replaced.

12 Field coil replacement involves the use of a wheel operated screwdriver, a soldering iron, caulking and riveting. This operation is considered to be beyond the scope of most owners. Therefore, if the field coils are at fault either purchase a rebuilt dynamo, or take the casing to a BLMC garage or electrical engineering works for new field coils to be fitted.

13 Next check the condition of the commutator (arrowed in photo). If it is dirty and blackened as shown, clean it with a petrol dampened rag. If the commutator is in good condition the surface will be smooth and quite free from pits or burnt areas, and the insulated segments clearly defined.

14 If, after the commutator has been cleaned, pits and burnt spots are still present, wrap a strip of glass paper round the commutator taking great care to move the commutator $\frac{1}{4}$ of a turn every ten rubs till it is thoroughly clean (photo).

15 In extreme cases of wear, the commutator can be mounted in a lathe and, with the lathe turning at high speed, a very fine cut may be taken off the commutator. Then polish it with glass paper. If it has worn so that the insulators between the segments are level with the top of the segments, then undercut the insulators to the depth indicated in Fig. 10:6. The best tool to use for this purpose is half a hacksaw blade ground to a thickness of the insulator, and with the handle end of the blade covered in insulating tape to make it comfortable to hold. The sort of finish the surface of the commutator should have when completed is shown in the photo.

16 Check the bush bearing (arrowed in photo) in the commutator end bracket for wear by noting if the armature spindle rocks when placed in it. If worn it must be renewed.

17 The bush bearing can be removed by a suitable extractor or by screwing an inch tap four or five times into the bush. The tap, complete with bush, is then pulled out of the end bracket.

18 NOTE: The bush bearing is of the porous bronze type and, before fitting a new one, it is essential that it is allowed to stand in SAE 30 engine oil for at least 24 hours before fitment. In an emergency the bush can be immersed in hot oil (100°C) for 2 hours.

19 Carefully fit the new bush into the end plate, pressing it in until the end of the bearing is flush with the inner side of the end plate. If available, press the bush in with a smooth shouldered mandrel the same diameter as the armature shaft.

10 Dynamo - repair and reassembly

1 To renew the ball bearing fitted to the drive end bracket, drill out the rivets which hold the bearing retainer plate to the end bracket and lift off the plate.

2 Press out the bearing from the end bracket and remove the corrugated and felt washers from the bearing housing.

3 Thoroughly clean the bearing housing and the new bearing, and pack with high melting point grease.

4 Place the felt washer and corrugated washer in that order in the end bracket bearing housing (photo).

5 Then fit the new bearing as shown (photo).

6 Gently tap the bearing into place with the aid of a suitable drift (photo).

7 Replace the bearing plate and fit three new rivets (photo).

8 Open up the rivets with the aid of a suitable cold chisel (photo).

9 Finally peen over the open end of the rivets with the aid of a ball hammer as illustrated.

10 Refit the drive end bracket to the armature shaft. Do not try and force the bracket on but, with the aid of a suitable socket abuting the bearing, tap the bearing on gently, so pulling the end bracket down with it (photo).

11 Slide the spacer up the shaft and refit the woodruff key (photo).

12 Replace the fan and pulley wheel and then fit the spring washer and nut and tighten the latter. The drive bracket end of the dynamo is now fully assembled as shown (photo).

13 If the brushes are little worn and are to be used again then ensure that they are placed in the same holders from which they were removed. When refitting brushes either new or old, check that they move freely in their holders. If either brush sticks, clean with a petrol moistened rag and if still stiff, lightly polish the sides of the brush with a very fine file until the brush moves quite freely in its holder.

14 Tighten the two retaining screws and washers which hold the wire leads to the brushes in place (photo).

15 It is far easier to slip the end piece with brushes over the commutator, if the brushes are raised in their holders as shown in the photo, and held in this position by the pressure of the springs resting against their flanks.

16 Refit the armature to the casing and then the commutator end plate, and screw up the two through bolts.

17 Finally, hook the ends of the two springs off the flanks of the brushes and onto their heads so the brushes are forced down into contact with the armature.

11 Starter motor - general description

One of four types of starter motor have been fitted to the Maxi depending on the date of the manufacture and the destined market.

All starter motors are interchangeable and engage with a common flywheel starter ring gear. With the inertia type starter motor, the relay is fitted to the rear of the front grille, whereas the pre-engaged type has the solenoid switch on the top of the motor.

The principle of operation of the inertia type starter motor is as follows: When the ignition switch is turned, current flows from the battery to the starter motor solenoid switch which causes it to become energized. Its internal plunger moves inwards and closes an internal switch so allowing full starting current to flow from the battery to the starter motor. This causes a powerful magnetic field to be induced into the field coils which causes the armature to rotate.

Mounted on helical splines is the drive pinion which, because of the sudden rotation of the armature, is thrown forwards along the armature shaft and so into engagement with the flywheel ring gear. The engine crankshaft will then be rotated until the engine starts to operate on its own and, at this point, the drive pinion is thrown out of mesh with the flywheel ring gear.

The pre-engaged starter motor operates by a slightly different method using end face commutator brushes instead of brushes located on the side of the commutator.

The method of engagement on the pre-engaged starter differs considerably in that the drive pinion is brought into mesh with the starter ring gear before the main starter current is applied.

When the ignition is switched on, current flows from the battery to the solenoid which is mounted on the top of the starter motor body. The plunger in the solenoid moves inwards so causing a centrally pivoted engagement lever to move in such a manner that the forked end pushes the drive pinion into mesh with the starter ring gear. When the solenoid plunger reaches the end of its travel, it closes an internal contact and full starting current flows to the starter field coils. The armature is then able to rotate the crankshaft so starting the engine.

A special one way clutch is fitted to the starter drive pinion so that when the engine just fires and starts to operate on its own, it does not drive the starter motor.

12 Starter motor (M35G) - testing on engine

1   If the starter motor fails to operate, then check the condition of the battery by turning on the headlamps. If they glow brightly for several seconds and then gradually dim, the battery is in an uncharged condition.

2   If the headlamps glow brightly and it is obvious that the battery is in good condition then check the tightness of the battery wiring connections (and in particular the earth lead from the battery terminal to its connection on the bodyframe). Check the tightness of the connections at the relay switch and at the starter motor. Check the wiring with a voltmeter for breaks or shorts.

3   If the wiring is in order then check that the starter motor switch is operating. To do this, press the rubber covered button in the centre of the relay switch under the bonnet. If it is working, the starter motor will be heard to 'click' as it tries to rotate. Alternatively check it with a voltmeter.

4   If the battery is fully charged, the wiring in order, and the switch working but the starter motor fails to operate then it will have to be removed from the car for examination. Before this is done, however, ensure that the starter pinion has not jammed in mesh with the flywheel. Check by turning the square end of the armature shaft with a spanner. This will free the pinion if it is stuck in engagement with the flywheel teeth.

13 Starter motor (M35G) - removal and replacement

1   Disconnect the positive and then the negative terminals from the battery. Also disconnect the starter motor cable from the terminal on the starter motor end cover.

2   Undo and remove the two bolts which secure the starter motor to the clutch and flywheel housing. Lift the starter motor away by manipulating the drive gear out from the ring gear area and then from the engine compartment (Fig. 10:7).

3   Refitting is the reverse procedure to removal. Make sure that the starter motor cable, when secured in position by its terminal, does not touch any part of the body or power unit which could damage the insulation.

14 Starter motor (M35G) - dismantling and reassembly

1   With the starter motor on the bench, loosen the screw on the cover band and slip the cover band off. With a piece of wire bent into the shape of a hook, lift back each of the brush springs in turn and check the movement of the brushes in their holders by pulling on the flexible connectors. If the brushes are so worn that their faces do not rest against the commutator, or if the ends of the brush leads are exposed on their working face, they must be renewed.

2   If any of the brushes tend to stick in their holders then wash them with a petrol moistened cloth and, if necessary, lightly polish the sides of the brush with a very fine file until the brushes move quite freely in their holders.

3   If the surface of the commutator is dirty or blackened, clean it with a petrol dampened rag. Secure the starter motor in a vice and check it by connecting a heavy gauge cable between the starter motor terminal and a 12 volt battery.

4   Connect the cable from the other battery terminal to earth in the starter motor body. If the motor turns at high speed it is in good order.

5   If the starter motor still fails to function or if it is wished to renew the brushes, then it is necessary to further dismantle the motor.

6   Lift the brush springs with the wire hook, and lift all four brushes out of their holders one at a time.

7   Remove the terminal nuts and washers from the terminal post on the commutator end bracket.

8   Unscrew the two through bolts which hold the end plates together and pull off the commutator end bracket. Also remove the driving end bracket which will come away complete with the armature.

9   At this stage, if the brushes are to be renewed, their flexible connectors must be unsoldered and the connectors of new brushes soldered in their place. Check that the new brushes move freely in their holders as detailed above. If cleaning the commutator with petrol fails to remove all the burnt areas and spots, then wrap a piece of glass paper round the commutator and rotate the armature.

10   If the commutator is very badly worn, remove the drive gear as detailed below. Then mount the armature in a lathe and with the lathe turning at high speed, take a very fine cut out of the commutator and finish the surface by polishing with glass paper. DO NOT UNDERCUT THE MICA INSULATORS BETWEEN THE COMMUTATOR SEGMENTS.

11   With the starter motor dismantled, test the four field coils for an open circuit. Connect a 12 volt battery with a 12 volt bulb in one of the leads between the field terminal post and the tapping point of the field coils to which the brushes are connected. An open circuit is proved by the bulb not lighting.

12   If the bulb lights, it does not necessarily mean that the field coils are in order, as there is a possibility that one of the coils will be earthed to the starter yoke or pole shoes. To check this, remove the lead from the brush connector and place it against a clean portion of the starter yoke. If the bulb lights, the field coils are earthing. Replacement of the field coils calls for the use of a wheel operated screwdriver, a soldering iron, caulking and riveting operations and is beyond the scope of the majority of owners. The starter yoke should be taken to a reputable electrical engineering works for new field coils to be fitted. Alternatively, purchase an exchange Lucas starter motor.

13   If the armature is damaged, this will be evident after visual inspection. Look for signs of burning, discolouration, and for conductors that have lifted away from the commutator.

14   With the starter motor stripped down, check the condition of the bushes. They should be renewed when they are sufficiently worn to allow visible side movement of the armature shaft.

15   The old bushes are simply driven out with a suitable drift and the new bushes inserted by the same method. As the bushes are of the phosphor bronze type it is essential that they are allowed to stand in engine oil for at least 24 hours before fitment. Alternatively soak in oil at 100°C for 2 hours.

16   To dismantle the starter motor drive, first use a press

to push the retainer clear of the circlip which can then be removed. Lift away the retainer and main spring.

17   Slide the remaining parts with a rotary action of the armature shaft.

18   It is most important that the drive gear is completely free from oil, grease and dirt. With the drive gear removed, clean all parts thoroughly in paraffin. UNDER NO CIRCUMSTANCES OIL THE DRIVE COMPONENTS. Lubrication of the drive components could easily cause the pinion to stick.

19   Reassembly of the starter motor drive is the reverse sequence to dismantling. Use a press to compress the spring and retainer sufficiently to allow a new circlip to be fitted to its groove on the shaft. Remove the drive from the press.

20   Reassembly of the starter motor is the reverse sequenc to dismantling.

---

15   Starter motor (M35J) – testing on engine

The test procedure for this type of starter motor is basically identical to that for the Lucas M35G and full information will be found in Section 12.

---

16   Starter motor (M35J) – removal and refitting

The removal and refitting sequence for this type of starter motor is basically identical to that for the Lucas M35G and full information will be found in Section 13.

---

17   Starter motor (M35J) – dismantling and reassembly

---

1   With the starter motor on the bench, first mark the relative positions of the starter motor body to the two end brackets.

2   Undo and remove the two screws and spring washers securing the drive end bracket to the body. The drive end bracket, complete with armature and drive, may now be drawn forwards from the starter motor body.

3   Lift away the thrust washer from the commutator end of the armature shaft.

4   Undo and remove the two screws securing the commutator end bracket to the starter motor body. The commutator end bracket may now be drawn back about an inch allowing sufficient access so as to disengage the field bushes from the bracket. Once these are free, the end bracket may now be completely removed.

5   With the motor stripped, the brushes and brush gear may be inspected. To check the brush spring tension, fit a new brush into each holder in turn and, using an accurate spring balance, push the brush on the balance tray until the brush protrudes approximately 1/16 inch from the holder. Make a note of the reading which should be approximately 28 ounces. If the spring pressures vary considerably the commutator end bracket must be renewed as a complete assembly.

6   Inspect the brushes for wear and fit a new brush which is nearing the minimum length of 3/8 inch. To renew the end bracket brushes, cut the brush cables from the terminal posts and, with a small file or hacksaw, slot the head of the terminal posts to a sufficient depth to accommodate the new leads. Solder the new brush leads to the posts.

7   To renew the field winding brushes, cut the brush leads approximately $\frac{1}{4}$ inch from the field winding junction and carefully solder the new brush leads to the remaining stumps, making sure that the insulation sleeves provide adequate cover.

8   If the commutator surface is dirty or blackened, clean it with a petrol dampened rag. Carefully examine the commutator for signs of excessive wear, burning or pitting. If evident it may be reconditioned by having it skimmed at the local engineering works or BLMC dealer who possesses a centre lathe. The thickness of the commutator must not be less than 0.08 inch. For minor reconditioning, the commutator may be polished with glass paper. DO NOT UNDERCUT THE MICA INSULATORS BETWEEN THE COMMUTATOR SEGMENTS.

9   With the starter motor dismantled, test the field coils for open circuit. Connect a 12 volt battery with a 12 volt bulb in one of the leads between each of the field brushes and a clean part of the body. The lamp will light if continuity is satisfactory between the brushes, windings and body connection.

10   Replacement of the field coils calls for the use of a wheel operated screwdriver, a soldering iron, caulking and riveting operations and is beyond the scope of the majority of owners. The starter motor body should be taken to an automobile electrical engineering works for new field coils to be fitted. Alternatively purchase an exchange Lucas starter motor.

11   Check the condition of the bushes and they should be renewed when they are sufficiently worn to allow visible side movement of the armature shaft.

12   To renew the commutator end bracket bush, drill out the rivets securing the brush box moulding and remove the moulding, bearing seal retaining plate and felt washer seal.

13   Screw in a $\frac{1}{2}$ inch tap and withdraw the bush with the tap.

14   As the bush is of the phosphor bronze type it is essential that it is allowed to stand in engine oil for at least 24 hours before fitment. Alternatively soak in oil at 100°C for 2 hours.

15   Using a suitable diameter drift, drive the new bush into position. Do not ream the bush as its self lubricating properties will be impaired.

16   To remove the drive end bracket bush it will be necessary to remove the drive gear as described in paragraphs 18 and 19.

17   Using a suitable diameter drift remove the old bush and fit a new one as described in paragraphs 14 and 15.

18   To dismantle the starter motor drive, first use a press to push the retainer clear of the circlip which can then be removed. Lift away the retainer and main spring.

19   Slide off the remaining parts with a rotary action of the armature shaft.

20   It is most important that the drive gear is completely free from oil, grease and dirt. With the drive gear removed, clean all parts thoroughly in paraffin. UNDER NO CIRCUMSTANCES OIL THE DRIVE COMPONENTS. Lubrication of the drive components could easily cause the pinion to stick.

21   Reassembly of the starter motor drive is the reverse sequence to dismantling. Use a press to compress the spring and retainer sufficiently to allow a new circlip to be fitted to its groove on the shaft. Remove the drive from the press.

22   Reassembly of the starter motor is the reverse sequence to dismantling.

---

18   Starter motor (M35J pre-engaged) – testing on engine

The testing procedure is basically similar to the M35G starter described in Section 12. However, note the following instructions before removing the starter.

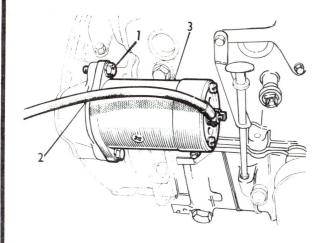
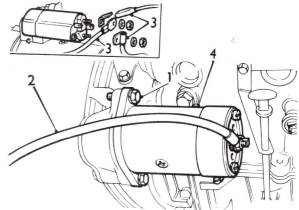

FIG. 10:7 M35G STARTER MOTOR REMOVAL

No.	Description	No.	Description
1	Starter motor securing bolts	3	Starter motor body
2	Heavy duty cable		

FIG. 10:9 M35J PRE-ENGAGED STARTER MOTOR REMOVAL

No.	Description	No.	Description
1	Starter motor securing bolts	3	Solenoid electrical connections
2	Heavy duty cable	4	Starter motor body

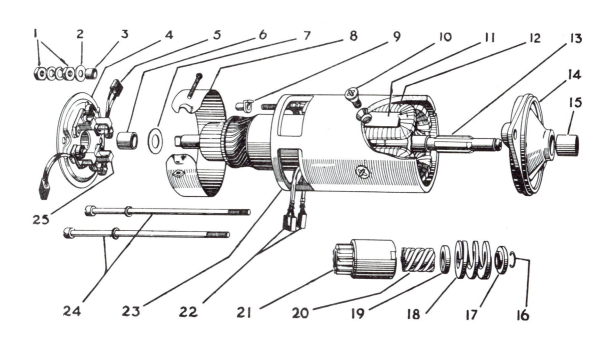

FIG. 10:8 M35G STARTER MOTOR COMPONENTS

No.	Description	No.	Description	No.	Description	No.	Description
1	Terminal nuts and washers	8	Cover band	15	Bush	22	Brushes
2	Insulating washer	9	Insulating bush	16	Jump ring	23	Yoke
3	Insulating bush	10	Pole securing screw	17	Retainer	24	Through bolts
4	End plate	11	Pole piece	18	Main spring	25	Brush box
5	Brush	12	Field coil	19	Thrust washer		
6	Bush	13	Shaft	20	Sleeve		
7	Thrust washer	14	End bracket	21	Pinion and barrel assembly		

Ensure that the pinion gear has not jammed in mesh with the flywheel due either to a broken solenoid spring or dirty pinion gear splines. To release the pinion, engage a low gear and, with the ignition switched off, rock the car backwards and forwards which should release the pinion from mesh with the ring gear. If the pinion still remains jammed the starter motor must be removed for further examination.

19 Starter motor (M35J pre-engaged) - removal and replacement

1   Disconnect the positive and then the negative terminals from the battery.
2   Make a note of the electrical connections at the rear of the solenoid and disconnect the top heavy duty cable. Also release the two Lucar terminals situated below the heavy duty cable. There is no need to undo the lower heavy duty cable at the rear of the solenoid (Fig. 10:9).
3   Undo and remove the two bolts which hold the starter motor in place and lift away upwards.
4   Replacement is a straightforward reversal of the removal sequence. Check that the electrical cable connections are clean and firmly attached to their respective terminals.

20 Starter motor (M35J pre-engaged) - dismantling and reassembly

1   Detach the heavy duty cable, linking the solenoid STA terminal to the starter motor terminal, by undoing and removing the securing nuts and washers (Fig. 10:11).
2   Undo and remove the two nuts and spring washers securing the solenoid to the drive end bracket.
3   Carefully withdraw the solenoid coil unit from the drive end bracket.
4   Lift off the solenoid plunger and return spring from the engagement lever.
5   Remove the rubber sealing block from the drive end bracket.
6   Remove the retaining ring (spire nut) from the engagement lever pivot pin and withdraw the pin.
7   Unscrew and remove the two drive end bracket securing nuts and spring washers and withdraw the bracket.
8   Lift away the engagement lever from the drive operating plate.
9   Extract the split pin from the end of the armature and remove the shim washers and thrust plate from the commutator end of the armature shaft.
10 Remove the armature, together with its internal thrust washer.
11 Withdraw the thrust washer from the armature.
12 Undo and remove the two screws securing the commutator end bracket to the starter motor body.
13 Carefully detach the end bracket from the yoke, at the same time disengaging the field brushes from the brush gear. Lift away the end bracket.
14 Move the thrust collar clear of the jump ring, and then remove the jump ring. Withdraw the drive assembly from the armature shaft.
15 Inspection and renovation is basically the same as for the Lucas M35G starter motor and full information will be found in Section 14. The following additions necessitated by the fitting of the solenoid coil should be noted:
16 If a bush is worn, so allowing excessive side movement of the armature shaft, the bush must be renewed. Drift out the old bush with a piece of suitable diameter rod, preferably with a shoulder on it to stop the bush collapsing.
17 Soak a new bush in engine oil for 24 hours or if time does not permit, heat in an oil bath at $100^{\circ}C$ for two hours prior to fitting.
18 As new bushes must not be reamed after fitting it must be pressed into position using a small mandrel of the same diameter as the bush and with a shoulder on it. Place the bush on the mandrel and press into position using a bench vice.
19 Use a test light and battery to test the continuity of the coil windings between terminal STA and a good earth point on the solenoid body. If the light fails to come on, the solenoid should be renewed.
20 To test the solenoid contacts for correct opening and closing, connect a 12 volt battery and a 60 watt test light between the main unmarked Lucar terminal and the STA terminal. The light should not come on.
21 Energise the solenoid with a separate 12 volt supply connected to the small unmarked Lucar terminal and a good earth on the solenoid body.
22 As the coil is energised the solenoid should be heard to operate and the test lamp should light with full brilliance.
23 The contacts may only be renewed as a set, ie moving and fixed contacts. The fixed contacts are part of the moulded cover.
24 To fit a new set of contacts, first undo and remove the moulded cover securing screws.
25 Unsolder the coil connections from the cover terminals.
26 Lift away the cover and moving contact assembly.
27 Fit a new cover and moving contact assembly, soldering the connections to the cover terminals.
28 Refit the moulded cover securing screws.
29 Whilst the motor is apart, check the operation of the drive clutch. It must provide instantaneous take up of the drive in one direction and rotate easily and smoothly in the opposite direction.
30 Make sure that the drive moves smoothly on the armature shaft splines without binding or sticking.
31 Reassembly of the starter motor is the reverse sequence to dismantling. The following additional points should be noted:
32 When assembling the drive, always use a new retaining ring (spire nut) to secure the engagement lever pivot pin.
33 Make sure that the internal thrust washer is fitted to the commutator end of the armature shaft before the armature is fitted.
34 Make sure that the thrust washers and plate are assembled in the correct order and are prevented from rotating separately by engaging the collar pin with the locking piece on the thrust plate.

21 Starter motor (2M100 pre-engaged) - testing on engine

The test procedure for this type of starter motor is basically identical to that for the Lucas M35J pre-engaged starter motor and the M35G. Full information will be found in Sections 12 and 18.

22 Starter motor (2M100 pre-engaged) - removal and replacement

The removal and refitting sequence for this type of starter motor is basically identical to that for the Lucas M35J

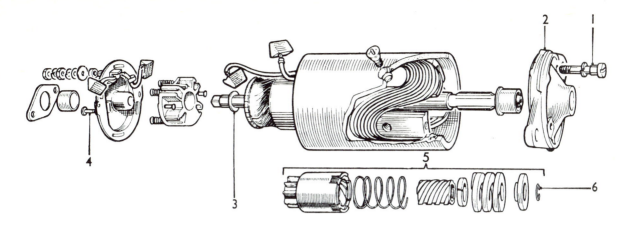

FIG. 10:10 M35J INERTIA STARTER MOTOR COMPONENTS

No. Description	No. Description	No. Description	No. Description
1 Drive end bracket securing screws	2 Drive end bracket 3 Thrust washer	4 Commutator end bracket securing screws	5 Drive assembly 6 Jump ring

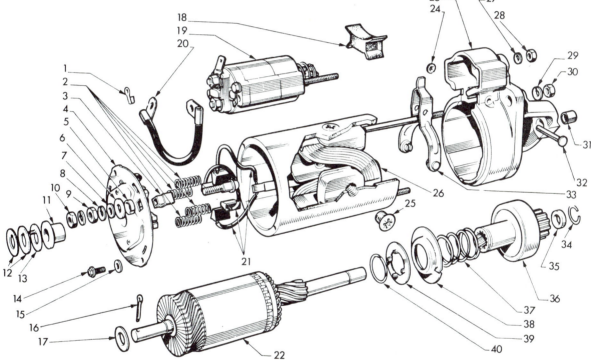

FIG. 10:11 M35J (PRE-ENGAGED) STARTER MOTOR COMPONENTS

No. Description	No. Description	No. Description	No. Description
1 Hook	12 Washers	22 Armature	31 Bush
2 Brush springs	13 Tabbed washer	23 Starter drive cover and starter motor end plate	32 Lever swivel pin
3 Insulator	14 Bolt	24 Pin retaining ring	33 Actuating lever
4 End plate and brush holder	15 Washer	25 Field coil retaining screw	34 Circlip
5 Spacer	16 Split pin	26 Field coils	35 Spacer
6 Washer	17 Washer	27 Washer	36 Pinion
7 Washer	18 Grommet	28 Nut	37 Spring
8 Lockwasher	19 Solenoid assembly	29 Lockwasher	38 Clutch spring backplate
9 Nut	20 Cable assembly	30 Nut	39 Tabbed washer
10 Nut	21 Brush assembly		40 Retaining ring
11 Bush			

pre-engaged type starter motor. Full information will be found in Section 19.

23 Starter motor (2M100 pre-engaged) - dismantling and reassembly

1 Undo and remove the nut and spring washer that secures the connecting link between the solenoid and starter motor at the solenoid 'STA' terminal. Carefully ease the connecting link out of engagement of the terminal post on the solenoid.

2 Undo and remove the two nuts and spring washers that secure the solenoid to the drive end bracket.

3 Carefully ease the solenoid back from the drive end bracket, lift the solenoid plunger and return spring from the engagement lever, and completely remove the solenoid.

4 Recover the shaped rubber block that is placed between the solenoid and starter motor body.

5 Carefully remove the end cap seal from the commutator end cover.

6 Ease the armature shaft retaining ring (spire nut) from the armature shaft. NOTE: The retaining ring must not be reused, but a new one obtained ready for fitting.

7 Undo and remove the two long through bolts and spring washers.

8 Detach the commutator end cover from the yoke, at the same time disengaging the field brushes from the brush box moulding.

9 Lift away the thrust washer from the armature shaft.

10 The starter motor body may now be lifted from the armature and drive end assembly.

11 Ease the retaining ring (spire nut) from the engagement lever pivot pin. NOTE: The retaining ring must not be reused, but a new one obtained ready for fitting.

12 Using a parallel pin punch of suitable size, remove the pivot pin from the engagement lever and drive end bracket.

13 Carefully move the thrust collar clear of the jump ring, and slide the jump ring from the armature shaft.

14 Slide off the thrust collar, and finally remove the roller clutch drive and engagement lever assembly from the armature shaft.

15 For inspection and servicing information of the brush gear, commutator, and armature refer to Section 17, paragraphs 5 to 8 inclusive.

16 To test the field coils refer to Section 17, paragraphs 9 and 10.

17 Check the condition of the bushes and if they show signs of wear remove the old ones and fit new as described in Section 17, paragraphs 11 to 17. Disregard the reference in paragraph 16 to the removal of the drive gear as this will have already been done.

18 Whilst the motor is apart, check the operation of the drive clutch. It must provide instantaneous take up of the drive in one direction and rotate easily and smoothly in the opposite direction.

19 Make sure that the drive moves smoothly on the armature shaft splines without binding or sticking.

20 Reassembling the starter motor is the reverse sequence to dismantling. The following additional points should be noted:

21 When assembling the drive end bracket always use a new retaining ring (spire nut) to secure the engagement lever pivot pin.

22 Make sure that the internal thrust washer is fitted to the commutator end of the armature shaft before the armature end cover is fitted.

23 Always use a new retaining ring (spire nut) onto the armature shaft to a maximum clearance of 0.010 inch between the retaining ring and the bearing brush shoulder. This will be the armature end float.

24 Tighten the through bolts to a torque wrench setting of 8 lb ft and the nuts securing the solenoid to the drive bracket to 4.5 lb ft.

24 Control box - general description

1 The control box is positioned on the right hand wing valance and comprises three units: two separate vibrating armature - type single contact regulators and a cut out relay. One of the regulators is sensitive to change in current and the other to changes in voltage.

2 Adjustments can be made only with a special tool which resembles a screwdriver with a multi-toothed blade. This can be obtained through Lucas agents.

3 The regulators control the output from the dynamo depending on the state of the battery and the demands of the electrical equipment, and ensure that the battery is not overcharged. The cut out is really an automatic switch and connects the dynamo to the battery when the dynamo is turning fast enough to produce a charge. Similarly it disconnects the battery from the dynamo when the engine is idling or stationary so that the battery does not discharge through the dynamo.

25 Cut-out and regulator contacts - maintenance

1 Every 12,000 miles check the cut-out and regulator contacts. If they are dirty or rough or burnt, place a piece of fine glass paper (DO NOT USE EMERY PAPER OR CARBORUNDUM PAPER) between the cut-out contacts, close them manually and draw the glass paper through several times.

2 Clean the regulator contacts in exactly the same way, but use emery or carborundum paper and not glass paper. Carefully clean sets of contacts from all traces of dust with a rag moistened in methylated spirits.

26 Regulator - adjustment

1 The regulator requires very little attention during its service life, and if there should be any reason to suspect its correct functioning, tests of all circuits should be made to ensure that they are not the reason for the trouble.

2 These checks include the tension of the fan belt, to make sure that it is not slipping and so providing only a very low charge rate. The battery should be carefully checked for possible low charge rate due to a faulty cell, or corroded battery connections.

3 The leads from the generator may have been crossed during replacement, and if this is the case, then the regulator points will have stuck together as soon as the generator starts to charge. Check for loose or broken leads from the generator to the regulator.

4 If, after a thorough check, it is considered advisable to test the regulator, this should be carried out only by an electrician who is well acquainted with the correct method, using test bench equipment.

5 Pull off the Lucas connections from the two adjacent control box terminals 'B'. To start the engine it will now be necessary to join together the ignition and battery leads

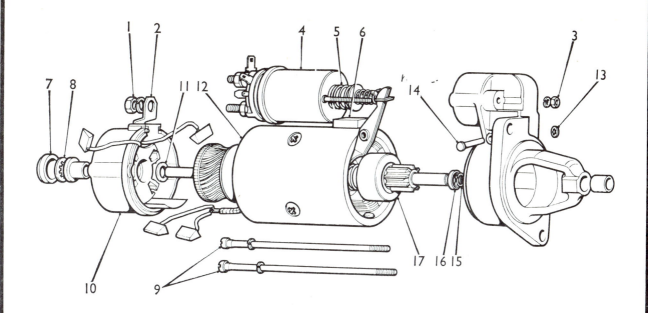

FIG. 10:12 LUCAS 2M100 PRE - ENGAGED STARTER MOTOR

No.	Description	No.	Description	No.	Description	No.	Description
1	Connecting link securing nut	5	Solenoid plunger and return		(spire nut)	13	Retaining ring (spire nut)
2	Connecting link		spring	9	Through bolts	14	Pivot pin
3	Solenoid to drive end bracket	6	Rubber block	10	Commutator end cover	15	Thrust collar jump ring
	securing nut	7	End cap seal	11	Thrust washer	16	Thrust collar
4	Solenoid	8	Armature shaft retaining ring	12	Yoke	17	Roller clutch drive

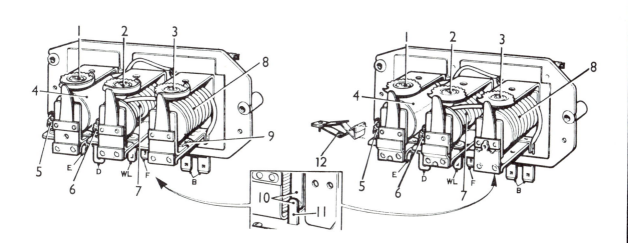

FIG. 10:13 LUCAS RB340 CONTROL BOX

No.	Description	No.	Description	No.	Description	No.	Description
1	Adjustment cam - voltage	4	Voltage regulator	7	Current regulator	10	Cut-out contacts
2	Adjustment cam - current	5	Voltage contacts	8	Cut-out relay	11	Fixed contact bracket
3	Adjustment cam - cut-out	6	Current contacts	9	Armature back stop	12	Clip

A Early units prior to 37563 identified by flanged adjustment cams

with a suitable wire.

6   Connect a 0-20 volt voltmeter between terminal 'D' on the control box and terminal 'WL'. Start the engine and run it at 3,000 rpm. The reading on the voltmeter should be steady and lie between the limits detailed in the specification.

7   If the reading is unsteady this may be due to dirty contacts. If the reading is outside the specified limits stop the engine and adjust the voltage regulator in the following manner:

8   Take off the control box cover and start and run the engine at 3,000 rpm. Using the correct tool, turn the voltage adjustment cam anti-clockwise to raise the setting and clockwise to lower it. To check that the setting is correct, stop the engine, and then start it and run it at 3,000 rpm noting the reading. Refit the cover and the connections to the 'WL' and 'D' terminals.

27   Current regulator - adjustment

1   The output from the current regulator should equal the maximum output from the dynamo which is 22 amps. To test this it is necessary to bypass the cut-out by holding the contacts together.

2   Remove the cover from the control box and with a bulldog clip hold the cut out contacts together.

3   Pull off the wires from the adjacent terminals 'B' and connect a 0-40 moving-coil ammeter to one of the terminals and to the leads.

4   All the other connections, including the ignition, must be made to the battery.

5   Turn on all the lights and other electrical accessories and run the engine at 3,000 rpm. The ammeter should give a steady reading between 19 and 22 amps. If the needle flickers it is likely that the points are dirty. If the reading is too low, turn the special Lucas tool clockwise to raise the setting and anti-clockwise to lower it.

28   Cut-out - adjustment

1   Check the voltage required to operate the cut out by connecting a voltmeter between the control box terminals 'D' and 'WL'. Remove the control box cover, start the engine and gradually increase its speed until the cut out closes. This should occur when the reading is between 12.7 to 13.3 volts.

2   If the reading is outside these limits turn the cut out adjusting cam by means of the adjusting tool, a fraction at a time clockwise to raise the voltage, and anti-clockwise to lower it.

3   To adjust the drop off voltage, bend the fixed contact blade carefully. The adjustment to the cut out should be completed within 30 seconds of starting the engine as otherwise heat build-up from the shunt-coil will affect the readings.

4   If the cut out fails to work, clean the contacts, and if there is still no response, renew the cut out and regulator unit.

29   Starter motor solenoid - removal and replacement

1   The starter motor solenoid, for models with the inertia type starter motor, is located behind the front grille (Fig.10:14).

2   To remove the solenoid, first disconnect the positive and then the negative terminals from the battery.

3   Make a note of the electrical cable connections and then

release the two Lucar connectors. Disconnect the two heavy duty cables by undoing and removing the securing nuts.

4   Unscrew and remove the two setscrews holding the solenoid to the front grille. Lift away the solenoid.

5   Refitting is the reverse sequence to removal.

30   Flasher unit and circuit - fault tracing and rectification

The flasher unit is enclosed in a small metal container and is operated when the ignition is on by composite switch mounted on the steering column (Fig. 10:15).

If the flasher unit fails to operate, or works either very slowly or very rapidly, check out the flasher indicator circuit as described below, before assuming there is a fault in the unit itself.

1   Examine the direction indicator bulbs front and rear for broken filaments (see Sections 39 and 40).

2   If the external flashers are working, but the internal flasher warning lights on one or both sides have ceased to function, check the filaments and replace as necessary.

3   With the aid of the wiring diagram check all the flasher circuit connections if a flasher bulb is sound but does not work.

4   In the event of total indicator failure, check the 7 - 8 fuse.

5   With the ignition switched on, check that current is reaching the flasher unit by connecting a voltmeter between the 'plus' or 'B' terminal and earth. If this test is positive, connect the 'plus' or 'B' terminal and the 'L' terminal and operate the flasher switch. If the flasher bulb lights up the flasher unit itself is defective and must be replaced as it is not possible to dismantle and repair it.

31   Windscreen wiper arms - removal and replacement

1   Before removing a wiper arm, turn the windscreen switch on and off to ensure the arms are in their normal parked position parallel with the bottom of the windscreen.

2   To remove the arm, pivot the arm back and pull the wiper arm head off the splined drive, at the same time easing back the clip with a screwdriver.

3   When replacing an arm, place it so it is in the correct relative parked position and then press the arm head onto the splined drive till the retaining clip clicks into place.

32   Windscreen wiper mechanism - Fault diagnosis and rectification

Should the windscreen wipers fail, or work very slowly then check the terminals for loose connections, and make sure the insulation of the external wiring is not broken or cracked. If this is in order, then check the current the motor is taking by connecting up a 0 - 20 ammeter in the circuit and turning on the wiper switch. Consumption should be between 1.5 and 3.4 amps.

If no current is passing, check fuse 5. If the fuse has blown, replace it after having checked the wiring of the motor and other electrical circuits serviced by this fuse for short circuits. If the fuse is in good condition, check the wiper switch.

If the wiper takes a very high current, check the wiper blades for freedom of movement. If this is satisfactory, check the gearbox cover and gear assembly for damage and measure the end float which should be between 0.002 to 0.008 inch.

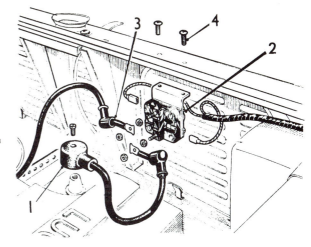

FIG. 10:14 STARTER MOTOR SOLENOID

No.	Description	No.	Description
1	Battery terminal	3	Heavy duty cable
2	Solenoid	4	Solenoid bracket securing screws

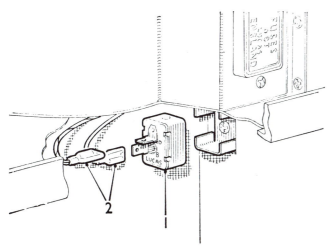

FIG. 10:15 FLASHER UNIT LOCATION

No.	Description	No.	Description
1	Flasher unit	2	Flasher unit cables

FIG. 10:16 WINDSCREEN WIPER ARM AND BLADE CONNECTIONS

No.	Description	No.	Description
1	Arm locking clip	4	Blade location on arm
2	Wheelbox spindle	5	Rubber insert
3	Blade locking clip	6	Insert stiffener

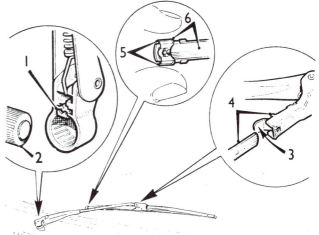

The end float is set by the thrust screw. Check that excessive friction in the cable connecting tubes, caused by too small a curvature, is not the cause of the high current consumption.

If the motor takes a very low current, ensure that the battery is fully charged. Check the brush gear, after removing the commutator end bracket, and ensure that the brushes are free to move. If necessary, renew the tension spring. If the brushes are very worn they should be replaced with new ones. The armature may be checked by substitution.

33 Windscreen wiper blades - changing wiping arc.

If it is wished to change the area through which the wiper blades move, this is simply done by removing each arm in turn from each splined drive, and then replacing it on the drive in a slightly different position.

34 Windscreen wiper motor - removal and replacement

1 Remove the windscreen wiper arms by lifting the blades and pulling the arms off the splined drive shafts, at the same time easing back the clip with a screwdriver (Fig. 10:17).
2 Disconnect the positive and then the negative terminal from the battery.
3 Release the electric cable terminal block from the connector for the windscreen wiper motor located next to the motor.
4 Undo the nut which secures the outer cable to the windscreen wiper motor housing (Fig. 10:18).
5 Undo and remove the two screws that secure the motor retaining bracket to the inner wing valance.
6 Carefully draw the wiper motor from the outer cable, at the same time the inner cable will be drawn out of the outer cable.
7 Refitting the wiper motor and inner cable is the reverse sequence to removal. Take care in feeding the inner cable through the outer cable and engaging the inner cable with each wiper wheelbox spindle.

35 Windscreen wiper motor - dismantling, inspection and reassembly

1 Refer to Fig. 10:19 and remove the four gearbox cover retaining screws (2) and lift away the cover (1). Release the circlip (4) and flat washer (5) securing the connecting rod (3) to the crankpin on the shaft and gear (7). Lift away the connecting rod (3) followed by the second flat washer (5).
2 Release the circlip (4) and washer (5) securing the shaft and gear (7) to the gearbox body (9).
3 De-burr the gear shaft and lift away the gear (7) making a careful note of the location of the dished washer (8).
4 Scribe a mark on the yoke assembly (15) and gearbox (9) to ensure correct reassembly and unscrew the two yoke bolts (14) from the motor yoke assembly. Part the yoke assembly including armature from the gearbox body. As the yoke assembly has residual magnetism ensure that the yoke is kept well away from metallic dust.
5 Unscrew the two screws securing the brush gear and the terminal and switch assembly and remove both the assemblies.
6 Inspect the brushes for signs of excessive wear. If the main brushes are worn to a limit of 3/16 inch or the narrow section of the third brush is worn to the full width of the brush fit a new brush gear assembly. Ensure that the three brushes

move freely in their boxes. If a push type spring gauge is available, check the spring rate which should be between 5 to 7 ounces when the bottom of the brush is level with the bottom of the slot in the brush box. Again, if the spring rate is incorrect, fit a new brush gear assembly.
7 If the armature is suspect take it to an automobile electrician to test for open or short circuiting.
8 Inspect the gear wheel for signs of excessive wear or damage and fit a new one if necessary.
9 Reassembly is the reverse procedure to dismantling but there are several points that require special attention.
10 Use only Ragosine Listate grease to lubricate the gear wheel teeth and cam, the armature shaft worm gear, connecting rod and its connecting pin, the cross head slide and cable rack and wheelbox gear wheels.
11 Use only Shell Turbo 41 oil to lubricate the bearing bushes, the armature shaft bearing journals (sparingly), the gear wheel shaft and crankpin, the felt washer in the yoke bearing (thoroughly soak) and the wheelbox spindles.
12 The yoke assembly fixing bolts should be tightened using a torque wrench set to 14 lb ft.
13 When a replacement armature is to be fitted, slacken the thrust screw so as to provide end float for fitting the yoke
14 The thrust disc inside the yoke bearing should be fitted with the concave side towards the end face of the bearing. The dished washer fitted beneath the gear wheel should have its concave side towards the gear wheel as shown in Fig. 10:19.
15 The larger of the two flat washers is fitted underneath the connecting rod and the smaller one on top, under the retaining circlip.
16 To adjust the armature end float, tighten the thrust screw and then turn back one quarter of a turn so giving an end float of between 0.004 and 0.008 inch. The gap should be measured under the head of the thrust screw. Fit a shim of suitable size beneath the head, and tighten the screw.

36 Horns - fault tracing and rectification

1 If a horn works badly or fails completely, first check the wiring leading to it for short circuits and loose connections. Also check that the horn is firmly secured and that there is nothing lying on the horn body.
2 The horn should never be dismantled, but it is possible to adjust it. This adjustment is to compensate for wear of the moving parts only and will not affect the tone. To adjust the horn proceed as follows:

a) On either the Lucas 9H or 6H models there is a small adjustment screw on the broad rim of the horn nearly opposite the two terminals. Do not confuse this with the large screw in the centre.
b) Turn the adjustment screw anti-clockwise until the horns just fail to sound. Then turn the screw a quarter of a turn clockwise which is the optimum setting.
c) It is recommended that if the horn has to be reset in the car, the fuse 2 should be removed and replaced with a piece of wire, otherwise the fuse will continually blow due to the continuous high current required for the horn in continual operation.
d) With twin horns, the horn which is not being adjusted should be disconnected while adjustment of the other takes place.

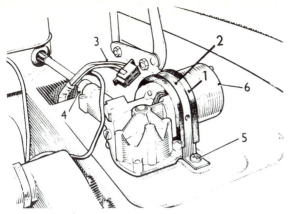

FIG. 10:17 WINDSCREEN WIPER MOTOR REMOVAL

No.	Description	No.	Description
1	Rubber insulating pad	4	Rack securing nut
2	Motor retaining bracket	5	Retaining bracket securing screws
3	Terminal block	6	Wiper motor

FIG. 10:18 WINDSCREEN WIPER RACK AND WHEELBOX AS-SEMBLY

No.	Description	No.	Description
1	Screen washer jet	7	Gear spindle retaining nut
2	Air intake grille	8	Spindle finisher
3	Air intake grille securing screws	9	Rack outer cable
		10	Gear housing retaining nuts
4	Washer tube	11	Cover plate, gear and spindle assembly
5	Plenum chamber baffle plate		
6	Wiper motor mounting platform		

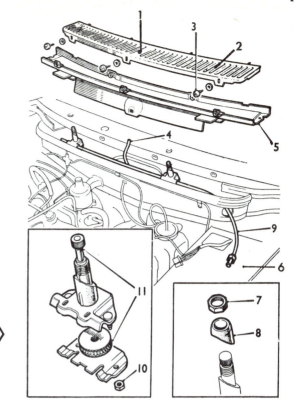

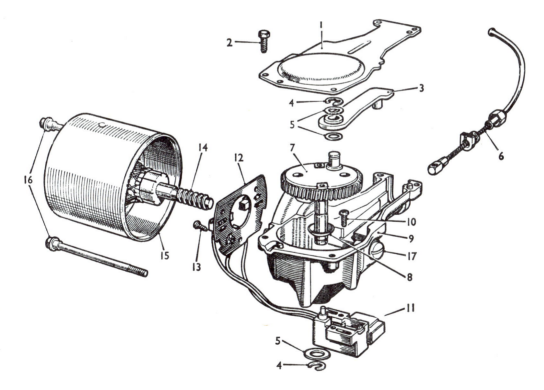

FIG. 10:19 WINDSCREEN WIPER MOTOR

No.	Description	No.	Description	No.	Description	No.	Description
1	Gearbox cover	6	Cross-head	10	Screw for limit switch	14	Armature
2	Screw for cover	7	Shaft and gear	11	Limit switch assembly	15	Yoke assembly
3	Connecting rod	8	Dished washer	12	Brush gear	16	Yoke bolts
4	Circlip	9	Gearbox	13	Screw for brush gear	17	Armature thrust screw
5	Plain washers						

37 Headlight units - removal and replacement

1   Sealed beam, or renewable bulb light units are fitted depending on the market for which the car was originally destined.
2   The method of gaining access to the light unit for replacement is identical for all types of light units and bulbs.
3   Undo and remove the screw securing the rim and carefully lift off the rim (Fig. 10:20).
4   Undo and remove the three screws securing the light unit retaining plate to the light assembly body. Lift away the retaining plate.
5   Draw the light unit forwards away from the light assembly body.
6   To remove the sealed beam unit, detach the three pin connector from the reflector and lift away the light unit.
7   On spring clip type bulb holders, detach the three pin connector and disengage the spring clip from the reflector lugs. The bulb may now be lifted away.
8   When a cap type bulb holder is fitted, press and turn the cap in an anti-clockwise direction. Lift off the cap and then the bulb.
9   Refitting the sealed beam unit is the reverse sequence to removal.
10   When replacing a bulb in a spring clip type bulb holder, make sure that the pip on the bulb flange engages in the slot in the reflector. Refit the spring clip, ensuring that the coils in the clip are resting on the base of the bulb and that the legs of the clip are fully engaged under the reflector lugs.
11   With the cap type bulb holder, make sure that the notch in the bulb flange locates on the ridge in the reflector. Engage the cap lugs in the reflector slots. Press in and turn the cap in a clockwise direction.
12   Place the three lugs on the outer edge of the light unit in the slots formed in the lamp body. Replace the retaining plate and secure with the three screws.
13   Finally replace the outer rim and secure with the one retaining screw.

38 Headlight beam - adjustments

The headlights may be adjusted for both vertical and horizontal beam position by the two screws, these being shown in Fig. 10:20. For vertical movement screw (9) should be used and horizontal movement screw (10).

They should be set so that on full or high beam, the beams are set slightly below parallel with a level road surface. Do not forget that the beam position is affected by how the car is normally loaded for night driving, and set the beams loaded to this position.

Although this adjustment can be approximately set at home, it is recommended that this be left to the local garage who will have the necessary equipment to do the job more accurately.

39 Side and front flasher bulbs - removal and replacement

1   Undo and remove the two screws securing the lamp lens to the lamp body and lift away the lens taking care not to damage the seal (Fig. 10:21).
2   Either bulb is retained by a bayonet fixing, so to remove a bulb push in slightly and rotate in an anti-clockwise direction.

3   To gain access to a direction indicator side reflector bulb, remove the screw securing the lens and lift away the lens. A single filament bayonet cap bulb is fitted.

40 Stop, tail and rear flasher bulbs - removal and replacement

1   Undo and remove the three screws securing the lamp lens to the lamp body and lift away the lens taking care not to damage the seal (Fig. 10:22).
2   Two bulbs are used, the lower one being of the double filament type, and are retained in position by a bayonet fixing. To remove a bulb, push in slightly and rotate in an anti-clockwise direction.
3   The lower, double filament bulb has offset pins on the bayonet fixing, so it is not possible to fit it the wrong way round.

41 Number plate and reverse light bulbs - removal and replacement

1   Undo and remove the two screws securing the cover to the lamp body and lift away the cover (Fig. 10:24).
2   Lift away the relevant lens and remove the bulb by pushing in slightly and rotating in an anti-clockwise direction.
3   Refitting is the reverse sequence to removal.

42 Instrument operation - testing

The bi-metal resistance equipment for the fuel and thermal type temperature gauges comprises an indicator head and transmitter with the unit connected to a common voltage stabilizer. This item is fitted because the method of operation of the equipment is voltage sensitive, and a voltage stabilizer is necessary to ensure a constant voltage supply at all times.

Special test equipment is necessary when checking correct operation of the voltage stabilizer, fuel gauge and temperature so, if a fault is suspect, the car must be taken to the local BLMC garage who will have this equipment.

There are, however, several initial checks that can be carried out without this equipment and should be performed as follows:
1   Connect a 0 - 20 voltmeter across the 2 terminal (bottom fuse) of the fuse block and a good earth on the car body.
2   Switch on the ignition and note the reading on the meter. It should be approximately 12 volts.
3   Start the engine and run at a fast idle speed of between 1,000 to 1,100 rpm. The ignition warning light should be out and the meter registering between 12 and 14 volts.
4   Next make sure that the instrument panel wiring multi connector plug is correctly fitted to the back of the panel.
5   Finally the wiring harness to the multi connector plug should be checked for continuity and all instrument earth connections checked for tightness.
6   Should the cause of the trouble not have been found, further tests will have to be carried out by the local BLMC dealer.

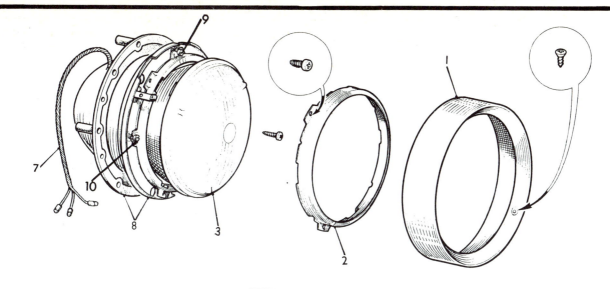

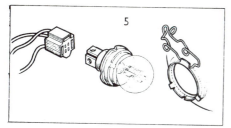

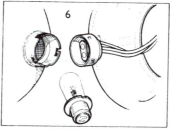

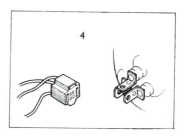

FIG. 10:20 HEADLIGHT UNIT COMPONENT PARTS

No.	Description	No.	Description	No.	Description	No.	Description
1	Outer rim		nector	6	Cap type bulb holder	8	Back shell
2	Light unit retaining rim	5	Spring clip type bulb holder and	7	Wiring to rear of light unit	9	Vertical adjustment screw
3	Light unit		connector		assembly	10	Horizontal adjustment screw
4	Sealed beam light unit con-						

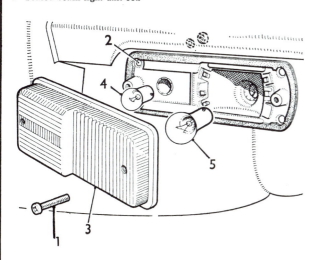

FIG. 10:21 FRONT AND SIDE FLASHER LIGHT UNIT

No.	Description	No.	Description
1	Light lens securing screw	4	Sidelamp bulb
2	Light body and seal	5	Flasher bulb
3	Light lens		

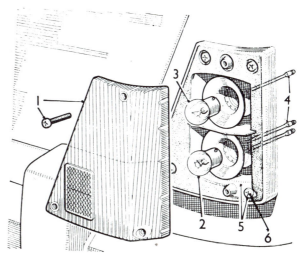

FIG. 10:22 STOP, TAIL AND REAR FLASHER LIGHT UNIT

No.	Description	No.	Description
1	Light lens and securing screw	4	Electric cables
2	Stop and tail light bulb	5	Light body and seal
3	Flasher bulb	6	Light body securing screw

43   Instrument panel and printed circuit (cable gear change models) - removal and replacement

1   Disconnect the positive and then the negative terminals from the battery.

2   Working beneath the instrument panel undo and remove the three screws and plain washers securing the instrument panel to the facia (Fig. 10:26).

3   Release the speedometer cable from the rear of the instrument.

4   Withdraw the multi pin wiring plug from the instrument panel.

5   The instrument panel may now be removed by moving it downwards slightly to disengage the upper mounting lugs and lifting away the complete instrument panel.

6   If it is necessary to remove the instrument panel printed circuit refer to Section 45 and remove the fuel and temperature gauges.

7   Refer to Section 49 and remove the voltage stabilizer.

8   The three voltage stabilizer terminals should next be removed, these being held by small self tapping screws (Fig. 10:27).

9   Remove the seven bulb holders from the printed circuit board.

10   Using a knife, thin screwdriver or pliers, very carefully remove the four pins that secure the printed circuit board to the rear of the instrument panel.

11   The printed circuit board may now be removed from the rear of the instrument panel.

12   Refitting the printed circuit and instrument panel is the reverse sequence to removal.

44   Speedometer head and cable (cable gear change models) - removal and replacement

1   Refer to Section 43 paragraphs 1 to 5 and remove the instrument panel.

2   Locate and then remove the two self tapping screws that retain the instrument moulding to the facia panel (Fig. 10:28).

3   Slacken the centre retaining screw and remove the instrument moulding together with the tubes for the warning lights.

4   Release the three clips and carefully withdraw the instrument cowl assembly.

5   Remove the seat slip ring mask assembly.

6   Undo and remove the two screws with shaped plain washers and lift away the speedometer lead. It is not necessary to remove the speedometer mounting rubber.

7   Refitting the speedometer head is the reverse sequence to removal.

8   Should it be necessary to remove the speedometer cable, it should first be released from the rear of the speedometer lead and then from the transmission unit connection. Next, release the rubber clip retaining the speedometer cable to the air cleaner intake tube. The speedometer cable may now be withdrawn from the car.

9   Refitting the speedometer cable is the reverse sequence to removal but the following additional points should be noted:

a)   Well lubricate the inner cable by withdrawing it and lightly greasing it except for 8 inches at the speedometer end. Refit the inner cable and wipe away excess grease.

b)   It is important that there is approximately 3/8 inch of inner cable projecting from the outer cable at the speedometer end.

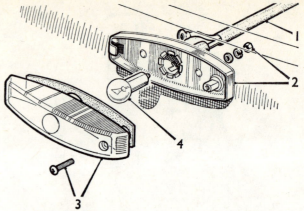

FIG. 10:23 DIRECTION INDICATOR SIDE REPEATER LIGHT UNIT

No.	Description	No.	Description
1	Feed cables	3	Light lens and securing screw
2	Light body and securing nuts	4	Bulb

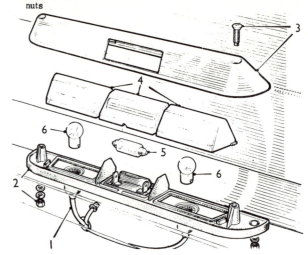

FIG. 10:24 NUMBER PLATE AND REVERSE LIGHT UNIT

No.	Description	No.	Description
1	Feed cables	4	Light lenses
2	Light body and securing nuts	5	Reverse lamp bulb
3	Light lens cover and securing screws	6	Number plate bulbs

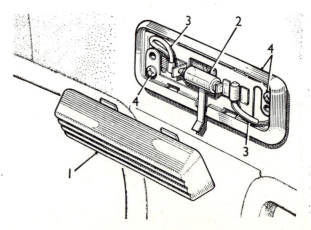

FIG. 10:25 INTERIOR LIGHT UNIT

No.	Description	No.	Description
1	Lens	3	Feed cable
2	Bulb	4	Light body and securing screws

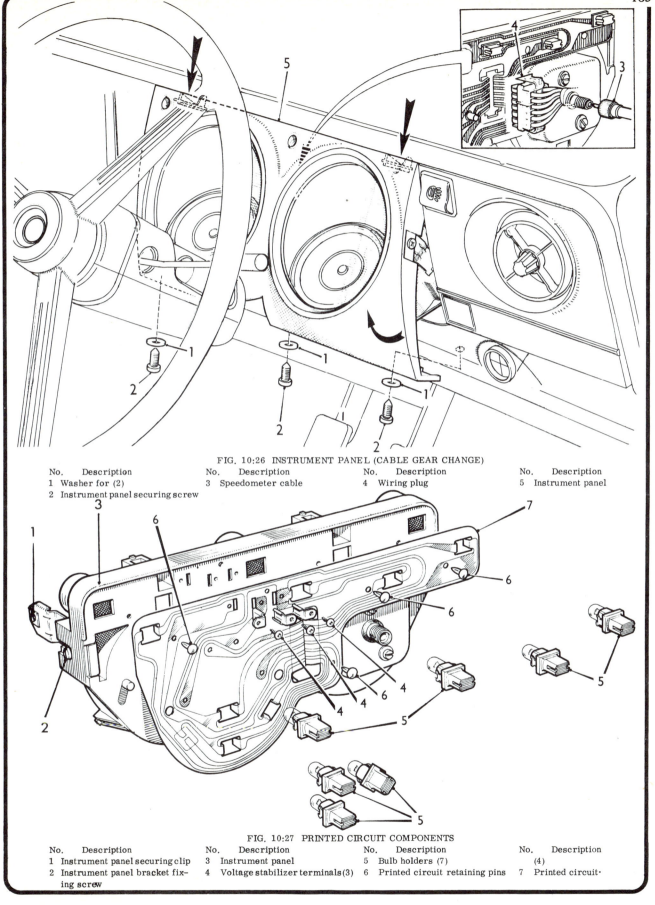

FIG. 10:26 INSTRUMENT PANEL (CABLE GEAR CHANGE)

No.	Description	No.	Description	No.	Description	No.	Description
1	Washer for (2)	3	Speedometer cable	4	Wiring plug	5	Instrument panel
2	Instrument panel securing screw						

FIG. 10:27 PRINTED CIRCUIT COMPONENTS

No.	Description	No.	Description	No.	Description	No.	Description
1	Instrument panel securing clip	3	Instrument panel	5	Bulb holders (7)		(4)
2	Instrument panel bracket fixing screw	4	Voltage stabilizer terminals(3)	6	Printed circuit retaining pins	7	Printed circuit·

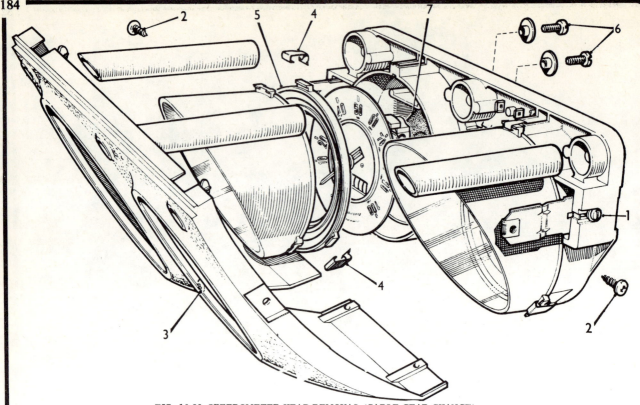

FIG. 10:28 SPEEDOMETER HEAD REMOVAL (CABLE GEAR CHANGE)

No.	Description	No.	Description	No.	Description	No.	Description
1	Instrument panel	3	Centre retaining screw	5	Seat slip ring		screws and washers
2	Side screws retaining instrument moulding	4	Cowl assembly retaining clips	6	Speedometer head retaining	7	Speedometer mounting rubber

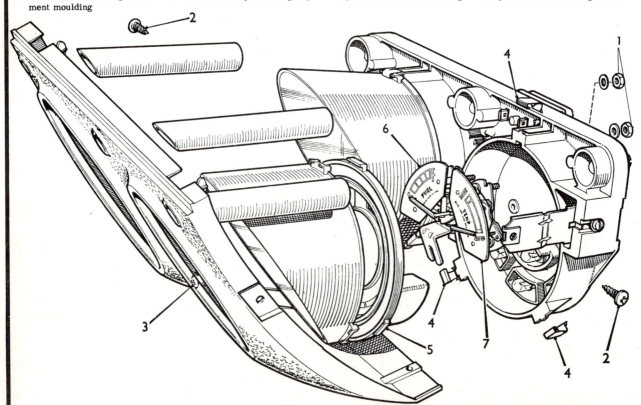

FIG. 10:29 FUEL AND TEMPERATURE GAUGES REMOVAL (CABLE GEAR CHANGE)

No.	Description	No.	Description	No.	Description	No.	Description
1	Gauge securing nuts		ment moulding	4	Cowl assembly retaining clips	6	Fuel gauge
2	Side screws retaining instru-	3	Centre retaining screw	5	Mask assembly	7	Temperature gauge

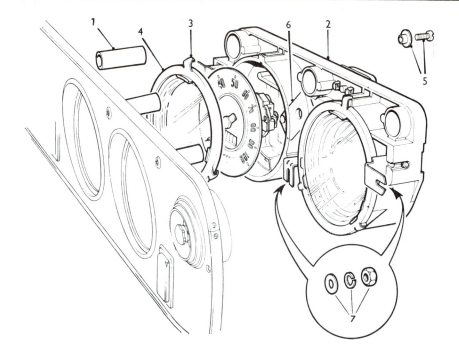

FIG. 10:30 SPEEDOMETER HEAD REMOVAL (ROD GEAR CHANGE)

No.	Description	No.	Description	No.	Description	No.	Description
1	Warning light tube	4	Glass rim assembly		screws and washers	7	Instrument panel securing
2	Instrument panel	5	Speedometer head retaining	6	Speedometer mounting rubber		nuts and washers
3	Glass rim retaining clips						

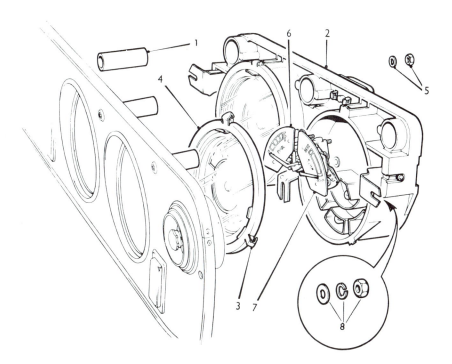

FIG. 10:31 FUEL AND TEMPERATURE GAUGES REMOVAL(ROD GEAR CHANGE)

No.	Description	No.	Description	No.	Description	No.	Description
1	Warning light tube	4	Glass rim assembly	6	Fuel gauge	8	Instrument panel securing
2	Instrument panel	5	Gauge securing nuts	7	Temperature gauge		nuts and washers
3	Glass rim retaining clips						

c)   The positioning of the cable is important so that there is a minimum of 6 inches bend radius at any point and furthermore no bend within 2 inches at either end of the cable.
d)   The cable retaining clips must not be overtightened.
e)   Do not overtighten the connections at either end of the cable. These must be finger tight only.

45   Fuel and temperature gauge (cable gear change models) - removal and replacement

1   Refer to Section 43 paragraphs 1 to 5 and remove the instrument panel.
2   Locate and then remove the two self tapping screws that retain the instrument moulding to the facia panel (Fig. 10.29).
3   Slacken the centre retaining screw and remove the instrument moulding together with the tubes for the warning lights.
4   Release the three clips and carefully withdraw the instrument cowl assembly.
5   Remove the seat slip ring/mask assembly.
6   Undo and remove the nuts and plain washers that secure the two gauges, and lift away the fuel and temperature gauges. Take extreme care not to touch the needles as these are fragile and easily bent.
7   Refitting is the reverse sequence to removal.

46   Instrument panel and printed circuit (rod gear change models) - removal and replacement

1   Refer to Chapter 12/14, and remove the facia panel.
2   Undo and remove the three retaining nuts and carefully withdraw the instrument panel together with the tubes for the warning lights.
3   To detach the printed circuit from the instrument panel is basically identical to that for cable gear change models. Full information will be found in Section 43, paragraphs 6 to 11 inclusive.
4   Refitting the printed circuit and instrument panel is the reverse sequence to removal.

47   Speedometer head and cable (rod gear change models) - removal and replacement.

1   Refer to Section 46 and remove the instrument panel.
2   Using a screwdriver or a knife, carefully ease up the glass rim retaining clips and lift away the glass rim assembly (Fig. 10:30).
3   Undo and remove the two screws and shaped plain washers which secure the speedometer lead and lift it away. It is not necessary to remove the speedometer mounting rubber.
4   Refitting is the reverse sequence to removal.
5   Removal and replacement of the speedometer drive cable is basically identical to the cable gear change models and full information will be found in Section 44 paragraphs 8 and 9.

48   Fuel and temperature gauge (rod gear change models) - removal and replacement

1   Refer to Chapter 12/14, and remove the facia panel.
2   Undo and remove the three retaining nuts and carefully withdraw the instrument panel together with the tubes for the warning lights (Fig. 10:31).

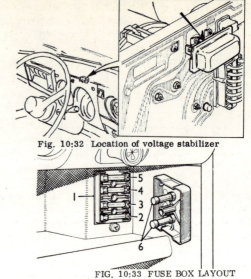

Fig. 10:32 Location of voltage stabilizer

FIG. 10:33 FUSE BOX LAYOUT

No.	Description	No.	Description
1	Fuse box	4	15 amp rated fuse
2	35 amp rated fuse	5	35 amp rated fuse
3	15 amp rated fuse	6	Spare fuses

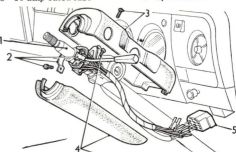

FIG. 10:34 DIRECTION INDICATOR, HORN AND HEADLAMP FLASHER SWITCH

No.	Description	No.	Description
1	Column with steering wheel removed		screws
2	Switch retaining screws	4	Lower cowel and securing screws
3	Upper cowel and securing	5	Multi pin connector

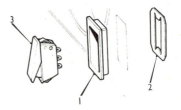

FIG. 10:35 PANEL SWITCHES (rod gear change models)

1   Bezel   3   Switch
2   Retaining plate

Fig. 10:36 Panel switches (cable gear change models)

3   Using a knife or screwdriver, carefully ease up the glass rim retaining clips and lift away the glass rim assembly.
4   Undo and remove the nuts and plain washers that secure the two gauges and lift away the fuel and temperature gauges. Take extreme care not to touch the needles as these are fragile and easily bent.
5   Refitting is the reverse sequence to removal.

49   Voltage stabilizer - removal and replacement

1   The voltage stabilizer is a push fit into the rear of the instrument panel printed circuit board (Fig. 10:32).
2   Before removal, as a safety precaution disconnect the positive and then the negative terminals from the battery.
3   Carefully pull the voltage stabilizer from the rear of the printed circuit.
4   Refitting is the reverse sequence to removal. Note that the terminals of the stabilizer are offset, so it cannot be fitted the wrong way round.

50   Fuses

All fuses are mounted in block form and located on the right hand side panel between the facia panel and parcel shelf. There are four fuses in the electrical circuit and a further two spares in the cover. The layout is shown in Fig. 10:33.

Fuse 2   This has a 35 amp rating and protects the equipment which operates independent of the ignition switch. These include the horn, interior light and headlamp flasher circuit.

Fuse 3   This has a 35 amp rating and protects the right hand panel, side and tail lamps.

Fuse 4   This has a 35 amp rating and protects the left hand panel, side and tail lamps.

Fuse 5   This has a 35 amp rating and protects the circuits which operate only when the ignition switch is on. These include the windscreen wipers, direction indicators, brake lights, heater booster fan, heated backlight and cigar lighter (when fitted).

If any of the fuses blow due to a short circuit, or similar trouble, trace the source of trouble and rectify before fitting a new fuse.

51   Direction indicator, horn and headlamp flasher switch - removal and replacement

Cable gear change models
1   Refer to Chapter 11/15, and remove the steering wheel.
2   For safety reasons disconnect the battery positive and then negative terminals.
3   Undo and remove the screw securing the top half of the switch cowl and lift away the cowl half (Fig. 10:34).
4   Undo and remove the two screws securing the bottom half of the switch cowl and lift away the cowl half.
5   Disconnect the wiring loom multi pin plug from the socket which is located beneath the facia panel.
6   Undo and remove the switch bracket clamp screw and release the bracket. Lift away the switch complete with wiring.
7   Refitting is the reverse sequence to removal.

Rod gear change models
The sequence for removal of the switch combination is basically identical to that for the cable gear change models with the exception that the instructions given in paragraphs 3 and 4 should be reversed.

53   Switches - removal and refitting

Panel switch (Cable gear change models)
1   Using a screwdriver, ease one side of the switch away from the panel. It will be necessary to pack the other side of the switch and lifting up under the flange (Fig. 10:36).
2   Push and lift under the flange on the other side of the switch and withdraw from the panel.
3   Note the electrical cable connections and remove the switch complete with bezel.
4   Using screwdrivers ease the bezel retaining clips and separate the switch from the bezel.
5   Refitting is the reverse sequence to removal.

Panel switch (Rod gear change models)
1   Remove the facia board (see Chapter 12, Section 12).
2   Depress the spring leaves at each end of the switch to remove the retaining plate.
3   Draw the switch out of the panel. Before disconnecting any of the leads, note where each one is fitted.
4   Depress the spring leaves at each end of the switch to remove the switch bezel.
5   Refitting is the reverse sequence to removal.

Ignition switch
Refer to Chapter 11/16 for full information.

Brake light switch
Refer to Chapter 9/24 for full information.

KEY TO WIRING DIAGRAM

Use the one diagram key to identify components on these wiring diagrams. Refer to the appropriate wiring diagram and disregard any additional numbered items appearing in the key.

No.	Description	No.	Description
1.	Dynamo	36.	Windscreen wiper switch
2.	Control box	37.	Windscreen wiper motor
3.	Battery	38.	Ignition/starter siwtch
4.	Starter solenoid	39.	Ignition coil
5.	Starter motor	40.	Distributor
6.	Lighting switch	42.	Oil pressure switch
7.	Headlamp dip switch	43.	Oil pressure warning lamp
8.	RH headlamp	44.	Ignition warning lamp
9.	LH headlamp	45.	Speedometer
10.	Main beam warning lamp	46.	Water temperature gauge
11.	RH sidelamp	47.	Water temperature transmitter
12.	LH sidelamp	49.	Reverse lamp switch
14.	Panel lamps	50.	Reverse lamp
15.	Number plate lamps	57.	Cigar lighter *
16.	RH stop/tail lamp	60.	Radio *
17.	LH stop/tail lamp	64.	Bi-metal instrument voltage stabilizer
18.	Stop lamp switch	67.	Line fuse, 35 amp
19.	Fuse block	77.	Electric windscreen washer *
20.	Interior lamp	78.	Windscreen washer switch *
21.	RH door switch	83.	Induction heater and thermostat *
22.	LH door switch	84.	Suction chamber heater *
23.	Horn	110.	RH repeater flasher
24.	Horn-push	111.	LH repeater flasher
25.	Flasher	115.	Rear window demist switch *
26.	Direction indicator and headlamp flasher switch	116.	Rear window demist unit *
27.	Direction indicator warning lamps	139A.	Alternative connection - lead added to harness from nine-way socket to headlamp when existing lead is not required *
28.	RH front flasher lamp	150.	Rear window demist warning lamp *
29.	LH front flasher lamp	152.	Hazard warning lamp *
30.	RH rear flasher lamp	153.	Hazard warning switch *
31.	LH rear flasher lamp	154.	Hazard warning flasher unit *
32.	Heater blower switch *	158.	Printed circuit instrument panel *
33.	Heater blower motor *	159.	Brake pressure warning lamp and lamp test-push *
34.	Fuel gauge	164	Ballast resistor
35.	Fuel gauge tank unit		

*Accessory or optional extra when fitted.

Cable Colour Code

N. Brown	P. Purple	W. White
U. Blue	G. Green	Y. Yellow
R. Red	LG. Light Green	B. Black
	O. Orange	

When a cable has two colour code letters the first denotes the main colour and the second denotes the tracer colour

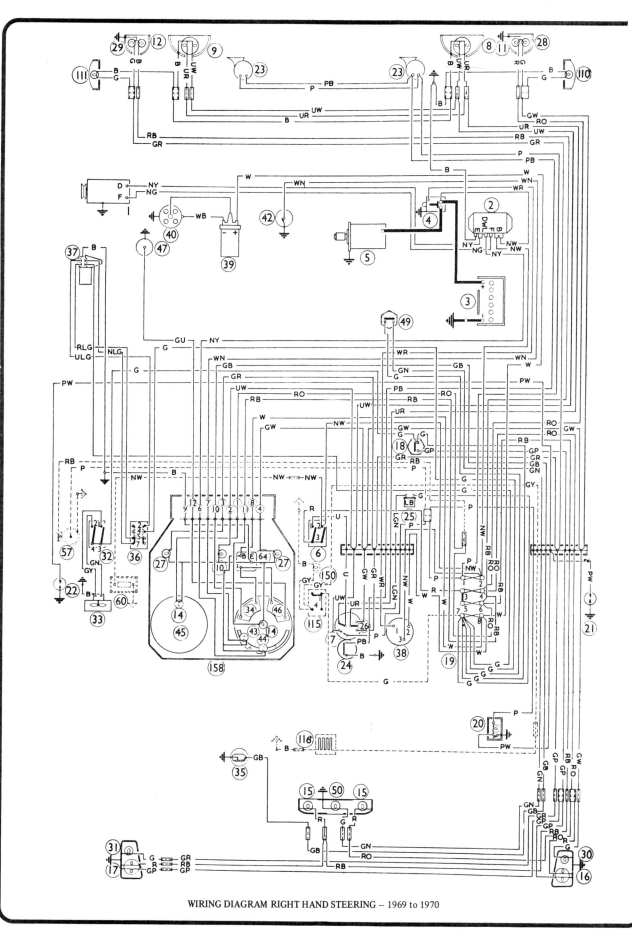

Wiring Diagram Right Hand Steering – 1969 to 1970

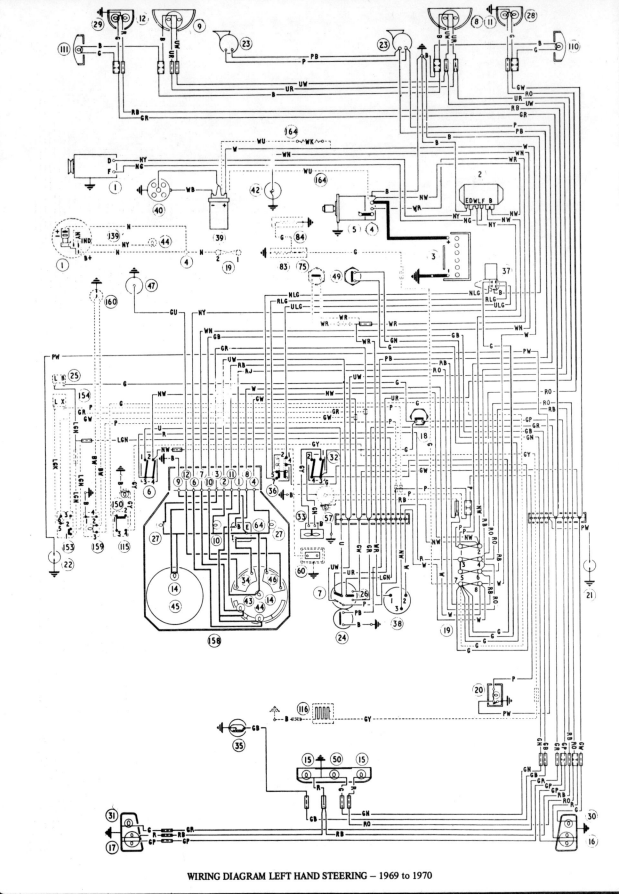

WIRING DIAGRAM Left Hand Steering – 1969 to 1970

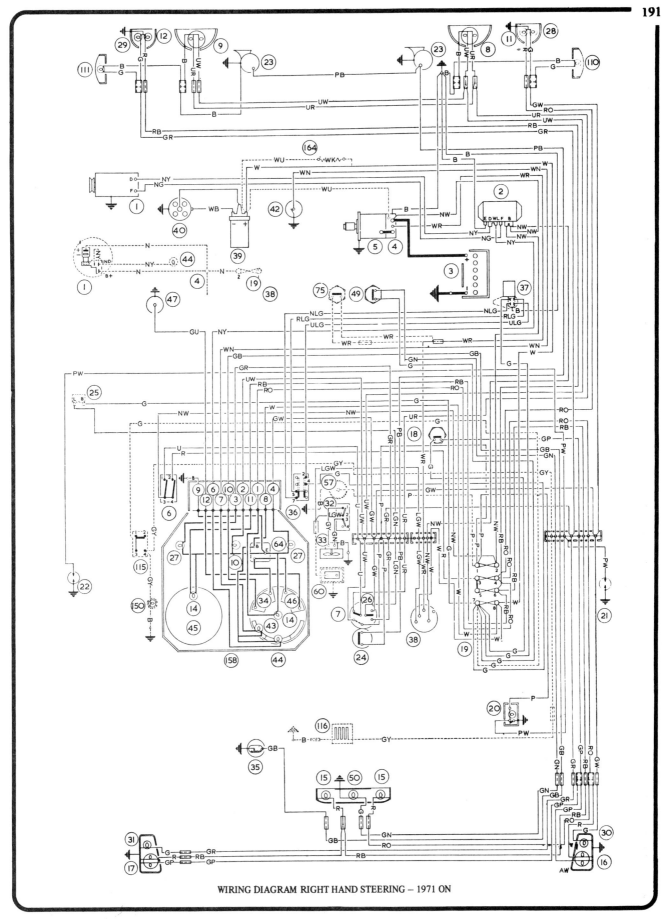

WIRING DIAGRAM RIGHT HAND STEERING – 1971 ON

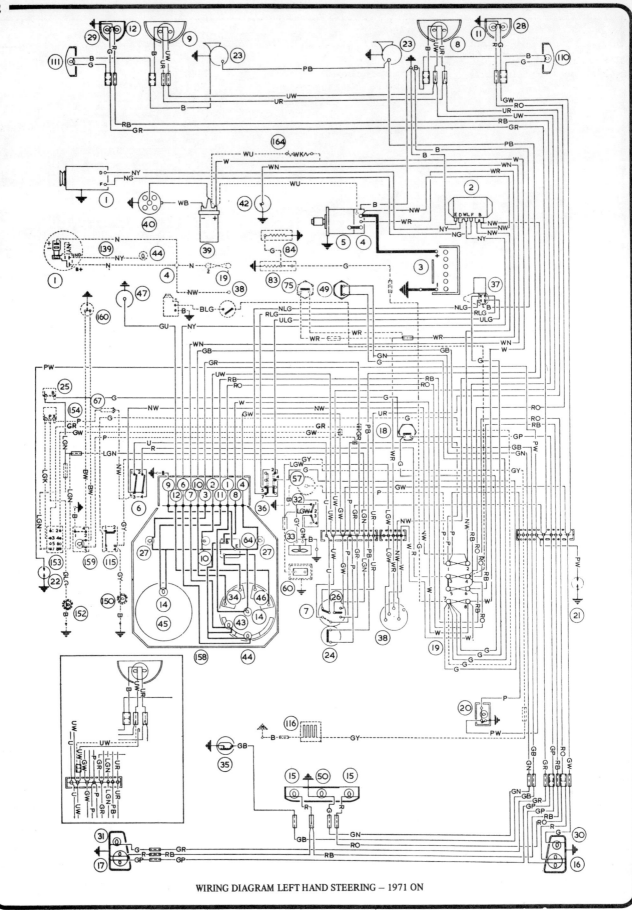

WIRING DIAGRAM LEFT HAND STEERING – 1971 ON

Fault Finding Chart - Electrical system

Cause	Trouble	Remedy
SYMPTOM: STARTER MOTOR FAILS TO TURN ENGINE		
No electricity at starter motor	Battery discharged	Charge battery.
	Battery defective internally	Fit new battery.
	Battery terminal leads loose or earth lead not securely attached to body	Check and tighten leads.
	Loose or broken connections in starter motor circuit	Check all connections and check any that are loose.
	Starter motor switch or solenoid faulty	Test and replace faulty components with new.
Electricity at starter motor: faulty motor	Starter motor pinion jammed in mesh with ring gear	Disengage pinion by turning squared end of armature shaft.
	Starter brushes badly worn, sticking, or brush wires loose	Examine brushes, replace as necessary, tighten down brush wires.
	Commutator dirty, worn, or burnt	Clean commutator, recut if badly burnt.
	Starter motor armature faulty	Overhaul starter motor, fit new armature.
	Field coils earthed	Overhaul starter motor.
SYMPTOM: STARTER MOTOR TURNS ENGINE VERY SLOWLY		
Electrical defects	Battery in discharged condition	Charge battery.
	Starter brushes badly worn, sticking, or brush wires loose	Examine brushes, replace as necessary, tighten down brush wires.
	Loose wires in starter motor circuit	Check wiring and tighten as necessary.
SYMPTOM: STARTER MOTOR OPERATES WITHOUT TURNING ENGINE		
Dirt or oil on drive gear	Starter motor pinion sticking on the screwed sleeve	Remove starter motor, clean starter motor drive.
	Pinion or ring gear teeth broken or worn	Fit new gear ring, and new pinion to starter motor drive.
SYMPTOM: STARTER MOTOR NOISY OR EXCESSIVELY ROUGH ENGAGEMENT		
Lack of attention or mechanical damage	Pinion or ring gear teeth broken or worn	Fit new ring gear, or new pinion to starter motor drive.
	Starter drive main spring broken	Dismantle and fit new main spring.
	Starter motor retaining bolts loose	Tighten starter motor securing bolts. Fit new spring washer if necessary.
SYMPTOM: BATTERY WILL NOT HOLD CHARGE FOR MORE THAN A FEW DAYS		
Wear or damage	Battery defective internally	Remove and fit new battery.
	Electrolyte level too low or electrolyte too weak due to leakage	Top up electrolyte level to just above plates
	Plate separators no longer fully effective	Remove and fit new battery.
	Battery plates severely sulphated	Remove and fit new battery.
	Fan/dynamo belt slipping	Check belt for wear, replace if necessary, and tighten.
	Battery terminal connections loose or corroded	Check terminals for tightness, and remove all corrosion.
	Dynamo not charging properly	Remove and overhaul dynamo.
	Short in lighting circuit causing continual battery drain	Trace and rectify.
	Regulator unit not working correctly	Check setting, clean, and replace if defective
SYMPTOM: IGNITION LIGHT FAILS TO GO OUT, BATTERY RUNS FLAT IN A FEW DAYS		
Dynamo	Fan belt loose and slipping, or broken	Check, replace, and tighten as necessary.
	Brushes worn, sticking, broken, or dirty	Examine, clean, or replace brushes as necessary.
	Brush springs weak or broken	Examine and test. Replace as necessary.
	Commutator dirty, greasy, worn, or burnt	Clean commutator and undercut segment separators.
	Armature badly worn or armature shaft bent	Fit new or reconditioned armature.

Cause	Trouble	Remedy
Dynamo not charging	Commutator bars shorting	Undercut segment separations.
	Dynamo bearings badly worn	Overhaul dynamo, fit new bearings.
	Dynamo field coils burnt, open, or shorted	Remove and fit rebuilt dynamo.
	Commutator no longer circular	Recut commutator and undercut segment separators.
	Pole pieces very loose	Strip and overhaul dynamo. Tighten pole pieces.
Regulator or cut-out fails to work correctly	Regulator incorrectly set	Adjust regulator correctly.
	Cut-out incorrectly set	Adjust cut-out correctly.
	Open circuit in wiring of cut-out and regulator unit	Remove, examine, and renew as necessary.

Failure of individual electrical equipment to function correctly is dealt with alphabetically, item by item, under the headings listed below:

FUEL GAUGE

Fuel gauge gives no reading	Fuel tank empty!	Fill fuel tank.
	Electric cable between tank sender unit and gauge earthed or loose	Check cable for earthing and joints for tightness.
	Fuel gauge case not earthed	Ensure case is well earthed.
	Fuel gauge supply cable interrupted	Check and replace cable if necessary.
	Fuel gauge unit broken	Replace fuel gauge.
Fuel gauge registers full at the time	Electric cable between tank unit and gauge broken or disconnected	Check over cable and repair as necessary.

HORN

Horn operates all the time	Horn-push either earthed or stuck down	Disconnect battery earth. Check and rectify source of trouble.
	Horn cable to horn push earthed	Disconnect battery earth. Check and rectify source of trouble.
Horn fails to operate	Blown fuse	Check and renew if broken. Ascertain cause
	Cable or cable connection loose, broken or disconnected	Check all connections for tightness and cables for breaks.
	Horn has an internal fault	Remove and overhaul horn.
Horn emits intermittent or unsatisfactory noise	Cable connections loose	Check and tighten all connections.
	Horn incorrectly adjusted	Adjust horn until best note obtained.

LIGHTS

Lights do not come on	If engine not running, battery discharged	Push-start car, charge battery.
	Light bulb filament burnt out or bulbs broken	Test bulbs in live bulb holder.
	Wire connections loose, disconnected or broken	Check all connections for tightness and wire cable for breaks.
	Light switch shorting or otherwise faulty	By-pass light switch to ascertain if fault is in switch and fit new switch as appropriate.
Lights come on but fade out	If engine not running battery discharged	Push-start car, and charge battery.
Lights give very poor illumination	Lamp glasses dirty	Clean glasses.
	Reflector tarnished or dirty	Fit new reflectors.
	Lamps badly out of adjustment	Adjust lamps correctly.
	Incorrect bulb with too low wattage fitted	Remove bulb and replace with correct grade
	Existing bulbs old and badly discoloured	Renew bulb units.
	Electrical wiring too thin not allowing full current to pass	Rewire lighting system.
Lights work erratically - flashing on and off, especially over bumps	Battery terminals or earth connection loose	Tighten battery terminals and earth connection.
	Lights not earthing properly	Examine and rectify.

Cause	Trouble	Remedy
	Contacts in light switch faulty	By-pass light switch to ascertain if fault is in switch and fit new switch as appropriate.
WIPERS Wiper motor fails to work	Blown fuse	Check and replace fuse if necessary.
	Wire connections loose, disconnected, or broken	Check wiper wiring. Tighten loose connections.
	Brushes badly worn	Remove and fit new brushes.
	Armature worn or faulty	If electricity at wiper motor remove and overhaul and fit replacement armature.
	Field coils faulty	Purchase reconditioned wiper motor.
Wiper motor works very slowly and takes excessive current	Commutator dirty, greasy, or burnt	Clean commutator thoroughly.
	Drive to wheelboxes too bent or unlubricated	Examine drive and straighten out severe curvature. Lubricate.
	Wheelbox spindle binding or damaged	Remove, overhaul, or fit replacement.
	Armature bearings dry or unaligned	Replace with new bearings correctly aligned
	Armature badly worn or faulty	Remove, overhaul, or fit replacement armature.
Wiper motor works slowly and takes little current	Brushes badly worn	Remove and fit new brushes.
	Commutator dirty, greasy, or burnt	Clean commutator thoroughly.
	Armature badly worn or faulty	Remove and overhaul armature of fit replacement.
Wiper motor works but wiper blades remain static	Driving cable rack disengaged or faulty.	Examine and if faulty, replace.
	Wheelbox gear and spindle damaged or worn	Examine and if faulty, replace.
	Wiper motor gearbox parts badly worn	Overhaul or fit new gearbox.

Chapter 11 Suspension, dampers and steering

Contents

Specifications

Front suspension	Independant. Hydrolastic displacers interconnected front and rear. Mounted crosswise in subframe. Swivel axles ball jointed to upper and lower arms.
Rear suspension	Independant with trailing radius arms. Rubber and ball jointed to Hydrolastic displacers - mounted horizontally.

Suspension trim
    (Wheel arch to hub centre)
    Front (cable gear change)... ... ... 14.1 ± 0.25 in (358 ± 6.4 mm)
         (rod gear change) ... ... 14.0 ± 0.25 in (356 ± 6.4 mm)
    Rear ... ... 14.6 ± 0.25 in (370.8 ± 6.4 mm)
         (cable gear change)... ... ...   245 lb/sq in* (17.2 Kg/cm^2)
         (rod gear change) ... ...   225 lb/sq in* (15.8 Kg/cm^2)
    * The pressure must be adjusted to give correct trim height.

Steering
    Make ... ...   Cam gear
    Type ... ...   Rack and pinion with steering lock. Rubber joint in column.
Steering wheel diameter:
    Cable gear change   ... ...   16.25 in (413 mm)
    Rod gear change... ... ...   15 in (381 mm)
Steering wheel turns - lock to lock:
    Cable gear change 3.9
    Rod gear change 4.2
Front suspension data (unladen):
    Front wheel alignment:
        Cable gear change   ... ...   1/16 in (1.6 mm) toe-in
        Rod gear change ... ...   1/16 in to 1/8 in (1.6 to 3.8 mm) toe-in
        Swivel hub inclination 12º
Camber angle:
    Cable gear change   ... ...   1º positive
    Rod gear change... ... ... $1\frac{1}{2}º \pm \frac{3}{4}º$ positive
Castor angle:
    Cable gear change   ... ...   4º positive
    Rod gear change... ... ...   4º $\pm$ 1º positive

Specifications

Rear suspension data (unladen):
    Camber angle:

Cable gear change	0°
Rod gear change...	$0^o \pm 1^o$
Rear wheel alignment:	
Cable gear change	Parallel
Rod gear change...	0 to 1/16 in (0 to 1.6 mm) toe-in
Wheels	$4\frac{1}{2}$ C x 13 disc
Tyres...	155 – 13 Dunlop SP68 Tubeless
	Goodyear Tubeless
	Radial ply

Tyre pressures

Front*	26lb/sq in (1.8 Kg/cm^2)
Rear*	24lb/sq in (1.7 Kg/cm^2)

      * All motoring conditions.

Torque wrench settings	lb ft	Kg m
Front suspension:		
Upper and lower ballpin assembly	45	6.2
Lower arm to body	15	2.1
Lower arm pivot nuts	50	6.9
Sub-frame to body	25	3.4
Sub-frame to dash lower panel...	15	2.1
Hub nut (align to next hole)	150	20.7
Ballpin assembly to swivel hub...	38 to 45	5.2 to 6.2
Mud shield to swivel hub	17 to 25	2.35 to 3.46
Diving flange to brake disc	38 to 45	5.3 to 6.22
Caliper unit to swivel hub bolts	40 to 50	5.53 to 6.91
Suspension arm pivot bolt...	20	2.8
Road wheel nuts...	50	6.9
Rear suspension:		
Support brackets to body	25	3.4
Suspension pivot nuts...	50	6.9
Pivot joint to housing and body...	65	9
Rear arch springs to body...	15	2.1
Outer bearing retaining bolt	60	8.3
Outer bearing to body fixing bolts	30	4.1
Hub nut (align to next hole)	60	8.3
Pivot joint to reaction lever	70 to 80	9.7 to 11
Cap nut – ball joints	70 to 80	9.7 to 11
Steering:		
Steering wheel nut	32 to 37	4.4 to 5.1
Column coupling to pinion...	15	2.1
Balljoint to steering arms...	25	3.4
Rack cover plate	12 to 18	1.7 to 2.5
Balljoint locking ring...	33 to 37	4.6 to 5.1
Ball end locknuts	35 to 40	4.8 to 5.5
Steering shear screws	18	2.5

1   General description

The hydrolastic suspension system makes use of a special displacer unit at each wheel. The front and rear displacer units are connected together front to rear, on each side, by strong metal tubes and flexible piping.

Made from sheet steel and rubber, as shown in Fig. 11:4, each displacer unit comprises a lower and upper chamber housing, and a nylon reinforced diaphragm together with a compressed rubber conical spring. Damper valves in the top of the fluid separating chamber perform the function normally done by separate shock absorbers on other cars.

The displacer units are filled with a mixture of water, alcohol and anti-corrosive additives. They work in the following manner:

When either of the front wheels hits a bump, the piston moves up with the suspension and displaces the diaphragm. This increases the pressure in the unit and so forces some fluid from the lower to the upper chamber.

This causes the rubber spring to deflect and to transfer some liquid via the interconnecting pipe to the rear displacer unit on the same side. As the fluid enters the rear top chamber, it pushes down on the piston which results in the rear of the car being raised. This occurs far more quickly than it takes to describe.

The same process happens when a rear wheel meets a bump, but in reverse, as the fluid is now forced into one of

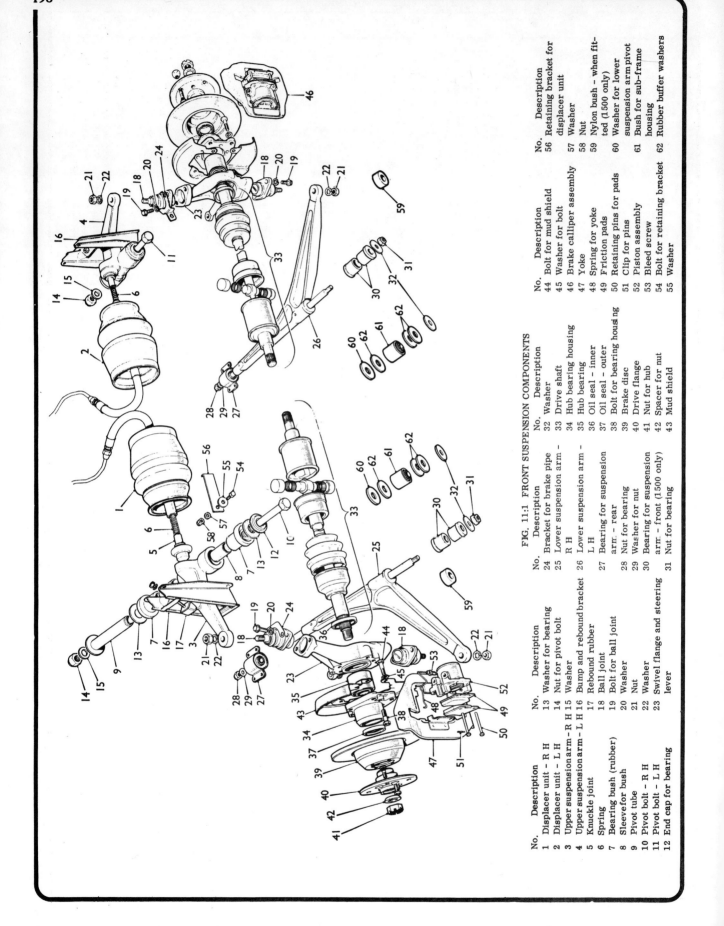

FIG. 11:1 FRONT SUSPENSION COMPONENTS

No.	Description	No.	Description	No.	Description	No.	Description
1	Displacer unit - R H	13	Washer for bearing	24	Bracket for brake pipe	44	Bolt for mud shield
2	Displacer unit - L H	14	Nut for pivot bolt	25	Lower suspension arm - R H	45	Washer for bolt
3	Upper suspension arm - R H	15	Washer	26	Lower suspension arm - L H	46	Brake calliper assembly
4	Upper suspension arm - L H	16	Bump and rebound bracket	27	Bearing for suspension arm - rear	47	Yoke
5	Knuckle joint	17	Rebound rubber	28	Nut for bearing	48	Spring for yoke
6	Spring	18	Ball joint	29	Washer for nut	49	Friction pads
7	Bearing bush (rubber)	19	Bolt for ball joint	30	Bearing for suspension arm - front (1500 only)	50	Retaining pins for pads
8	Sleeve for bush	20	Washer	31	Nut for bearing	51	Clip for pins
9	Pivot tube	21	Nut	32	Washer	52	Piston assembly
10	Pivot bolt - R H	22	Washer	33	Drive shaft	53	Bleed screw
11	Pivot bolt - L H	23	Swivel flange and steering lever	34	Hub bearing housing	54	Bolt for retaining bracket
12	End cap for bearing			35	Hub bearing	55	Washer
				36	Oil seal - inner	56	Retaining bracket for displacer unit
				37	Oil seal - outer	57	Washer
				38	Bolt for bearing housing	58	Nut
				39	Brake disc	59	Nylon bush - when fitted (1500 only)
				40	Drive flange	60	Washer for lower suspension arm pivot
				41	Nut for hub	61	Bush for sub-frame housing
				42	Spacer for nut	62	Rubber buffer washers
				43	Mud shield		

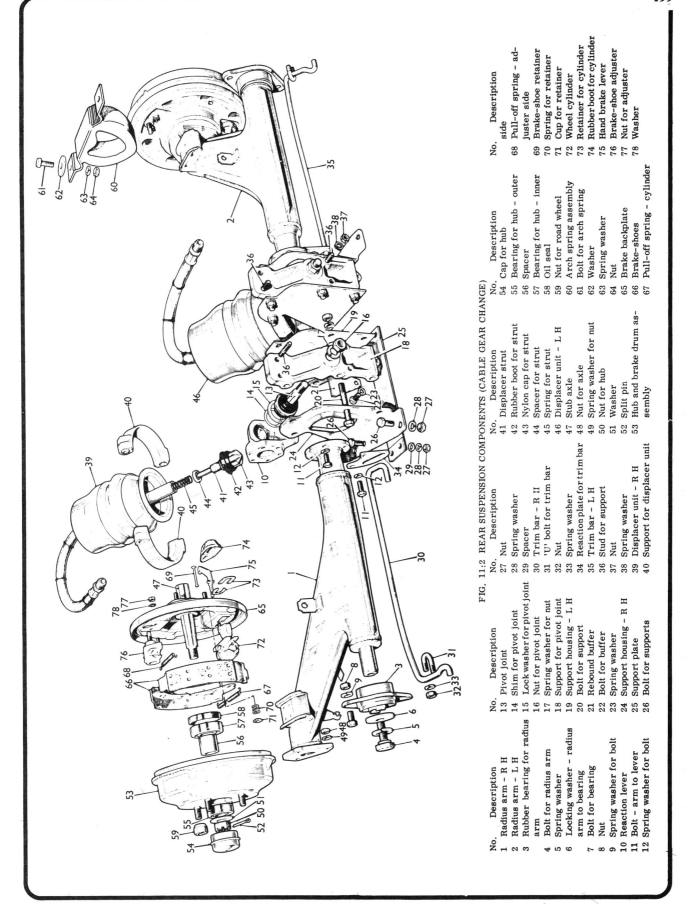

FIG. 11:2 REAR SUSPENSION COMPONENTS (CABLE GEAR CHANGE)

No.	Description	No.	Description	No.	Description	No.	Description
1	Radius arm – R H	13	Pivot joint	27	Nut	41	Displacer strut	54	Cap for hub
2	Radius arm – L H	14	Shim for pivot joint	28	Spring washer	42	Rubber boot for strut	55	Bearing for hub – outer
3	Rubber bearing for radius arm	15	Lock washer for pivot joint	29	Spacer	43	Nylon cap for strut	56	Spacer
4	Bolt for radius arm	16	Nut for pivot joint	30	Trim bar – R H	44	Spacer for strut	57	Bearing for hub – inner
5	Spring washer	17	Spring washer for nut	31	'U' bolt for trim bar	45	Spring washer for strut	58	Oil seal
6	Locking washer – radius arm to bearing	18	Support for pivot joint	32	Nut	46	Displacer unit – L H	59	Nut for road wheel
7	Bolt for bearing	19	Support housing – L H	33	Spring washer	47	Stub axle	60	Arch spring assembly
8	Nut	20	Bolt for support	34	Reaction plate for trim bar	48	Nut for axle	61	Bolt for arch spring
9	Spring washer	21	Rebound buffer	35	Trim bar – L H	49	Spring washer for nut	62	Washer
10	Reaction lever	22	Bolt for buffer	36	Stud for support	50	Nut for hub	63	Spring washer
11	Bolt – arm to lever	23	Spring washer	37	Nut	51	Washer	64	Nut
12	Spring washer for bolt	24	Support housing – R H	38	Spring washer	52	Split pin	65	Brake backplate
		25	Support plate	39	Displacer unit – R H	53	Hub and brake drum as-	66	Brake-shoes
		26	Bolt for supports	40	Support for displacer unit		sembly	67	Pull-off spring – cylinder side
								68	Pull-off spring – adjuster side
								69	Brake-shoe retainer
								70	Spring for retainer
								71	Cup for retainer
								72	Wheel cylinder
								73	Retainer for cylinder
								74	Rubber boot for cylinder
								75	Hand brake lever
								76	Brake-shoe adjuster
								77	Nut for adjuster
								78	Washer

the front displacer units. In this way it is possible to obtain a very comfortable ride with a minimum of rolling and pitching.

The front displacer units are mounted horizontally in the cross tube which is formed in the front sub frame. The displacer units react against upper wishbones with lower arms providing a fore and aft location. The swivel axles are ball jointed top and bottom. The upper wishbones are fitted with Simplex bonded rubber bushes, whilst the lower arms are mounted at the front end in Silentbloc rubber bushes, and at the rear in Metalastic bonded rubber bushes.

The rear displacers are mounted centrally at the rear and react against short balljoint - mounted levers coupled to the trailing arms. Torsional type trim bars are fitted which react against the trailing arms. The trailing arms are mounted at their outer end in metalastic bonded rubber bushes.

Rack and pinion steering is fitted to models covered by this manual. Positioned at each end of the rack is a balljoint which is attached to the inner end of the tie rod. The balljoint, and part of the tie rod, is enclosed in a rubber gaiter which is held in position by a clip at each end. It protects the ball joint and rack, preventing road dust and dirt entering and causing premature wear.

The outer end of the tie rod is threaded for adjustment, and is adjusted by shims between the end cover and pinion housing, whilst backlash between the pinion and rack is controlled by shims between the cover plate yoke and the pinion housing.

2   Front hubs - removal and replacement

1   Refer to Chapter 9/12, paragraphs 1 to 7 inclusive and remove the brake disc assembly.
2   Undo and remove the nut securing the steering arm swivel ball joint and, using a universal ball joint separator, release the ball joint from the steering arm.
3   Undo and remove the two bolts and spring washers securing the lower suspension arm ball joint to the swivel flange.
4   Using a universal three legged puller and suitable thrust block, carefully draw the hub assembly from the drive shaft.
5   Should the inner track of the hub bearing be retained on the drive shaft, it will be necessary to remove it using the universal puller, and binding the legs together with wire to stop them springing off the inner track when the puller centre bolt is screwed in.
6   To dismantle the swivel hub for overhaul, unscrew the six bolts securing the bearing housing to the swivel flange and withdraw the bearing housing from the swivel flange.
7   Lift away the brake disc shield from the swivel flange.
8   Using a screwdriver, ease the oil seal from the swivel flange and also from the bearing housing. New oil seals will be required for refitting.
9   Using a vice and suitable diameter tube to locate on the outer track of the bearing, press the bearing from the housing.
10   Thoroughly wash all parts, except for the oil seals which must be renewed, and carefully examine the bearing housing and swivel flange for signs of wear, damage and cracks. Obtain new parts as necessary.
11   Inspect the bearing for wear, by reassembling if the inner track has parted from the assembly and holding the inner track. Rotate the outer track and feel for signs of roughness or excessive movement. Look for pit marks or signs of overheating due to lack of lubricant. If the bearing assembly is suspect always obtain a new assembly.

12   To reassemble, first pack the bearing assembly with Castrol LM Grease and place the two oil seals in clean oil. Allow to soak for a few minutes.
13   Using a suitable diameter piece of metal tube, carefully drift the oil seal into the swivel flange. The lip of the oil seal must face inwards.
14   With the vice and packing, press the bearing assembly into the housing.
15   In a similar manner to that described in paragraph 13, fit the second disc shield to the swivel flange followed by the bearing housing, and secure with the six bolts.
16   Refit the brake disc shield to the swivel flange followed by the bearing housing, and secure with the six bolts.
17   Refitting the swivel flange assembly is now the reverse sequence to removal but it will be necessary to make up a tool like the one shown in Fig. 7:6 to enable the assembly to be drawn onto the drive shaft.

3   Rear hubs - removal and replacement

1   Refer to Chapter 9/4, paragraphs 1 to 6 inclusive and remove the rear brake drum and hub assembly.
2   Should the inner track of the inside bearing still be in position on the rear hub axle, it will be necessary to draw it off using a universal puller and binding the legs together with wire to stop them springing off the inner track when the puller centre bolt is screwed in.
3   Using a screwdriver, ease the oil seal from the centre of the drum/hub assembly noting which way round the seal is fitted.
4   Using a soft metal drift, drive out the inner track of the inner bearing. Lift out the distance piece, noting that the reduced internal diameter or interally shouldered end is fitted next to the outer bearing.
5   The soft metal drift is now used again to drive out the inner track of the outer bearing.
6   Finally drift out the outer tracks of both the inner and outer bearings.
7   Thoroughly wash all parts, except for the oil seal which must be renewed, and carefully examine the hub and shaft for wear, damage and cracks. Obtain new parts as necessary.
8   Inspect the bearings for wear by reassembling and holding the inner track. Rotate the outer track and feel for signs of roughness or excessive movement. Look for pit marks or signs of overheating due to lack of lubricant. If a bearing assembly is suspect, always obtain a new assembly.
9   To reassemble, first pack the bearing assembly with Castrol LM Grease. Place the new oil seal in clean oil and allow to soak for a few minutes.
10   Reassembly is now the reverse sequence to dismantling with the exceptions mentioned in the following paragraphs:
11   The bearing spacer must be fitted with its reduced internal diameter or internally shouldered end next to the outer bearing.
12   When refitting the new oil seal, the lip must face inwards and the outer edge be flush with its housing.
13   The hub dust caps must not be filled with grease, but fitted dry.

4   Rear hub axle - removal and replacement

1   Refer to Chapter 9/4, paragraphs 1 to 6 inclusive and remove the rear brake and hub assembly.

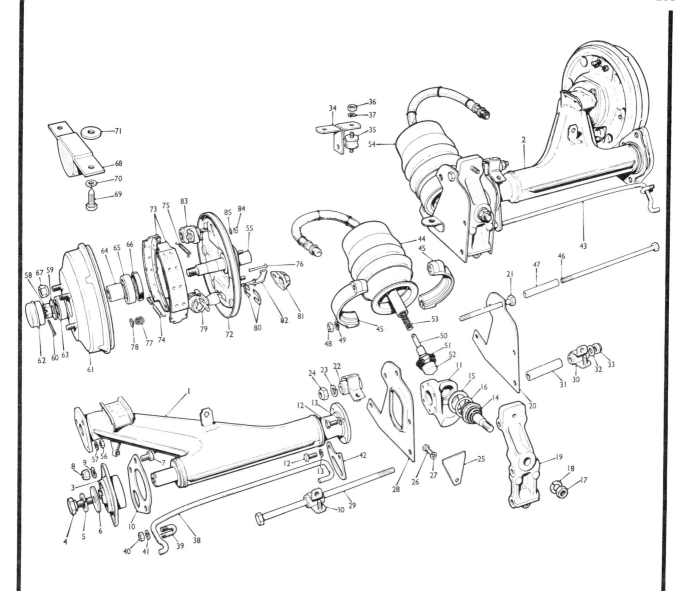

FIG. 11:3 REAR SUSPENSION COMPONENTS (ROD GEAR CHANGE)

No.	Description	No.	Description	No.	Description	No.	Description
1	Radius arm - R H	22	Upper mounting bracket	44	Displacer unit - R H	66	Oil seal
2	Radius arm - L H	23	Nut for support bolt	45	Support for displacer unit	67	Nut for road wheel
3	Rubber bearing for radius arm	24	Spring washer	46	Bolt for displacer support	68	Arch spring assembly
4	Bolt for radius arm	25	Rebound buffer	47	Distance tube for support bolt	69	Bolt for arch spring
5	Spring washer for bolt	26	Bolt for buffer	48	Nut for displacer support bolt	70	Spring washer
6	Locking washer - radius arm to bearing	27	Spring washer	49	Spring washer	71	Washer
7	Bolt for bearing	28	Support housing - R H	50	Displacer unit strut	72	Brake backplate
8	Nut	29	Lower bolt for support	51	Rubber boot for strut	73	Brake -shoes
9	Spring washer	30	Lower mounting bracket	52	Nylon cap for strut	74	Pull-off spring - cylinder side
10	Lashing plate	31	Distance tube for support bolt	53	Spring for strut	75	Pull-off spring - adjuster side
11	Reaction lever	32	Flat washer	54	Displacer unit - L H	76	Brake-shoe retainer
12	Bolt - arm to lever	33	Nut for support bolt	55	Stub axle	77	Spring for retainer
13	Spring washer	34	Exhaust pipe mounting bracket	56	Nut for axle	78	Cup for retainer
14	Pivot joint	35	Rubber mounting	57	Spring washer	79	Wheel cylinder
15	Shim for pivot joint	36	Nut for rubber mounting	58	Nut	80	Retainer for cylinder
16	Lock washer for pivot joint	37	Spring washer	59	Washer	81	Rubber boot for cylinder
17	Nut	38	Trim bar - R H	60	Split pin	82	Hand-brake lever
18	Spring washer	39	'U' bolt for trim bar	61	Hub and brake-drum assembly	83	Brake-shoe adjuster
19	Support for pivot joint	40	Nut for bolt	62	Cap for hub	84	Nut for adjuster
20	Support housing - L H	41	Spring washer	63	Bearing for hub - outer	85	Washer
21	Upper bolt for support	42	Reaction plate for trim bar	64	Spacer for bearings		
		43	Trim bar - L H	65	Bearing for hub - inner		

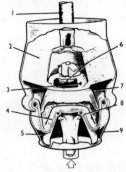

FIG. 11:4 HYDROLASTIC SUSPENSION DISPLACER UNIT

No.	Description	No.	Description
1	Interconnecting pipe	6	Damper valves
2	Rubber spring	7	Fluid-separating member
3	Damper bleed	8	Rubber diaphragm (nylon-reinforced)
4	Butyl liner		
5	Tapered piston	9	Tapered cylinder

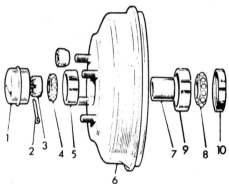

FIG. 11:5 REAR HUB COMPONENTS

No.	Description	No.	Description
1	Dust cap	6	Brake drum
2	Split pin	7	Spacer
3	Castellated nut	8	Race and inner track (inner bearing)
4	Race and inner track (outer bearing)	9	Outer track (inner bearing)
5	Outer track (outer bearing)	10	Oil seal

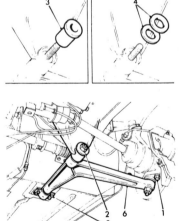

FIG. 11:6 FRONT LOWER SUSPENSION ARM

No.	Description	No.	Description
1	Lower swivel ball joint securing bolts		hers
2	Nut and special washer	5	Suspension arm rear bearing housing securing bolts
3	Sub frame housing rubber bush	6	Lower suspension arm asembly
4	Lower arm rubber buffer was-		

2   Extract the split pin, and lift away the plain washer locking the clevis pin securing the handbrake cable yoke to the wheel cylinder handbrake lever. Lift away the clevis pin.

3   Wipe the top of the brake master cylinder reservoir and unscrew the cap. Place a piece of thick polythene over the reservoir and refit the cap. This is to stop the hydraulic fluid syphoning out.

4   Using an open ended spanner, carefully unscrew the hydraulic pipe connection union to the rear of the wheel cylinder.

5   Undo and remove the three nuts with spring washers securing the hub axle and backplate to the radius arm.

6   Using a tapered soft metal drift, carefully drive the hub axle and backplate from the radius arm and separate the hub axle from the backplate.

7   Refitting is the reverse sequence to removal. It will be necessary to bleed the brake hydraulic system as described in Chapter 9/3.

5   Lower suspension arm (front) - removal and replacement

1   Apply the handbrake and chock the rear wheels. Jack up the front of the car and place on firmly based stands. Remove the road wheel.

2   Undo and remove the two bolts with spring washers that secure the lower swivel ball joint to the swivel flange (Fig. 11:6).

3   Undo and remove the large nut and special plain washer from the suspension arm front bearing shaft.

4   Cable gear change models only. Carefully ease out the rubber bush from the sub frame housing, exposed when the nut and washer were removed as in the previous paragraph.

5   Rod gear change models only. Lift away the rubber buffer washers from the sub frame housing, exposed when the nut and washer were removed as in paragraph 3.

6   Undo and remove the four bolts with spring washers securing the suspension arm rear bearing housing to the body.

7   The lower suspension arm assembly may now be lifted away from the sub frame housing.

8   Rod gear change models only. Remove the rubber buffer washer and large washer from the suspension arm.

9   Cable gear change models only. Remove the nylon bush (if fitted), or the rubber bush, from the suspension arm.

10   Undo and remove the nut and spring washer securing the swivel ball joint to the suspension arm.

11   Using a universal ball joint separator, part the ball joint from the suspension arm.

12   Undo and remove the rear bearing retaining nut and ease off the rear bearing.

13   Inspect all bushes for signs of wear or oil contamination and, if either is evident, obtain new parts.

14   To reassemble, first refit the rear bearing and retaining nut but do not tighten fully yet.

15   Refit the swivel ball joint and secure with the retaining nut and spring washers.

16   Cable gear change models only. Refit the rubber bush or nylon bush as was originally fitted.

17   Rod gear change models only. Fit the large washer, making sure the chamfer is facing towards the rear of the suspension arm, and then the rubber buffer washer.

18   Refitting the suspension arm assembly is the reverse sequence to removal. It is very important that all fixings are finally tightened with the car on the ground in the normal unladen condition.

19   The front wheel alignment must be checked and further information will be found in Section 23.

6   Upper suspension arm (front) - removal and replacement

1   Before commencing work, refer to Section 13 where information will be found on depressurisation of the hydrolastic suspension. Unless the equipment is close at hand at a BLMC garage it is recommended that the work in this Section should not be attempted, but entrusted to a garage.
2   Reference in this Section is made to the left hand side or right hand side of the car. This is relevant to which side the upper suspension arm is fitted and not to the driver's position.
3   Left hand side only. Working in the engine compartment undo and remove the two bolts, plain and rubber washers that secure the radiator top mounting bracket to the cowling (Fig. 11:7).
4   Chock the rear wheels and apply the handbrake. Jack up the front of the car and place on firmly based axle stands. Remove the road wheel.
5   The suspension may now be depressurised. For this it is usually necessary to use special equipment, but it may be done by unscrewing the valve cap and, using a large jam jar to catch the fluid, very carefully depressing the centre of the valve. Do not depress it fully as the hydrolastic suspension is pressurized to approximately 245 lb/sq inch. Use a small screwdriver for this job.
6   Left hand side only. Undo and remove the two bolts with plain and rubber washers that secure the radiator lower mounting bracket to the radiator.
7   Left hand side only. Carefully move the radiator sufficiently for the upper suspension arm pivot bolt to be removed later on.
8   Wipe the top of the brake master cylinder reservoir and unscrew the cap. Place some thick polythene over the top of the reservoir and replace the cap. This is to stop hydraulic fluid syphoning out when the brake pipe is disconnected.
9   Using an open ended spanner, disconnect the brake pipe at its connection with the flexible hose.
10   With a small garage jack, or suitable packing, support the weight of the hub assembly.
11   Undo and remove the two bolts and spring washers that secure that upper swivel ball joint to the swivel.
12   Undo and remove the nut and spring washer from the upper suspension arm pivot and then withdraw the pivot bolt.
13   Undo and remove the four bolts that secure the bump stop and rebound plate.
14   Carefully lower the hub assembly and lift away the bump stop and rebound plate.
15   The upper suspension arm may now be lifted from the front suspension sub frame.
16   If the bearing fitted into the inner end of the suspension arm requires renewal, this is a job best left to the local BLMC garage who will have the necessary tools and equipment to do the job in a satisfactory manner.
17   Refitting is the reverse sequence to removal but the following additional points should be noted:
18   Before refitting the suspension arm, make sure that the displacer unit spring is positioned correctly.

19   The knuckle joint assembly and suspension arm bearing surfaces must be lubricated with PBC (Polybutylcuprysil) or Rocol Folliac J166 Grease.

20   Provided the BLMC garage is only a short distance away, the suspension may be completely assembled, the brakes bled and then the car driven very slowly to his premises to have the suspension pressurised again.

7   Radius arm (rear) - removal and replacement

1   Refer to Section 10 and remove the trim bar.
2   Extract the split pin locking the handbrake cable yoke clevis pin at the handbrake lever on the brake/backplate. Lift away the plain washer and withdraw the clevis pin. Note that the head of the clevis pin is uppermost (Fig. 11:8).
3   Wipe the top of the brake master cylinder reservoir and unscrew the cap. Place some thick polythene over the top of the reservoir and replace the cap. This is to stop hydraulic fluid syphoning out when the brakepipe is disconnected.
4   Using an open ended spanner, disconnect the brake pipe at its connection with the flexible hose located at the centre of the radius arm.
5   Undo and remove the radius arm to bearing retaining bolt, spring washer and bearing locating washer from the outer bearing.
6   Undo and remove the bolt that secures the lashing plate. (Rod gear change model only).
7   The two bolts securing the outer bearing may now be removed and then, using a suitable drift, drive the bearing and housing assembly outwards from the body.
8   Undo and remove the four bolts and spring washers that secure the radius arm to the reaction lever.
9   The complete radius arm and hub assembly may now be lifted away from under the car.
10   Release the brake pipe from the clip on the radius arm.
11   Undo and remove the three nuts and spring washers that secure the hub shaft to the radius arm and, using a suitable diameter drift, drive the hub and shaft assembly from the radius arm.
12   Refitting the rear radius arm is the reverse sequence to removal. It is important that the retaining boss of the radius arm aligns with the lugs of the outer bearing before fitting the locating washer and bolt.

8   Reaction lever assembly - removal and replacement

Rod gear change models
1   Refer to Section 7 and remove the rear radius arm.
2   Refer to Section 12 and remove the two rear displacer units.
3   Using a garage jack, support the reaction lever assembly.
4   Raise the rear seat cushion and undo and remove the two nuts with spring and plain washers. Also remove the six bolts with spring and plain washers, all these fixings securing the reaction lever assembly to the underside of the body.
5   Lift away the reaction lever assembly from under the car.
6   Refitting is the reverse sequence to removal. Note that the two uppermost bolts have the largest diameter plain washers under their heads.

Cable gear change models
1   Follow the previous sequence for removal, paragraphs 1 to 3 inclusive.
2   Undo and remove the two nuts and spring washers from the outer support plate securing bolts.
3   Raise the rear seat cushion and undo and remove the six nuts with washers securing the reaction lever assembly to the underside of the body.
4   Lift away the reaction lever assembly from under the car.
5   Refitting is the reverse sequence to removal.

9   Reaction lever assembly - dismantling and reassembly

Rod gear change models

1   Undo and remove the two upper bolts that secure the side support plates to the reaction lever assembly (Fig. 11:9).
2   Undo and remove the long bolt and s p a c e r that holds the two side support plates together.
3   Undo and remove the large diameter nut and spring washer that secures the reaction pivot. Carefully push the reaction lever and pivot assembly from the housing support.
4   Lift away the spring from the pivot joint.
5   Unlock and remove the pivot joint housing, complete with ball pin and top socket, using a long box spanner. Lift away the lock washers and shims.
6   The reaction lever assembly is now completely dismantled and should be washed and wiped dry ready for inspection.
7   Check the components of the ball pin and socket assembly for signs of wear. If evident, a new assembly must be obtained. Generally inspect the side support plates and reaction lever for evidence of strain, elongation of bolt holes, and bent long through bolts. Obtain new parts as necessary.
8   To reassemble, first fit the ball pin, top socket and housing leaving out the lock washer and shims. Screw the housing down until no end play exists between the ball pin and seating.
9   Hold the threaded end of the ball pin and make sure it can be rotated about its axis. Then m e a s u r e the gap between the housing and reaction lever with feeler gauges.
10   Remove the ball pin and housing assembly and fit a new lock washer, shims to the thickness of the measured gap less 0.036 inch for the thickness of the lock washer and has 0.009 to 0.013 inch for the required preload.
11   Refit and tighten the housing assembly to a torque wrench setting of 70 to 80 lb ft using either a long socket or a box spanner with socket on the end to give the required connection to the torque wrench.
12   Reassembly is now the reverse sequence to removal.

Cable gear change models

1   Follow the dismantling sequence f o r rod gear change models with the exception of paragraph 2 and the first half of paragraph 3.
2   When the ball pin and top socket have been removed, the bottom socket in the reaction lever may be removed.
3   Inspection and reassembly is the same procedure as for rod gear change models except for the difference in dismantling as noted in the first paragraph of this subsection.

10   Trim bar - removal and replacement

1   Before commencing work refer to Section 6, paragraphs 1 and 13, where information will be found on depressurisation of the hydrolastic suspension.
2   Chock the front wheels. Jack up the rear of the car and support on firmly based stands. Remove the road wheel.
3   Depressurise the system.
4   Using a small jack, raise the hub until the radius arm compresses the rear wheel arch stop.
5   Undo and remove the two nuts and spring washers from the 'U' bolt that secures the trim bar to the body (Fig. 11:11)
6   Undo and remove the two bolts and spring washers that secure the reaction plate to the radius arm.
7   The trim bar and reaction plate may now be lifted away from under the car.

8   Refitting is the reverse sequence to removal. Provided the BLMC garage is only a short distance away, the suspension may be left deflated and the car driven very slowly to the garage to have the suspension pressurised again.

11   Displacer unit (front) - removal and replacement

1   Refer to Section 6 and remove the upper suspension arm.
2   Working in a similar manner to the removal of a brake or clutch flexible hose, disconnect the displacer hose from the steel suspension pipe (Fig. 11:12).
3   Undo and remove the clip nut, bolt and spring washer securing the outer end of the displacer hose to the body.
4   Undo and remove the nut, bolt, plain and spring washer securing the displacer unit retaining bracket and lift away the displacer unit.
5   Refitting is the reverse sequence to removal. It is important that the bearing surfaces of the knuckle joint assembly and upper s u s p e n s i o n arm are l u b r i c a t e d with PBC (Polybutylcuprysil) or Rocol Folliac J166 Grease.

12   Displacer unit (rear) - removal and replacement

Rod gear change

1   Before commencing work refer to Section 6, paragraphs 1 and 13 where information will be found on depressurisation of the hydrolastic suspension.
2   Depressurise the system.
3   Chock the front wheels. Jack up the rear of the car and support on firmly based stands. Remove the road wheels.
4   Left hand side only. For safety reasons disconnect the battery. Refer to Chapter 3/21, and remove the fuel tank. Also completely remove the exhaust system from the car.
5   Undo and remove the c l i p nut, bolt, plain and spring washer securing the outer end of the displacer hose to the body (Fig. 11:13).
6   Working in a similar manner to the removal of a brake flexible hose, disconnect the displacer hose from the steel suspension pipe.
7   Undo and remove the two bolts that secure the displacer unit supports, making a note that distance tubes are fitted on the bolts between the support plates.
8   The displacer may now be lifted away from the underside of the car.
9   Finally remove the spring, knuckle joint assembly and nylon cap.
10   Refitting is the reverse sequence to removal but the following additional points should be noted:
a)   It is important that the bearing surfaces of the knuckle joint assembly and reaction lever are lubricated with PBC (Polybutylcuprysil) or Rocol Folliac J166 Grease.
b)   When reassembling the knuckle joint, the rubber boot of the knuckle joint must be fitted to the nylon cap before refitting into the reaction lever.
c)   The d i s p l a c e r supports must be fitted with their flat faces towards the rear of the car.

Cable gear change

1   Refer to the instructions above for the rod gear change paragraphs 1, 3 and 4.
2   Undo and remove the two long through bolts, nuts and spring washers securing the displacer unit supports (Fig. 11:14).
3   Undo and remove the four nuts, bolts, spring and plain

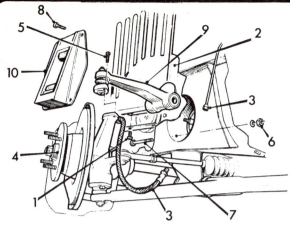

FIG. 11:7 FRONT UPPER SUSPENSION ARM

No.	Description	No.	Description
1	Engine to radiator lower bracket bolts	6	Suspension arm pivot bolt nut
2	Radiator	7	Pivot bolt
3	Brake pipe	8	Bump stop and rebound plate securing bolts
4	Hub assembly	9	Suspension arm
5	Upper swivel ball joint securing bolt		

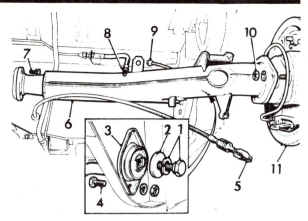

FIG. 11:8 REAR RADIUS ARM

No.	Description	No.	Description
1	Radius arm to bearing retaining bolt	7	Radius arm to reaction lever securing bolts
2	Locating washer	8	Radius arm assembly
3	Bearing and housing assembly	9	Flexible brake hose
4	Lashing plate securing bolts	10	Hub shaft securing nuts
5	Hand brake cable	11	Hub and shaft assembly
6	Outer bearing securing bolts		

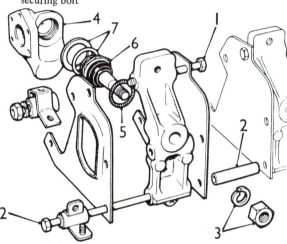

FIG. 11:9 REACTION LEVER COMPONENTS (ROD GEAR CHANGE)

No.	Description	No.	Description
1	Side support plates to reaction lever securing upper bolts		retaining nut and washer
2	Side support plates to reaction lever securing lower bolt and spacer	4	Reaction lever pivot assembly
		5	Spring
3	Reaction lever pivot	6	Ball pin and socket
		a	assembly
		7	Lock washers and shims

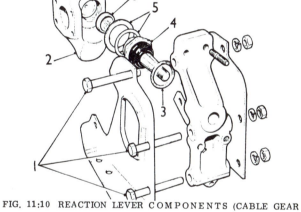

FIG. 11:10 REACTION LEVER COMPONENTS (CABLE GEAR CHANGE)

No.	Description	No.	Description
1	Side support plates to reaction lever securing bolts	4	Ball pin and socket assembly
2	Reaction lever pivot assembly	5	Lock washer and shims
3	Spring	6	Bottom socket

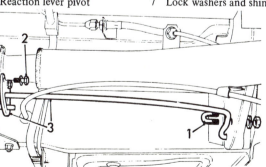

FIG. 11:11 TRIM BAR

No.	Description	No.	Description
1	'U' bolt		to radius arm
2	Bolts securing reaction plate	3	Trim bar and reaction plate

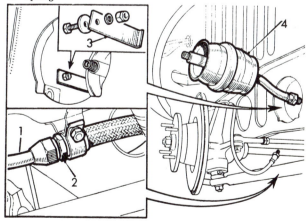

FIG. 11:12 FRONT DISPLACER UNIT REMOVAL

No.	Description	No.	Description
1	Suspension pipe	3	Body clip for hose/pipe connection
2	Displacer hose connection to suspension pipe	4	Displacer unit

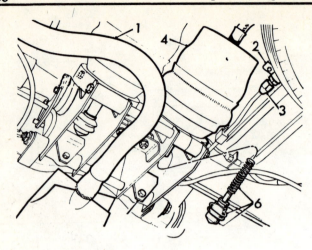

FIG. 11:13 REAR DISPLACER UNIT REMOVAL (ROD GEAR
                            CHANGE)

No.	Description	No.	Description
1	Exhaust system	4	Displacer unit
2	Displacer hose clip	5	Rebound rubber
3	Displacer unit hose connection to suspension pipe	6	Knuckle joint assembly

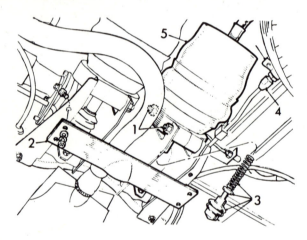

FIG. 11:14 REAR DISPLACER UNIT REMOVAL (CABLE GEAR
                            CHANGE)

No.	Description	No.	Description
1	Displacer unit support securing bolts	4	Displacer unit hose connection to suspension pipe
2	Tie plate	5	Displacer unit
3	Knuckle joint assembly		

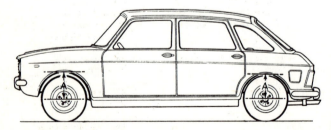

FIG. 11:15 TRIM HEIGHT CHECK
A. Measurement between hub centre and lower wing edge

washers securing the tie plate and lift away the tie plate.
Note which way round it is fitted.
5   Remove the knuckle joint assembly, spacers, nylon cap
and spring.
6   Undo and remove the clip nut, bolt, plain and spring
washer, securing the outer end of the displacer hose to the
body.
7   Working in a similar manner to the removal of a brake
flexible hose, disconnect the displacer hose from the steel
suspension pipe.
8   The displacer may now be lifted away from the underside
of the car.
9   Refitting is the reverse sequence to removal but the additional points noted for the rod gear change are also applicable. (See paragraph 10 of the previous sub section).

13   Trim height and displacer unit pressurisation

Should it be necessary to adjust the suspension height or
carry out work on the suspension which entails depressurisation or repressurisation of the hydrolastic suspension system,
it is advisable to ensure that there is a BLMC garage nearby
who can repressurise the system once the work has been
completed. When the need arises to depressurise the system
one method is given using a screwdriver to depress the valve
core and catch the fluid in a large jam jar (see Section 6,
paragraph 5), but it cannot be over emphasised that care
must be taken because of the high pressure involved.
     The car must be driven very slowly with the suspension
system in the deflated condition as the suspension will be up
against the bump rubbers. This is also the case when the
car has suffered accidental damage and the system has lost
the special fluid.
     The trim height of the car may be checked and adjusted
by altering the pressure within the system, the latter work
being carried out by the local BLMC garage. To check trim
height proceed as follows:
1   Remove any excess luggage from the car so that it is in
its normal unladen condition, and drive it onto a flat hard area.
2   Check and adjust the tyre pressures.
3   Bounce the car several times at the front and rear to allow the suspension to be in its normal ride condition.
4   Using a rule or tape, check the trim height and compare
the results with those figures given in the 'Specifications' at the
beginning of this Chapter (Fig. 11:15).
5   The pressure may be increased to raise, or decreased
to lower, the trim height. Should the trim height be difficult
to obtain, further investigation will be necessary. The cause
of the trouble is usually found to be a faulty displacer or flexible hose.

14   Steering – special maintenance.

1   Lubrication of the rack and pinion during normal servicing is unnecessary as the lubricant is retained in the assembly by the rubber gaiters. However, should a loss occur
due to a leak from the rack housing or rubber gaiters, then
the correct amount of oil should be inserted using an oil can.
Obviously before replenishing is carried out, the source of
the leak must be found and rectified.
2   To top up the oil in the rack and pinion steering assembly,
remove the clip from the rubber gaiter on the right hand end
of the steering rack housing and rotate the steering wheel
until the rack is in the normal straight ahead position. Allow

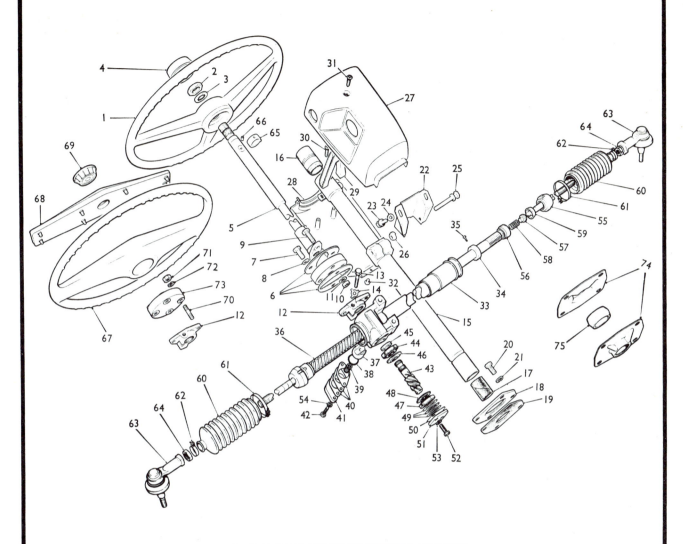

FIG. 11:16 RACK AND PINION STEERING ASSEMBLY

No.	Description	No.	Description	No.	Description	No.	Description
1	Steering-wheel - cable gear-change	18	Toe-plate	38	'O' ring for yoke	58	Spring for seat
2	Steering-wheel nut	19	Gasket	39	Damper spring	59	Tie-rod
3	Washer	20	Bolt	40	Shims	60	Gaiter
4	Steering-wheel motif - cable gear-change	21	Washer	41	Cover for damper	61	Clip for gaiter - large
5	Inner steering-column	22	Bracket for column	42	Bolt	62	Clip for gaiter - small
6	Coupling	23	Bolt for bracket (shear)	43	Pinion	63	Ball end assembly
7	Bolt - coupling to pinion flange	24	Washer	44	Bearing for pinion - upper	64	Locknut
8	Spring washer for bolt	25	Bolt for column (shear)	45	Oil seal	65	Trip for direction indicator switch
9	Bolt - column flange to coupling	26	Nut for bolt (captive)	46	Thrust washer	66	Screw for trip
10	Nut	27	Cowl for column - upper	47	Bearing for pinion - lower	67	Steering-wheel
11	Washer	28	Cowl for column - lower	48	Thrust washer	68	Steering-wheel pad
12	Pinion flange	29	Bracket for cowl	49	Shims	69	Steering-wheel motif
13	Pinch bolt	30	Screw for bracket	50	Gasket	70	Stud - coupling to pinion flange
14	Lock washer	31	Screw for cowl	51	Cover for pinion housing	71	Nut
15	Steering-column - outer	32	Screw for cowl	52	Bolt	72	Spring washer
16	Bush for column (plastic)	33	Rack housing	53	Washer	73	Flexible coupling
17	Bush for column (felt)	34	Bush for housing	54	Washer	74	Clamp plates
		35	Screw for bush	55	Ball housing	75	Bush for clamp plates
		36	Rack	56	Locking ring		
		37	Damper yoke	57	Seat		

Items 7, 8, 9 bracketed: cable gear change

Items 70, 71, 72, 73: Rod gear-change

any remaining oil to seep out, so that it is not overfilled. Using an oil can filled with the recommended grade of oil, insert the nozzle into the end of the rack housing and refill with not more than $\frac{1}{8}$ pint of Castrol Hypoy.

3   Reposition the gaiter and tighten the clip quickly to ensure minimum loss of oil, and then move the steering wheel from lock to lock very slowly to distribute the oil in the housing.

4   If at any time the car is raised and the front wheels are clear of the ground, do not use any excessive force or rapid movement when moving the wheels, especially from one lock to the other, otherwise damage could occur to the steering mechanism.

15   Steering wheel – removal and replacement

1   Cable gear change models. Ease the motif from the centre of the steering wheel hub.

2   Rod gear change models. Using a knife ease the steering wheel pad from the steering wheel spokes by releasing the eight clips positioned in pairs along the length of the pad.

3   With a pencil or scriber mark the relative positions of the steering wheel hub and column so that they may be correctly aligned upon reassembly.

4   Using a socket or box spanner, unscrew the steering wheel retaining nut. Lift away the nut and shakeproof washer.

5   Undo and remove the screw that retains the top half of the switch cowl.

6   Lift the top half of the switch cowl from the column.

7   Undo and remove the screws that retain the lower half of the switch cowl and lift away the bottom half of the switch cowl.

8   Remove the steering wheel by thumping the rear of the rim adjacent to the spokes with the palms of the hands which should loosen the hub splines from the column splines. Lift away the steering wheel.

9   Replacement is the reverse procedure to removal. Align the two marks previously made to ensure the spokes are in the correct position. Refit the shakeproof washer and nut and tighten to a torque wrench setting of 32 to 37 lb ft.

16   Steering lock and ignition/starter switch – removal and replacement

1   Refer to Section 18 or 19, as applicable, and remove the steering column.

2   Refer to Chapter 10/51, and remove the direction indicator switch assembly.

3   Using an 'Easy Out' or other suitable means undo and remove the three special shear retaining screws. If a tool is available they can be drilled out very carefully (Fig. 11:17).

4   The housing and lock assembly may now be lifted away from the column.

5   Refitting the housing and lock assembly is the reverse sequence to removal. New shear screws must be used and tightened until the heads shear at the waisted point. This will occur at a torque wrench setting of approximately 18 lb ft.

17   Steering column top bush – removal and replacement

1   Refer to Chapter 10/51, and remove the direction indicator and headlamp flasher switch.

2   With a pencil or scriber, mark the exact position of the

direction indicator switch trip relative to the inner column.

3   Using a small screwdriver, undo and remove the trip grub screw and slide off the trip ring.

4   Completely remove the direction indicator switch.

5   With a small centre punch or a hook made from thin sheet steel, carefully draw out the old top bush.

6   Refitting the new bush is the reverse sequence to removal, but the following additional points should be noted:

a)   The new bush should be fitted with the chamfered end of the bush entering the outer column first.

b)   Make sure the depression in the outer column engages with the slot in the bush.

18   Steering column (rod gear change) – removal and replacement

1   For safety reasons disconnect the battery.

2   Disconnect the column switch wiring loom at the multipin connector located below the facia.

3   Refer to Section 15 and remove the steering wheel.

4   Undo and remove the four bolts, nuts and spring washers that secure the toe plates. Carefully ease the two toe plates and the rubber grommet, which is between the two plates, up the steering column.

5   Undo and remove the two nuts and spring washers that secure the steering column coupling to the pinion flange.

6   Using a small hacksaw blade, cut a screwdriver slot in the head of the shear bolt that secures the column to the mounting bracket. With a screwdriver unscrew the shear bolt. The shear bolt nut is locked to the bracket so do not try to turn it.

7   The complete steering column assembly may now be lifted away from inside the car. Take care not to touch the headlining with the steering wheel end of the column.

8   To refit the column, first make sure the wheels are in the straight ahead position.

9   Turn the inner column until it is in the straight ahead position and place it in its approximate fitted position.

10   Using a new shear bolt, attach the steering column to its mounting bracket but do not fully tighten it yet.

11   Refit the steering wheel in its original marked position and make sure that the column, gear and steering wheel are all in the straight ahead position.

12   Refit the two nuts with spring washers that secure the column coupling to the pinion flange, and fully tighten.

13   Ease the two toe plates and rubber grommet down the steering column and replace the four nuts, bolts and spring washers.

14   Carefully tighten the steering column to mounting shear bolt, until the hexagon head shears at the waisted joint.

15   Replace the steering wheel shakeproof washer and securing nut and tighten to a torque wrench setting of 32 to 37 lb ft.

16   Reconnect the steering column switch wiring loom multipin connector and finally the two battery terminals.

19   Steering column (cable gear change) – removal and replacement

1   Undo and remove the two bolts that secure the steering pinion flange to the coupling.

2   For safety reasons disconnect the battery.

3   Disconnect the column switch wiring loom at the multipin connector located below the facia.

4   Undo and remove the four bolts, nuts and spring washers

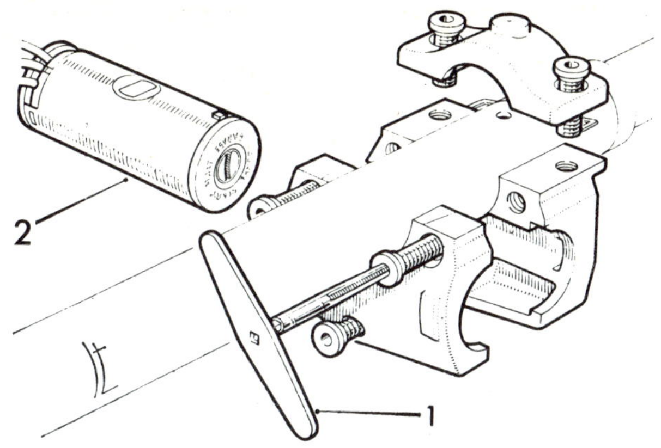

FIG. 11:17 STEERING LOCK AND IGNITION STARTER SWITCH REMOVAL

No.	Description	No.	Description
1	'Easy out' used to remove shear screw	2	Housing and lock assembly

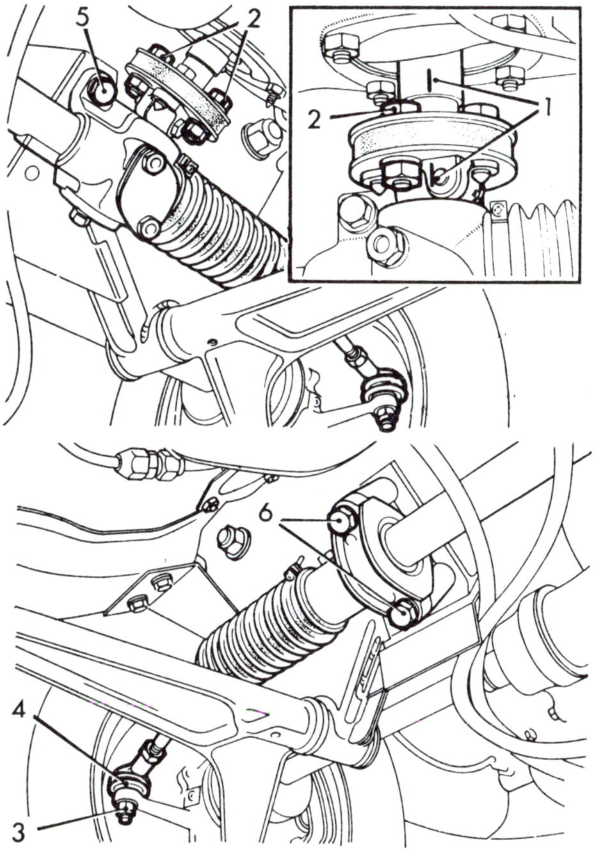

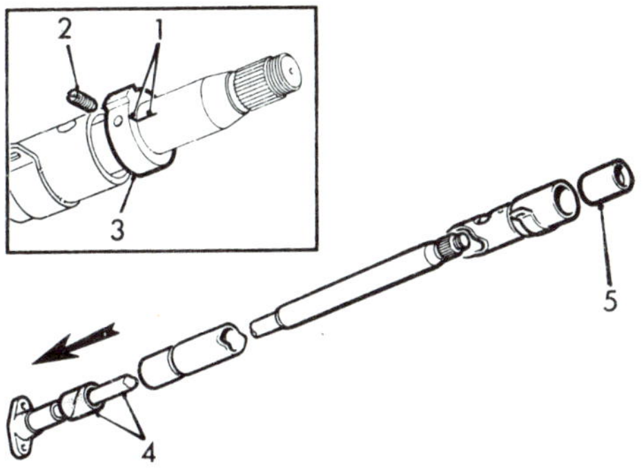

FIG. 11:18 STEERING COLUMN COMPONENTS

No.	Description	No.	Description
1	Alignment marks	4	Lower column and felt bush
2	Grub screw	5	Upper felt bush
3	Trip ring		

FIG. 11:19 STEERING GEAR REMOVAL

No.	Description	No.	Description
1	Alignment marks	4	Ball joint
2	Steering column coupling securing bolts	5	Pinion housing to body securing bolts
3	Steering arm swivel ball joint nut	6	Steering gear clamp securing bolts

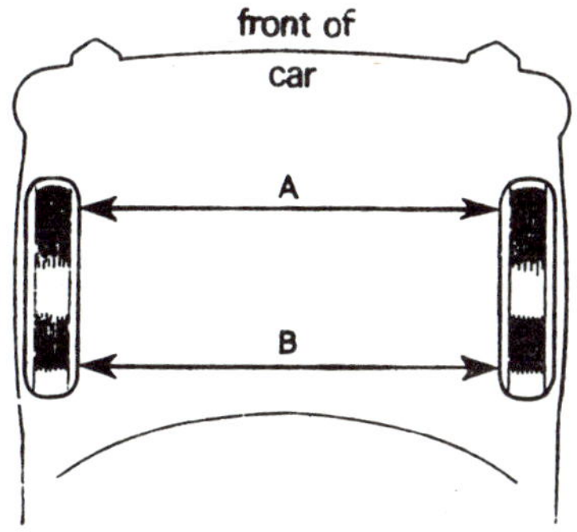

FIG. 11:20 FRONT WHEEL ALIGNMENT
Dimension 'A' must be 1/16 inch less than dimension 'B'

that secure the toe plates. Carefully ease the two toe plates and rubber grommet, which is located between the two plates, up the steering column.

5　Refer to Section 15 and remove the steering wheel.

6　Undo and remove the screw that retains the top half of the switch cowl.

7　Lift the top of the switch cowl from the column.

8　Undo and remove the screws that retain the lower half of the switch cowl and lift away the lower half.

9　Using a small hacksaw blade, cut a screwdriver slot in the head of the shear bolt that secures the column to the mounting bracket. With a screwdriver unscrew the shear bolt. The shear bolt nut is locked to the bracket so do not try to turn it.

10　The complete steering column assembly may now be lifted away from inside the car. Take care not to touch the headlining with the steering wheel end of the column.

11　To refit the column first make sure the wheels are in the straight ahead position.

12　Turn the inner column until it is in the straight ahead position and place it in its approximate fitted position.

13　Using a new shear bolt, attach the steering column to its mounting bracket but do not fully tighten it yet.

14　Refit the steering wheel in its original marked position and make sure that the column, gear and steering wheel are all in the straight ahead position.

15　Carefully tighten the steering column to mounting shear bolt until the hexagon head shears at the waisted joint.

16　Refitting is now the reverse procedure to removal. The steering wheel nut must be tightened to a torque wrench setting of 32 to 37 lb ft.

20　Steering column – dismantling, overhaul and reassembly

1　Refer to Chapter 10/51, and remove the combined direction indicator switch.

2　Refer to Section 16 of this Chapter and remove the steering lock and ignition/starter switch.

3　With a pencil or scriber, mark the exact position of the direction indicator switch trip relative to the inner column (Fig. 11:18).

4　Using a small screwdriver, undo and remove the trip grub screw and slide off the trip ring.

5　The inner column may now be drawn downwards from the outer column. Recover the lower felt bush should it come away from the outer column.

6　If the upper plastic bush has worn, it may be removed by drifting it out using a long metal drift.

7　Undo and remove the two bolts that secure the flexible coupling to the inner column should it have deteriorated.

8　The two toe plates and rubber grommet may now be slid from the outer column.

9　Inspect the rubber grommet between the two toe plates and if it has worn or distorted, a new grommet should be obtained.

10　Reassembly is the reverse sequence to removal. The inner column should be entered into the outer column and positioned so that about 3 inches of the inner column slender position is still visible. Fit the felt bush round the slender position and into its housing. Press the felt inner bush and inner column fully home.

21　Steering gear – removal and replacement

1　Apply the handbrake, chock the rear wheels, jack up the front of the car and support on firmly based stands.

2　Turn the steering wheel until it is in the straight ahead position.

3　Using a scriber or file, mark the pinion housing, coupling and column flange so that they may be correctly refitted (Fig. 11:19).

4　Undo and remove the two nuts, bolts and spring washers from the steering column coupling flange.

5　Undo and remove the nut on each of the two steering arm ball joints and, using a universal ball joint separator, release the ball joints from the steering arms.

6　Undo and remove the two bolts and spring washers that secure the pinion housing to the body.

7　Undo and remove the two bolts and spring washers that secure the steering gear clamp.

8　Carefully move the steering gear assembly to the left sufficiently to disengage it from between the right hand lower suspension arm and sub frame.

9　The steering gear may now be withdrawn from below the right hand side of the body.

10　Refitting the steering gear is the reverse sequence to removal.

22　Steering gear – dismantling, overhaul and reassembly

It is not possible to make any adjustments to the rack and pinion steering gear unless it is removed from the car. With it removed, it is recommended that it be dismantled and the whole unit examined before making any adjustments. This will save having to remove the unit again later because of initial non-detection of wear. If wear is bad, it is best to fit an exchange reconditioned unit.

1　Hold the rack at the pinion body between the soft faces fitted to the jaws of a vice.

2　Ease back the tabs on the pinion flange securing bolt lock washer and unscrew the securing bolt (Fig. 11:16).

3　Turn the pinion until the rack is in the straight ahead position. Note the relative position of the pinion marking (this being either a slot or an arrow should point downwards) the marking on the pinion flange, and their relative positions to a longitudinal centre line of the steering gear. Withdraw the flange.

4　Slacken the ball end locknuts and unscrew the two ball ends from the tie rods.

5　Unscrew the rubber gaiter securing clips to the housing and tie rods and completely remove the clips.

6　Ease the tie rod end of one of the gaiters from contact with the tie rod and allow the oil to drain out - approximate capacity $\frac{1}{3}$ pint.

7　The two rubber gaiters may now be removed.

8　Remove the two damper housing cover plate securing bolts and spring washers and lift away the cover plate, joint washer and packing shims. Place these shims to one side so that they can be replaced as a set upon reassembly. Lift out the damper spring and finally the damper.

9　Remove the bolts and spring washers securing the pinion end cover and lift away the end cover, joint washer and shims. Also lift out the lower thrust washer, bearing and bearing race. The pinion may now be withdrawn from the pinion housing.

10　Lift away the upper bearing race, bearing and thrust

washer.

11   Using a screwdriver, ease out the pinion shaft oil seal. This should be discarded and a new one obtained.

12   With a pin punch, open the indentations in the lock nut clear of the milled slots in the ball joint housing. For this operation use a 'C' spanner of suitable size. This will release the tie rod, ball seat and seat tension spring. Repeat this operation for the other end of the rack.

13   Very carefully, withdraw the rack from the pinion end of the housing, so preventing the teeth damaging the bush in the other end of the housing.

14   Remove the bush retaining screw and extract the bush and its housing from the rack housing.

15   Thoroughly clean all parts with paraffin. Carefully inspect the teeth on the rack and also the pinion for chipping, roughness, uneven wear, hollows or fractures.

16   Carefully inspect the component parts of the inner ball joints for wear or ridging and renew as necessary.

17   The outer track rod joints cannot be dismantled and, if worn, must be renewed as a complete assembly. Examine the component parts of the damper and renew any parts that show signs of wear. Pay particular attention to the oil seals and as a precautionary measure it is always best to renew them.

18   As it is difficult to refill the rack and pinion assembly with oil once it is fitted to the car, make sure that the rubber gaiters are sound before refitting them. If they are in the least bit torn or perished complete loss of oil could occur later and they would then have to be renewed.

19   To reassemble, first fit a new bush into the housing so that the flats of the bush are offset to the bush retaining screw hole in the housing.

20   Insert a metal rod into the bush so that it acts as a support preventing the bush distorting and drill a hole 0.119 inch (3 mm) in diameter through the existing hole in the housing and then through the bush. Coat the threaded portion, and under the head of the screw, with a thick non-setting oil resistant sealer and install it so securing the bush in the rack housing. Check that the screw does not protrude into the bore of the bush.

21   Carefully position the top pinion housing bearing race, bearing and thrust washer into the pinion housing.

22   The rack may now be inserted into the housing, but care must be taken not to allow the teeth to score the bushes. Move the rack into the straight ahead position.

23   Insert the pinion so that the mark ie, slot or arrow on the splined end, is pointing down towards the damper.

24   Refit the lower thrust washer, bearing race and the bearing.

25   Position some shims on the lower bearing so as to provide a gap of approximately 0.010 inch between the face of the housing and housing cover.

26   Refit the housing cover, and evenly tighten the securing bolts until the cover is held securely. Using feeler gauges, determine the clearance between the housing and end cover.

27   Remove the cover and adjust the thickness of the shims so as to give a clearance of 0.007 to 0.009 inch. Allow 0.006 inch for the compressed thickness of the cover gasket. This clearance will then give a bearing pre-load of 0.001 to 0.003 inch.

28   Assemble the shim pack so that a 0.060 inch shim is on the top of the pack and then place it against the cover.

29   Refit the cover and new gasket, and secure with the two bolts and spring washers. It is important that the bolt which is fitted nearest to the damper cover has its threads coated with a sealing compound. Tighten the two bolts to a torque wrench setting of 12 to 28 lb ft.

30   Screw a new ball housing locking ring onto the rack to the limits of the thread.

31   Refit the seat spring, seat, tie rod and ball housing. Tighten the ball housing until the tie rod is just nipped.

32   Screw the locking ring back to the ball housing and check that the tie rod is still pinched. Now slacken the ball housing back one eighth of a turn so as to allow full movement of the tie rod.

33   Tighten the locking ring onto the housing, making sure that the housing does not turn, to a front torque wrench setting of 33 to 37 lb ft.

34   Lock the ball housing and locking ring by using a small chisel and driving the clips of the locking ring into the slots in the housing.

35   Fit the damper yoke, damper cover and cover gasket, leaving out the damper spring, 'O' ring and shims.

36   Replace the cover securing bolts and spring washers, and slowly tighten whilst at the same time turning the pinion backwards and forwards through 180 degrees until the point is reached where it is just possible to rotate the pinion with it held between the fingers.

37   Using feeler gauges, measure the clearance between the cover and its seating on the cover.

38   Remove the cover and fit the 'O' ring, damper spring and shims to the thickness of the feeler gauge plug 0.002 to 0.005 inch. Refit the damper cover and tighten the two bolts to a torque wrench setting of 12 to 18 lb ft.

39   Using a tube of suitable diameter, fit a new pinion seal to the housing.

40   Refit the two gaiters and secure the housing end clips. Also tighten the clip to the tie rod furthest from the pinion.

41   Using a squirt type oil can with the nozzle under the free end of the rubber gaiter insert ⅓ pint of Castrol Hypoy. Tighten the remaining gaiter securing clip.

42   Move the rack until it is in its central position and mark the pinion for correct reconnection when refitting to the car. The total rack travel is 6.36 inches; to the mid way position is 3.18 inches. There are also 3.9 turns of the pinion from one full lock to the other.

43   Refit the ball ends and lock nuts. Screw on both ball ends an equal distance onto each tie rod. Tighten the locknuts just sufficiently to prevent the ball ends turning, before the rack and pinion assembly is reconnected.

44   The assembly is now ready for refitting to the car.

23   Front wheel alignment

1   The front wheels are correctly aligned when they are turning in at the front 1/16 inch as shown in Fig. 11:20. It is important that this measurement is taken on a centre line drawn horizontally and parallel to the ground through the centre line of the hub. The exact point should be in the centre of the sidewall of the tyre and not on the wheel rim which could be distorted and give inaccurate readings.

2   The adjustment is effected by loosening the lock nut on each tie rod ball joint and also slackening the rubber gaiter clip holding it to the tie rod, and turning both tie rods equally until the adjustment is correct.

3   This is a job best left to your local BLMC garage as accurate alignment requires the use of special equipment. If the wheels are not in alignment, tyre wear will be heavy and uneven and the steering will be stiff and unresponsive.

Cause	Trouble	Remedy
SYMPTOM: STEERING FEELS VAGUE, CAR WANDERS AND FLOATS AT SPEED		
General wear or damage	Tyre pressure uneven	Check pressures and adjust as necessary.
	Dampers worn	Test, and replace if worn.
	Steering gear ball joints badly worn	Fit new ball joints.
	Suspension geometry incorrect	Check and rectify.
	Steering mechanism free play excessive	Adjust or overhaul steering mechanism.
	Front suspension and rear suspension pick-up points out of alignment	Normally caused by poor repair work after a serious accident. Extensive rebuilding necessary.
SYMPTOM: STIFF & HEAVY STEERING		
Lack of maintenance or accident damage	Tyre pressure too low	Check pressures and inflate tyres.
	No oil in steering gear	Top up steering gear.
	No grease in steering and suspension ball joints	Clean nipples and grease thoroughly.
	Front wheel toe-in incorrect	Check and reset toe-in.
	Suspension geometry incorrect	Check and rectify.
	Steering gear incorrectly adjusted too tightly	Check and readjust steering gear.
	Steering column badly misaligned	Determine cause and rectify (usually due to bad repair after severe accident damage and difficult to correct).
SYMPTOM: WHEEL WOBBLE & VIBRATION		
General wear or damage	Wheel nuts loose	Check and tighten as necessary.
	Front wheels and tyres out of balance	Balance wheels and tyres and add weights as necessary.
	Steering ball joints badly worn	Replace steering gear ball joints.
	Hub bearings badly worn	Remove and fit new hub bearings.
	Steering gear free play excessive	Adjust and overhaul steering gear.
	Front springs weak or broken	Inspect and renew as necessary.

Chapter 12 Bodywork and underframe

Contents

1 General description

The combined body and underframe is of all welded steel construction. This makes a very strong and torsionally rigid shell. There are four forward hinged doors and one full height tailgate at the rear. The windscreen is slightly curved and is of the Zebra Zone toughened safety glass type. The front seats recline fully whilst the rear seat folds flat to provide a 'van' type load area.

The facia and instrument panel are relieved in black to prevent glare.

The instruments are contained in two dials located above the steering column and are supplemented with a range of easy access controls. A heater and ventilation system is fitted incorporating a full flow system with outlet ducts at instrument panel level.

2 Maintenance - body and chassis

1 The condition of the bodywork is of considerable importance as it is on this that the second-hand value of the car will mainly depend. It is much more difficult to repair neglected bodywork than to renew mechanical assemblies. The hidden portions of the body, such as the wheel arches, the underframe and the engine compartment are equally important, although obviously not requiring such frequent attention as the immediately visible paintwork.

2 Once a year, or every 12,000 miles, it is advisable to visit the local BLMC main agent and have the underside of body steam cleaned. This will take about 1½ hours. All traces of dirt and oil will be removed and the underside can then be inspected carefully for rust, damaged hydraulic pipes, frayed electrical wiring and similar maladies. The car should be greased on completion of this job.

3 At the same time the engine compartment should be cleaned in a similar manner. If steam cleaning facilities are not available, then brush 'Gunk' or a similar cleaner over the whole of the engine, and engine compartment, with a stiff brush, working it well in where there is an accumulation of oil and dirt. Do not paint the ignition system, and protect it with oily rags when the 'Gunk' is washed off. As the 'Gunk' is washed away it will take with it all traces of oil and dirt, leaving the engine looking clean and bright.

4 The wheel arches should be given particular attention, as under sealing can easily come away here, and stones and dirt thrown up from the road wheels can soon cause the paint to chip and flake, and so allow rust to set in. If rust is found, clean down the bare metal with wet and dry paper. Paint on an anti-corrosive coating such as 'Kurust', or if preferred red lead, and renew the undercoating and top coat.

5 The bodywork should be washed once a week or when dirty. Thoroughly wet the car to soften the dirt, and then wash the car down with a soft sponge and plenty of clean water. If the surplus dirt is not washed off very gently it will in time wear the paint as surely as wet and dry paper. It is best to use a hose if this is available. Give the car a final wash down and then dry with a soft chamois leather to prevent the formation of spots.

6 Spots of tar and grease thrown up from the road can be removed by a rag dampened in petrol.

7 Once every six months, or every three months if wished, give the bodywork and chromium trim a thoroughly good wax polish. If a chromium cleaner is used to remove rust on any of the cars plated parts, remember that the cleaner also removes part of the chromium so use only when absolutely necessary.

3   Maintenance - upholstery and carpets

1   Remove the carpets or mats, and thoroughly vacuum clean the interior of the car every three months, or more frequently if necessary.

2   Beat out the carpets and vacuum clean them if they are very dirty. If the upholstery is soiled apply an upholstery cleaner with a damp sponge and wipe off with a clean dry cloth.

4   Minor body repairs

1   Major damage must be repaired by your local BLMC garage, but there is no reason way you cannot beat out, repair and respray minor damage yourself. The essential items which the owner should gather together to ensure a really professional job are:

a)   A plastic filler such as Holts 'Cataloy'.

b)   Paint whose colour matches exactly that of the bodywork, either in a can for application by a spray gun or in a aerosol can.

c)   Fine cutting paste.

d)   Fine and medium grade wet and dry paper.

2   Never use a metal hammer to knock out small dents as the blows tend to scratch and distort the metal. Knock out the dent with a mallet or rawhide hammer and press on the underside of the dented surfaces a metal dolly or smooth wooden block roughly contoured to the normal shape of the damaged area.

3   After the worst of the damaged area has been knocked out, rub down the dent and surrounding area with medium wet and dry paper and thoroughly clean away all traces of dirt.

4   The plastic filler comprises a paste and hardener which must be thoroughly mixed together. Mix only a small portion at a time as the paste sets hard within five to fifteen minutes depending on the amount of hardener used.

5   Smooth on the filler with a knife or stiff plastic to the shape of the damaged portion and allow to thoroughly dry, a process which takes approximately six hours. After the filler has dried it is likely that it will have contracted slightly so spread on a second layer of filler if necessary.

6   Smooth down the filler with fine wet and dry paper wrapped round a small flat block of wood, and continue until the whole area is perfectly smooth and it is impossible to feel where the filler joins the rest of the paintwork.

7   Spray on from an aerosol can, or with a spray gun, an anti-rust undercoat, smooth down with wet and dry paper, and then spray on two coats of the final finish using a circular motion.

8   When thoroughly dry, polish the whole area with a fine cutting paste to smooth the re-sprayed area into the remainder of the wing or panel and to remove the small particles of paint spray which will have settled round the area.

9   This will leave the area looking perfect with not a trace of the previous unsightly dent.

5   Major chassis and body repairs.

1   Major chassis and body repair work cannot be successfully undertaken by the average owner. Work of this nature should be entrusted to a competent body repair specialist who should have the necessary jigs, welding and hydraulic equipment as well as skilled panel beaters to ensure a proper job is done.

2   If the damage is severe, it is vital that on completion of the repair the chassis is in correct alignment. Less severe damage may also have twisted or distorted the chassis although this may not be visible immediately. It is therefore always best on completion of repair to check for twist and squareness to ensure that all is correct.

3   To check for twist, position the car on a clean level floor, place a jack under each jacking point, raise the car and take off the wheels. Raise or lower the jacks until the sills are parallel with the ground. Depending where the damage occured, using an accurate scale, take a measurement from the vertical to the floor and determine a datum which may be calculated using a known correct dimension. This should then be added to the dimensions given in the table.

4   Check the underside for twist by taking measurements at the four suspension mountings as indicated in Fig. 12:2. If it is impossible to get comparable readings it is an indication that the body is twisted.

5   After checking for twist, check for squareness by taking a series of measurements on the floor. Drop a plum line and bob weight from the lettered and dimensioned points on the chassis frame to the floor and mark these points with chalk. Draw a straight line between each point and measure and mark the middle of each line. A line drawn on the floor starting at the front and finishing at the rear should be quite straight and pass through the centres of the other lines. Diagonal measurements can also be made as a check for squareness.

6   Front door - dismantling and reassembly

a)   Interior door handle and trim

1   Make sure the window is fully closed and then undo and remove the screw and washer that secures the window regulator handle. Lift away the handle and its escutcheon (Fig. 12:4).

2   Carefully, using a screwdriver, ease the two halves of the plastic bezel from the control unit, the top half upwards and the bottom half downwards.

3   Undo and remove the two screws that secure the arm rest to the door. Lift away the arm rest.

4   Insert a screwdriver blade between the lower edge of the trim panel and the door and very carefully lever the pad retaining clips from the door panel plugs. Lift away the trim panel.

5   Refitting the trim panel and interior handle is the reverse sequence to removal. Note that the locating dowel on the window handle escutcheon must be at the bottom.

b)   Door glass

1   Remove the interior handle and door trim panel as described in part (a) of this Section (Fig. 12:5).

2   Unscrew the trim panel finisher securing screws and lift away the finisher and door capping.

3   Carefully peel back the plastic cover from the door inner panel.

4   Undo and remove the two screws that secure the glass stop to the lower part of the door inner panel. Lift away the glass stop.

5   Carefully wind the glass down fully (refit the handle for this operation) and disengage the window regulator from the channel.

6   Tilt the glass inwards and lift it up so as to clear the top of the door. Lift away the glass from the door.

FIG. 12:1 HORIZONTAL ALIGNMENT DATA

No.	Description
1	Body shell

Code letter	Dimension	Location
A	56.58 in. (1287 mm)	Front bumper mounting hole
B	33.72 in. (854.49 mm)	Jig location slots
C	29.70 in. (754.4 mm)	Suspension tie-rod
D	27.36 in. (745.7 mm)	Suspension tie-rod
E	44.00 in. (1017.6 mm)	Service checking hole
F	42.74 in. (1085.6 mm)	Rear suspension
G	58.25 in. (1497.6 mm)	Rear bumper mounting hole
H	33.72 in. (856.50 mm)	Weld pin - sub-frame

No.	Description
2	Sub-frame assembly

Code letter	Dimension	Location
J	33.56 in. (752.4 mm)	Service checking hole-sub-frame
K	7.00 in. (177.8 mm)	Service checking hole to location pins
L	29.70 in. (654.4 mm)	Sub-frame to dash
M	6.59 in. (107.5 mm)	Location pins—sub-frame to dash

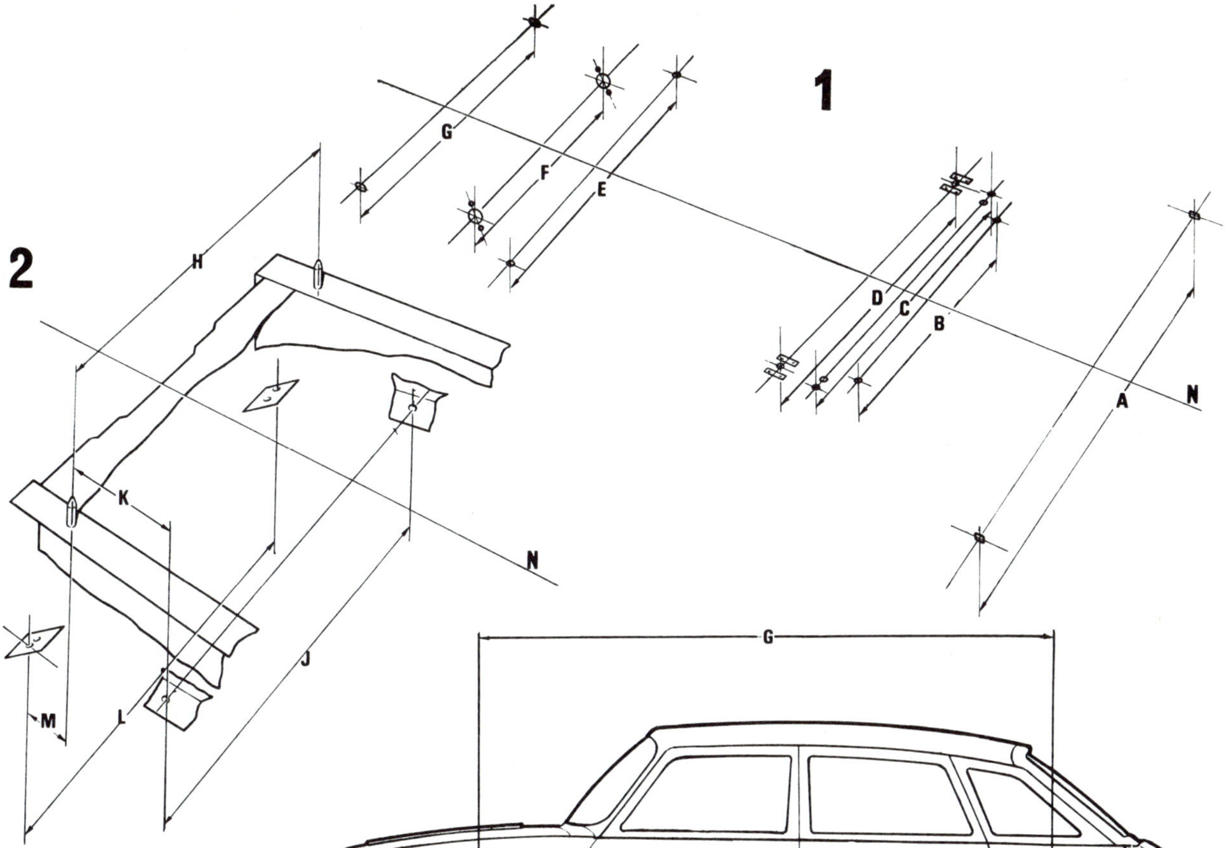

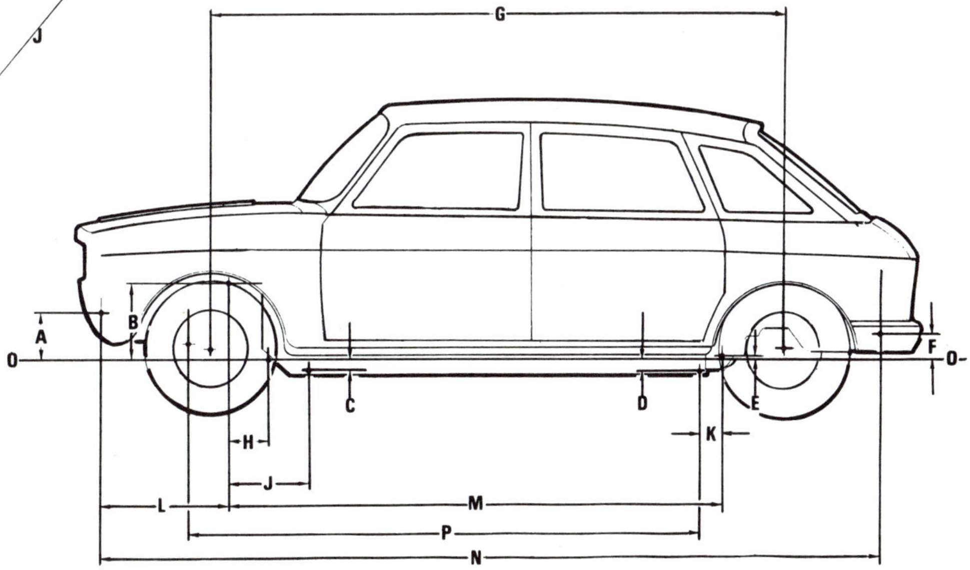

FIG. 12:2 VERTICAL ALIGNMENT DATA

Code letter	Dimension	Code letter	Dimension
A	8.82 in. (224 mm)	J	14.37 in. (365 mm)
B	11.70 in. (296.2 mm)	K	4.10 in. (104.2 mm)
C	2.36 in. (60 mm)	L	23.46 in. (595.9 mm)
D	3.05 in. (77.5 mm)	M	89.04 in. (2261.7 mm)
E	.88 in. (22.3 mm)	N	140.92 in. (3579.4 mm)
F	4.25 in. (108 mm)	O	Body line
G	103.50 in. (2628.9 mm)	P	91.94 in. (2335.3 mm)
H	6.68 in. (170.2 mm)		

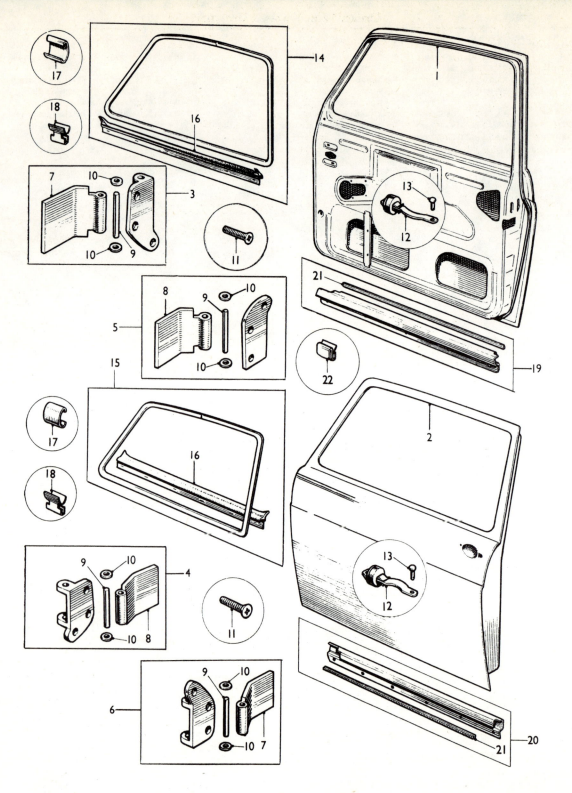

FIG. 12:3 DOOR COMPONENTS

No.	Description	No.	Description	No.	Description	No.	Description
1	R H door shell	7	Hinge leaf	13	Clevis pin	19	R H inner waist capping assembly
2	L H door shell	8	Hinge leaf	14	R H outer moulding assembly	20	L H inner waist capping assembly
3	R H door upper hinge assembly	9	Hinge pin	15	L H outer moulding assembly		
4	L H door upper hinge assembly	10	Brass washer	16	Weatherstrip	21	Weatherstrip
5	R H door lower hinge assembly	11	Screw	17	Moulding capping	22	Clip
6	L H door lower hinge assembly	12	Door check arm	18	Clip		

7   Refitting is the reverse sequence to removal.

c) Door glass regulator

1   Remove the interior handle and door trim panel as described in part (a) of this Section.
2   Temporarily refit the window regulator handle and check that the glass is in the fully raised position.
3   Retain the glass in the raised position by using tapered rubber or wooden wedges between the inner panel and the glass (Fig. 12:6).
4   Carefully peel back the plastic cover from the door inner panel.
5   Undo and remove the seven screws that secure the window regulator to the door inner panel.
6   Working inside the door, disengage the regulator from the glass channel.
7   Contact the window regulator assembly and withdraw it from the lower rear cut out in the door inner panel.
8   Refitting the window regulator assembly is the reverse sequence to removal. Well lubricate all moving parts with Castrol GTX.

d) Exterior door handle

1   Remove the interior handle and door trim panel as described in part (a) of this Section.
2   Carefully peel back the plastic cover from the door inner panel.
3   Undo and remove the two nuts and plain washers securing the exterior door handle to the door outer panel (Fig. 12:7).
4   Carefully disengage the link from the push button arm.
5   The exterior door handle may now be lifted away from the door.
6   To refit, first position the handle on the outer door panel and press the end of the link into the push button arm brush and secure it with the clip.
7   Refit the two plain washers and securing nuts.
8   Move the latch to the fully latched position and check the operation of the push button. A little free movement of the button must be felt before the sliding contactor begins to lift, and the latch must release from the striker before the push button is fully depressed.
9   To adjust the push button plunger screw, disconnect the push button link and lift the cranked push button arm. Turn the plunger screw in the required direction.
10   Reassembly is now the reverse sequence to dismantling

e) Door lock

1   Before the locking mechanism is considered to be defective, refer to Section 9 and make sure that the striker plate is adjusted correctly.
2   Remove the interior handle and door trim panel as described in part (a) of this Section.
3   Carefully peel back the plastic cover from the door inner panel.
4   Detach the latch release rod from its plastic clip.
5   Disconnect the lock control rod from the locking lever bush.
6   Undo and remove the three screws with shakeproof and plain washers securing the remote control to the door inner panel. Lift away the remote control assembly from the door.
7   Release the clip, and detach the latch release rod from the release lever bush.
8   Detach the clip and withdraw the lock control rod from the locking quadrant bush.
9   Carefully ease the window channel from the door channel

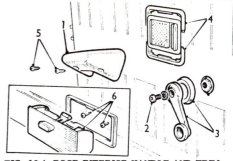

FIG. 12:4 DOOR INTERIOR HANDLE AND TRIM

No.	Description	No.	Description
1	Arm rest	4	Door lock remote control plastic bezel
2	Window regulator handle retaining screw	5	Arm rest retaining screws
3	Window regulator handle and escutcheon	6	Ash tray and retaining screws

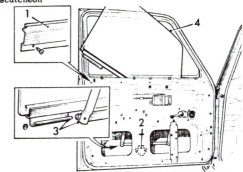

FIG. 12:5 DOOR GLASS REMOVAL

No.	Description	No.	Description
1	Trim pad finisher		channel
2	Glass stop retaining screws	4	Door glass
3	Regulator disengaged from		

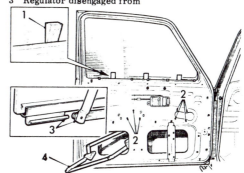

FIG. 12:6 DOOR GLASS REGULATOR REMOVAL

No.	Description	No.	Description
1	Tapered wedge		channel
2	Regulator retaining screws	4	Regulator assembly contracted
3	Regulator disengaged from		

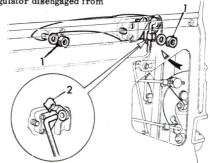

FIG. 12:7 EXTERIOR DOOR HANDLE REMOVAL

No.	Description	No.	Description
1	Handle securing nuts		push button arm
2	Disengagement of link from		

and move it to one side. Note this channel is retained in position with adhesive.

10   Release the clip and detach the push-button link from the contactor slide bush.

11   Next release the clip, and detach the key operated link from the latch locking lever bush.

12   Undo the four latch securing screws and lift away the latch assembly.

13   Release the two legged spring collar and withdraw the lock complete with link from outside the door. It is not necessary to disturb the self adhesive washer under the lock head.

14   To remove the striker, first remove the seat belt anchor bolt and ease away the door post trim panel with a screwdriver.

15   Unscrew the two striker retaining screws and lift away the cover plate.

16   To reassemble, if the striker and cover plate have been removed these should first be refitted. Lightly tighten the two securing screws and replace the door post trim panel and seat belt anchor bolt.

17   Make sure that the plastic bush is correctly fitted in the operating arm of the key operated lock. The bush must be inserted towards the keyslot end with the link retaining clip fitted under its head.

18   It should be noted that the locks are handed. When fitted, the operating arm must be inclined towards the door shut face with the key slot inverted.

19   Carefully press the lock link into the plastic bush towards the key slot end and retain in position with the clip.

20   Make sure that the self adhesive washer is fitted to the lock and then fit the spring collar.

21   Insert the lock assembly into the door aperture and press it firmly home.

22   Fit the plastic bushes into the locking lever and latch release lever, towards the latch, with the spring clips fitted under the heads of the bushes.

23   Fit the bush into the slide contactor, away from the latch, so that the spring clip is fitted on the tail end of the bush.

24   Insert the bush into the latch locking lever towards the latch, with the clip fitted under the head of the bush.

25   Pass the latch operating levers, latch release lever first, through the aperture in the door shut face.

26   Secure the latch in position with the four retaining screws

27   Move the latch disc to the fully latched position.

28   Push the key operated link inwards into the latch locking lever bush and retain with the clip.

29   Push the push-button link outwards into the sliding contactor bush and retain with the clip.

30   Check the operation of the push button and adjust the plunger screw in the required direction until there is a little free movement of the button before the sliding contactor begins to lift.

31   Press the end of the latch release rod upwards into its plastic clip.

32   Next press the end of the lock control rod into its bush in the locking lever.

33   Locate the control rods in their respective guides.

34   Position the remote control unit on the door inner panel and hold it in position with the three bolts, shakeproof and plain washers. Do not tighten fully yet.

35   Press the latch release rod into the bush in the latch release lever.

36   Move the control unit towards the latch, without compressing the rod spring, until the latch release lever is up against

its stop. Should control unit movement be restricted by the screw slot, enlarge the slot using a round file.

37   Move the latch disc to the closed position.

38   Check the operation of the latch release lever. It should release the striker before the full range of its movement is reached.

39   Move the latch disc to the closed position.

40   Adjust the screwed end pivot on the lock control rod until it fits freely into its bush in the locking quadrant.

41   Press the pivot into its bush and secure the rod with the clip.

42   Check the operation of the safety locking lever and the key. Lubricate all moving parts with Castrol GTX.

43   Refit the door interior panel plastic cover, door trim panel and interior handle which is the reverse sequence to that described in part (a) of this Section.

---

7   Rear door – dismantling and reassembly

The sequence for dismantling and reassembling the rear door is basically identical to that for the front door. Full information will be found in the previous Section.

---

8   Front and rear door – removal and refitting

---

1   Disconnect the door check strap by extracting the split pin and withdrawing the clevis pin. Note that its head is positioned uppermost. Take care that the door is not opened too far with the check strap disconnected, otherwise the wing or door panel could be dented.

2   Using a pencil, accurately mark the outline of the hinge relative to the door, to assist refitting. It is desirable to have an assistant to take the weight of the door once the two hinges have been released.

3   Undo and remove the three screws that secure each hinge to the door and lift away the complete door assembly (Fig. 12:3).

4   For storage, it is best to stand the door on an old blanket and allow it to lean against a wall also suitably padded at the top to stop scratching.

5   Refitting the door is the reverse sequence to removal. If, after fitting, adjustment is necessary, it should be done at the hinges to give correct alignment, or the striker reset if the door either moves up or down on final closing.

---

9   Striker plate – adjustment

---

1   It is important that before attempting to close the door after a lock has been refitted, the latch disc is in the open position. Operate the push button several times and then pull a screwdriver through the latch opening.

2   Whilst adjustments are being made, it is not necessary to slam the door as zero torque locks are fitted.

3   If the striker plate has been removed, tighten the screws just sufficiently to allow the door to close and latch.

4   Firmly press the door inwards, or pull it outwards without depressing the push button, until it lines up with the general contour of the body.

5   Open the door and, with a soft pencil, mark the outline of the striker plate to establish its new horizontal position.

6   Note that the over-travel stop tends to twist the striker during adjustment, so this must be corrected making the loop at right angles to the door hinge axis.

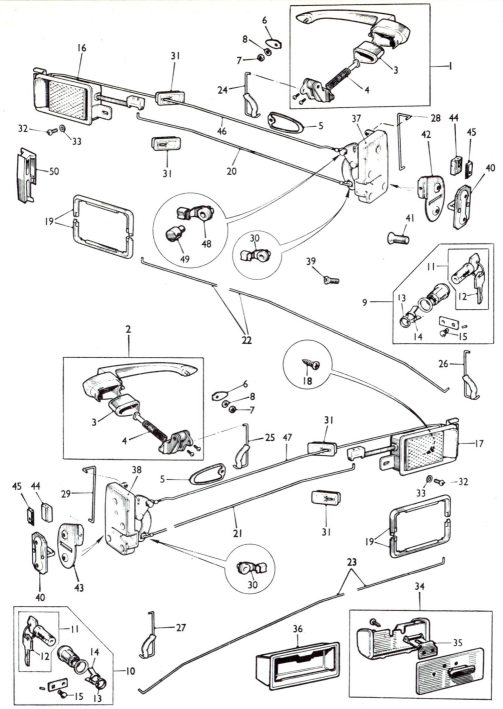

FIG. 12:8 COMPONENT PARTS OF DOOR LOCK ASSEMBLIES

No.	Description	No.	Description	No.	Description	No.	Description
1	Door handle assembly	14	Retaining clip	27	Handle push-button rod	39	Screw
2	Door handle assembly	15	Operating stud	28	Private lock rod	40	Striker
3	Push-button	16	Remote control	29	Private lock rod	41	Screw
4	Spring	17	Remote control	30	Clip	42	Striker plate
5	Washer	18	Screw	31	Grommet	43	Striker plate
6	Washer	19	Bezel	32	Screw	44	Seal
7	Nut	20	Remote control rod	33	Shakeproof washer	45	Retainer
8	Spring washer	21	Remote control rod	34	Ashtray assembly	46	Lock operating rod
9	Door lock assembly	22	Remote control rod	35	Spring	47	Lock operating rod
10	Door lock assembly	23	Remote control rod	36	Ashtray case	48	Clip
11	Barrel assembly	24	Handle push-button rod	37	Door lock	49	Adjustment pin
12	Key	25	Handle push-button rod	38	Door lock	50	Guide link
13	Spring clip	26	Handle push-button rod				

7   Retighten the striker screws.

8   Using the method of trial and error, position the striker accurately until the door can be closed easily, without rattling, and with no apparent lifting or dropping.

9   Close the door and check the adjustment by pressing on the door to see that the striker has not been set too far in. A fractional movement should be possible as the seals are compressed.

10   Door rattles – tracing and rectification

1   The commonest cause of door rattles is a misaligned, loose or worn striker plate but other causes can be:

a)   Loose door handles, window winder handles, or door hinges.

b)   Loose, worn or misaligned door lock components.

c)   Loose or worn remote control mechanism.

2   It is quite possible for door rattles to be the result of a combination of the above faults so a careful examination must be made to determine the causes of the rattles.

3   If the loop of the striker plate is worn, and as a result the door rattles, renew it and adjust as described in Section 9.

4   Should the hinges be worn, they must be renewed and then adjusted as described in Section 3.

11   Windscreen and backlight glass – removal and replacement

1   Windscreen replacement is no light task. Leave this to the specialist if possible. Instructions are given below however.

2   Refer to Chapter 10/31, and remove the windscreen wiper arms.

3   Using a screwdriver, carefully prise up the end of the moulding finisher strip and withdraw it from its slot in the moulding.

4   The assistance of a second person should now be enlisted, ready to catch the glass when it is released from its aperture.

5   Working inside the car, commencing at one top corner, press the glass and ease it from the rubber moulding.

6   Remove the rubber moulding from the windscreen aperture.

7   Now is the time to remove all pieces of glass if the screen has shattered. Use a vacuum cleaner to extract as much as possible. Switch on the heater boost motor and adjust the controls to 'Screen defrost' but watch out for flying pieces of glass which might be blown out of the ducting.

8   Carefully inspect the rubber moulding for signs of splitting or deterioration. Clean all traces of sealing compound from the rubber moulding and windscreen aperture flange.

9   To refit the glass, first place the rubber seal onto the aperture flange.

10   Lubricate the channel in the seal with a concentrated soap and water solution, or with washing up liquid.

11   Place the lower edge of the glass in the channel and, using a piece of plastic or tapered wood, ease the rubber lip over the glass.

12   The finisher strip must next be fitted to the moulding and for this a special tool is required. An illustration of this tool is shown in Fig. 12:9, and a handyman should be able to make up an equivalent using netting wire and a wooden file handle.

13   Fit the eye of the tool into the groove and feed in the finisher strip.

14   Push the tool around the complete length of the moulding, feeding the finisher into the channel as the eyelet opens it. The back half beds the finisher into the moulding.

12   Facia board (rod gear change) – removal and refitting

1   For safety reasons, disconnect the positive and negative terminals from the battery.

2   Release the choke control cable from the carburettor choke linkage.

3   Refer to Section 24 and remove the glovebox.

4   Refer to Section 21 and remove the heater controls as described in paragraphs 5 to 8 inclusive.

5   Undo and remove the four screws and cup washers that secure the facia to the body. Note that the longest of the four screws is located at the top centre position (Fig. 12:10).

6   Draw the facia forwards by about three inches and detach the fresh air pipes from the facia ventilators.

7   Detach the two tubes from the windscreen washer pump. Note which way round they are fitted.

8   Unscrew the knurled nut securing the speedometer outer cable to the rear of the instrument.

9   Note the electrical cable connections to the rear of the switches and release these connections from their terminals.

10   Detach the multi pin plug from the rear of the instrument panel.

11   Remove the facia board from its location, whilst at the same time drawing the choke control cable through its rubber grommet.

12   Refitting is the reverse sequence to removal. The choke cable should be fed through the grommet in the engine bulkhead as the facia board is refitted.

13   Facia panel (cable gear change) – removal and refitting

1   For safety reasons disconnect the positive and negative terminals from the battery.

2   Release the choke control cable from the carburettor choke linkage.

3   Disconnect the control cable from the heater valve.

4   Refer to Chapter 11/18, and remove the steering column.

5   Refer to Chapter 10/43, and remove the instrument panel.

6   Refer to Section 24 of this Chapter and remove the glovebox.

7   Disconnect the demister tubes from the facia ducts.

8   Disconnect the fresh air pipe from the facia ventilators (Fig. 12:11).

9   Note the electrical cable connections to the rear of the switches and release these connections from their terminals.

10   Unscrew the windscreen washers pump from its push.

11   Disconnect the heater control cables from the heater unit.

12   Unscrew and remove the self tapping screws and plain washers that secure the lower edge of the facia panel.

13   Unscrew and remove the bolts with shakeproof and plain spring washers that secure the upper half of the facia panel.

14   Very carefully release the finished trim from the body flange on each door aperture in the vacinity of the facia panel.

15   Draw the facia panel from the body and lift away from the inside of the car.

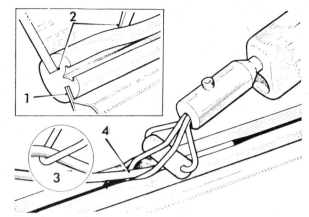

FIG. 12:9 FINISHER STRIP REFITTING TOOL

No.	Description	No.	Description
1	Windscreen glass aperture flange	4	Eye of tool inserted in finisher groove
2	Easing rubber lip over glass		ugh wire loop
3	Finisher strip threaded thro-		

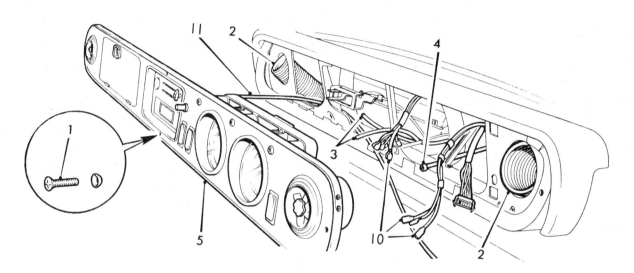

FIG. 12:10 FACIA BOARD (ROD GEAR CHANGE)

No.	Description	No.	Description	No.	Description
1	Retaining screws	3	Windscreen washer pump pipes	4	Speedometer cable
2	Fresh air pipes			5	Facia board

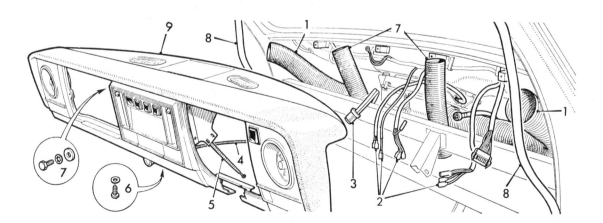

FIG. 12:11 FACIA PANEL (CABLE GEAR CHANGE)

No.	Description	No.	Description	No.	Description	No.	Description
1	Fresh air pipes	4	Heater valve control cable	7	Facia upper retaining screw	8	Door aperture finisher trim
2	Electric cables	5	Heater control cable				
3	Speedometer cable	6	Facia lower retaining screw				

This sequence of photographs deals with the repair of the dent and scratch (above rear lamp) shown in this photo. The procedure will be similar for the repair of a hole. It should be noted that the procedures given here are simplified - more explicit instructions will be found in the text

In the case of a dent the first job - after removing surrounding trim - is to hammer out the dent where access is possible. This will minimise filling. Here, the large dent having been hammered out, the damaged area is being made slightly concave

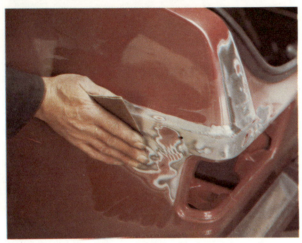

Now all paint must be removed from the damaged area, by rubbing with coarse abrasive paper. Alternatively, a wire brush or abrasive pad can be used in a power drill. Where the repair area meets good paintwork, the edge pf the paintwork should be 'feathered', using a finer grade of abrasive paper

In the case of a hole caused by rusting, all damaged sheet-metal should be cut away before proceeding to this stage. Here, the damaged area is being treated with rust remover and inhibitor before being filled

Mix the body filler according to its manufacturer's instructions. In the case of corrosion damage, it will be necessary to block off any large holes before filling - this can be done with zinc gauze or aluminium tape. Make sure the area is absolutely clean before ...

... applying the filler. Filler should be applied with a flexible applicator, as shown, for best results: the wooden spatula being used for confined areas. Apply thin layers of filler at 20-minute intervals, until the surface of the filler is slightly proud of the surrounding bodywork

Initial shaping can be done with a Surform plane or Dreadnought file. Then, using progressively finer grades of wet-and-dry paper, wrapped around a sanding block, and copious amounts of clean water, rub-down the filler until really smooth and flat. Again, feather the edges of adjoining paintwork

The whole repair area can now be sprayed or brush-painted with primer. If spraying, ensure adjoining areas are protected from over-spray. Note that at least one-inch of the surrounding sound paintwork should be coated with primer. Primer has a 'thick' consistency, so will fill small imperfections

Again, using plenty of water, rub down the primer with a fine grade of wet-and-dry paper (400 grade is probably best) until it is really smooth and well blended into the surrounding paint-work. Any remaining imperfections can now be filled by carefully applied knifing stopper paste

When the stopper has hardened, rub-down the repair area again before applying the final coat of primer. Before rubbing-down this last coat of primer, ensure the repair area is blemish-free - use more stopper if necessary. To ensure that the surface of the primer is really smooth use some finishing compound

The top coat can now be applied. When working out of doors, pick a dry, warm and wind-free day. Ensure surrounding areas are protected from over-spray. Agitate the aerosol thoroughly, then spray the centre of the repair area, working outwards with a circular motion. Apply the paint as several thin coats.

After a period of about two-weeks, which the paint needs to harden fully, the surface of the repaired area can be 'cut' with a mild cutting compound prior to wax polishing. When carrying out bodywork repairs, remember that the quality of the finished job is proportional to the time and effort expended

16 Refitting is the reverse sequence to removal. As the facia panel is being finally positioned, feed the choke and heater valve control cables through the engine bulkhead grommets.

14 Facia panel (rod gear change) - removal and refitting

1 Refer to Section 12 and remove the facia board.
2 Remove the trim pad from the facia support (Fig. 12:12).
3 Completely remove the ashtray.
4 Undo and remove the nut, shakeproof washer and plain washer securing the facia support to each end of the facia panel.
5 Undo and remove the facia support lower securing screws and carefully draw away the facia support.
6 Disconnect the bonnet control cable from the bonnet lock and then release the control cable from its support clips on the inner wing valance.
7 Disconnect the heater control cable from the heater valve.
8 Detach the demister tubes from the facia ducts.
9 Undo and remove the facia panel lower securing screws and plain washers located at each end of the facia panel.
10 Undo and remove the facia panel upper securing bolts with shakeproof and plain washers.
11 Carefully release the finished trim from the body flange on each door aperture in the area of the facia panel.
12 The facia panel may now be drawn rearwards and lifted away from inside the car.
13 Refitting is the reverse sequence to removal. As it is being finally positioned, feed the bonnet and heater valve control cables through the grommets in the engine bulkhead.

15 Parcel shelf - removal and refitting

Cable gear change
1 Refer to Chapter 11/19, and remove the steering column.
2 Undo and remove the four screws that secure the parcel shelf to the body (Fig. 12:13).
3 Undo and remove the two screws and plain washers that secure the fuse box located on the right hand side of the parcel shelf.
4 Carefully draw the parcel shelf rearwards and lift away from inside the car.
5 Refitting is the reverse sequence to removal.

Rod gear change
1 Using a hacksaw, cut a screwdriver slot in the head of the shear bolt that secures the steering column to the mounting bracket.
2 Unscrew and remove the shear bolt. It should be noted that the nut of the shear bolt is locked to the bracket and cannot be turned.
3 Follow the instructions given in paragraphs 2 to 4 inclusive for cable gear change models.
4 Refitting is the reverse sequence to removal. A new shear bolt attaching the steering column to the mounting bracket must be used and tightened until the hexagon head shears at the waisted point.

16 Radiator grille (rod gear change) - removal and refitting

1 Unscrew the self tapping screw securing each headlamp rim and, with a screwdriver, ease each rim from the light unit body.

2 Undo and remove the four self tapping screws and plain washers securing the top of the radiator grille to the body.
3 Carefully lift the grille upwards, so releasing the four legs from their rubber inserts in the front valance.
4 Refitting the radiator grille is the reverse sequence to removal.

17 Tailgate - removal and refitting

1 Using a screwdriver, carefully remove the two outer hinge finishers.
2 The help of an assistant should be obtained to take the weight of the tailgate.
3 Undo and remove the two bolts, nuts and washers that secure each rim to the body and tailgate. Note which way round the rims are fitted as they must not, under any circumstances, be fitted the wrong way round.
4 Undo and remove the two nuts from each pair of hinge studs exposed as described in paragraph 1.
5 Carefully remove the tailgate from the rear of the car.
6 Refitting the tailgate is the reverse sequence to removal.

18 Tailgate lock (cable gear change) - removal and refitting

Push button lock
1 Undo and remove the self tapping screws that secure the tailgate trim pad and then carefully lever the trim pad from the tailgate with a wide bladed screwdriver.
2 Recover the plastic retaining pegs as they are released when the trim pad is removed.
3 Disengage the latch operating rods from the operating bracket.
4 Unscrew the lock retaining ring and remove the operating bracket. For this a blunt chisel can be used to start movement of the lock retaining ring.
5 Lift away the push button lock assembly.
6 Using a pair of circlip pliers, remove the circlip and withdraw the spring seat and spring from the push button assembly.
7 The push button lock barrel may now be withdrawn.
8 Refitting is the reverse sequence to removal. Make sure that the operating rod bushes are pressed into the lock operating bracket towards its spring with the retaining clips fitted between the heads of the bushes and the bracket. Lubricate all moving parts with a little Castrol GTX.

Latch type lock
1 Undo and remove the self tapping screws that secure the tailgate trim pad and then carefully lever the trim pad from the tailgate with a wide bladed screwdriver.
2 Recover the plastic retaining pegs as they are released when the trim pad is removed.
3 Disengage the latch operating rods from the operating bracket.
4 Undo and remove the latch unit securing screws for each latch unit and then withdraw each latch unit complete with operating rod.
5 Finally detach the rod from each latch unit.
6 To refit, first check that the brushes for the operating rods are fitted into the latch lever of each latch unit from the spring side of the lever with the clip fitted on the tail end of the bush.
7 Press the control rods into their bushes from the tailgate side and retain each with its clip.

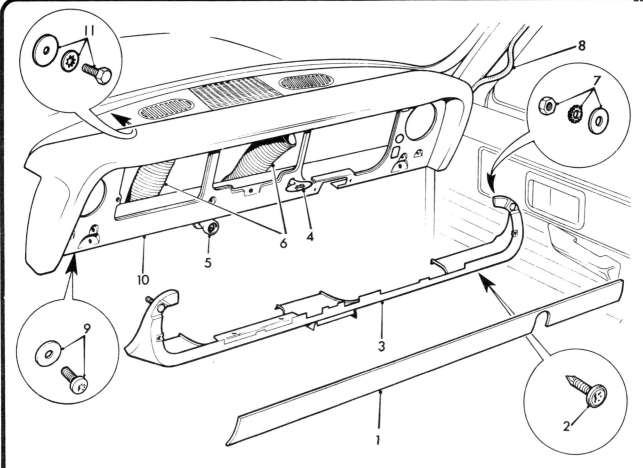

FIG. 12:12 FACIA PANEL (ROD GEAR CHANGE)

No.	Description	No.	Description	No.	Description	No.	Description
1	Trim pad	4	Bonnet control cable	7	Facia support retaining nut	10	Facia panel
2	Facia support lower securing screws	5	Heater control cable	8	Door aperture finisher trim	11	Facia panel upper securing screws
3	Facia support	6	Demister tubes	9	Facia lower securing screws		

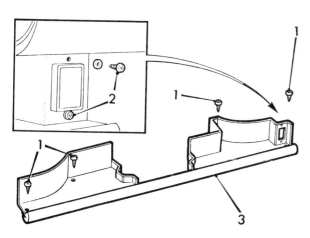

FIG. 12:13 PARCEL SHELF

No.	Description	No.	Description
1	Parcel shelf securing screws	3	Parcel shelf
2	Fusebox retaining screws		

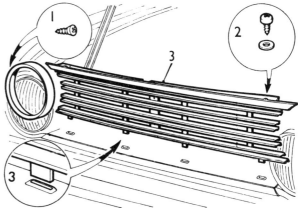

FIG. 12:14 RADIATOR GRILLE ATTACHMENT

No.	Description	No.	Description
1	Headlamp rim securing screw		screws and plain washers
2	Radiator grille securing	3	Grille legs

8   Refit the latch units to the tailgate.
9   Each latch should now be manually set to the closed position.
10 Adjust the pegs on the operating rods until they correctly align in their respective bushes. Press the pegs into the bushes and retain the rods with the clips.
11 Depress the push button and make sure that the two latches release at the same time. Lubricate all moving parts with Castrol GTX.

Adjustment
1   Move the latch disc to the closed position and then depress the push button. Make sure that there is a definite free movement of the push button before the sliding contactor begins to rise and also that the latch is released from the striker before the push button is fully depressed.
2   To adjust the push button plunger it is first necessary to disconnect the push button link. Next lift the cranked push button arm and turn the plunger screw in the required direction.
3   Slacken the dovetail alignment guide securing screws and close the tailgate. Check its alignment with the body.
4   Adjust the positions of the strikers until the tailgate closes under the pressure applied to the centre of the tailgate and the latch/es fully engages in the striker/s.
5   Check that the striker/s is not set too far in by applying pressure to the tailgate and checking that slight movement is possible as the seals are compressed.
6   Finally tighten the alignment guide securing screws.

---

19   Tailgate lock (rod gear change) - removal and refitting

Turn button lock
1   Using a wide bladed screwdriver, carefully lever the trim pad from the tailgate.
2   Recover the plastic retaining pegs as they are released when the trim pad is removed.
3   Disengage the latch operating rods from the operating plate.
4   Unscrew and remove the screw that retains the operating plate to the turn button lock and withdraw the plate.
5   Unscrew the lock retaining ring. For this a blunt chisel can be used to start movement of the lock retaining ring.
6   Lift away the turn button lock assembly.
7   Using a small screwdriver, ease the small circlip from the lock assembly. Lift away the spring.
8   Insert the key into the lock barrel and turn the key in a clockwise direction.
9   Slide off the threaded sleeve from the lock assembly.
10 Using a small diameter parallel pin punch, carefully drift out the retaining pin from the lock assembly and withdraw the turn-button lock barrel.
11 Refitting the lock is the reverse sequence to removal. Make sure that the ends of the spring are engaged in the slot in the threaded sleeve and the groove in the lock barrel housing. Lubricate all moving parts with Castrol GTX.

Latch type lock
1   Using a wide bladed screwdriver, carefully lever the trim pad from the tailgate.
2   Recover the plastic retaining pegs as they are released when the trim pad is removed.
3   Disengage the latch operating rods from the operating plate.
4   Unscrew and remove the screws and shakeproof washers

that secure the end latch unit. Lift away each latch unit complete with operating rod.
5   Detach the rod from each latch unit.
6   To refit, first make sure that the operating rod bushes are pressed into the lock operating plate towards the lock assembly spring, with the retaining clips fitted between the leads of the bushes and the operating plate.
7   Make sure also that the bushes for the operating rods are fitted into the latch of each latch unit from the spring side of the lever, with the clip fitted on the tail end of the bush.
8   Next press the control rods into their bushes in the latch units from the tailgate side and retain each with its clip.
9   Refit the latch units to the tailgate.
10 Each latch should now be manually set to the closed position.
11 Adjust the pegs on the operating rods until they align with their respective bushes. Press the pegs into the bushes and retain the rods with the clips.
12 Move the turn button anti-clockwise and check that both latches release at the same time. Lubricate all moving parts with Castrol GTX.

Adjustment
For full information refer to Section 13.

---

20   Bonnet - removal and refitting

1   Using a soft pencil, mark the outline position of both the hinges at the bonnet to act as a datum for refitting.
2   With the help of an assistant to take the weight of the bonnet, undo and remove the two lower stay retaining screws.
3   Undo and remove the hinge to bonnet securing bolts with plain and spring washers. There are two bolts to each hinge.
4   Lift away the bonnet and put in a safe place so that it will not be scratched.
5   Refitting the bonnet is the reverse sequence to removal.

---

21   Bonnet lock and control cable (rod gear change) - removal and refitting

---

1   Disconnect the positive and negative terminals from the battery.
2   Slacken the locknut and detach the cable from the trunnion at the lock lever (Fig. 12:16).
3   Detach the outer cable from the clip on the bonnet lock and from the clips on the right hand wing valance.
4   Undo and remove the screws that secure the glove box lid support.
5   Undo and remove the two screws and plain washer that secure the glove box lid striker.
6   Undo and remove the glove box side and lower end retaining screws and draw the glove box rearwards.
7   Unscrew the nut and shakeproof washer that secures the outer cable to the facia panel.
8   The inner and outer cable can now be withdrawn from the large body grommet.
9   Detach the bonnet lock return spring from the bonnet lock platform.
10 Undo and remove the bolts, shakeproof and plain washers that secure the lock to the front cross panel. Lift away the bonnet lock assembly.
11 Should it be necessary to remove the locking pin assembly on the underside of the bonnet, undo and remove the two retaining bolts with shakeproof and plain washers. Lift away

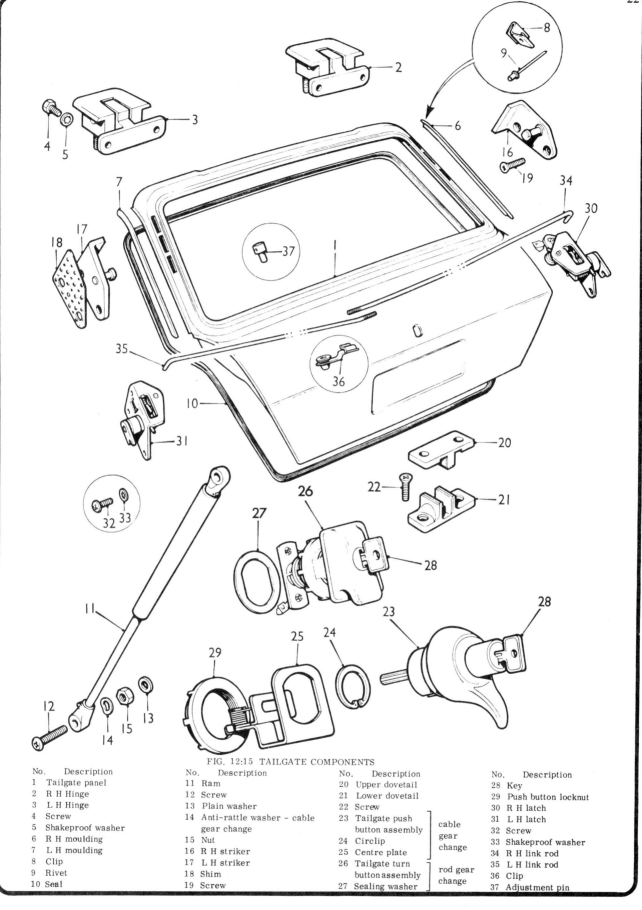

FIG. 12:15 TAILGATE COMPONENTS

No.	Description	No.	Description	No.	Description		No.	Description
1	Tailgate panel	11	Ram	20	Upper dovetail		28	Key
2	R H Hinge	12	Screw	21	Lower dovetail		29	Push button locknut
3	L H Hinge	13	Plain washer	22	Screw		30	R H latch
4	Screw	14	Anti-rattle washer - cable gear change	23	Tailgate push button assembly	cable gear change	31	L H latch
5	Shakeproof washer	15	Nut	24	Circlip		32	Screw
6	R H moulding	16	R H striker	25	Centre plate		33	Shakeproof washer
7	L H moulding	17	L H striker	26	Tailgate turn button assembly	rod gear change	34	R H link rod
8	Clip	18	Shim	27	Sealing washer		35	L H link rod
9	Rivet	19	Screw				36	Clip
10	Seal						37	Adjustment pin

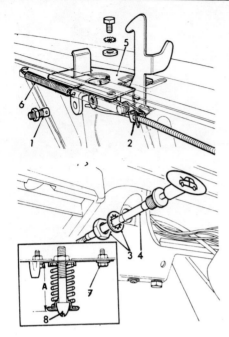

FIG. 12:16 BONNET LOCK AND CONTROL ASSEMBLY

No.	Description	No.	Description
1	Lock lever trunnion to cable connection	5	Bonnet lock assembly
2	Cable retaining clip	6	Lock return spring
3	Cable securing nut and shakeproof washer	7	Locking pin assembly retaining screws
4	Cable assembly	8	Locking pin

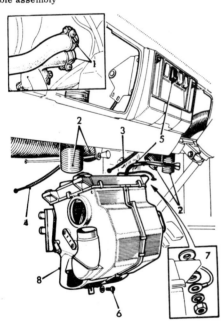

FIG. 12:17 HEATER UNIT REMOVAL (CABLE GEAR CHANGE)

No.	Description	No.	Description
1	Heater pipe connections	6	Heater lower retaining screw
2	Demister and fresh air flexible hoses	7	Heater securing nut and earth cable
3	Temperature control cable	8	Heater assembly
4	Air control cable		
5	Blower control switch		

the locking pin assembly.

12   Refitting is the reverse sequence to removal but the following additional points should be noted:

a)   If the locking pin assembly has been removed, it should be set so that there is a distance of 2 inches between the outer edge of the thimble and the bonnet panel.

b)   The bonnet lock cable must be threaded through the same body grommet as the choke cable.

c)   Lubricate all moving parts with Castrol GTX.

---

22   Heater unit - removal and refitting

Cable gear change

1   Disconnect the positive and then the negative terminals from the battery.

2   Refer to Chapter 2/2, and drain the complete cooling system.

3   Slacken the clips securing the small bore water hoses to the heater unit on the engine side of the bulkhead. Detach the hoses (Fig. 12:17).

4   Refer to Section 15 and remove the parcel shelf.

5   Refer to Chapter 10/43, and remove the instrument panel.

6   Refer to Section 24 and remove the glovebox.

7   Detach the demister and fresh air flexible hoses from the heater unit.

8   Disconnect the temperature control cable from the heater flap and detach the cable from its retaining clip.

9   Disconnect the air control cable from the heater flap and detach the cable from its retaining clip.

10   Make a note of the electrical cable connections at the blower control switch and detach the two Lucar connectors.

11   Unscrew and remove the heater unit lower retaining screw and plain washer from beneath the heater unit.

12   Unscrew and remove the four nuts and washers that secure the heater unit. Note that there is an earth cable located under the right hand rear nut.

13   Place some polythene sheeting over the carpeting so any water left in the heater matrix does not stain the carpeting. Very carefully lift away the heater unit.

14   Refitting the heater unit is the reverse sequence to removal.

Rod gear change

1   Disconnect the positive and then the negative terminals from the battery.

2   Refer to Chapter 2/2, and drain the complete cooling system.

3   Slacken the clips securing the small bore water hoses to the heater unit on the engine side of the bulkhead. Detach the hoses (Fig. 12:19).

4   Refer to Section 23 and remove the glove box.

5   Using a small screwdriver, unscrew the grub screws that secure the control knobs to the heater controls. Remove the two knobs.

6   With a knife, carefully prise away the heater control masking plate.

7   Undo and remove the two bolts and shakeproof washers that secure the heater controls to the facia board.

8   Disconnect the temperature and air control cables from the heater. Detach the cables from the retaining clips.

9   Refer to Section 15 and remove the parcel shelf.

10   Detach the demister hoses from the heater unit.

11   Make a note of the electrical cable connections at the blower control switch and detach the two Lucar connectors.

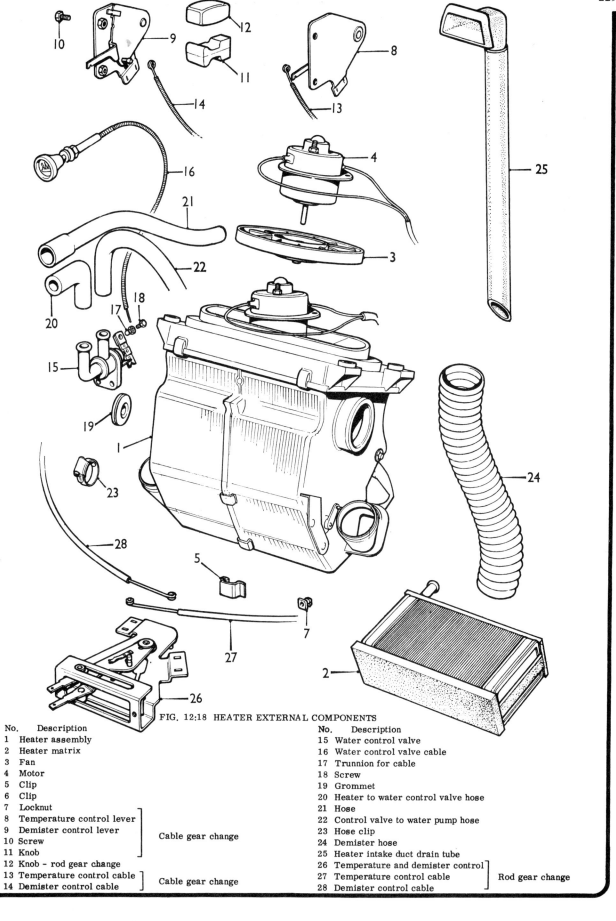

FIG. 12:18 HEATER EXTERNAL COMPONENTS

No.	Description		No.	Description
1	Heater assembly		15	Water control valve
2	Heater matrix		16	Water control valve cable
3	Fan		17	Trunnion for cable
4	Motor		18	Screw
5	Clip		19	Grommet
6	Clip		20	Heater to water control valve hose
7	Locknut		21	Hose
8	Temperature control lever		22	Control valve to water pump hose
9	Demister control lever	Cable gear change	23	Hose clip
10	Screw		24	Demister hose
11	Knob		25	Heater intake duct drain tube
12	Knob – rod gear change		26	Temperature and demister control
13	Temperature control cable	Cable gear change	27	Temperature control cable	Rod gear change
14	Demister control cable		28	Demister control cable

12   Removal is now identical to that for the cable gear change. Refer to paragraphs 11 to 13 inclusive of 'Cable gear change' above.

13   Refitting the heater unit is the reverse sequence to removal.

23   Heater unit - dismantling and reassembly

1   Release the spring from the heater flap.

2   Rod gear change models only. Disconnect the control cables from the heater and detach the cables from the retaining clips.

3   Release the six clips that secure the booster fan motor mounting plate. Lift away the plate complete with fan, motor and electric cables.

4   Lift up the fan mounting plate and, with a soldering iron, unsolder the booster fan motor cables from the resistance.

5   Release the spring clip that secures the fan to the motor spindle. Withdraw the fan.

6   Undo and remove the three long bolts, plain washers and nut that secure the motor. Lift away the motor.

7   Release the clips from the ends of the control flap mounting spindles.

8   Unscrew and remove the screws that secure the backing plate.

9   Remove the lower mounting bracket.

10   Release the clips retaining the two halves of the casing.

11   Carefully part the casing halves and lift away the matrix.

12   Disconnect the control cables from the control levers and detach the cables from the retaining clips.

13   Reassembly of the heater unit is the reverse sequence to removal.

24   Glovebox - removal and refitting

Cable gear change

1   Unscrew and remove the screw and plain washer that secures the lid support to the lid.

2   Unscrew and remove the three hinge screws and plain washers and lift away the lid.

3   Undo and remove the three glovebox retaining screws, two plain washers and lid striker. Note which way round the striker is fitted.

4   Carefully draw the glovebox compartment rearwards.

5   Refitting is the reverse sequence to removal.

Rod gear change

1   Undo and remove the screws that secure the glovebox lid support.

2   Undo and remove the two screws and plain washers that secure the glovebox lid striker.

3   Undo and remove the glovebox side and lower end retaining screws and draw the glovebox compartment rearwards.

4   Refitting is the reverse sequence to removal.

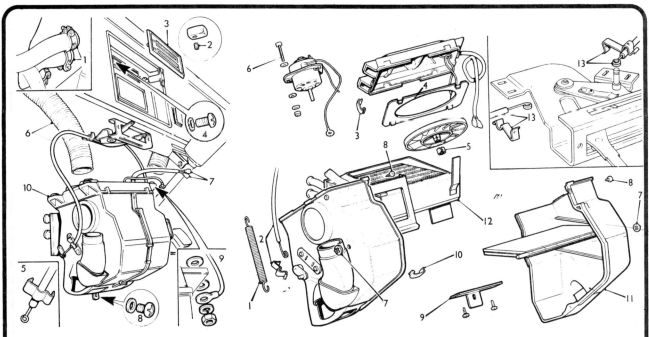

FIG. 12:19 HEATER UNIT REMOVAL (ROD GEAR CHANGE)

1   Heater pipe
2   Heater control knob
3   Heater control masking plate
4   Heater control to facia board securing screws
5   Heater control cables securing clips
6   Heater demist hoses
7   Blower control switch connections
8   Heater lower retaining screw
9   Heater securing nut and earth cable
10 Heater assembly

FIG. 12:20 HEATER INTERNAL COMPONENTS

No.   Description
1   Flap control spring
2   Control cables and securing clips
3   Clip - booster fan motor mounting plate
4   Fan mounting baffle plate
5   Clip - fan to motor spindle
6   Motor securing bolts
7   Clip - control flap mounting

No.   Description
    spindle
8   Backing plate securing screws
9   Lower mounting bracket
10 Casing clips
11 Casing half
12 Heater matrix
13 Control cable attachment to control levers

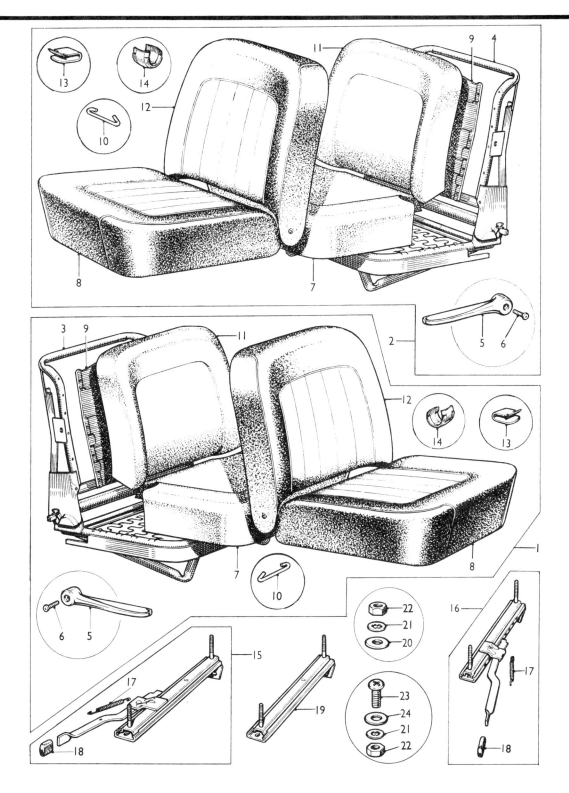

FIG. 12:21 FRONT SEAT COMPONENTS

No.	Description	No.	Description	No.	Description	No.	Description
1	R H seat assembly	7	Cushion pad	13	Clip	19	Slide
2	L H seat assembly	8	Cushion cover	14	Clip	20	Plain washer
3	R H seat frame	9	Squab diaphragm	15	Locking slide assembly	21	Shakeproof washer
4	L H seat frame	10	Diaphram hook	16	Locking slide assembly	22	Nut
5	Handle	11	Squab pad	17	Spring	23	Screw
6	Screw	12	Squab cover	18	Knob	24	Plain washer

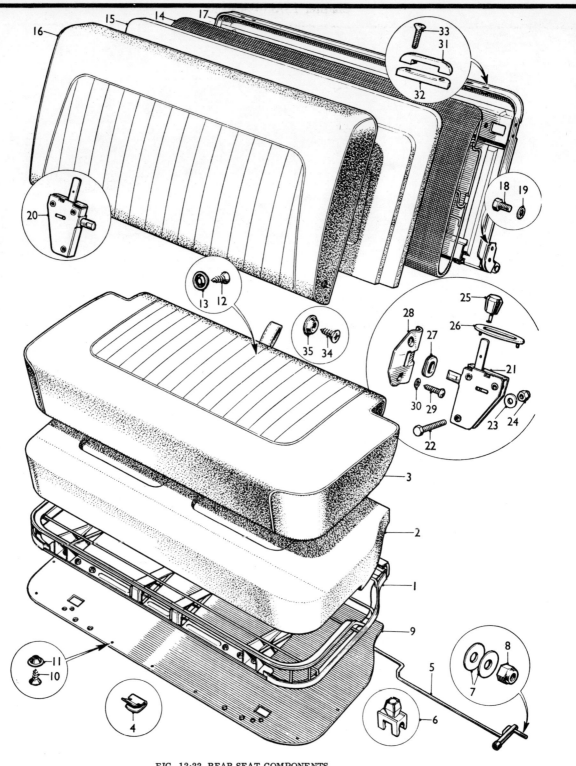

FIG. 12:22 REAR SEAT COMPONENTS

No.	Description	No.	Description	No.	Description	No.	Description
1	Rear cushion frame	10	Screw	19	Lock washer	28	Lock striker plate
2	Rear cushion pad	11	Cup washer	20	R H squab lock	29	Screw
3	Rear cushion cover	12	Screw	21	L H squab lock	30	Lock washer
4	Clip	13	Cup washer	22	Screw	31	Squab support hasp
5	Rear cushion support	14	Rear squab spring case	23	Plain washer	32	Squab hasp backing plate
6	Clip	15	Rear squab pad	24	Locknut	33	Screw
7	Plain washer	16	Rear squab pad cover	25	Knob	34	Screw
8	Locknut	17	Squab panel	26	Lock escutcheon	35	Cup washer
9	Rear cushion bottom liner	18	Screw	27	Grommet		

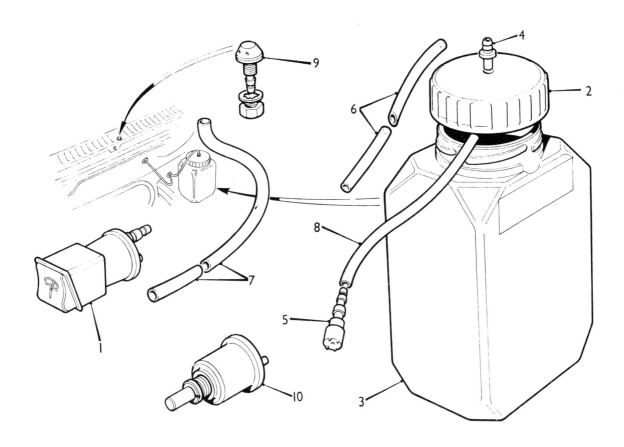

FIG. 12:23 WINDSCREEN WASHER COMPONENTS

No.	Description	No.	Description	No.	Description	No.	Description
1	Windscreen washer pump (cable gearchange)	3	Reservoir	6	Reservoir to pump tube	9	Jet
2	Reservoir cap	4	Connector	7	Pump to jet tube	10	Windscreen washer pump (rod gearchange)
		5	Non - return valve	8	Pick - up tube		

25 Windscreen washer control - removal and refitting

Cable gear change
1   Remove the glovebox (see previous Section).
2   Disconnect the pipes from the pump then unscrew the pump from the rear of the pushbutton.
3   Ease the pushbutton from the facia.

4   Installation is the reverse of the removal procedure.

Rod gear change
1   Remove the glovebox (see previous Section).
2   Remove the heater controls from the facia (see Section 22).
3   Disconnect the pipes from the pump then unscrew the pump bezel.
4   Ease the pump from the facia panel.
5   Installation is the reverse of the removal procedure.

Chapter 13 Supplement

Contents

1.   Specifications

Note: The specifications given in this Section are those which differ from the ones given in the earlier Chapters of this manual.

Engine (1750HL)

Compression ratio	9.5 : 1
Idle speed	800 rpm
Fast idle speed	1100 to 1200 rpm

Valve clearance *

Inlet	0.014 to 0.016 in. (0.35 to 0.40 mm)
Exhaust	0.017 to 0.019 in. (0.43 to 0.48 mm)

    * Adjust only if less than 0.012 in. (0.31 mm)

Oil capacity with automatic transmission ... ...   13 Imp. pints (15.6 US pints/7.4 litres)

Fuel system and carburation (1750HL)

Carburettor type	Twin SUHS6
Needle	BBR, spring loaded
Jet size	0.100 in.
Piston spring	Red

Ignition system (1750HL)

Ignition timing	11º BTDC at 1000 rpm (stroboscopic/vacuum pre-disconnected)

Automatic transmission (1750 and 1750HL)

Type	Automotive Product Mark III E

Ratios:

Fourth	.. ..	1.00 : 1
Third	.. ..	1.45 : 1
Second	.. ..	1.81 : 1
First	.. ..	2.61 : 1
Reverse	.. ..	2.61 : 1

Road speed at 1000 rpm in fourth gear	.. .. ..	17.2 mph
Speedometer gear ratio	.. ..	15/6

Final drive (automatic transmission)

Ratio	.. ..	3.800 : 1

Electrical system

Alternator type	.. ..	Lucas 16ACR or 17ACR	
Minimum brush length	.. ..	0.2 in. (5 mm) protruding beyond brush box moulding	
Brush spring pressure	.. ..	9 to 13 oz (255 to 368 gm) with brush face flush with face of brush box moulding	

	16 ACR	**17 ACR**	
Field winding resistance at 20°C (68°F):			
Pink winding	43 ohms ± 5%	4.2 ohms ± 5%	4.3 ohms ± 5%
Green winding	−	3.2 ohms ± 5%	
Purple winding	3.3 ohms ± 5%	−	
Current flow	3 amps	3 amps	
Alternator output at 6000 alternator rpm	34 amps at 14V	36 amps at 14V	

Suspension, dampers and steering (1750HL)

Tyre size	.. ..	165 - 13 radial ply

2 Introduction

The Maxi HL and Maxi automatic were added to the then current range of Maxi models in October 1972.

Maxi HL

The 1748 cc ohc engine was updated on HL models to produce 95 bhp at 5350 rpm which is an increase of ten per cent over the standard production unit. This was achieved by fitting new pistons which raised the compression ratio to 9.5:1, and fitting two SU HS6 carburettors to a new inlet manifold. The exhaust system was uprated to accommodate the new carburettors. In addition a wider overlap camshaft was fitted.

The exterior styling makes the vehicle easily distinguishable from its 1500 and 1750 counterparts by the fitment of a full width grille finished in matt black with horizontal bars and a chrome surround. An HL badge is fitted to the lower near side of the grille.

At the rear a matching motif is fitted to the left-hand side of the tailgate.

Fitted to the sides are chrome strips with a coloured insert to match the body colour. This runs along the waist and across the tailgate. In addition distinctive hub caps and wheel trims are fitted. Tyre size is increased to 165 x 13.

Internally the general standard of the trim has been improved. The front and rear seats are finished in brushed-nylon cloth fluted areas, colour matched to the body and trim. Thick fully fitted carpets cover the whole floor area.

The dashboard is finished in a new safety padded PVC material and houses a calibrated 110 mph speedometer, fuel gauge, temperature gauge together with warning lights for the direction indicators, headlight main beam, oil pressure and ignition.

Standard features in the HL include electrically operated windscreen washers, a cigar lighter, sporting leatherbound steering wheel and wood grain gear lever knob together with a dipping rear view mirror and electrically heated rear window. Padded companion boxes are fitted to both front doors.

Maxi automatic

The maxi automatic is based on the manual transmission 1750 model. The automatic transmission is available as a factory fitted optional extra. It is of the Automotive Products 'Mark III E' type and was specially developed for the maxi.

This transmission is compact and versatile and comprises basically a hydraulic torque converter and automatic transmission with four forward speeds and reverse. Gearchanges are effected by means of hydraulically operated multi-plate clutches and brake bands. Gearchanges are controlled automatically by a speed sensing mechanical governor. This can be overridden at anytime by a driver's manual control in the form of a selector lever mounted centrally between the front seats.

The new automatic transmission is available on Maxi HL models also.

Engine

3 Engine and transmission (automatic) - removal and replacement

1   The sequence of operations listed in this Section is not critical, as the position of the person undertaking the work, or the tool in his hand, will determine to a certain extent the order in which the work is tackled. Obviously the power unit cannot be removed until everything is disconnected from it; the following sequence will ensure nothing is forgotten. (Fig. 13.1).

2   Remove the plastic ignition shield.

3   Refer to Chapter 2, and drain the cooling system.

4   Preferably whilst the engine is warm, place a container having a capacity of at least 10 pints under the transmission unit drain plug and unscrew the drain plug.

5   Using a soft pencil mark the outline position of both the hinges at the bonnet to act as a datum for refitting.

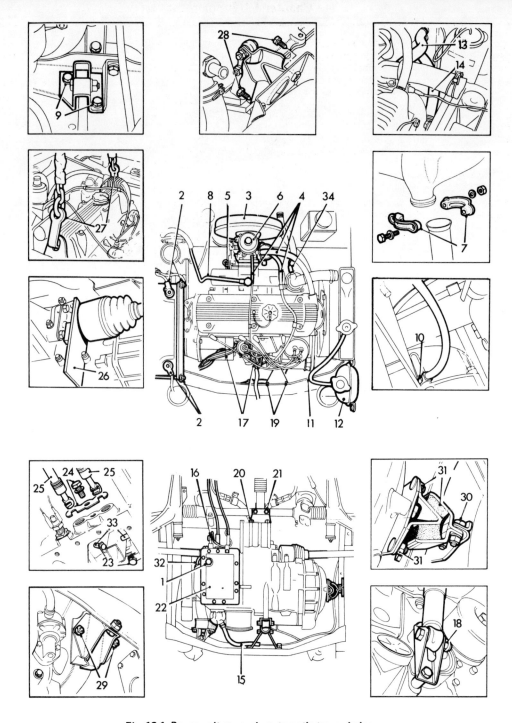

Fig. 13.1. Power unit removal - automatic transmission
Summary of items to be disconnected

1 Drain plug	9 Engine steady bracket	18 Engine damper bracket	28 Engine left-hand rear mounting bolts
2 Battery terminals and clamp	10 Earth cable	19 Damper mounting bracket	29 Engine left-hand front mounting nuts and bolts
3 Air cleaner	11 Radiator spill pipe	20 Exhaust bracket bolts	
4 Fuel hoses and breather pipe	12 Expansion tank	21 Exhaust pipe 'U' bolt	30 Engine right-hand mounting bolts
5 Kickdown rod	13 Heater hose - thermostat housing	22 Cover plate	31 Engine right-hand mounting
6 Carburettor installation	14 Heater hose - water pump	23 Park lock securing bolts	32 Speedometer cable
7 Exhaust manifold to downpipe clamp	15 Main fuel line	24 Control cable retainer and securing bolt	33 Control cable attachment
8 Vacuum pipe	16 Oil pressure switch	25 Control cables	34 Thermal transmitter
	17 Electrical connections to starter, alternator/dynamo, coil and distributor	26 Driveshaft removal tool	
		27 Engine sling	

6 With the help of a second person to take the weight of the bonnet, undo and remove the two lower stay retaining screws.

7 Undo and remove the hinge to bonnet securing bolts with spring and plain washers. There are two bolts to each hinge.

8 Lift away the bonnet and put in a safe place so that it will not be scratched.

9 Disconnect the positive and then the negative terminals from the battery.

10 Undo and remove the nuts and plain washers holding the battery clamp bar to the support rods and lift away the clamp bar and two rods.

11 Lift away the battery from its tray. The tray may next be lifted away.

12 Undo and remove the two nuts and shake proof washers securing the air cleaner to the carburettor air intake flange. Lift away the air cleaner.

13 Disconnect the fuel pipe, vacuum pipe and engine breather pipe from the carburettor installation.

14 Disconnect the 'kick-down' rod from the carburettor linkage.

15 Remove the carburettor installation from the manifold and tie it well clear of the engine.

16 Disconnect the exhaust downpipe from the exhaust manifold.

17 Disconnect the servo unit vacuum pipe from the inlet manifold.

18 Disconnect the engine steady from the subframe.

19 Detach the earth cable from the torque converter cover.

20 Disconnect the spill pipe from the radiator filler neck.

21 Remove the expansion tank.

22 Disconnect the heater hose from the thermostat housing.

23 Disconnect the heater hose from the water pump.

24 Disconnect the fuel feed pipe from the fuel pump.

25 The following cables should be disconnected:
Thermal transmitter, oil pressure switch, inhibitor switch, distributor, ignition coil, dynamo/alternator.

26 Remove the rubber strap that supports the thermal transmitter wire to the radiator top hose.

27 Chock the rear wheels, apply the handbrake, jack-up the front of the car and support it under the lower suspension arms with axle stands.

28 Detach the engine damper from the bracket on the engine.

29 Undo and remove the bolts that secure the damper mounting bracket to the subframe and remove the bracket. Note that the right-hand top bolt secures the petrol pipe support clip and spacer.

30 Slacken the exhaust bracket 'U' bolt securing nuts.

31 Undo and remove the two nuts that secure the exhaust pipe bracket to the differential housing.

32 Now slide the exhaust pipe bracket down the exhaust pipe.

33 Move the gear selector lever to the 'D' position.

34 Remove the control cable retainer and then slacken the two outer control cable nuts.

35 Carefully pull the outer cables out of the transmission casing.

36 Disconnect the inner control cable from the end of the detent rod, and the second inner control cable from the park lock control rod.

37 Withdraw the control cables from the transmission casing.

38 Refer to Chapter 7, and release the driveshafts from their locator rings in the differential unit. It is important that when releasing the left-hand drive shaft the large rectangular block welded to the tool must face the left-hand roadwheel to avoid damage to the differential case.

39 The car may now be lowered to the ground again.

40 Using a rope or chain support the weight of the complete power unit.

41 Undo and remove the bolts that secure the engine left-hand rear mounting to the subframe.

42 Undo and remove the bolts that secure the engine left-hand front mounting to the subframe bracket.

43 Undo and remove the bolts that secure the engine right-hand mounting to the subframe bracket.

44 Undo and remove the bolts that secure the engine right-hand mounting to the plate attached to the torque converter cover. Remove the engine mounting.

45 Detach the rubber strap that supports the speedometer cable to the heater hose.

46 The power unit should now be lifted slightly until the converter cover plate is clear of the petrol pipe. Take care not to damage the servo vacuum pipe against the master cylinder as the power unit is lifted.

47 Disconnect the speedometer cable from the transmission unit.

48 Move the engine as far as possible to the right-hand side of the car and disengage the left-hand driveshaft.

49 Move the engine as far as possible to the left-hand side of the car and disengage the right-hand driveshaft.

50 Temporarily secure the driveshafts with string or wire to prevent damage or interference during final removal of the power unit.

51 The power unit may now be lifted up and away from the front of the car.

52 Refitting the power unit is the reverse sequence to removal and will not present any problems if care is taken. It will be necessary to adjust the selector control cables as described later in this Chapter.

---

4   Automatic transmission unit - separation from engine

---

1 Before the automatic transmission can be separated from the engine the complete power unit must be removed from the car.

2 Remove the starter motor securing bolts and lift away the starter motor (Figs. 13.2 and 13.3).

3 Undo and remove the bolts securing the converter end cover and lift away the end cover.

4 Undo and remove the converter retaining bolts and lockwasher.

5 It is now desirable to use a special tool (18G 1222) to remove the converter. Do not attempt to remove the converter by other means otherwise expensive damage can result.

6 Using a hook shaped tool remove the converter housing oil seal if it is to be renewed.

7 Undo and remove the converter housing securing bolts and lift away the converter housing.

8 Withdraw the oil connection (valve) from the crankcase and follow this with the forward clutch oil feed pipe.

9 The nut securing the input sprocket must next be removed. For this a large socket and sprocket holding tool is desirable - the latter can be improvised.

10 Carefully remove the primary drive chain and sprockets as an assembly.

11 Should the radiator still be in position on the power unit this must be removed (Chapter 2).

12 Refer to Chapter 4, and remove the distributor.

13 The oil pump driveshaft must next be removed. It is best drawn upwards with a piece of plastic tube wedged over the end.

14 Remove the oil filter from the side of the transmission unit.

15 Remove the fuel pump and recover the pushrod.

16 Remove the radiator lower mounting bracket from the engine.

17 Remove the engine mounting securing nuts and bolts and lift away the mountings.

18 Undo and remove the nuts and bolts that secure the transmission unit casing to the underside of the crankcase.

19 The engine may now be lifted up and away from the transmission unit.

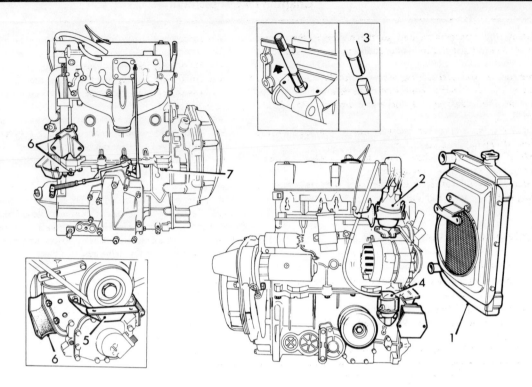

Fig. 13.2. Separating engine from automatic transmission
Summary of items to be disconnected - external

1	Radiator	3	Distributor drive	5	Radiator mounting bracket	7 Securing nuts and
2	Distributor	4	Fuel pump	6	Mountings	bolts

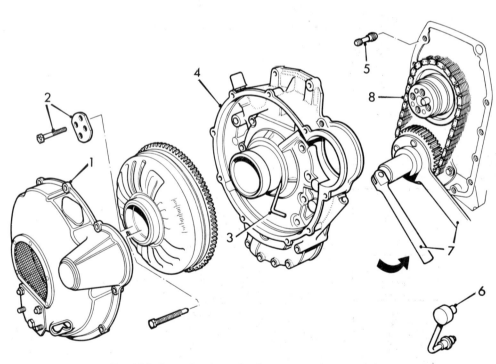

Fig. 13.3. Separating the engine from automatic transmission
Summary of items to be disconnected - internal

1	Converter end cover	3	Oil seal removal (when necessary)	5	Oil connection (valve)	7 Input sprocket nut removal
2	Converter retaining bolts and lockwasher	4	Converter housing	6	Forward clutch oil feed pipe	8 Primary drive chain and sprockets

20 Refitting the transmission unit to the engine is the reverse sequence to removal but the following additional points should be noted:

a) *If the torque converter is being renewed, the three small dowel holes in the new torque converter must be line reamed with those in the crankshaft. If necessary oversize dowels are available.*

b) *Tighten the input sprocket retaining nut to a torque wrench setting of 110 lb f ft (15.2 kg f m).*

c) *Apply a little Loctite grade 'HVX' to the crankshaft spigot where it enters the torque converter.*

d) *Tighten the torque converter securing bolts to a torque wrench setting of 60 lb f ft (8.3 kg f m).*

Fuel system and carburation

5   Twin carburettor installation - removal and replacement

1   For safety reasons, disconnect the battery.
2   Undo and remove the two wing nuts and lift off the air cleaner assembly (Fig. 13.4).
3   Detach the throttle return spring(s) from their anchor brackets.

4   Disconnect the throttle cable from the carburettor and remove the cable trunnion and return spring(s).
5   Disconnect the mixture control cable from the carburettor.
6   Disconnect the engine breather pipe at the 'Y' shaped junction.
7   Disconnect the fuel pipe and the fuel bridge pipe from the carburettor.
8   Detach the vacuum advance pipe.
9   Undo and remove the eight nuts securing the carburettor installation to the inlet manifold.
10   Lift off the throttle cable abutment bracket and the return spring anchor bracket(s).
11   The two carburettors and interconnecting linkage may now be lifted away.
12   Refitting the twin carburettor installation is the reverse sequence to removal. It will be necessary to adjust the throttle and mixture control cables. Also if the carburettors have been dismantled they will have to be reset.

6   Twin carburettor installation - adjustment and tuning

1   It is pointless trying to adjust a twin carburettor installation until the engine and ignition systems are correctly set. The following items should be checked:

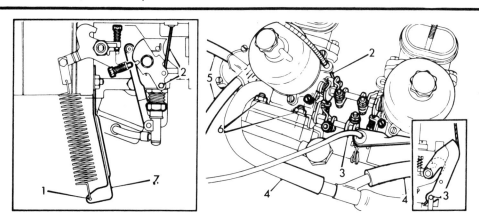

Fig. 13.4. Twin carburettor installation - removal

| 1 | Throttle return spring | 3 | Throttle cable | 5 | Fuel delivery pipes | 7 | Return spring anchor |
| 2 | Mixture control cable attachments | 4 | Engine breather pipes | 6 | Securing nuts | | bracket |

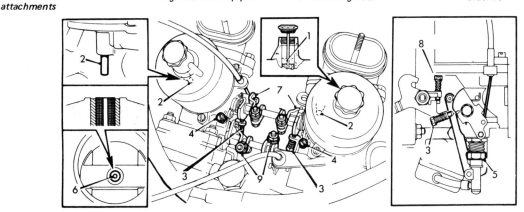

Fig. 13.5. Twin carburettor installation - adjustment items

1	Damper	4	Throttle adjustment screw	6	Jet and bridge - detail	8	Throttle adjustment screws
2	Lifting pin	5	Jet adjustment nut	7	Mixture control link pins	9	Throttle connectors
3	Fast idle screw						

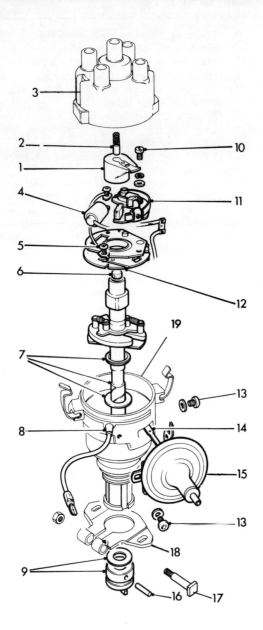

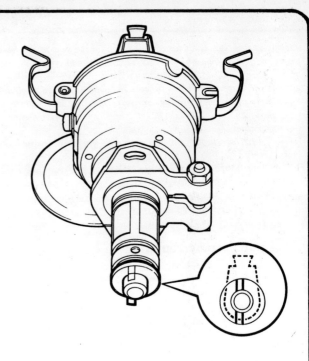

Fig. 13.7. The correct position of the driving dog on the 45D4 distributor

Fig. 13.6. The 45D4 distributor - exploded view

1	Rotor	10	Contact set securing screw
2	Carbon brush and spring	11	Contact set
3	Cap	12	Base plate
4	Condenser (capacitor)	13	Vacuum unit retaining screws and washers
5	Base plate securing screw	14	Vacuum unit link
6	Felt pad	15	Vacuum unit
7	Shaft assembly with steel washer and spacer	16	Parallel pin
8	Low tension lead and grommet	17	Pinch bolt and nut
		18	Lock plate
9	Drive dog and thrust washer	19	Distributor body

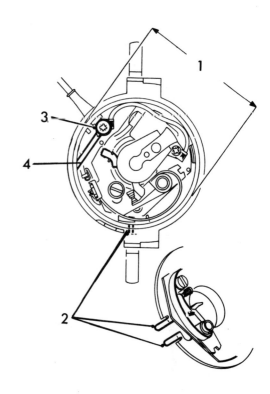

Fig. 13.8. Installing the 45D4 distributor base plate

1 Dimension across distributor cap register
2 Downward pointing prongs on baseplate
3 Earth lead
4 Slot in base plate

Ignition timing
Valve tappet clearance
Distributor contact breaker points
Spark plugs

2 Remove the air cleaner assembly.
3 Top-up the carburettor piston dampers with engine oil (Fig. 13.5).
4 Check that the throttle operates correctly.
5 Check that the mixture control returns fully and that the control has 1/16 inch (2 mm) free-play before the cable starts to pull on the lever.
6 Make sure that there is a small clearance between the fast idle screws and their cams.
7 Raise each caburettor lifting pin, release the pin and ensure that the piston falls freely onto the bridge of the carburettor. This is indicated by a metallic click.
8 Automatic transmission models. Select 'P' postion.
9 Start the engine and run it at a fast idle speed until it reaches normal operating temperature and then run for a further five minutes.
10 Increase the engine speed to 2500 rpm for thirty seconds. Tuning can now begin. If adjustments cannot be completed within three minutes increase the engine speed to 2500 rpm again for thirty seconds and then resume tuning. Repeat this procedure at three minute intervals until tuning is completed.
11 First check the engine idle speed and adjust if necessary (see Specifications).
12 Using either a vacuum synchronizing device or a piece of rubber tubing held adjacent to the ear check the carburettors for balance.
13 If the balance is not correct, release the throttle connector and adjust the balance by turning the throttle adjustment screw on one of the carburettors.
14 When the balance is correct, adjust the idle speed by turning the throttle adjusting screw on each carburettor by the same amount.
15 Recheck the carburettor balance and retighten the throttle connector.
16 Should it be found that it is not possible to obtain a smooth idle speed and balance is not achieved adjust the idle speed mixture.
17 Stop the engine and remove both suction chambers, and pistons. Turn both jet adjusting nuts up until each jet is flush with the bridge of its carburettor or as high as possible without exceeding the bridge height.
18 Make sure that both jets are in the same relative position to the bridge of their respective carburettors.
19 Turn the jet adjusting nut on each carburettor down two complete turns.
20 Refit the pistons and suction chambers and top-up the oil level in the piston dampers.
21 Restart the engine and run it at idle speed.
22 Turn the jet adjusting nut on both carburettors in the same direction one flat at a time, up to weaker or down to richen until the fastest speed is obtained.
23 Now turn both nuts up slowly until the speed first begins to fall.
24 Turn the nuts down equally very slowly by the minimum amount until the maximum speed is regained.
25 Re-check the idle speed and carburettor intake balance. Adjust as necessary with the throttle adjusting screws.
26 Set the throttle interconnection levers so that the throttles open simultaneously. Slacken one of the levers and re-tighten so that both link pins just contact the lower edge of the levers.

27 Check that the mixture control has 1/16 inch (2 mm) free-play before the cable starts to pull on the levers. If necessary adjust the link pins so that the levers more simultaneously.
28 Unscrew the fast idle screws well clear of their cams. Pull out the mixture control knob until the linkage is about to move the carburettor jets and leave the control in this position.
29 Turn each fast idle adjusting screw until it just contacts its cam and then turn each screw by an equal amount to give the correct fast idle speed (see Specificcations).
30 Return the mixture control and stop the engine. Refit the air cleaner assembly

Ignition system

7 Lucas 45D4 distributor - dismantling

1 Spring back the cap retaining clips and remove the cap.
2 Pull off the rotor arm and extract the felt pad from the cam.
3 Remove the two vacuum unit retaining screws, tilt the unit to disengage the link from the plate then remove the unit.
4 Push the low tension lead and its grommet into the distributor body.
5 Remove the screw which retains the baseplate.
6 Carefully lever the slotted segment of the baseplate from its retaining groove then lift out the baseplate assembly.
7 Drive out the drive dog parallel retaining pin then remove the dog and thrust washer.
8 Draw out the shaft assembly, steel washer and spacer.
9 Push the moving contact spring inwards and detach the electrical connector from the spring loop.
10 Remove the screw to release the earthing lead and the capacitor (condenser).
11 Remove the single screw and lift out the contact set.

8 Lucas 45D4 distributor - inspection and repair

1 Thoroughly wash all the mechanical parts in petrol and wipe them dry using a lint-free cloth.
2 Check the contact breaker points, as described in Chapter 4, Section 3. Check the distributor cap for signs of tracking, indicated by a thin black line between the segments. Replace the cap if evident.
3 If the metal portion of the rotor arm is badly burned or loose, renew the arm. If slightly burnt, clean the arm with a fine file. Check that the carbon brush moves freely in the centre of the distributor cover.
4 Do not dismantle the advance mechanism beyond removal of the control springs. If any of the moving parts, or the cam, are worn or damaged, a replacement shaft assembly must be obtained.
5 Check the fit of the shaft in its bearing. If excessive play exists, a replacement distributor must be obtained.
6 Check the baseplate assembly. If the spring between the plates is damaged, or the plates do not move freely, a replacement assembly must be obtained.

9 Lucas 45D4 distributor - reassembly

1 The reassembly procedure is essentially the reverse of the removal procedure. However, the following points must be noted:
a. A trace of a general purpose grease or petroleum-jelly (Vaseline) should be applied to the contact pivot post.
b. Lubricate the spacer and steel washer with a molybdenum disulphide dry lubricant such as Rocal MP (Molypad) before fitting them on the shaft.
c. Install the thrust-washer with the pipe towards the drive dog.
d. Fit the drive dog so that the driving tongues are parallel with the rotor arm electrode and to the left of its centreline (see Fig.

13.7). If a new shaft has been used, it must be drilled through the hole in the drive dog. Whilst drilling, push the shaft from the cam end, pressing the dog and washer against the body shank.

e.   Secure the pin in the drive dog by means of a centre-punch. If the shaft is new, tap the drive end to flatten the washer pipe to ensure correct endfloat.

f.   Position the baseplate assembly so that the two downward pointing prongs can straddle the screw hole below the cap clip. Press the plate into the body to engage it in the undercut.

g.   Accurately measure the dimension across the distributor cap register on the body at right angles to the slot in the baseplate. Position the earth lead then fit and tighten the baseplate securing screw. Remeasure the dimension across the cap register; if this is not at least 0.06 in (0.15 mm) greater than that first measured, the baseplate assembly must be renewed.

h.   Check that the baseplate prongs still straddle the screw hole. Refit the vacuum unit, engaging the operating arm with the pin of the moving plate.

j.   Set the contact points gap to that specified.

Automatic transmission

10   Automatic transmission - general description

The automatic transmission fitted to models covered by this manual incorporates a three element hydraulic torque converter, with a maximum torque conversion ratio of 2:1, coupled to a bevel gear train which provides four forward gears and reverse.

Power from the engine is transmitted from the crankshaft converter output gear to the transmission unit by a drive chain.

The final drive is transmitted from a drive gear to a conventional type differential unit which in turn transmits engine power through driveshafts employing constant velocity joints to the wheels.

The complete gear train assembly, including the reduction gear and differential unit runs below and parallel to the crankshaft and is

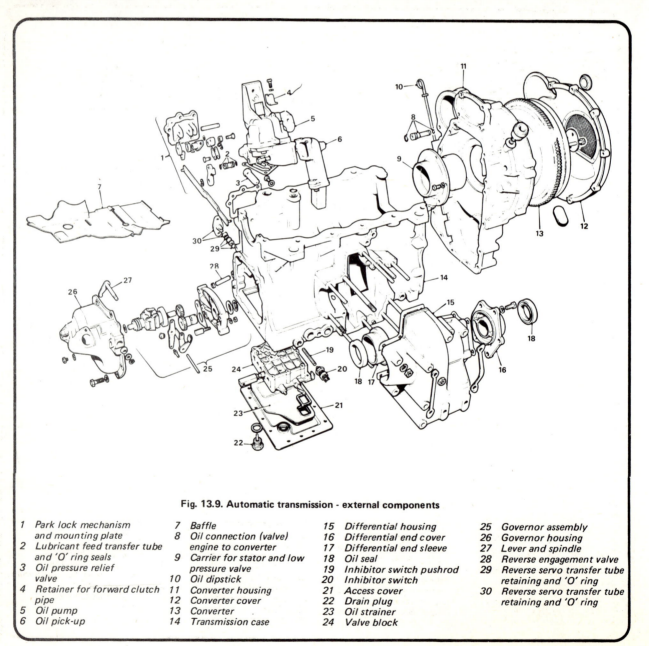

Fig. 13.9. Automatic transmission - external components

1 Park lock mechanism and mounting plate	7 Baffle	15 Differential housing	25 Governor assembly
2 Lubricant feed transfer tube and 'O' ring seals	8 Oil connection (valve) engine to converter	16 Differential end cover	26 Governor housing
3 Oil pressure relief valve	9 Carrier for stator and low pressure valve	17 Differential end sleeve	27 Lever and spindle
4 Retainer for forward clutch pipe	10 Oil dipstick	18 Oil seal	28 Reverse engagement valve
5 Oil pump	11 Converter housing	19 Inhibitor switch pushrod	29 Reverse servo transfer tube retaining and 'O' ring
6 Oil pick-up	12 Converter cover	20 Inhibitor switch	30 Reverse servo transfer tube retaining and 'O' ring
	13 Converter	21 Access cover	
	14 Transmission case	22 Drain plug	
		23 Oil strainer	
		24 Valve block	

housed in the transmission casing which also serves as the engine sump.

The gear trains are controlled by a selector lever within a gated quadrant marked in seven positions. It is mounted centrally on the floor panel.

The reverse, neutral and drive positions are for normal automatic driving with the first, second, third and fourth positions used for manual operation or override as required by the driver.

This allows the system to be used as a fully automatic four speed transmission, from rest to maximum speed with the gears changing automatically according to throttle position and load. Should a lower ratio be required to obtain greater acceleration, an instant full throttle position (kick-down) on the accelerator immediately produces a ratio change.

Complete manual control of all four forward gears by the use of the selector lever provides rapid changes. However, it is very important that downward changes are effected at the correct road speeds

otherwise serious damage may result to the automatic transmission unit. The second, third and top gears provide engine braking whether in automatic or manual control positions. In first gear a free wheel condition exists when decelerating.

Manual selection to third or second gear gives the engine braking and also allows the driver to stay in a particular lower gear to suit road conditions or when descending steep hills.

Due to the complexity of the automatic transmission unit, if performance is not up to standard, or overhaul is necessary, it is imperative that this be undertaken by the local BLMC garage who will have the equipment for accurate fault diagnosis and rectification. It is important that the fault is diagnossised before the unit is removed from the car.

The contents of the following Sections is therefore solely general and servicing information.

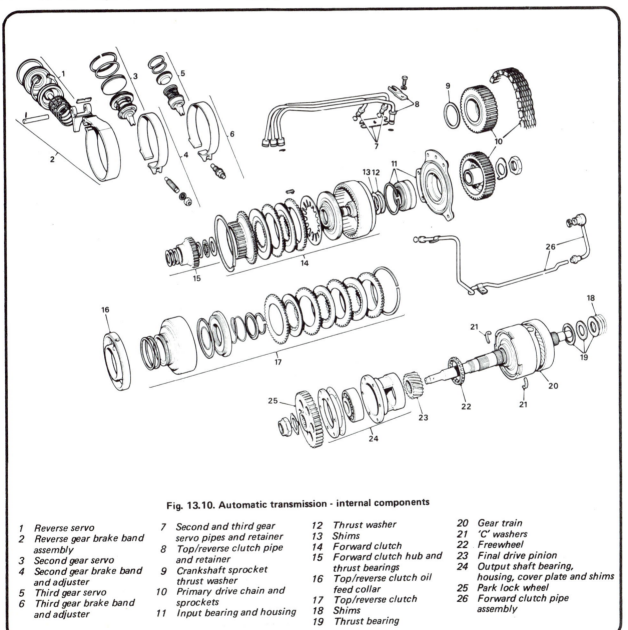

Fig. 13.10. Automatic transmission - internal components

1 Reverse servo	7 Second and third gear	12 Thrust washer	20 Gear train
2 Reverse gear brake band	servo pipes and retainer	13 Shims	21 'C' washers
assembly	8 Top/reverse clutch pipe	14 Forward clutch	22 Freewheel
3 Second gear servo	and retainer	15 Forward clutch hub and	23 Final drive pinion
4 Second gear brake band	9 Crankshaft sprocket	thrust bearings	24 Output shaft bearing,
and adjuster	thrust washer	16 Top/reverse clutch oil	housing, cover plate and shims
5 Third gear servo	10 Primary drive chain and	feed collar	25 Park lock wheel
6 Third gear brake band	sprockets	17 Top/reverse clutch	26 Forward clutch pipe
and adjuster	11 Input bearing and housing	18 Shims	assembly
		19 Thrust bearing	

11 Automatic transmission - lubrication

The sequence for checking the oil level, draining and refilling the engine/automatic transmission unit is basically identical to that for manual transmission models. The total oil capacity is however, 13 Imp. pints (15.6 US pints, 7.4 litres). It is very important that **no oil additives** are used otherwise operation of the automatic transmission unit will be impaired.

12 Automatic transmission - removal and replacement

The automatic transmission unit may only be detached once the complete power unit has been removed from the car. If the unit has developed a fault this must be investigated and positively identified before the unit is removed so the advice of the local BLMC garage must be sought.

Full information on this sequence will be found in Sections 3 and 4, of this Chapter.

13 Automatic transmission control cables - removal, replacement and adjustment

1   For safety reasons, disconnect the battery.
2   Move the gear selector lever to the 'D' position.
3   Unscrew the knob from the control lever (Fig. 13.11).
4   Carefully pull the nacelle from the selector mechanism.
5   Drain the engine/transmission oil.
6   Undo and remove the bolts and spring washers securing the access cover to transmission unit. Lift away the access cover and gasket.
7   Carefully pull the oil strainer off the end of the pick-up pipe.
8   Undo and remove the bolt and spring washer securing the park lock guide lug from the valve block.
9   Undo and remove the bolt and spring washer securing the control cable retainer to the rear of the automatic transmission unit.
10   Disconnect the control cables from the detent rod and the park lock control rod.
11   The control cables may now be withdrawn from the transmission casing.
12   Unscrew the two outer cable securing nuts from the selector mechanism.
13   Unscrew the two inner cables from the selector assembly and remove the cables from the assembly.
14   To refit the cables first screw the two inner cables into their forks in the selector assembly. Make quite sure that each cable is fully screwed in. To allow for subsequent alignment at the transmission end now unscrew the cables one complete turn only.
15   Screw on the two outer cable nuts and tighten finger tight.
16   Refitting is now the reverse sequence to removal. It will be necessary to adjust the control cables as described later in this Section. Finally, check the adjustment of the reverse light and starter inhibitor switches as described in subsequent Sections.
17   To check the cable adjustment first move the selector lever to the 'P' position and then release the brakes. Rock the car to-and-fro to ascertain if the parking pawl has engaged. If it has the park lock cable adjustment is correct.
18   Move the selector lever to the 'N' position and start the engine.
19   Select the '1' position, release the brakes and drive the car forwards slowly. Once the car starts to move select 'N'. The drive should now be disconnected.

20   If the drive is felt to be disconnected during each of the described tests the gear selector cable adjustment is correct.
21   To carry out any adjustments first stop the engine and move the selector lever to the 'R' position.
22   Slacken the box nut on whichever cable requires adjustment. Hold the cable close to the box nut and pull the cable out from the selector mechanism.
23   When the cable cannot be pulled out any further tighten the box nut.
24   Check the cable adjustment and also that the engine can only be started with the selector lever in the 'N' or 'P' position.

14 Automatic transmission selector mechanism - removal, overhaul and replacement

1   Refer to the previous Section, and remove the control cables.
2   Remove the front carpeting from the interior.
3   Make a note of and disconnect the electrical wiring at the snap connectors (Fig. 13.12).
4   Undo and remove the earth cable terminal securing screw.
5   Undo and remove the six screws securing the housing to the floor and lower the selector mechanism through the floor.
6   To dismantle the selector mechanism first remove the screw to the left of the reverse light switch and then remove the reverse light switch (Fig. 13.13).
7   Undo and remove the two cable connector unions from the front of the selector mechanism body.
8   Unscrew the selector knob locknut.
9   Remove the 'E' clip and withdraw the forward pin.
10   Remove the 'E' clip and withdraw the centre pin.
11   Remove the 'E' clip and washer from the outside end of each of the two short pins.
12   Move the left-hand fork to the bottom of its actuating slot and remove the pin, fork and plate.
13   Move the right-hand fork to the bottom of its actuating slot and remove the pin, fork and plate.
14   Remove the 'E' clip and withdraw the actuator pivot pin.
15   The actuator assembly may now be withdrawn from the frame.
16   Finally remove the bolt and separate the selector lever and spring from the actuator.
17   Inspect all parts for wear and obtain new as necessary.
18   Reassembly of the selector mechanism and then replacement is the reverse sequence to removal. All the 'E' clips should be renewed and lubricate all sliding surfaces with a little 'Duckhams Laminoid 'O' grease'.

15 Automatic transmission 'kick-down' linkage - adjustment

1   For this adjustment to be correctly achieved a special gauge tool kit is required. It has a BLMC part number '18G 1234'. If this tool is available follow the details given in this Section, otherwise leave to the local BLMC garage (Fig. 13.14).
2   Check that the slots in the 'kick-down' lever and its spindle are in line.
3   Remove the plug from the governor housing and screw in the spindle from the special tool until a stop is felt. The governor should now be fully collapsed.
4   Clean the setting holes in the bellcrank lever and transmission case.
5   Rotate the bellcrank lever anticlockwise and insert the peg of the special tool through the lever and into the hole in the transmission case.
6   Using the special gauge check the length of the 'kick-down' spring. If necessary, slacken the locknut and rotate the adjuster to

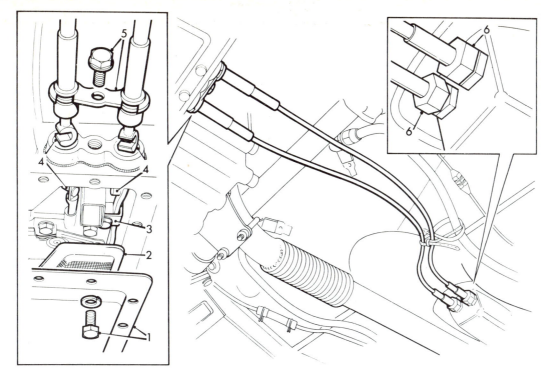

Fig. 13.11. Automatic transmission control cables

1	Access cover and securing bolts	4	Control cables, detent rod and park lock control rod
2	Oil strainer	5	Control cable retainer securing bolt
3	Park lock guide lug	6	Outer cable nuts

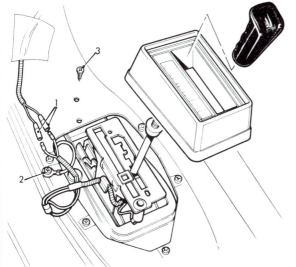

Fig. 13.12. Selector mechanism - attachments

1 Electrical cable snap connectors
2 Earth cable securing screw
3 Mechanism securing screws

Fig. 13.13. Exploded view of selector mechanism

1 Reverse light switch and screw
2 Connectors
3 Knob locknut
4 'E' clip and forward pin
5 'E' clip and centre pin
6 'E' clip and short pin
7 Left-hand fork assembly
8 Right-hand fork assembly
9 'E' clip and actuator pivot pin
10 Actuator assembly
11 Selector lever and spring assembly

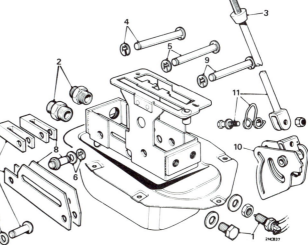

set the spring length to match the gauge. Tighten the locknut again.

7   Check that the throttle is fully open. If not slacken the locknut on the carburettor rod and adjust the rod until the throttle is fully open and then retighten the locknut.

8   Remove the peg and spindle of the special tool. Refit the plug to the governor housing.

9   Make sure that the throttle is fully open when the throttle pedal is fully depressed. If necessary adjust the throttle cable.

10   The car should now be driven and the Kick-down' change speeds noted. These should occur at the following speeds when 'D' is selected:

a)   1 - 2 change at 26 - 33 mph (42 - 53 kph)
b)   2 - 3 change at 37 - 43 mph (60 - 70 kph)
c)   3 - 4 change at 57 - 65 mph (92 - 105 kph)

11   If the gearchanges occur at low speeds, slacken the locknut and rotate the adjuster to increase the 'kick-down' spring load. Re-tighten the locknut.

12   If the gearchanges occur at high speeds, slacken the locknut and rotate the adjuster to decrease the 'kick-down' spring load. Retighten the locknut.

---

16   Automatic transmission starter inhibitor switch - adjustment

---

1   Move the selector lever to the 'N' or 'P' position.

2   Disconnect the two cable terminal connectors from the inhibitor switch. Slacken the locknut.

3   Connect a test light and battery across the switch terminals.

4   Unscrew the switch from the transmission casing until the test light goes out.

5   Now screw the switch into the transmission casing until the test light comes on. Screw the switch in a further half turn and retighten the locknut.

6   Check that the test light only comes on when the selector lever is in the 'P' or 'N' positions.

7   Remove the test light and battery and reconnect the terminal connectors to the inhibitor switch.

---

17   Automatic transmission reverse light switch - adjustment

---

1   Move the selector lever to the 'R' position.

2   Disconnect the two cable terminal connectors from the reverse light switch. Slacken the locknut.

3   Connect a test light and battery across the switch terminals.

4   Unscrew the switch from the selector mechanism until the test light goes out.

5   Screw the switch into the selector mechanism until the test light comes on. Screw the switch in a further half turn and retighten the locknut.

6   Check that the test light only comes on when the selector lever is in the 'R' position.

7   Remove the test light and battery and reconnect the terminal connectors to the reverse light switch.

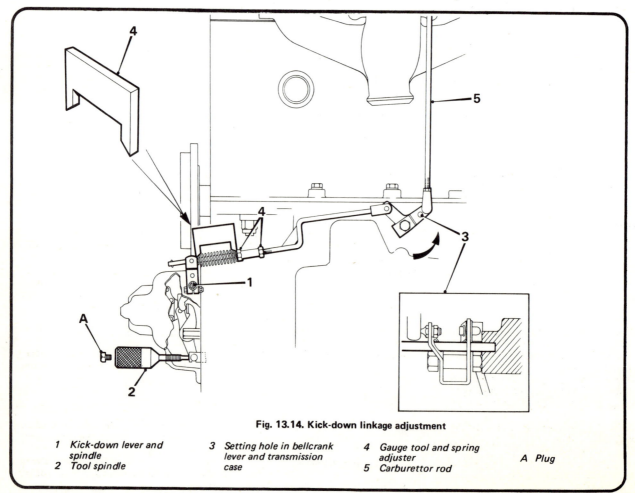

Fig. 13.14. Kick-down linkage adjustment

| 1 Kick-down lever and spindle | 3 Setting hole in bellcrank lever and transmission case | 4 Gauge tool and spring adjuster | A Plug |
| 2 Tool spindle | | 5 Carburettor rod | |

18   Automatic transmission - fault diagnosis

To enable a complete fault diagnosis sequence to be carried out certain special tools and equipment are necessary. These will be found at the local BLMC garage so it is best to leave the checking of any suspected faults to them. Also it is important that the fault be found before the unit is removed from the car. There are however several checks that the reader can carry out before seeking the advice of a specialist.

Preliminary check
a)   Check oil level.
b)   Check engine idle speed.
c)   Check adjustment of selector lever cables, inhibitor switch and 'kick-down' linkage.

Road test

Test	Fault	Rectification
1 Check the throttle with the pedal fully depressed	a. Throttle not fully open	1a. Adjust the throttle cable.
2 Check that the starter will operate only when 'P' and 'N' are selected	a. Starter will not operate in 'P' and 'N'	2a. Adjust the inhibitor switch.
	b. Starter operates in all positions	2b. Check the inhibitor switch and its wiring for short-circuiting.
3 Check the adjustment of both control cables	a. One or both cables out of adjustment	3a. Adjust the cables.
4 Position the car on a slope, select 'P' and release the brakes. Repeat this test with the car facing in the opposite direction	a. The park lock fails to hold the car in one or both positions	4a. Remove and check the park lock mechanism.
5 Apply the hand and foot brakes, and with the engine idling, select 'R' from 'N' and '1' from 'N'	a. Excessive bump on engagement of 'R' or '1'	5a. Reduce engine idle speed.
	b. Engine stalls on engagement of 'R' or '1'	5b. Increase engine idle speed.
	c. Excessive bump on engagement of 'R' when idle speed is correct	5c. Check the reverse engagement valve or, when fitted, the reverse accumulator for sticking or other damage (BLMC garage).
6 Select '1', release the brakes and check that the car drives forward but that there is no engine braking when the throttle is released	a. Car does not drive forward	6a. Remove and check the forward clutch if satisfactory renew the freewheel.
	b. Engine braking can be felt	6b. Renew the freewheel (BLMC garage).
7 Select '1' and drive away, using the manual gear-change to select '2' and '3' progressively as the road speed increases. When the road speed is above 25 mph (40 kmph) select 'D' and release the throttle pedal	a. Drive in '1' but not in '2'	7a. Check the second gear brake band adjustment. If satisfactory, check the second gear servo. (BLMC garage)
	b. Drive in '1' and '2' but not in '3'	7b. Check the third gear brake band adjustment. If satisfactory, check the third gear servo. (BLMC garage)
	c. Drive in '1', '2' and '3', but no upward gear-change (to fourth gear) on selecting 'D'	7c. Check the kick-down linkage adjustment. 7d. If correct, check the governor for freedom of operation. If the governor is satisfactory, remove and check the top/reverse clutch. (BLMC garage)
8 Stop the car, select 'D' and accelerate up through the gears using 'kick-down'. Check that the gear-changes occur at the following road speeds: 1-2 change at 26 to 33 mph (42 to 53 kmph) 2-3 change at 37 to 43 mph (60 to 70 kmph) 3-4 change at 57 to 65 mph (92 to 105 kmph)	a. Gear-changes occur at low speeds	8a. Check the kick-down linkage adjustment.
	b. Gear-changes occur at high speeds	8b. Check the kick-down linkage adjustment. If correct, check the governor for freedom of operation.
9 Stop the car, select 'R' and drive the car backwards	a. Car will not drive backwards	9a. Check reverse gear brake band adjustment. If satisfactory, check the reverse servo. (BLMC garage)
	b. Delay in engaging reverse	9b. Check the reverse engagement valve or, when fitted, the reverse accumulator. (BLMC garage)

19 Differential unit (automatic transmission) - removal and replacement

1   Refer to Section 3, and remove the complete power unit.
2   Undo and remove the bolts and spring washers securing the differential end cover to the differential housing (Fig. 13.15). Lift away the end cover and recover any shims fitted to the right-hand side of the differential housing.
3   Unlock and then remove the differential housing nuts and lockwashers.
4   Using a soft faced hammer carefully tap the differential housing from the securing studs. Lift away the housing.
5   Lift out the differential end sleeve.
6   The complete differential assembly can now be removed.
7   Remove the 'O' ring seal from the end sleeve.
8   Remove the oil seals from the differential end cover and end sleeve.
9   To reassemble first dip new oil seals and a new 'O' ring seal in engine oil and fit them to the differential end cover and end sleeve.
10   Fit the end sleeve to the transmission casing, making sure that the sleeve locates correctly on its dowel.
11   Fit the differential assembly into the transmission casing and push it hard against the end sleeve.
12   Fit the differential housing and tighten the nuts sufficiently to hold the bearings firmly but not so tight as to prevent lateral movement of the differential assembly.
13   It is now necessary to adjust the bearing preload. First fit the differential end cover leaving out the gasket and shims.
14   Tighten the end cover bolts in a diagonal manner just sufficiently to ensure full contact of the cover spigot with the bearing, without applying any preload.
15   Using feeler gauges, measure the gap between the cover flange and differential housing at not less then three positions around the circumference. If necessary adjust the bolt tightness to equalise the gap. Be careful not to overtighten as it will only distort the cover flange.
16   Should the situation arise where no gap exists between the flange and housing, remove the end cover and add a known thickness of shims between the cover and the bearing to produce a gap. The thickness of shims fitted must be included in the calculation of the preload shim requirement.
17   The compressed thickness of the new side cover gasket is 0.008 inch and the required preload is 0.001 to 0.002 inch. The clearance between the cover flange and casing must be adjusted by shims to give the required preload.

To act as a guide the following sample calculation is given:

Measured clearance		0.007 inch
Gasket compressed thickness		0.008 inch
(gasket thickness minus clearance)	=	0.008 - 0.007 inch
	=	0.001 inch
Add required preload of 0.001 - 0.002 inch	=	0.002 inch
Shim thickness required	=	0.002 inch

Note: Shims are available in 0.002 and 0.003 inch thicknesses.
18   Remove the end cover, fit the required thickness of shims and a new gasket. Refit the end cover and tighten the bolts to a torque wrench setting of 18 lb f ft (2.5 kg f m).
19   Fully tighten the differential housing nuts, 5/16 inch 18 lb f ft (2.5 kg f m) and 3/8 inch 25 lb f ft (3.5 kg f m). Lock the nuts by bending over the lock tabs.
20   The power unit may now be refitted to the car.

20 Differential unit (automatic transmission) - dismantling and reassembly

The sequence is basically identical to that for the manual transmission model, as described in Chapter 8, Section 3.

Electrical system

21 Alternator - general description

The Lucas 16 or 17ACR series alternator is fitted to later models. The main advantage of the alternator over the dynamo lies in its ability to provide a high charge at low revolutions. Driving slowly in heavy traffic with a dynamo invariably means no charge is reaching the battery. In similar conditions even when the wipers, heater, lights and perhaps radio switched on, the alternator will ensure a charge reaches the battery.

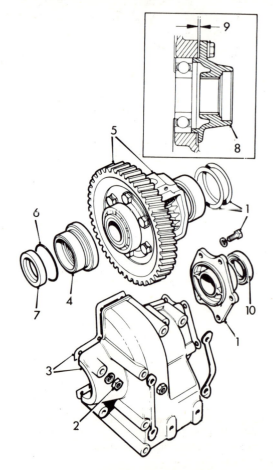

Fig. 13.15. Differential unit removal

1	Differential end cover	7	Oil seal
2	Housing nuts	8	End cover less shims
3	Housing and gasket	9	End cover to differential
4	End sleeve		housing gap
5	Differential assembly	10	Oil seal
6	'O' ring seal		

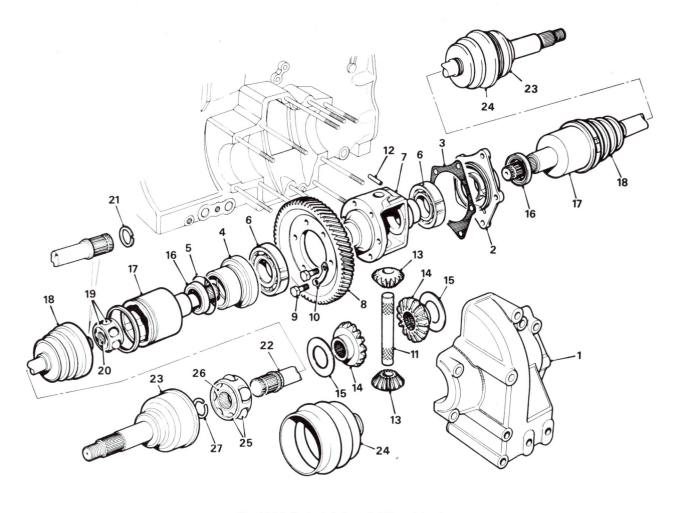

Fig. 13.16. Exploded view of differential unit

1 Differential housing	7 Differential cage	14 Differential gear	21 Spring ring
2 Differential end cover	8 Crownwheel	15 Thrust washer	22 Shaft
3 Gasket	9 Bolt for crown wheel	16 Oil seal	23 Constant velocity joint
4 Differential end sleeve	10 Lock washer for bolt	17 Pot joint outer	outer member
5 'O' ring seal	11 Differential pin	member	24 Rubber boot
6 Differential carrier	12 Roll pin for differential	18 Rubber boot	25 Balls and cage
bearing	pin	19 Balls and cage	26 Inner member
	13 Differential pinion	20 Inner member	27 Spring ring

An important feature of the alternator is a built in output control regulator, based on 'thick film' hybrid integrated micro - circuit technique, which results in the alternator being a self contained generating and control unit.

The system provides for direct connection of a charge light, and eliminates the need for a field switching relay and warning light control unit - necessary with former systems.

The alternator is of the rotating field ventilated design and comprises, principally, a laminated stator on which is wound a star connected 3 phase output winding, a twelve pole rotor carrying the field windings - each end of the rotor shaft runs in ball race bearings which are lubricated for life, natural finish diecast end brackets, incorporating the mounting lugs, a rectifier for converting the AC output of the machine to DC for battery charging, and an output control regulator.

The rotor is belt driven from the engine through a pulley to the rotor shaft, a pressed steel fan adjacent to the pulley draws cooling air through the alternator. This fan forms an integral part of the alternator specification. It has been designed to provide adequate airflow with a minimum of noise and to withstand the high stresses associated with maximum speed. Rotation is clockwise viewed on the drive end. Maximum continuous rotor speed is 12500 rpm. Rectification of alternator output is achieved by six silicone diodes housed in a rectifier pack and connected as a 3 phase full wave

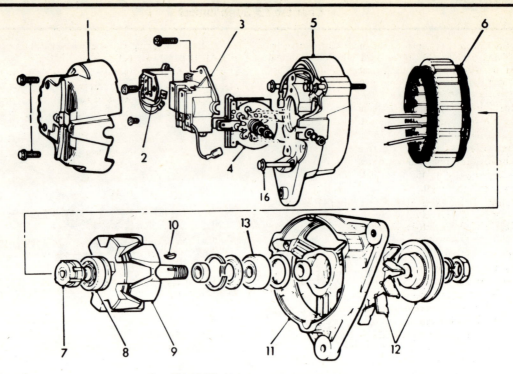

Fig. 13.17. Alternator component parts

1	Moulded end cover	4	Rectifier pack
2	Connector	5	Slip ring end bracket
3	Brush box assembly	6	Stator winding

7	Slip ring moulding	11	Drive end bracket
8	End bearing (slip ring)	12	Fan and pulley
9	Pressure ring	13	End bearing (drive end)
10	Key		

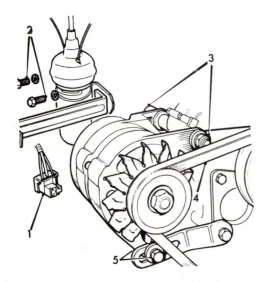

Fig. 13.18. Alternator attachments

1 Terminal block
2 Coil securing bolts
3 Alternator mounting bolt
4 Alternator adjustment strap and lock bolt

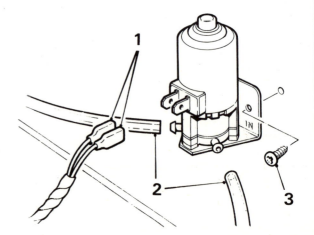

Fig. 13.19. The electrically operated windscreen washer pump

1 Lucar connectors   3 Pump securing screws
2 Pipes

bridge. The rectifier pack is attached to the outer face of the slip ring end bracket and contains also three 'field' diodes; at normal operating speeds, rectified current from the stator output windings flows through these diodes to provide self excitation of the rotor field, via brushes bearing on face type slip rings.

The slip rings are carried on a small diameter moulded drum attached to the rotor shaft outboard of the rotor shaft axle, while the outer ring has a mean diameter of 0.75 inch (19.05 mm). By keeping the mean diameter of the slip rings to a minimum, relative speeds between brushes and rings and hence wear, are also minimal. The slip rings are connected to the rotor field winding by wires carried in grooves in the rotor shaft.

The brush gear is housed in a moulding screwed to the outside of the slip ring end bracket. This moulding thus encloses the slip ring and brush gear assembly, and together with the shielded bearing protects the assembly against entry of dust and moisture.

The regulator is set during manufacture and requires no further attention. Briefly the 'thick film' regulator comprises resistors and conductors screen printed onto a square aluminium substrate. Mounted on the substrate are Lucas semi-conductors consisting of three transistors, a voltage reference diode and a field rectification diode, and two capacitors. The internal connections between these components and the substrate are made by Lucas patented connectors. The whole assembly is housed in a recess in an aluminium heat sink, which is attached to the slip ring end bracket. Complete hermetic sealing is achieved by a silicone rubber enscapulant to provide environmental protection.

Electrical connections to external circuits are brought out to Lucar connector blades, these being grouped to accept a moulded connector socket which ensures correct connections.

22 Alternator - maintenance

1 The equipment has been designed for the minimum amount of maintenance in service, the only items subject to wear being the brushes and bearings.
2 Brushes should be examined after 60,000 miles (100,000 km) and renewed if necessary. Any servicing of the alternator other than brush renewal should be left to the local BLMC garage or auto electrical specialists.
3 The bearings are pre-packed with grease for life and should not require any further attention.

23 Alternator - removal and replacement

1 For safety reasons, disconnect the battery.
2 Remove the ignition shield.

3 Release the spring clip and withdraw the connector from its socket in the alternator cover (Fig. 13.18).
4 To give better access undo and remove the two bolts and spring washers securing the ignition coil and move it away from the engine.
5 Undo and remove the adjusting link bolt and mounting bolt.
6 Detach the drive belt from the alternator pulley and lift the alternator from the engine.
7 Refitting the alternator is the reverse sequence to removal. The fan belt should be set to give lateral play of 0.5 in (13 mm) on the longest run.

24 Alternator brush - removal and replacement

1 With the alternator on the bench and the exterior clean undo and remove the two end cover securing screws. Lift away the end cover (Fig. 13.17).
2 To inspect the brushes correctly the brush holder moulding should be removed by undoing the securing bolts and disconnecting the 'Lucar' connector to the diode plates.
3 With the brush holder moulding removed and the brush assemblies still in position check that they protrude from the face of the moulding by at least 0.2 inch (5 mm). Also check that when depressed, the spring pressure is 7-10 oz (198-283 gms) when the end of the brush is flush with the face of the brush moulding. To be done with any accuracy this requires a push type spring scale.
4 Should either of the foregoing requirements not be fulfilled the spring assemblies must be renewed. This can be done by simply removing the holding screws of each assembly, discarding the old ones, and fitting new assemblies.
5 With the brush holder moulding removed the slip rings on the face end of the rotor are exposed. These can be cleaned with a petrol soaked cloth and any signs of burring can be removed very carefully with fine glass paper. On no account should any other abrasive be used or any attempt at machining be made.
6 Reassembly is the reverse order to dismantling. Make sure that leads which may have been connected to any of the screws are reconnected correctly.

25 Electrically operated windscreen washer pump - removal and installation

1 Disconnect the leads from the pump terminals.
2 Remove the pipes from the pump nozzles.
3 Remove the two pump securing screws and lift away the pump.
4 Installation is the reverse of the removal procedure, but note that the reservoir pipe connects to the pump 'IN' nozzle and the green lead connects to the pump positive (+) terminal.

Key to wiring diagram

Use the one diagram key to identify components on these wiring diagrams. Refer to the appropriate wiring diagram and disregard any additional numbered items appearing in the key

No.	Description	No.	Description
1	Alternator or dynamo †	39	Ignition coil
2	Control box	40	Distributor
3	Battery	42	Oil pressure switch
4	Starter solenoid	43	Oil pressure warning lamp
5	Starter motor	44	Ignition warning lamp
6	Lighting switch	45	Headlamp flasher switch
7	Headlamp dip switch	46	Water temperature gauge
8	Headlamp - dipped beam	47	Water temperature transmitter
9	Headlamp - main beam	49	Reverse lamp switch
10	Main beam warning lamp	50	Reverse lamp
11	RH sidelamp	57	Cigar lighter *
12	LH sidelamp	60	Radio *
14	Panel lamps	64	Bi-metal instrument voltage stabilizer
15	Number plate lamps	67	Line fuse *
16	Stop lamps	75	Automatic transmission inhibitor switch *
17	RH tail lamp	76	Automatic transmission gear selector indicator lamp *
18	Stop lamp switch		
19	Fuse block	77	Electric windscreen washer *
20	Interior lamp	78	Windscreen washer switch *
21	Door switch	83	Induction heater and thermostat *
22	LH tail lamp	84	Suction chamber heater *
23	Horn	110	RH repeater flasher
24	Horn-push	111	LH repeater flasher
25	Flasher unit	115	Rear window demist switch *
26	Direction indicator switch	116	Rear window demist unit *
27	Direction indicator warning lamps(s)	139	Alternative connections when alternator is fitted *
28	RH front flasher lamp	150	Rear window demist warning lamp *
29	LH front flasher lamp	152	Hazard warning lamp *
30	RH rear flasher lamp	153	Hazard warning switch *
31	LH rear flasher lamp	154	Hazard warning flasher unit *
32	Heater blower switch *	158	Printed circuit instrument panel
33	Heater blower motor *	159	Brake pressure warning lamp and lamp test-push *
34	Fuel gauge	160	Brake pressure differential switch *
35	Fuel gauge tank unit	164	Ballast resistor *
36	Windscreen wiper switch	266	Headlamp wiper motor *
37	Windscreen wiper motor	267	Headlamp washer motor *
38	Ignition/starter switch	268	Headlamp wipe/wash switch *

* Optional or special market fitment circuits shown dotted
† For the charging circuit on 1972 models equipped with a dynamo

Cable colour code

N	Brown	P	Purple	W	White
U	Blue	G	Green	Y	Yellow
R	Red	LG	Light Green	B	Black
		O	Orange	K	Pink

When a cable has two colour code letters the first denotes the main colour and the second denotes the tracer colour

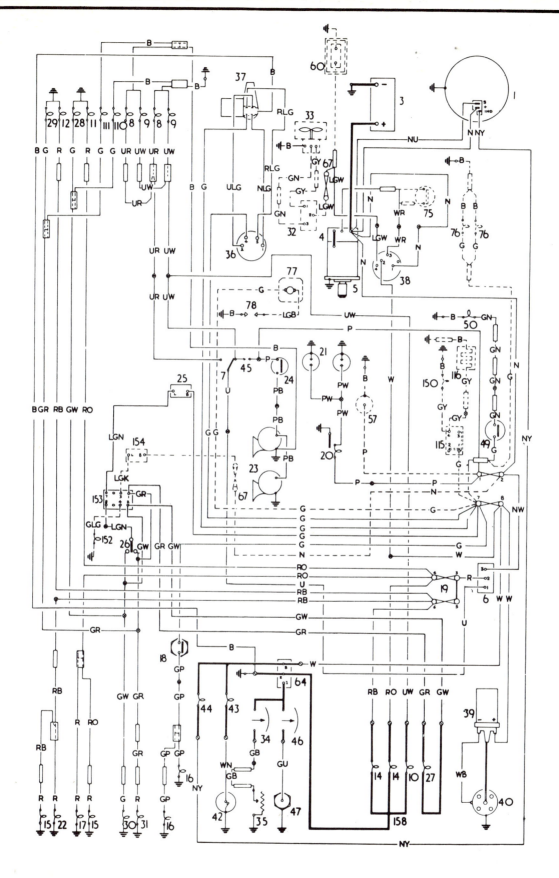

Wiring diagram - 1972 models onwards

Index

**Printed by
J. H. HAYNES & Co. Ltd
Sparkford Yeovil Somerset
ENGLAND**